Interaction Flow Modeling Language

Interaction Flow Modeling Language

Model-Driven UI Engineering of Web and Mobile Apps with IFML

Marco Brambilla
*Professor of Software Engineering,
Politecnico di Milano, Milano, Italy*

Piero Fraternali
*Professor of Web Technologies,
Politecnico di Milano, Milano, Italy*

AMSTERDAM • BOSTON • HEIDELBERG • LONDON
NEW YORK • OXFORD • PARIS • SAN DIEGO
SAN FRANCISCO • SYDNEY • TOKYO

Morgan Kaufmann is an imprint of Elsevier

Acquiring Editor: Steve Elliot
Editorial Project Manager: Kaitlin Herbert
Project Manager: Priya Kumaraguruparan
Cover Designer: Mark Rogers

Morgan Kaufmann is an imprint of Elsevier
225 Wyman Street, Waltham, MA 02451, USA

ISBN: 978-0-12-800108-0

For information on all MK publications
visit our website at www.mkp.com

Working together
to grow libraries in
developing countries

www.elsevier.com • www.bookaid.org

Contents

Foreword

A decade and a half ago, on the strength of a relatively new modeling language standard and a notion that software development needed to be more abstract, the Object Management Group (OMG) took a leap of faith and launched an effort known as the Model Driven Architecture (MDA). The idea was simple: like other, better-established engineering disciplines, software development should begin with abstract models, models that could be organized, evaluated, tested & shared before the targeted system was built. After all, it's much easier (and less expensive) to change a system when it's in a high-level (but precise) language, than to change it after it has been fully built (or worse, fielded with customers and users).

Oddly, many fought the idea. We at OMG were convinced by other engineering disciplines; after all, no ship is launched without first architecting the design on paper (or online) and considering various important aspects. An important aspect for a ship, which is best ascertained at design time rather than at launch time, is its center of gravity (CG). After all, the CG of a ship had better be below the water line; if it isn't below the water line at launch time, it will be soon after (as the Swedes discovered to their chagrin at the 10 August 1628 launch of the great warship Vasa, which sank 1300 m into its maiden voyage in Stockholm harbor). Evaluation of models can save quite a lot of time, money and effort, and the MDA approach has had a salutatory effect on software development in the 21st century. The best systems are fully architected and designed, with those designs evaluated before development begins. Even better, though one cannot automate the construction of a ship or a building from its blueprints, in the software realm one can automate the construction of a software system from its blueprint (model), and many telecommunications, banking & military systems are in fact built that way today.

Another major trend of the 21st century is "computing everywhere." Fewer and fewer complex systems are implemented without computing infrastructure today. The music industry, the news industry, the telecommunications industry and the banking industry have been totally disrupted by computing interfaces – music travels by MP3 instead of by physical records and tapes; news travels by text & HTML instead of by newsprint paper; voice travels by voice-over-IP (VoIP) instead of regular telecommunications channels; and money is by far more virtual than paper or metal today. This has necessitated the construction of thousands of user interfaces to access services and functions; dropping a tape into a tape recorder was quite simple and straightforward, but every MP3 player in the world has a different user interface, and some of them are quite bizarre and non-intuitive.

These two trends, modeling and computing everywhere, haven't quite caught up with each other. From the launch of the first international multi-market standard modeling language (the Unified Modeling Language, or UML, in September 1997) to 2013, there has been no standard way to model user interfaces. This problem is made even worse when one considers that many software systems need to be executable on multiple computing platforms – after all, you want to listen to music on your desktop computer, your laptop computer, your music player, perhaps even your wristwatch and your hearing aid. Necessarily these different computing platforms have different user interfaces – have you ever seen a screen on a hearing aid? – and while software modeling languages have for decades supported execution on multiple computing platforms, they have not supported multiple interfaces on multiple computing platforms.

This is more important than it might sound. One of the major software product failures of the second decade of this millennium has been the attempt by major software vendors to support a single user interface concept on all computing platforms (including servers, desktop computers, laptop computers and telephones). The touch-screen concept makes sense for telephones (with their relatively small screens and our relatively large fingers); it makes less sense for many on desktops and laptops (where generally there is a full-size keyboard available, and many computing users would prefer to use that keyboard and mouse); it makes no sense for servers (which are generally "headless," that is, without screens at all.

What is needed, of course, is to apply the concept of abstract models to user interfaces, and this the new OMG Interaction Flow Modeling Language (IFML) is designed to do. Becoming a fully-recognized standard in March, 2014, the IFML allows the system modeler to capture the user interaction and content of the front-end (user interface) of any system (including software systems) and model the control behavior of that system's front-end.

Clearly this is a major breakthrough for systems modeling in general, and software design in particular. With a standard modeling language (fully integrated with other OMG MDA modeling languages through shared underlying modeling structure), a systems designer can capture the control flow of both the system and the interface to that system, and then map the system and interface to whatever infrastructure needs to be delivered. Whether that system runs on a server in the cloud, or on a watch on the user's wrist, or in an embedded system in one's body, the system designer can expect to have both consistent execution of the system and consistent interface to that system. This is clearly a very powerful concept for designing portable and interoperable systems.

In this book, you will learn the concepts of portable design of IFML models, and how to apply those models in real-world systems. Real, executable, fully-worked examples show you how to use IFML in practice, integrate with UML models, and how to rely on the shared MDA infrastructure of OMG modeling languages. While it's worth taking a look at the standard itself to understand its structure, this book is an invaluable guide to how to use the standard to good effect in real systems, whether software systems, software-driven systems, or any other engineered systems that feature a software front-end. This book belongs on the bookshelf of every system designer that depends on software interfaces.

Richard Mark Soley, Ph.D.
Chairman and Chief Executive Officer,
Object Management Group, Inc.,
Moscow, Russian Federation,
23 October 2014

Introduction

In the last twenty years, capabilities such as information browsing, hypertext-style navigation, multimedia content fruition, form-based interaction, and interface personalization have become widespread. They are found in consumer applications, business information systems, and even human–machine interfaces for industrial control. More and more embedded systems are equipped with sophisticated GUIs. Powerful interaction functionalities are implemented on top of a variety of technologies and platforms whose boundaries are becoming less distinguishable: window-based interfaces for desktop and client–server architectures, pure-HTML web pages, rich Internet applications, and mobile apps. This convergence in technologies is well portrayed by the HTML 5 initiative, which seeks to establish a coherent set of concepts and common technological grounds for the development of a broad variety of interaction front-ends.

However, the emergence of such an unprecedented mix of devices, technological platforms, and communication channels is not accompanied by the maturation of approaches for creating a platform independent model (PIM) that can be used to express interaction design decisions independently of the implementation platform. In addition, front-end design is a complex task where many requirements, perspectives, and disciplines intersect: graphic design and aesthetics, enterprise visual identity, interaction design, usability, multi-screen support, offline-online usage, integration with backend business logic and data, and coherence with the enterprise organization models (e.g., business process compliance).

Front-end development, therefore, continues to be a costly and inefficient process, where the collision of many complex factors imposes continuous reworking and refinement of the implementation. The situation is made worse by the scarcity of automation in mainstream software production methods, which causes low reuse of design artifacts across the interfaces of different projects and high overhead for ensuring cross-platform portability of applications. In this context, the role of a PIM-level interaction modeling language is to provide a stable set of concepts that can be used to characterize the essential aspect of the user's interaction with a software application interface: the provision of stimuli, the capturing and processing of such stimuli by the application logic, and the update of the interface based on such processing. The PIM should be designed for change. The stable core of concepts should be accompanied by a native extension mechanism capable of accommodating new forms of interactions and interface renditions (e.g., gestural stimuli and renditions in 3D or augmented reality devices).

A PIM-level interaction modeling language—seamlessly integrated with other modeling perspectives for the design of complete software solutions—brings several benefits:

- It permits the explicit representation of the different perspectives of the front end (content, interface organization, interaction and navigation options, and connection with the business logic and the presentation style).
- It raises the abstraction level of the front-end specification, isolating it from implementation-specific issues.
- It improves the coordination of work in the development process by allowing the allocation of interaction requirement specifications and their implementation to different roles in the team.
- It enables the communication of interface and interaction design to nontechnical stakeholders, enabling the early validation of requirements.
- With the proper tool support, it allows automatic checks on the interface models, not only for the correct use of the modeling constructs but also for desirable properties of the portrayed interface such as uniformity of the interaction style and usability of the interface.

To address these needs, the OMG (Object Management Group) adopted the Interaction Flow Modeling Language (IFML) as a standard in July 2014. This book offers a structured introduction to this new modeling language. The spirit is not that of a reference manual for the illustration of the formal concepts that constitute the language, but rather that of a practical guide book showing the language at work through a progression of examples, design patterns, and best practices. After reading the book, the should have a clear understanding of how to exploit IFML in practice and integrate it into mainstream enterprise software development standards.

As IFML gets implemented by tool vendors, the reader will be able to try out the examples provided in the book and even generate partial or full applications from the models.

1.1 WHAT IFML IS ABOUT

IFML supports the specification of the front end of applications independently of the technological details of their realization. It addresses the following questions of front-end modeling:

- **The composition of the view**: What are the visualization units that compose the interface, how are they organized, and which ones are displayed simultaneously and which in mutual exclusion?
- **The content of the view**: What content elements are displayed from the application to the user, and what input is acquired from the user and supplied to the application?
- **The commands**: What interaction events are supported?
- **The actions**: What business components are triggered by the events?

- **The effects of interaction**: What is the effect of events and action execution on the state of the interface?
- **The parameter binding**: What data items are communicated between the elements of the user interface and the triggered actions?

IFML expresses the abovementioned aspects using a visual modeling language based on the OMG standards. Its technical foundations lie on the OMG Model Driven Architecture (MDA) framework. This grants seamless integration with the specifications of the other layers of the software system. The specification consists of five main technical artifacts:

- The IFML metamodel specifies the structure and semantics of the IFML constructs using the OMG Meta Object Facility (MOF).
- The IFML Unified Modeling Language (UML) profile defines a UML-based syntax for expressing IFML models. In particular, the UML Profile for IFML is based on the use of UML components (both basic components and packaging components), classes, and other concepts, which may concur with hierarchical structures or dependencies.
- The IFML visual syntax offers a concrete representation based on a unique diagram. This compacts all aspects of the user interface that are otherwise expressed separately with UML class diagrams, state machine, and composite structure diagrams.
- The IFML textual syntax offers a textual alternative, equivalent to the visual syntax, for expressing IFML models.
- The IFML XMI provides a model exchange format for tool portability.

This book adopts the IFML visual syntax as a concrete vehicle for conveying the user interaction models because it is close to UML—and thus familiar to developers—and because it is very compact.

1.2 THE IFML DESIGN PRINCIPLES

Designing a modeling language for the front end is a complex and multidisciplinary task where many perspectives intersect. A good modeling language should pay attention to coverage (i.e., the ability to represent complex application front ends but also to model usability and understandability). The latter goals require addressing all the factors that contribute to make a modeling language quick to learn, simple to use, easy to implement by tool vendors, and open to extensibility. The design of IFML adheres as much as possible to the following "golden" rules:

- **Conciseness**: the number of diagram types and concepts needed to express the salient interface and interaction design decisions is kept to the minimum. In particular, the IFML visual syntax conveys the front-end model using a single diagram. This design simplifies the model editing and maintenance processes, because references between different types of diagrams need not be maintained and only the internal coherence among the various elements of a single type of diagram must be preserved.

- **Inference from the context**: whenever something can be deduced from existing parts of the model, inference rules at the modeling level automatically apply default modeling patterns and details, avoiding the need for modelers to specify redundant information. For example, parameter passing rules between different model elements, which are ubiquitous and cumbersome to specify, are inferred from the context as often as possible.

- **Extensibility**: adaptation to novel requirements, interaction modalities, and technologies must be planned in the language design. IFML builds upon a small set of core concepts that capture the essence of interaction: the interface (containers), stimuli (events), content (components and data binding), and dynamics (flows and actions). By design, these concepts are meant to be extended to mirror the evolution of technologies and devices. Thus, IFML incorporates standard means for defining new concepts, such as novel interface components or event types. The OMG standard already comprises examples of extensions, and this book illustrates many more cases that ease the specification of web, desktop, and mobile applications. Time and practice will show if the core of IFML is sufficiently technology neutral to enable extension to novel interaction paradigms that are possibly very different from the ones for which the language was initially conceived.

- **Implementability**: models that lack adequate tool support and cannot be used to produce the code are quickly abandoned. IFML is a platform-independent language but has been designed with executability in mind. This is obtained through model transformations and code generators to ensure that models can be mapped easily into executable applications for various platforms and devices. Chapters 10 and 11 present some techniques for implementing IFML specifications in several platforms, discuss the tool support requested in general for making the language usable, and illustrate one specific tool that enables automation of the design process and code generation.

- **Not everything in the model**: sometimes the hardest choice in language design is what to leave out. IFML purposely ignores presentation aspects, because presentation is adversarial to abstraction (in graphic design, every pixel is important). It also delegates to external models the specification of aspects that, although relevant to the user interface, are not properly part of it. For example, the internal functioning of the actions triggered by the GUI can be described using an action model. If the action is the invocation of an object's method, this can be described by referencing a method in a UML class; if the action is the invocation of an orchestration of web services, this can be described using a SoaML[1] diagram; if the action is described by a complex behavior, this can be obtained by referencing a whole UML dynamic diagram (e.g., a sequence diagram or activity diagram). The content model underlying the application can be described with any structural diagram, such as a UML class diagram, a Common Warehouse Metamodel (CWM) diagram,[2] an Entity-Relationship diagram, or an ontology.

1.3 HOW TO READ THIS BOOK

This book is directed not only to the IT specialists but also to a wider audience of all the professionals involved in the construction of interactive applications, from stakeholders to user-experience creators. To address this target, we purged the book of any unnecessary formalism and academic discussion, and made intensive use of practical and motivating examples to explain each new concept introduced to the reader. The book should be approachable with limited effort by readers with a general background in software development and in basic database, mobile, and web technologies. Throughout the chapters, concepts are shown at work in the modeling of popular real-life interactive application interfaces. In the same way, development tasks are exemplified with the help of a running case taken from a popular online application. Our intention is to show things with the help of progressive examples, rather than to tell how things should be done.

While writing the book, we tried to cater to the needs of four main categories of readers:

- **Software designers/analysts**, whose main goal is learning IFML and understanding the design patterns and best practices that apply in practice. Another fundamental question that software designers want to address is how to integrate model-driven front-end design in current software development processes, with the objective of enabling fast prototyping of the interface connected to the application back end.
- **UI design professionals**, whose aim is to use IFML for specifying the dynamics of the interaction without developing software. Ultimately, IFML should allow the UI professionals to produce a high-level description of their interface concepts that is easily communicable to both IT and business stakeholders.
- **Executives with interests in the IT field**, whose purpose is to understand the role of IFML in organizing software projects and its value in terms of efficiency and cost reduction. Early validation of front-end requirements with customers, cross-project reuse, documentation and cross-team dissemination of design best practices, the unlocking of corporate knowledge from source code, and its preservation in technology-independent models are some of the factors where IFML impacts the key performance indicators of software projects.
- **Students,** whose objective is learning IFML, typically as part of an education path that comprises software development and software engineering disciplines. For students specializing in model-driven software engineering, an added value can be the study of an example of modeling language design. For all students, it may be interesting to try the examples of interface modeling illustrated in the book with the help of the online resources provided and of an IFML modeling and code generation tool. The knowledge afforded by the book can also be used to earn professional certification as an IFML modeler.

1.3.1 STRUCTURE OF THE BOOK

The book proceeds from the prerequisites of IFML (domain modeling), through the various facets of the language, and toward more practical aspects, including a gallery of design patterns, implementation, tool support, and integration within the MDA framework.

- Chapter 2 gives an introductory overview of the language, allowing readers to grasp its main concepts quickly.
- Chapters 3 addresses domain modeling, an activity complementary to front-end modeling. It positions IFML with respect to the established practices for modeling the objects of a domain, most notably the use of UML class diagrams. The chapter also discusses useful patterns that apply specifically to domain modeling for interactive applications.
- Chapters 4–7 provide a walkthrough of IFML, addressing both the standard primitives and the language extensions for specific purposes. Each construct is defined and immediately exemplified. The chapters also contain several design patterns that address typical requirements of application front-end design.
- Chapter 8 complements the feature-based illustration of IFML afforded in chapters 4–7 with a requirement-based view. Various functionalities of interest for desktop, mobile, web, and multiscreen applications are considered, and the design patterns that model them are discussed.
- Chapter 9 deepens the illustration of the concrete usage of IFML, switching from a pattern-based perspective to an application-based one. Two real-life applications are introduced and modelled.
- Chapter 10 and 11 respectively focus on how to convert IFML models into implemented software front ends, including the tool support available for doing so. The aim is to show how to reap the benefits of front-end modeling by quickly producing application prototypes and by generating the complete code of the application from the models with the help of code generation tools.
- Chapter 12 concludes the book by positioning IFML in the broader space of OMG languages and standards, with the aim of giving the reader a precise view on how to set up a coherent model-driven environment capable of spanning all the tiers and facets of application development: the front end, the business logic, the persistent data, and the interoperation with external services.

1.4 ON-LINE RESOURCES

The book is associated with several online resources. The web site at http://www.ifml.org/ offers a variety of materials dedicated to model-driven interface development and to IFML, including examples of modeling, design patterns, technical and research articles, teaching materials, and resources for developers and educators. In particular, the section at http://www.ifml.org/book/ is dedicated to this book. A contact form in the web site permits instructors to contact the book's authors to obtain further up-to-date teaching materials.

The site at http://www.webratio.com/ is the home of WebRatio, the model-driven engineering tool presented in Chapter 12. The WebRatio community hosts a wealth of materials on the usage of IFML, which can be tried out in practice with the tool. An evaluation program is available for trying the software, and academic licenses are granted upon request to researchers, teachers, and students willing to use the tool in educational activities.

1.5 BACKGROUND

The model-driven approach to application front-end development at the base of this book is the result of more than fifteen years of research work at Politecnico di Milano, the largest Italian IT School, accompanied by intense development activity in the industry at the international level. The first model-driven CASE tool for the front end, called AutoWeb, was designed by Piero Fraternali between 1996 and 1998 and focused on web hypertexts. The tool was used to develop several web applications and pioneered the possibility of automating the development of user interfaces—including the presentation aspects—starting from a high-level conceptual model.

The ancestor of IFML was a modeling language called Web Modelling Language (WebML), conceived in the context of the research project Web-Based Intelligent Information Infrastructures (W3I3, 1998–2000), supported by the European Commission. Since 1999, WebML has been used for the development of industrial web applications, both as part of research contracts with companies such as Microsoft and Cisco Systems, and in industrial projects with companies such as Acer Europe. In the fall of 2001, a team of WebML designers and developers founded a start-up company with the goal of developing, distributing, and marketing WebRatio, a tool suite based on WebML. Since then, model-driven development of web applications with WebRatio has been applied to thousands of applications worldwide, including very large projects in such industries as utilities (water and energy), finance, logistics, e-commerce, and more. This solid industrial experience has been the key to understanding what works and what does not in the model-driven development of user interfaces. This understanding has been distilled in the guidelines and design patterns illustrated in this book.

The last step of the long story behind the book is the IFML standardization process at the OMG. Here, the consensus process typical of a wide-scale international standardization effort has produced the refinement of many fundamentals aspects of the language, such as its compliance and integration with OMG standards, the general applicability to any class of interactive applications, and the provision of a model exchange format.

1.6 ACKNOWLEDGMENT

We would like to thank all the people that made this book possible. First of all, we wish to thank Stefano Ceri and the whole research group at Politecnico di Milano, where the WebML language originated. Secondly, all the people that in these years worked at WebRatio, starting with the founders Roberto Acerbis, Aldo Bongio, and Stefano Butti. The industrial experience collected there has been inspirational for continuous innovation. Third, the people that actually contributed to the specification and implementation of the IFML language within the OMG: Richard Soley, OMG Chairman, who encouraged and accompanied our initiative; the whole OMG team, the co-submitters of the standard; and people like Ed Seidewitz, Manfred Koethe, and Arne Berre that contributed their experience to the success of the standardization process. Finally, we want to thank the team at Morgan Kaffman, including Kaitlin Herbert and Andrea Dierna, who patiently took care of the whole process down to the final release of the book. Last—but not least—the reviewers of this book, Antonio Valecillo and Juha-Pekka Tolvanen, who provided us with extremely valuable comments and feedback on the first draft of the manuscript.

END NOTES

1. See http://www.omg.org/spec/SoaML/.
2. See http://www.omg.org/spec/cwm/.

IFML in a Nutshell

IFML supports the platform-independent description of graphical user interfaces for applications deployed or accessed on systems such as desktop computers, laptops, PDAs, mobile phones, and tablets. The main focus is on the structure and behavior of the application as perceived by the end user. The modeling language also incorporates references to the data and business logic that influence the user's experience. This is achieved respectively by referencing the domain model objects that provide the content displayed in the interface and the actions that can be triggered by interacting with the interface.

This chapter introduces the essential features of IFML: its scope, the design rules behind it, its main modeling elements, and its role in the development process. The chapter concludes with an initial example of the language.

2.1 SCOPE AND PERSPECTIVES

To understand the aim and scope of IFML better, it may be useful to refer to the well-known Model–View–Controller (MVC) software architecture of an interactive application,[1] shown in Figure 2.1. MVC distinguishes the application's internal status and business logic (Model), their representation in the user interface (View), and the rules governing the response to the user's interaction (Controller).

IFML mainly describes the view (i.e., the content of the front end and the user interaction mechanisms available in the interface). More precisely, IFML covers various aspects of the user interface:

- **View structure**: It expresses the general organization of the interface in terms of ViewContainers, along with their nesting relationships, visibility, and reachability.
- **View content**: It specifies what ViewContainers actually contain in terms of ViewComponents (i.e., elements for content display and data entry). ViewComponents that display content are further characterized by a ContentBinding, which expresses the source of the published content.
- **Events**: They are the occurrences that affect the state of the user interface. They can be produced by a user's interaction, by the application itself, or by an external system.

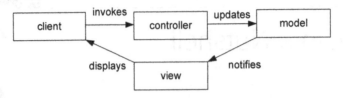

FIGURE 2.1

The Model–View–Controller architecture of an interactive application.

- **Event transitions**: They specify the consequences of an event on the user interface, which can be a change of the ViewContainer, an update of the content on
  display, the triggering of an action, or a mixture of these effects.
- **Parameter binding**: It clarifies the input–output dependencies between View-
  Components, view containers, and actions.

For the sake of conciseness, IFML condenses all these perspectives within only
one diagram type called an **Interaction Flow Diagram**. This is in contrast to other
modeling languages such as UML, which rely on multiple diagrams for conveying
the various facets of an application.

Besides describing the view part of the application, an IFML Interaction Flow
Diagram also provides the hooks to connect it with the model and controller parts:

- With respect to the controller, IFML represents the effects of the user's interactions. It defines the events produced in the view and the course of action taken
  by the controller in response to them, such as triggering a business component
  and updating the view.
- With respect to the model, IFML describes the data binding between the interface elements and the objects that embody the state of the application, as well
  the actions that are triggered by the user's interactions.

Figure 2.2 shows as an initial example the IFML model of a simple interface: the
view structure consists of three ViewContainers ("ProductCategories," "ProductOf-
Category," and "ProductInformation"), which reflect the top-level organization of
the GUI in three distinct pages. The model shows the content of each ViewContainer.
For example, the "ProductCategories" ViewContainer comprises one ViewComponent called "CategoryList." This notation represents the content of the respective
page in the GUI (i.e., a list of product categories). Events are represented in IFML
as circles. The "SelectCategory" event specifies that the "CategoryList" component
is interactive. In the GUI, the user can select one of the categories to access a list of
its products. The effect of the "SelectCategory" event is represented by the arrow
emanating from it (called InteractionFlow in IFML), which specifies that the triggering of the event causes the display of the "ProductOfCategory" ViewContainer and
the rendering of its "ProductList" ViewComponent (i.e., the list of products *of the
selected category*). The input–output dependency between the "CategoryList" and
the "ProductList" ViewComponents is represented as a parameter binding (the IFML

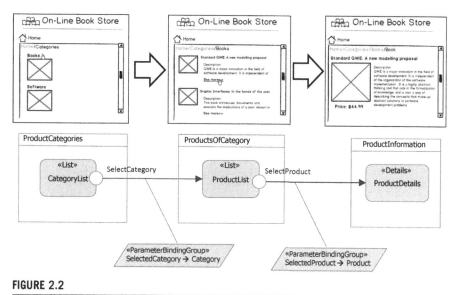

FIGURE 2.2

Example of an interface and its IFML specification.

ParameterBindingGroup element in Figure 2.2). The value of the "SelectedCategory" parameter, which denotes the object selected by the user in the "CategoryList" View-Component, is associated with the value of the input parameter "Category," which is requested for the computation of the "ProductList" ViewComponent.

2.2 OVERVIEW OF IFML MAIN CONCEPTS

An IFML diagram consists of one or more top-level *ViewContainers* (i.e., inter-face elements that comprise components for displaying content and supporting interactions).

Figure 2.3 contrasts two different organizations of the GUI: (a) an e-mail appli-cation (desktop or rich Internet application) consisting of a top-level container with embedded sub-containers at different levels, and (b) an e-commerce web site that organizes the user interface into different independent view containers corresponding to page templates.

Each view container can be internally structured in a *hierarchy of subcontainers.* For example, in a desktop or rich Internet application, the main window can contain multiple tabbed frames, which in turn may contain several nested panes. The child view containers nested within a parent view container can be displayed simultane-ously (e.g., an object pane and a property pane) or in *mutual exclusion* (e.g., two alternative tabs). In the case of mutually exclusive (XOR) containers, one could be the *default container,* which is displayed by default when the parent container is accessed. The meaning of a container can be specified more precisely by adding a

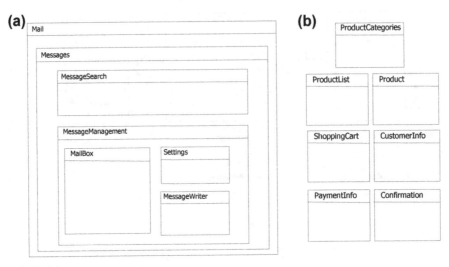

FIGURE 2.3

Example of different top-level interface structures.

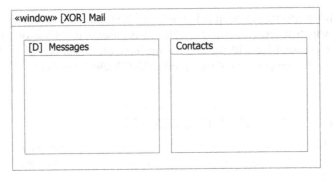

FIGURE 2.4

Example of mutually exclusive subcontainers.

stereotype to the general-purpose construct. For instance, a ViewContainer can be tagged as «window», as in the case of the "Mail" ViewContainer in Figure 2.4, to hint at the nature of its expected implementation.

In Figure 2.4, the "Mail" top-level container comprises two subcontainers, displayed alternatively: one for messages and one for contacts. When the top level container is accessed, the interface displays the "Messages" ViewContainer by default.

A ViewContainer can contain *ViewComponents,* which denote the publication of content (e.g., a list of objects) or the input of data (e.g., entry forms).

Figure 2.5 shows the notation for embedding ViewComponents within View-Containers. The "Search" ViewContainer comprises a "MessageKeywordSearch"

FIGURE 2.5

Example of ViewComponents within view containers.

ViewComponent that represents a form for searching; the "MailBox" ViewContainer comprises a "MessageList" ViewComponent that denotes a list of objects.

A ViewComponent can have *input and output parameters.* For example, a View-Component that shows the details of an object has an input parameter corresponding to the identifier of the object to display. a data entry form exposes as output parameters the values submitted by the user. and a list of items exports as output parameter the item selected by the user.

A ViewContainer and a ViewComponent can be associated with *events* to express that they support user interaction. For example, a ViewComponent can represent a list associated with an event for selecting one or more items, a form associated with an event for input submission, or an image gallery associated with an event for scrolling though the gallery. IFML events are mapped to *interactors*[2] in the implemented application. The way in which such interactors are rendered depends on the specific platform for which the application is deployed and is not captured by IFML. Rather, it is delegated to transformation rules from a platform-independent model (PIM) to a platform-specific model (PSM). For example, the scrolling of an image gallery may be implemented as a link in an HTML application and as a swipe gesture handler in a mobile phone application.

The effect of an event is represented by an *interaction flow,* which connects the event to the ViewContainer or ViewComponent affected by the event. For example, in an HTML web application the event produced by the selection of one item from a list may cause the display of a new page with the details of the selected object. This effect is represented by an interaction flow connecting the event associated with the list component in a top-level ViewContainer (the web page) with the ViewComponent representing the object detail, which is positioned in a different ViewContainer (the target web page). The interaction flow expresses a change of state of the user interface. The occurrence of the event causes a transition from a source to a target web page.

For example, in Figure 2.6 the "MailBoxList" ViewComponent shows the list of available mailboxes and is associated with the "MailBoxSelection" event, whereby the user can open the "MailBox" ViewContainer and access the messages of the mailbox selected in the "MessageList" ViewComponent .

An event can also cause the *triggering of an action,* which is executed prior to updating the state of the user interface. The effect of an event firing an action is represented by an interaction flow connecting the event to an action symbol (represented

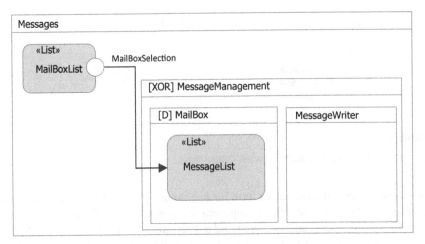

FIGURE 2.6

Example of interaction flow between ViewComponents.

by a hexagon). For example, in a mail management application, the user can select several messages from a list and choose to delete them. The selection event triggers a delete action, after which the ViewContainer is displayed again with an updated list. The result of action execution is represented by an interaction flow that connects the action to the affected ViewContainer or ViewComponent.

In Figure 2.7, the "Message toolbar" ViewContainer is associated with the events for deleting, archiving, and reporting mail messages. Such events are connected by a flow to an action symbol (a labeled hexagonal icon), which represents the business operation. The outgoing flow of the action points to the ViewContainer displayed after the action is executed; if the outgoing flow of an action is omitted, this means that the same ViewContainer from which the action was activated remains in view (as illustrated by the "Archive" and "Report" actions in Figure 2.7).

The model of Figure 2.7 does not express the objects on which the business actions operate. Such an *input–output dependency* between view elements (ViewContainers and ViewComponents) or between view elements and actions requires the specification of *parameter bindings* associated with interaction flows. More specifically, two kinds of interaction flows can host parameter bindings: *navigation flows*, which represent navigation between view elements, and *data flows*, which express data transfer only but are not produced by user interaction. Parameter binding rules are represented by annotations attached to navigation and data flows, as shown in Figure 2.8.

In Figure 2.7, the "MessageToolbar" ViewContainer has an input parameter "MessageSet" whose value is set to the messages selected from the "MessageList" ViewComponent when the user triggers the "MessageSelection" event. Another parameter binding rule is associated with the Delete, Archive and Report events; the value of the "MessageSet" parameter is bound to the "InputMessages" parameter of the triggered action.

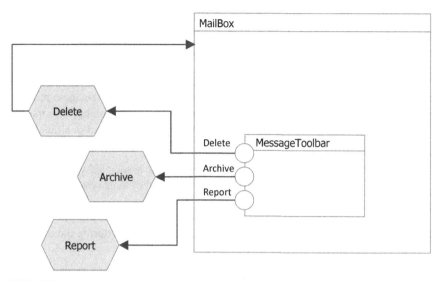

FIGURE 2.7

Example of events triggering business actions.

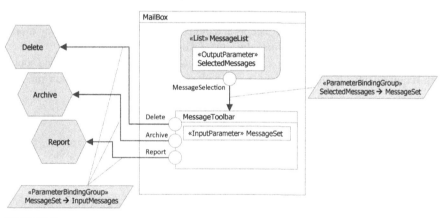

FIGURE 2.8

Example of parameter bindings used for expressing input–output dependencies.

2.3 ROLE OF IFML IN THE DEVELOPMENT PROCESS

The development of interactive applications is typically managed with agile approaches, which traverse several cycles of "problem discovery" / "design refinement" / "implementation." Each iteration of the development process generates a prototype or a partial version of the system. Such an incremental lifecycle is particularly appropriate for modern web and mobile applications, which must be deployed quickly and change frequently during their lifetime to adapt to user requirements. Figure 2.9 schematizes a possible development process and positions IFML within the flow of activities.

Requirements specification collects and formalizes the information about the application domain and expected functions. The input is the set of business requirements that motivate the application development and all the available information on the technical, organizational, and managerial context. The output is a functional specifications document comprising:

- the identification of the user roles and of the use cases associated with each role;
- a data dictionary of the essential domain concepts and of their semantic relationships; and
- the workflow embodied in each use case, which shows how the main actors (the user, the application, and possibly external services) interact during the execution of the use case.

In addition, nonfunctional requirements must also be specified, including performance, scalability, availability, security, and maintainability. When the application is directed to the general public, requirements about the look and feel and the usability of the interfaces assume special prominence among the nonfunctional requirements. User-centered design practices that rely on the construction of realistic mock-ups of the application functionality can be applied. These mock-ups can be used for the early validation of the interface concepts and then serve as the basis for creating more detailed and technical specifications during the front-end modeling phase.

Domain modeling[3] organizes the main information objects identified during requirements specification into a comprehensive and coherent domain model.

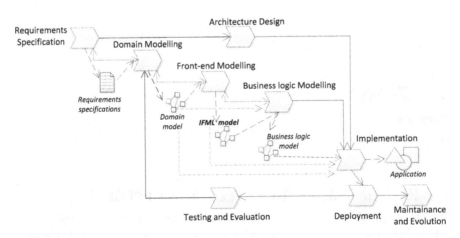

FIGURE 2.9

The role of IFML in the development process of an interactive application.

Domain modeling specifies the main information assets identified during requirements specification into a domain model, which is a (typically visual) representation of the essential objects, their attributes and associations. The first conceptual data modeling language, the Entity-Relationship model, was proposed in 1976, and ever since new modeling languages have been proposed, including UML. At the same time, modeling practices and guidelines have been consolidated; in particular, domain modeling for interactive applications exploits suitable design patterns, discussed in chapter 3. The entities and associations of the domain model identified during domain modeling are referenced in the front-end design models, to describe what pieces of data are published in the interface.

Front-end modeling maps the information delivery and data manipulation functionality dictated by the requirements use cases into a front-end model. Front-end modeling operates at the conceptual level, where IFML comes into play. The designer may use IFML to specify the organization of the front end in one or more top-level view containers, the internal structure of each view container in terms of subcontainers, the components that form the content of each view container, the events exposed by the view containers and components, and how such events trigger business actions and update the interface.

Business logic modeling specifies the business objects and the methods necessary to support the identified use cases. UML static and dynamic diagrams are normally employed to highlight the interfaces of objects and the flow of messages. Process-oriented notations—such as UML activity and sequence diagrams, BPMN process models, and BPEL service orchestrations—provide a convenient way to represent the workflow across objects and services. The actions specified in the business logic design can be referenced in the front-end model to show which operations can be triggered by interacting with the interface.

Data, front-end, and business-logic design are interdependent activities executed iteratively. The precedence order of Figure 2.9 is only illustrative. In some organizations, work could start from the design of the front end and the data objects and actions could be discovered at a later stage by analyzing what information is published in the interface and what operations are requested to support the interactions.

Architecture design is the process of defining the hardware, network, and software components that make up the architecture on which the application delivers its services to users. The goal of architecture design is to find the mix of these components that best meets the application requirements in terms of performance, security, availability, and scalability, and at the same time respects the technical and economic constraints of the project. The inputs of architecture design are the nonfunctional requirements and the constraints identified during business requirements collection and formalized in the requirements specifications. The output may be any specification that addresses the topology of the architecture in terms of processors, processes, and connections, such as UML deployment diagrams.

Implementation is the activity of producing the software modules that transform the data, business logic, and interface design into an application running on the selected architecture. **Data implementation** maps the domain model onto one or more data sources by associating the conceptual-level constructs with the logical data structures (e.g., entities and relationships to relational tables). **Business logic implementation** creates the software components needed to support the identified use cases. The implementation of individual components may benefit from the adoption of software frameworks, which organize the way in which fine-grain components are orchestrated and assembled into larger and more reusable functional units and also cater to nonfunctional requirements like performance, scalability, security, and availability. Business logic may also reside in external services, in which case implementation must address the orchestration of calls to remote components such as web APIs (Application Programming Interfaces). **Interface implementation** translates the conceptual-level ViewContainers and ViewComponents into the proper constructs in the selected implementation platform. ViewContainers may interoperate with business objects deployed either in the client layer or in the server layer.

Testing and evaluation verify the conformance of the implemented application to the functional and nonfunctional requirements. The most relevant concerns for interactive applications testing are:

- Functional testing: the application behavior is verified with respect to the functional requirements. Functional testing can be broken down into the classical activities of module testing, integration testing, and system testing.
- Usability testing: the nonfunctional requirements of ease of use, communication effectiveness, and adherence to consolidated usability standards are verified against the produced front end.
- Performance testing: the throughput and response time of the application must be evaluated in average and peak workload conditions. In case of inadequate level of service, the deployment architecture, including the external services, must be monitored and analyzed to identify and remove bottlenecks.

Deployment is the activity of installing the developed modules on top of the selected architecture. Deployment involves the data layer, the software gateways to the external services, and the business and presentation layer, where the interface modules and the business objects must be installed.

Maintenance and evolution encompass all the modifications applied after the application has been deployed in the production environment. Differently from the other phases of development, maintenance and evolution are applied to an existing system, which includes both the running application and its related documentation.

IFML models are the result of front-end design, but their production has important implications for other development activities as well.

- Domain modeling may specify entities and associations whose purpose is to aid the categorization and retrieval of the main business objects for a better user experience. We discuss this practice in chapter 3.
- Business logic modeling identifies the available operations and defines their possible outcomes and output, which affect the status of the interface. Chapter 6 discusses the interplay between front-end and business-logic modeling.

- Implementation may exploit model transformations and code generation to produce prototypes of the user interface or even fully functional code. In chapter 10 we discuss how to implement IFML models manually in some representative software platforms, and then in chapter 11 we exemplify the automation of the development activities achieved with model-driven tools.
- Testing and evaluation can be anticipated and performed on the IFML models rather than on the final code. Model checking may discover inconsistencies in the design of the front end (e.g., unreachable statuses of the interface) and suggest ways to refactor the user interface for better usability (e.g., recommend uniform design patterns for the different types of user interactions, such as searching, browsing, creating. modifying, and deleting objects).
- Finally, maintenance and evolution benefit most from the existence of a conceptual model of the application. Requests for changes are analyzed and turned into changes at the design level. Then, changes at the conceptual level are propagated to the implementation, possibly with the help of model-to-code transformation rules. This approach smoothly incorporates change management into the mainstream production lifecycle and greatly reduces the risk of breaking the software engineering process due to the application of changes solely at the implementation level.

2.4 A COMPLETE EXAMPLE

As a conclusion to this brief introduction of IFML, we present a simple, yet complete, example. The application is an online store where the user can browse products, such as books, music, and software, and add products to his shopping cart, as shown by the UML use case diagram of Figure 2.10.

The application has a web front end. In the "Browse books" use case, the user accesses a home page that contains a list of product categories. Clicking on a product category such as "Books" leads to a page displaying the summary data about all the items of that category. Clicking on a "See more" associated with one item's summary opens a page where the full details of the selected object are

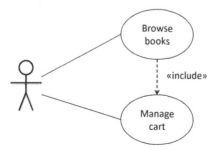

FIGURE 2.10

Use cases of the Bookstore application.

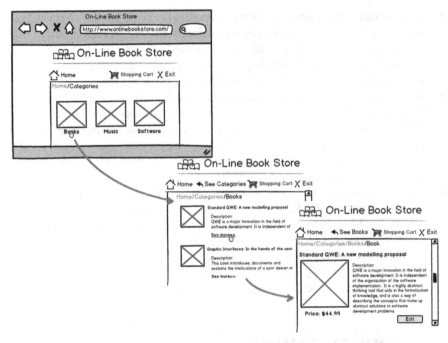

FIGURE 2.11

Mock-ups of the user interface supporting the "Browse books" use case.

presented. Figure 2.11 shows the mock-ups of the application front end supporting the "Browse books" use case.

When looking at the details of an item, the user can press the "Add to cart" button to add the item to his virtual shopping cart. A modal window appears where the user can specify the quantity of goods he wants to purchase. After submitting the desired quantity, a confirmation pop-up window is presented to acknowledge the addition of the product to the cart. Figure 2.12 shows the mock-ups of the interface supporting the "Manage cart" use case.

The IFML model of the Bookstore application contains the five ViewContainers shown in Figure 2.13.

The ViewContainers are annotated with stereotypes (such as H, for "Home," L for "Landmark," and "Modal" and "Modeless") that further specify their properties. These are discussed in chapter 4.

The ViewContainers definition is refined by specifying the ViewComponents they comprise, as illustrated in Figure 2.14.

Interactivity is represented by adding the relevant events and specifying the interaction flows they trigger, along with the parameter binding between the source and the target components of the interaction flows. The model of Figure 2.15 shows that the "CategoryList" ViewComponent supports an interactive event "SelectCategory," whereby the user can choose a category from the index. As a result, the

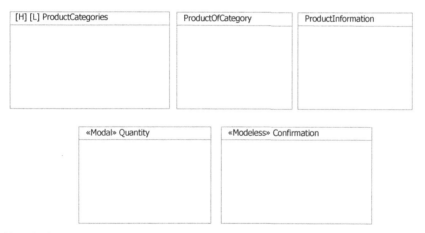

FIGURE 2.12

Mock-ups of the user interface supporting the "Manage cart" use case.

[H] [L] ProductCategories	ProductOfCategory	ProductInformation

«Modal» Quantity	«Modeless» Confirmation

FIGURE 2.13

IFML ViewContainers of the Bookstore application.

"ProductOfCategory" page is displayed, and the "ProductList" ViewComponent shows the items corresponding to the chosen category. The input–output dependency between the "CategoryList" and the "ProductList" ViewComponents is represented by the parameter binding group, which associates the "SelectedCategory" output parameter of the source component with the "Category" input parameter of the target component. The same modeling pattern is used to express the interaction

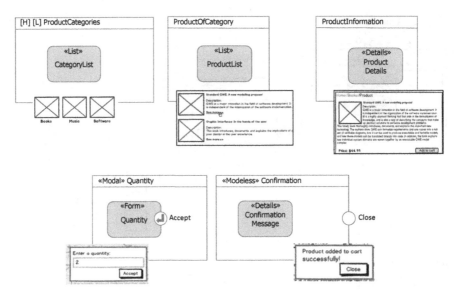

FIGURE 2.14

ViewComponents embedded in IFML ViewContainers, with their mock-up renditions.

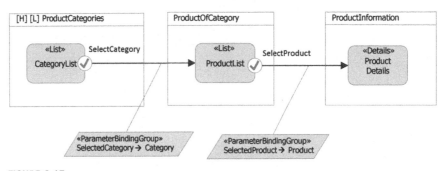

FIGURE 2.15

IFML events and interaction flows of the "Browse books" use case .

for selecting a product from the "ProductList" component and then accessing its data in the "ProductDetails" component.

Some event may trigger the execution of a piece of business logic. As an example, Figure 2.12 and Figure 2.16 show the activation of an action for inserting items in the shopping cart. After the user presses the "Add to cart" button associated with the "ProductDetails" component, a modal window appears asking for the quantity of items desired. The quantity submission event triggers the execution of the "Add

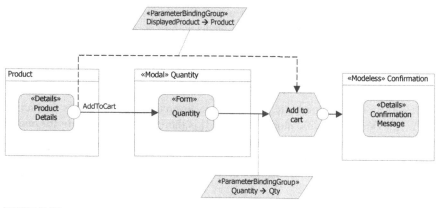

FIGURE 2.16

IFML events and interaction flows of the "Browse Products" use case.

to cart" action. The "Quantity" value from the Form ViewComponent and the "DisplayedProduct" parameter from the "ProductDetails" ViewComponent are submitted as input parameters to the "Add to cart" action. Once the action is completed, a confirmation window is displayed.

Notice that the binding of the "Quantity" output parameter is associated with an *interaction flow*, which denotes the effect of a submit event that requires the user's interaction. Conversely, the binding of the "DisplayedProduct" parameter is associated with a *data flow*, which merely expresses an input–output dependency automatically performed by the system and not triggered by a user's interaction.

2.5 SUMMARY OF THE CHAPTER

In this chapter we have provided a bird's-eye view of IFML. First, we positioned its concepts in the software architecture of an interactive application by referring them to the elements of the Model–View–Controller design pattern. We then summarized the essential concepts of the language: interfaces are modeled as one or more View-Containers, possibly nested hierarchically; ViewContainers comprise ViewCompo-nents that enable content display and data entry; and interactivity is expressed by Events associated with ViewContainers and ViewComponents, whose effect on the interface is denoted by InteractionFlows that connect the event to a ViewContainer, a ViewComponent, or an Action. The latter express a business operation triggered from the user interface. ViewContainers, ViewComponents, and Actions may have param-eters. In this case, the input–output dependencies between them are represented by parameter bindings associated with the InteractionFlows. These concepts have been illustrated in a small, yet complete, example. The chapter has also highlighted the role and benefits of IFML in the application development cycle.

2.6 BIBLIOGRAPHIC NOTES

Model-driven engineering basic principles are covered by various books, including [BCW12]. Domain-specific modelling (DSM) is thoroughly discussed in the books [Kelly08] and [Voelter13], which underline the motivations for adopting a higher level of abstraction in the development of applications, discuss the design principles and architecture of DSM, and contain several use cases that illustrate the approach in practice.

The processes and modeling language for web applications—a special class of interactive applications—have been addressed by James Conallen, who adapted UML and the Rational Unified Process to the specific context of web application development [Conallen99, Conallen00]. The resulting method includes the activities of requirements gathering, analysis, design, implementation, testing, deployment, configuration, and change management. In the design phase, ad hoc UML stereotypes are used to describe the components of web pages. In this way, page design is made visual according to one of the basic principles of the Rational Unified Process. A more recent textbook on web application modeling and code generation is [BBC03], which introduces the Web Modeling Language, a conceptual language similar to IFML but specifically tailored to web application development. The book presents a comprehensive method applied to a real-world use case and discusses the architectures and tools for code generation.

END NOTES

1. See, e.g., http://en.wikipedia.org/wiki/Mode-view-controller/.
2. By "interactor" we mean any interface widget that supports user interaction, such as a button, a link, or a check box.
3. "Domain modeling" is the locution normally employed in object-oriented method, whereas conceptual database design normally refers to "data modeling."

Domain modeling

The goal of domain modeling is the specification of the relevant information assets that constitute the application domain in a formal yet comprehensible and readable way. The activity of domain modeling produces a domain model, also called a conceptual schema by database designers. This embodies the available knowledge about the relevant concepts, their properties and relationships, and, in object-oriented modeling, the operations applicable to them. The reason why a book on interface modeling contains a chapter on domain modeling is that the interface model must refer to the objects that provide content to be published in the application front end. Furthermore, events triggered within the interface may cause the execution of operations, which may update objects and change the status of the interface.

Thus, domain modeling naturally interplays with the modeling of the business logic and of the front end of the application. The produced domain model also drives the implementation of the physical structures for data storage, update, and retrieval.

Domain modeling is one of the most consolidated disciplines of information technology. The resulting domain model can be regarded as a content model, which emphasizes the description of the information assets used by the application.

Many languages and guidelines have been proposed and are now consolidated for domain modeling. For this reason, we do not propose yet another domain modeling language but instead exploit UML class diagrams. The motivation for this choice is that IFML is an OMG standard based on UML, and thus using class diagrams makes one notation fit both domain and front-end modelling. As a more familiar alternative to UML class diagrams, information system and database designers may use the Entity–Relationship (E–R) model, which focuses only on entities, attributes, and relations but disregards the operations supported by objects. For the sake of expressing most IFML patterns illustrated in this book, only the UML class diagram features that are also present in the E–R model are necessary, and thus the two modeling languages can be considered almost equivalent.

The essential ingredients of the domain model in UML are *classes*, defined as blueprints abstracting the common properties of *objects* (also known as class *instances*), and *associations*, representing semantic connections between classes. Classes are characterized by typed attributes and by the operations applicable to their instances. Classes can also be organized in generalization hierarchies, which express the derivation of a specific concept from a more general one and imply inheritance of properties and behavior. Associations are characterized by multiplicity constraints

Category

Product

FIGURE 3.1

Graphic notation for classes.

that impose restrictions on the number of association instances in which an object may take part.

This chapter introduces the essential domain modeling concepts sufficient to specify the domain model of an interactive application. Examples are represented using UML notation. The bibliographic notes at the end of the chapter mention several textbooks on data and domain modeling in which the reader can find further examples and discussions of advanced data modeling constructs.

3.1 CLASSES

Classes are the central concept of the domain model.

> **CLASS**
>
> A class represents a description of the common features of set of objects of the real world. Examples of class are Person, Car, Product, and MailBox.

A class has a population, which is the set of objects that are described by the class. These objects are also called the **instances** of the class. For example, the population of class Person is a specific set of persons, while the population of class Car is a specific set of cars.

As is the case for all the concepts of the domain model, classes are specified using a graphical notation. They are denoted by means of rectangles with the class name at the top. Figure 3.1 shows two classes: "Category" and "Product."

3.2 ATTRIBUTES

Classes are further specified by means of attributes, which are the properties common to all instances of the class.

> **ATTRIBUTE**
>
> **Attributes** are the properties of objects that are relevant for application purposes. Examples of attributes are the name, address, and photo of a person. Attributes have values, which are typed.

In other words, the class is a descriptor of the common properties of a set of objects, and such properties are expressed as typed attributes.

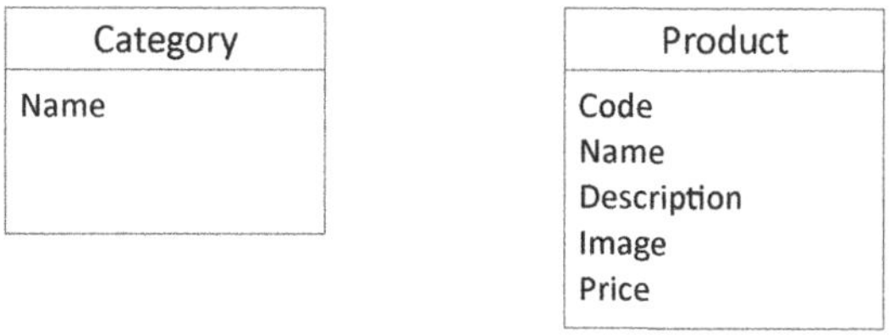

Category		Product	
Name		Code	
		Name	
		Description	
		Image	
		Price	

FIGURE 3.2

Graphic notation for classes and attributes.

Class instances are allowed to have null values for one or more attributes. However, a null value may represent different modeling situations and raises ambiguities in the interpretation of the properties of an instance:

- A null value may denote that a certain attribute does not apply to a specific class instance (for example, the driving license number for persons without a driving license).
- A null value may denote that the value of a certain attribute is unknown for a specific class instance (for example, the age or the marital status of a person).

Attributes are graphically represented inside the class box below the class name, as shown in Figure 3.2. In the example, the class "Category" is characterized by attribute "Name," and class "Product" by attributes "Code," "Name," "Description," "Image," and "Price."

3.3 IDENTIFICATION AND PRIMARY KEY

UML follows the object-oriented assumption that all the instances of a class are distinguishable by means of an internal identifier, which need not be specified explicitly in the class diagram. However, in information system and database modeling, it is customary to highlight domain attributes that are human readable and can be used to identify objects because they have unique values across the entire class population. Such attributes are called primary keys and have an important role in denoting objects in the user interface and in retrieving information about selected objects from the database.

PRIMARY KEY

A **primary key** is an attribute that can be used to identify the instances of the class uniquely. Examples of primary keys are the plate number of a car and the Social Security Number of a person.

A **composite primary key** is a set of attributes that can be used to identify the instances of the class uniquely. An example can be the pair code and year of delivery of an academic course.

Primary key attributes must satisfy a few restrictions not required for regular attributes. Their value must be **not null** for every instance of the class and **unique**, which means that there should not exist two class instances with the same value for the key attributes. UML does not provide a specific notation for expressing key attributes. One option is to add an OCL constraint to the relevant attribute, to denote that its value is not null and unique.

An example of such an OCL statement could be the following, which forces attribute "code" of class "Product" to be not null and unique (i.e., it must be a key):

```
Context Product
self.code <> null and Product.allInstances() -> forAll(c1,c2 | c1
<> c2 implies c1.code <> c2.code)
```

An effective way to handle the specification of key constraints is to create a UML stereotype of the general concept of attribute or of attribute group and associate the OCL constraints with such a stereotype so that it can be managed by any standard UML tool. An example of such notation is the addition of the «PK» stereotype to the primary key attributes.

In the rest of this book, we will use the convention of prefixing with «PK» the primary key attributes in class diagrams and assume that the implicit identity attribute of class instances is represented by an "OID" (object identifier) attribute, which is defined for all classes and thus can be omitted from the domain model diagrams.

Figure 3.3 shows the classes "Category" and "Product" completed with the specification of primary keys. Attribute "Name" is a key of class "Category," while the attribute "Code" is a key for class "Product."

OCL, which we have employed for expressing the key constraint, is a general-purpose textual language adopted as a standard by the OMG[1] for defining calculation rules and constraints on top of the basic UML models semantics. The language is *typed*, *declarative*, and *side effect-free*. *Typed* means that each OCL expression has a type, evaluates to a value of that type, and must conform to the rules and operations of that type. *Declarative* means that OCL does not include imperative constructs. *Side effect-free* implies that OCL expressions can query or constraint the state of the modeled system but not modify it.

OCL statements defining constraints are invariants embedded in the context of a specific type (e.g., a class or an association) called the *context type* of the constraint. The body of an OCL constraint is a Boolean condition that must be satisfied by all the instances of the context type.

The standard OCL library predefines the primitive and collection-related types (and their operations) that can be used in the definition of an OCL expression, together with quantifiers (such as *for all* and *exists*) and iterators (*select*, *reject*, *closure*, etc.). Access to

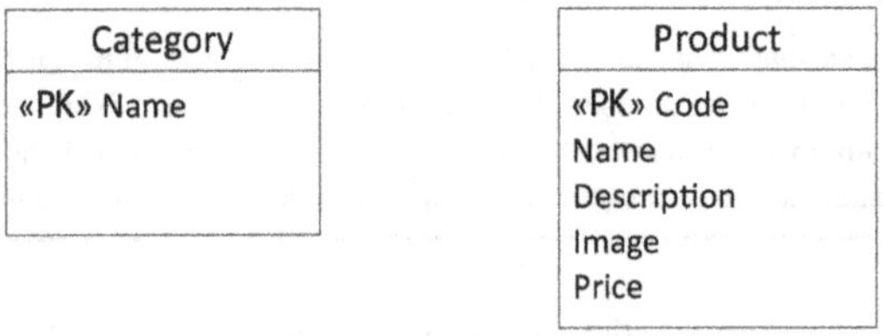

Category		Product
«PK» Name		«PK» Code
		Name
		Description
		Image
		Price

FIGURE 3.3

Notation for primary keys in class diagrams.

the properties of an object and navigation from an object to its related objects (via associations) is expressed using the dot notation, as shown in Figures 3.14 and 3.15.

Although we use OCL extensively in the examples throughout the book, the detailed explanation of all the features of the language is outside the scope of the book. The bibliographic notes provide hints for further readings on OCL.

3.4 ATTRIBUTE TYPE AND VISIBILITY

Attributes must be typed, which means that they assume values from well-defined domains (e.g., the set of integer or floating point numbers). Expressing attribute types in the domain model is good practice for making the specification more expressive and for driving implementation.

In the sequel, we assume that class attributes are associated with the usual data types supported by most programming languages and database products. Such data types may include string, text, integer, float, date, time, boolean, enumeration, blob, are url. The meanings of these types are summarized in Table 3.1.

Attribute types can be represented in class diagrams by means of a label positioned besides the attribute declaration in the class box. Figure 3.4 shows the classes "Category" and "Product" with the attributes types specified.

Table 3.1 Typical built-in data types

Data type	Description
string	A "short" sequence of characters
text	A "long" sequence of characters
integer	An integer numerical type
float	A floating point numerical type
date	A calendar date
time	A temporal instant of time
boolean	A true or false value
enumeration	A sequence of user-defined values
blob	A binary large object, for example an image or a video, which must be handled in a special way because of its size. Blob types can be further refined by expressing their MIME type (for example image/gif)
url	A uniform resource locator of a web resource

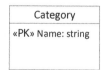

FIGURE 3.4

Graphic notation for attribute types.

Attributes are associated with access modifiers that denote their visibility. Access qualification is denoted by a symbol prefixing the attribute name, which can be:

- (+) the attribute is public, that is, visible globally;
- (-) the attribute is private, that is, visible only from objects of the owning class;
- (#) the attribute is protected, that is, visible only from objects of the owning class or of classes derived from it; or
- (~) the attribute has package visibility, that is, only objects of the classes in the same package can access it.

In classic object-oriented design, the general practice is to define class attributes as private and then specify access to them through appropriate getter and setter methods, as described in Section 3.5. Conversely, in information system and database modeling, visibility of attributes is not normally specified at the class level, as it is assumed that the domain model represents the available data objects and access is controlled at a global level, for example, by means of database permissions. In the rest of the book we follow the database approach and assume all attributes in the domain model to be public by default. This assumption simplifies the reference to content in the interface model, because it allows one to use attribute names directly rather that getter and setter methods.

3.5 OPERATIONS

In object-oriented modeling, classes are not only containers of information but also allow the specification of behavior, which is expressed by their operations.

OPERATION

Operations represent the actions allowed on the objects of a class. They are described by a name, a return value, and a (possibly empty) set of parameters.

Operations' parameters and return values are typed just as attributes are. Operations also have visibility, which can be public, private, protected, or package.

Examples of operations for a class "Product" are "buy," "applyDiscount," and "bundle." Besides operations that denote business actions, classes typically comprise operations for handling the access to the attributes in read and write mode. *Setter methods* are the operations that assign values to class attributes, whereas *getter methods* are those used to extract the value of an attribute. Furthermore, classes include *constructors*, which are operations for creating new instances of a class. Figure 3.5 shows the UML notation for representing operations in class diagrams.

As done for the implicit OID attribute of objects, we do not explicitly represent constructors, getters, and setters in the domain model and assume that they exist for all classes.

Category
«PK» Name: string
setName(string) addProduct(Product) removeProduct(Product)

Product
«PK» Code: integer Name: string Description: text Image: blob Price: float
setName(string) setDescription(text) setPrice(float) addToCart(Cart) ...

FIGURE 3.5

Representation of operations in class diagrams.

3.6 GENERALIZATION HIERARCHIES

The domain model allows the designer to organize classes into a hierarchy to highlight their common features.

GENERALIZATION

A **generalization hierarchy** (also called **is-a hierarchy**) connects a superclass and one or more subclasses, representing a specialization of the superclass. The hierarchy can be multilevel, because a subclass can in turn be a superclass of other subclasses.

Each subclass **inherits** the features (attributes, operations, and associations) defined in the superclass and may add locally defined features. For example, Figure 3.6 specifies that "Laptop" and "Tablets" are subclasses of class "Computer." "Laptop" has the additional attribute "HDinterface," denoting the type of hard disk interface, and "Tablet" has the additional attribute "Connectivity," denoting the type of connectivity (WiFi, 3G, or 4G). We say that "Computer" is specialized into "Laptop" and "Tablet," and conversely that "Laptop" and "Tablet" are generalized into "Computer."

When domain modeling has the purpose of specifying the persistent classes that form the data tier of an application, it is customary to assume a few restrictive hypotheses that simplify the form of generalization hierarchies and make them more easily implementable with conventional database technology.

1. Each class is defined as the specialization of at most one superclass. In technical terms, "multiple inheritance" is avoided.
2. Each instance of a superclass is specialized exclusively into one subclass.
3. Each class appears in at most one generalization hierarchy.

These restrictions reduce the expressive power of the domain model. For example, due to the first two constraints, an instance of class "Computer" cannot be a "Tablet" and a "Laptop" at the same time. However, a similar meaning can be conveyed by

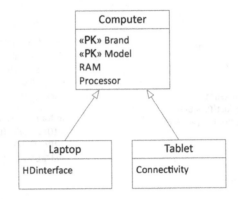

FIGURE 3.6

Graphic notation for IS-A hierarchies.

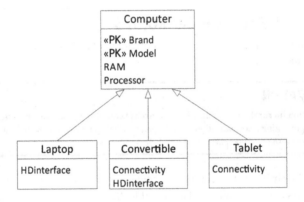

FIGURE 3.7

Generalization hierarchy approximating the use of multiple inheritance and nonexclusive specialization.

the diagram of Figure 3.7, which specializes class "Computer" into three subclasses: laptops, tablets, and convertibles. With this solution, the locally defined attributes of class "Laptop" and "Tablet" must be duplicated in class "Convertible."

3.7 ASSOCIATIONS

Classes do not exist in isolation but exhibit semantic connections to other classes called associations.

> **ASSOCIATION**
>
> An **association** represents a semantic connection between the objects of classes. Examples of associations are the connection between a product and the category to which it belongs or between a product and its accessories.

| Accessory | Options | Product |

FIGURE 3.8

Graphic notation for associations.

The meaning of the association is conveyed by the association's name, which is established by the designer. For example, the association between a product and the accessories available for it could be named "Options." The simplest form of association is the **binary association**, which connects two classes. Associations involving more than two classes, called **N-ary associations**, are also allowed. However, N-ary associations are more complex to understand and may raise subtle interpretation issues [GLM01]. In most cases, they can be equivalently replaced by multiple binary associations, as explained in Section 8.

Figure 3.8 shows the UML notation for associations, applied to the "Options" relationship between class "Product" and class "Accessory."

Each binary association is characterized by two **association ends** (also called **association roles**), each one expressing the function that one class plays in the association. For example, the association "Options" between an accessory and a product can be decomposed into two association roles, one from product to accessory, named "accessories," and one from accessory to product, named "product."

An association role/end can be regarded as the interpretation of the association from the viewpoint of one of the involved classes, that is, as an oriented connection between a source class and a destination class.

Association ends can be enriched with multiplicity constraints in terms of lower and upper bounds, denoting respectively the minimum and maximum number of objects of the destination class to which any object of the source class can be related.

- Relevant values for the multiplicity lower bound are zero or one. An association is said to be *optional* for its source class if the multiplicity lower bound is zero, and *mandatory* otherwise. Mandatory associations introduce existential dependencies between classes, because an object of the source class cannot exist without being associated with at least one object of the destination class.
- Relevant values for multiplicity lower bound are one or many. The latter option can be denoted as "*" (or as "N" in other notations such as E–R).

Based on their multiplicity constraint upper bound, associations are called "one-to-one" if both association ends multiplicity upper bound equals 1, "one-to-many" if one association end has multiplicity upper bound 1 and the other one has multiplicity upper bound N, or "many-to-many" if both association ends have multiplicity upper bound N.

In UML, multiplicity constraints are expressed by annotating the association ends with multiplicity indicators. Figure 3.9 shows how to represent association role names and multiplicity constraints: an accessory is associated with multiple products (multiplicity 1..*, placed at the side of class "Product"), and each product may be associated with several accessories (multiplicity 0..*, placed at the side of class

FIGURE 3.9

Graphic notations for association roles and multiplicity constraints.

"Accessory"). The role from "Accessory" to "Product" is mandatory, while the role from "Product" to "Accessory" is optional. The association is "many-to-many," because it connects one product to multiple accessories and one accessory to multiple products.

Association end names can be omitted from the diagram for better readability. In this case we assume default names as follows:

- An association end from class "A" to class "B" with multiplicity upper bound 1 is named by default after the name of the class in singular form.
- An association end from class "A" to class "B" with multiplicity upper bound * is named by default after the name of the class in plural form.

Defaults are not used when there is ambiguity, for example, when multiple associations exist between the same two classes or an association relates a class to itself. Figure 3.9 exemplifies the naming conventions assumed as default; thus the association end names could be omitted without ambiguity from the class diagram.

3.8 N-ARY ASSOCIATIONS AND ASSOCIATIONS WITH ATTRIBUTES

Most domain modeling languages, including UML, admit the specification of associations involving more than two classes, called N-ary associations, and of associations with attributes, represented with association classes. However, these constructs are less intuitive than binary relationships and also raise interpretation problems, such as those related to the meaning of multiplicity annotations [GLM01].

However, it is well known from the data modeling field that both these constructs can be represented using a combination of classes and binary associations. This practice requires slightly more modeling effort but makes the diagram interpretation more intuitive.

Figure 3.10 and Figure 3.11 show the representation of N-ary associations (actually ternary, for the sake of illustration) with equivalent binary associations and classes.

An N-ary association is equivalent to one "central" class and N binary associations connecting the central class to the participant classes of the N-ary association (Figure 3.10). Multiplicity constraints for the central class of the binary association have both upper and lower bounds equal to 1 to express the fact that an object of the central class must be connected to exactly one object of each one of the other classes.

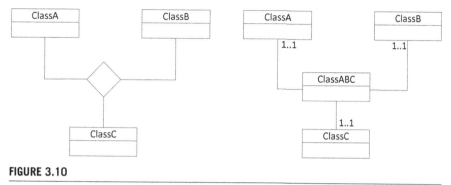

FIGURE 3.10

N-ary associations as a primitive construct (left) and as binary associations and classes (right).

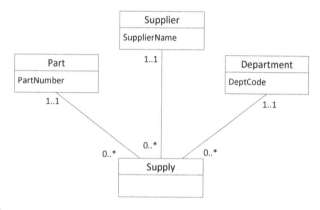

FIGURE 3.11

A ternary association, represented by the class "Supply" plus three binary associations.

This is done because it does not correspond to an object in the real world but is simply an artifact denoting the connection of N real world objects.

For example, the diagram in Figure 3.11 represents the supply of parts by suppliers to the departments of a company, which is a ternary association representable by means of three binary associations. Class "Supply" is the central class, which is connected to exactly one instance each of classes "Part," "Supplier," and "Department."

A (binary) association with attributes is equivalent to one "central" class connected by two binary associations to the participant classes of the association with attributes (Figure 3.12). As in the case of N-ary associations, multiplicity constraints of the binary associations must have both upper and lower bounds equal to 1 for the central class to express the fact that an object of such class must be connected to exactly one object of each of the other two classes, because it does not correspond to an object of the real world, but is a notation for denoting the attributes relevant to the connection of two real world objects.

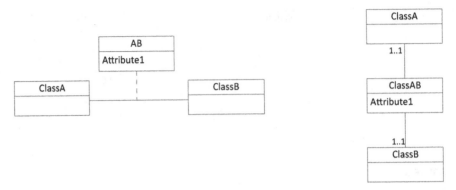

FIGURE 3.12

Association with attributes expressed with an UML association class "AB" (left) and an equivalent model using only binary associations and classes (right).

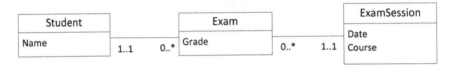

FIGURE 3.13

An association with attribute, represented by the class "Exam."

For example, the grade taken by a student in a given exam session could be represented using an association between the classes "Student" and "ExamSession," with an attribute "grade." The same situation can be equivalently modeled by replacing the association with attribute with a class "Exam," with an attribute "grade." The "Exam" class represents an individual exam taken by a student during an exam session. The resulting domain model, consisting solely of classes and associations without attributes, is represented in Figure 3.13.

N-ary associations with attributes are treated similarly: one central class is created, the association attributes are added to it, and then N binary associations are created between the central class and the other involved classes.

3.9 DERIVED INFORMATION AND THE OBJECT CONSTRAINT LANGUAGE (OCL)

In domain modeling, it may happen that the value of some attribute or association of a class can be determined from the value of some other elements of the model. For instance, the price after taxes of an article may be computed as the product of the price before taxes and the VAT, and the tracks published by an artist can be computed

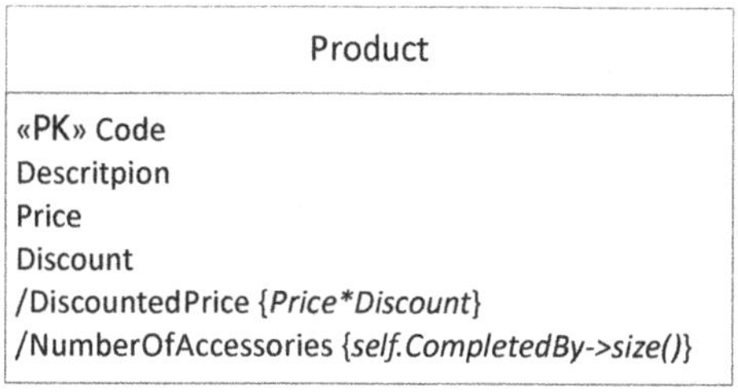

Product
«PK» Code
Descritpion
Price
Discount
/DiscountedPrice {*Price*Discount*}
/NumberOfAccessories {*self.CompletedBy->size()*}

FIGURE 3.14

Derived attributes.

by "joining" all the albums published by the artist to the tracks contained in each album. Attribute and associations that can be calculated are called *derived*.

UML includes a standard notation for characterizing attributes and associations as derived, and a language for expressing their computation rule.

- An attribute or association is denoted as derived by adding a slash character ("/") in front of the attribute or association name.
- The computation rule that defines the derived attribute or association is specified as an expression added to the declaration of the attribute or association.

Figure 3.14 shows two examples of derived attributes. Among its attributes, class "Product" includes two regular attributes, "Price" and "Discount," and two derived attributes: "/DiscountedPrice," computed as the value of the expression (Price*Discount), and "/NumberOfAccessories," computed as the values of the expression self.accessories -> size(). This expression counts the number of accessories associated with a product according to the "accessories" association role. The subexpression self.accessories is an example of path-expression, which is used for accessing the objects of an association owned by an object.

Figure 3.15 shows an example of derived association. Class "Product" is associated with class "Producer" by a derived association "/BrandedAccessories," which is the concatenation of the two associations between a product and its accessories and between an accessory and the company that produces it. The derivation rule is expressed on one of the two association roles by means of a path expression. In the example, the derivation rule is applied to the association role from class "Product" to class "Producer," and is formally specified by adding the OCL constraint to the role declaration:

```
context Product::BrandsOfAccessories:Set(Producer)
derive: self.accessories.producer
```

The examples of Figures 3.14 and 3.15 are formulated using the Object Constraint Language (OCL), which is the standard way for expressing constraints and derived information in UML. The use of OCL in domain modeling is important because it

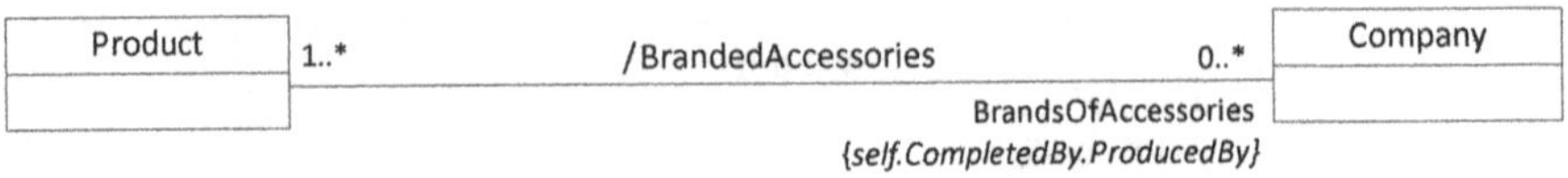

Product	1..*	/BrandedAccessories	0..*	Company

BrandsOfAccessories
{self.CompletedBy.ProducedBy}

FIGURE 3.15

Derived association.

permits the designer to convey more of the semantics of the application domain than would be possible with native UML constructs only, which are limited to simple restrictions such as visibility and multiplicity constraints.

3.10 DOMAIN MODELING PATTERNS AND PRACTICES

When designing the domain model for an interactive application that offers functionalities for data publication and management, some recurrent patterns and best practices can be exploited. They come from recognizing the role that information objects play in the application. Such roles can be summarized as follows:

- **Core objects**: These are the essential assets managed by the application that form the backbone of the domain model, around which the rest of the data schema is progressively built. Each core concept may require more than a single class to be represented, due to the presence of complex properties and internal components. For this reasons, core concepts become core submodels, which are sets of classes correlated by associations, collectively representing one core concept.
- **Interconnection objects**: These stem from the semantic associations between core concepts. In an interactive application they are used to construct links and indexes for navigating from one object to a related one. In the domain model, interconnection objects are denoted by associations between core classes that express the desired semantic connections.
- **Access objects**: These are auxiliary objects facilitating the construction of access mechanisms for optimizing the ease of use and effectiveness of the application in various ways:
  - by representing relevant categorizations over core objects, which can be used to express index hierarchies, progressively leading the user to the desired core objects;
  - by providing more precise keyword-based search mechanisms focused on well-defined categories of core objects; and
  - by clustering representative core objects into meaningful clusters, like the "pick of the day" or the "most popular objects." These collections offer the user a preview of the most interesting core objects.

Access objects are normally mapped into classes connected to the core classes by associations or specialization links. In the case of access objects, it is more appropriate to speak of access subschemas, because the same core object may be categorized or specialized in different ways, using multiple categorizing classes, associations, and specialized subclasses.

- Personalization objects: These are used to incorporate into the data model the relevant properties of the user needed for personalization purposes. For example, classes may be used to model user profile data and the groups in which the users participate, and associations may be used to connect the user and group classes to other classes in the application domain to represent aspects like object ownership or personal preferences. Groups can also denote roles played by the users, as is customary in role-based access control (RBAC) for regulating the access to the core objects.

The distinction between the different roles played by the classes and associations must take into account the application domain and the mission of the specific application. For instance, in an e-commerce web site for selling books, the author concept associated with the book concept could be considered either as a piece of core content or just as a property of books, not deserving the status of a core concept. A concept is core if it independently contributes to the achievement of the application's mission. In the book selling example, authors may qualify as core concepts if the site offers also information about authors, irrespective of books. In this case, the designer should treat authors as first-class objects, and, for example, publish their biography, interviews, and so on. As another example, the profile data about users are auxiliary content used for personalization in most e-commerce applications. Conversely, in a social network, data about people are the main asset, and profile data are the core content of the application.

3.11 THE PROCESS OF DOMAIN MODELING

The domain modeling process can be naturally structured as an incremental and iterative activity. Starting from an initial nucleus—typically consisting of the most important core concepts—the domain modeler can progressively extend the model by applying refinement operations:

- Adding a new core subschema or enriching an existing core subschema by detailing the internal properties and components of a core concept.
- Adding an interconnection subschema by drawing associations between core classes that express the semantic relationships between core concepts.
- Adding an access subschema by introducing a categorization class and connecting it to a core class, or by specializing a core class using a subclass that denotes a special collection.
- Adding a personalization subschema by introducing the user and role class, defining their properties, and connecting them to the core objects to express user- or role-related preferences and personal objects.

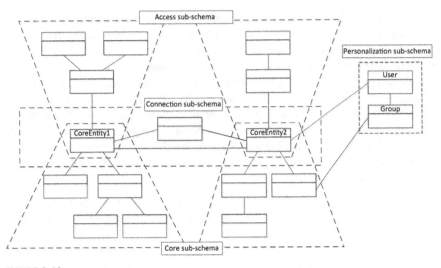

FIGURE 3.16

Data schema highlighting access, core, connection, and personalization subschemas.

Following the above domain modeling guidelines produces a domain model with a more regular structure, which is decomposed into modules with a well-identified purpose, as shown in Figure 3.16:

3.11.1 DESIGNING THE CORE SUBSCHEMA

The process of defining a core subschema from the description of the core concepts identified in the data requirements analysis is straightforward:

1. The core concept is represented by a class (called core class).
2. Properties with a single, atomic value become attributes of the core class. The identifying properties become the primary key of the core class.
3. Properties with multiple or structured values become internal components of the core class.

Internal components are represented as classes connected to the core class via a part-of association. Two cases are possible, which differ in the multiplicity constraints of the association connecting the component to the core class:

1. If the connecting association has a 1:1 multiplicity constraint for the component, the component is a proper subpart of the core concept. In this case, no instance of the internal component can exist in absence of the core class instance it belongs to, and multiple core objects cannot share the same instance of the internal component. Internal components of this kind are sometimes called "weak classes" in data modeling terminology, or "part-of components" in object-oriented terminology.

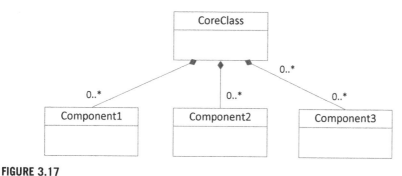

FIGURE 3.17

Typical core subschema.

2. If the association between the core class and the component has 0:* multiplicity for the internal component, the notion of "component" is interpreted in a broader sense. The internal component is considered a part of the core concept, even if an instance of it may exist independently of the connection to a core class instance and can be shared among different core objects. Nonetheless, the internal component is not deemed an essential data asset of the application and thus is not elevated to the status of a core concept.

Figure 3.17 illustrates the typical domain model of a core subschema, including one core class, two proper nonshared internal components, and one shared component.

Note that a shared component may be part of one or more concepts, but it is not treated as an independent object for the purpose of the application. Such a consideration is useful for building the front-end model, which should present or manage components as parts of their "enclosing" core concepts and not as standalone objects.

3.11.2 DESIGNING AN INTERCONNECTION SUBSCHEMA

Interconnection subschemas are patterns of associations introduced in the domain model for expressing semantic relationships between core objects, as illustrated in Figure 3.18.

At the two extremes, it is possible that all core concepts are related, which produces a completely connected graph of associations, or that all the core concepts of the application are unrelated. In the latter case, the interconnection subschema is empty, and the core concepts are isolated.

3.11.3 DESIGNING AN ACCESS SUBSCHEMA

Access subschemas are patterns of classes and associations that support the location and selection of core concepts. Identifying the needed access subschemas is less straightforward than identifying the other classes of subschemas. Hints as to the presence of access concepts can be found in the use case inventory, by carefully reviewing how users locate their objects of interest. An access subschema consists of two kinds of classes: categorizing classes and specialized subclasses.

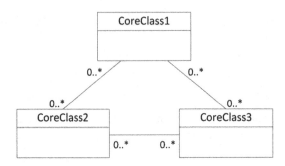

FIGURE 3.18

Typical connection subschema.

1. A categorizing class is a class connected via an association to a core class that plays the role of the categorized class, with the purpose of superimposing a classification hierarchy over the instances of the core class. For example, in an online portal application, the published news can be classified into categories by introducing a "NewsCategory" class into the domain model, with the role of categorizing class, and associating it to the class "NewsItem," which plays the role of the categorized class.

2. A specialized subclass is a class connected by an "is-a" association to a core class. The instances of this subclass share some common property that distinguishes them from the general case and can be exploited for facilitating access. Examples of this way of grouping special instances are commonly found in web applications and social networks in the form of "highlighted items," like editor's choices, specials of the day, recent news, and popular topics. In this case, the subclass denotes the restricted subgroup of instances of the superclass that are selected as members of the special collection.

Figure 3.19 pictorially represent a "canonical" access schema. A central class, labeled "Core," represents the core concept, and is surrounded by two classes representing access concepts, labeled "Access1," and "Access2," which denote alternative categorizations. The diagram contains also a subclass, labeled "SpecialCollection," which denotes a collection of representative core concepts.

Note that categorical concepts are treated as classes and not only as an internal property of the categorized class, because they may themselves store several pieces of information, like a representative image or some descriptive text, which illustrates the common features of core objects belonging to the category. The organization of categorical concepts can reflect the following three recurrent patterns:

- Categorical concepts can themselves be categorized, resulting in a hierarchy of categorizations. For example, hardware products can be classified by category

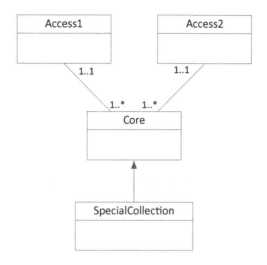

FIGURE 3.19

Typical access subschema.

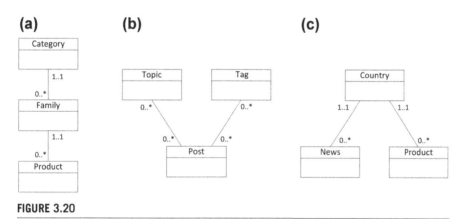

FIGURE 3.20

Three forms of categorization: hierarchical (a), multiple (b), and shared (c).

(computers or peripherals), then by family (PCs, servers, and laptops), then by commercial brand, and so on (Figure 3.20a).

- The same core concept may be subject to more than one categorization, providing multiple classifications. For example, blog posts may be organized by topic and by user generated tags (Figure 3.20b).
- Finally, the same categorical concept can be used to classify more than one core concept, resulting in a shared categorization. For example, the class "Country" may classify both news and products (Figure 3.20c).

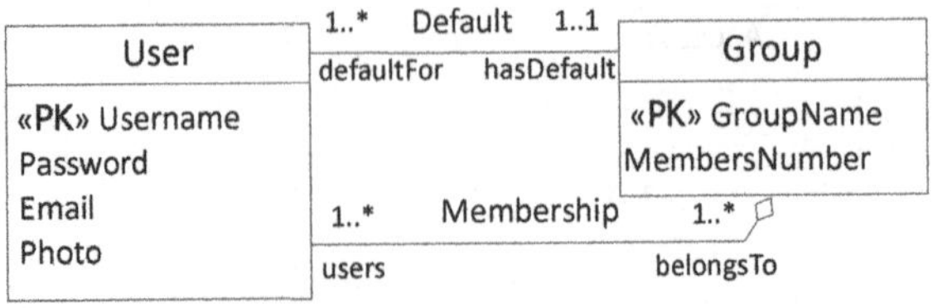

FIGURE 3.21

User and Group representations in the personalization data schema.

3.11.4 DESIGNING A PERSONALIZATION SUBSCHEMA

A personalization subschema consists of classes and associations describing properties of the users, relevant to the adaptation of the user interface. The properties captured by the personalization subschema typically comprise:

1. **Profile data**, which are the attributes—possibly complex—that characterize the individual users. Example of general-purpose profile attributes may be the name, address, location, sex, and age of a user. Profile data may also be application specific. For instance, in e-commerce applications profile attributes may include the total amount of expenditure, the date of the last visit or purchase, the feedback score of a buyer or seller, and so on.
2. **User groups**, which represents the identified clusters of users with homogeneous requirements or permissions. The typical usage of the user group concept is the clustering of users according to the role they are entitled to play in the application.
3. **Personalization associations**, which are semantic associations between core objects and the users or groups, denoting aspects such as the access rights of users or groups over core objects, the ownership of core objects by users or groups, the preference of users or groups for selected core objects, or the recommendation of core objects to users or groups.

Information about a user can be represented explicitly in the domain model. The model in Figure 3.21 is an example of a basic, yet typical, personalization subschema.

- Class "User" specifies information about the individuals who access the application. It includes basic properties such as username, password, photo, and e-mail.
- Class "Group" specifies information about clusters of users with homogeneous requirements. It includes collective properties, such as the group name, the number of members, and so on. The "Group" class can also be used to represent the roles of the users for access control purposes.
- A many-to-many association (called "Membership") connects class "User" and "Group," denoting that a user may belong to multiple groups and that a group clusters multiple users.
- A one-to-many association (called "Default") connects class "User" and "Group," denoting that a user may have one group as the default one among the groups he belongs to. This additional information is useful for assigning the

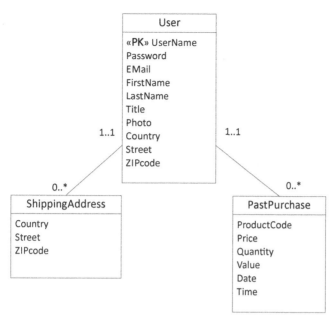

FIGURE 3.22

Domain-specific user profiles data for an e-commerce application.

user to the default group after he logs into the application. Note that in those applications where users are associated with a single group there is no need of the "Default" association.

The simple data schema of Figure 3.21 can be augmented with further elements to represent user information needed in a specific application domain.

Figure 3.22 shows an example in which the "User" class includes additional profile attributes, such as "FirstName," "LastName," "Title," "Country," "City," "Street," and "ZIPcode." Further classes can be included for modeling additional data of the user profile. For instance, the class "ShippingAddress" can be added to allow users to ship goods to multiple addresses. The class "LastPurchase" can be added for recording data about the last purchased products, like the price, the ordered quantity, the total order value, the purchase date and time, and the shipping address. Personalization data of this kind can be used, for example, for recommending products based on the past purchase history.

Personalization associations can also represent interface configuration preferences. An example of personalization association is reported in Figure 3.23, in the context of a personalized geo-referenced application publishing local information, like weather reports, events, and city guides. The preference associated with the user records the city where he is currently located and is represented by an association between class "User" and class "City," which permits the selection of specific content

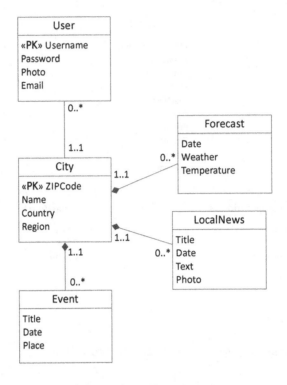

FIGURE 3.23

Basic domain model for a geo-localized newsfeed application.

based on the preferred city of the user, as denoted by the "Forecast," "LocalNews," and "CityGuideItem" components classes owned by class "City."

Note that the choice of making forecasts and local news part-of components of class "City," rather than shared components, is arguable and depends on the specific application and viewpoint of the modeler. This observation applies to most examples in the book, which should not be taken as the only possible models. Many of them may admit alternative variants in different contexts, based on the interpretation of requirements and even on the modeling style of the designer.

A personalization association may also denote information objects owned by individual users. The meaning of such an association may be that only the user who owns personal objects can access and manipulate them. This happens, for example, for the shopping cart in e-commerce applications. In other cases, personal objects are created and managed by their authors but are also available to other users. This happens, for example, in blog and content sharing platforms, where users publish content items for other users to view and comment.

The data schema of Figure 3.24 includes two personalization associations that relate each user with the articles and comments he has produced. Comments are also connected to the article with which they are associated.

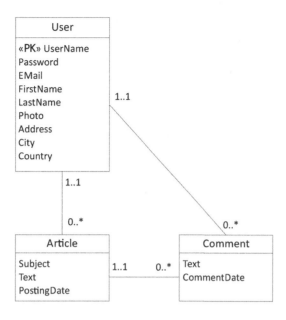

FIGURE 3.24

Basic domain model of a blog application.

The personalization subschema of the domain model describes the properties of users and the way they are clustered and associated with other domain objects. They are typically stored persistently (e.g., as the result of a user registration process). Exploiting the information of the personalization subschema for dynamically adapting the interface requires identifying the specific user at runtime and preserving his identity during the course of the interaction. In chapter 4, we introduce the IFML constructs for modeling interface adaptation: Context, ContextDimensions, and ContextVariables. A ContextVariable is a runtime-initialized object that can be used in the interface model. It can represent, among the other things, the authenticated user's identity and, if the application assigns specific roles to the authenticated user (e.g., as part of a RBAC scheme), also the current role of the user. In chapter 8, we will show how to model the login process, which is the typical way in which the ContextVariable with the authenticated identity of the user gets initialized at runtime.

3.12 RUNNING EXAMPLE

In this Section we start illustrating a running example that will support the description of interface modeling with IFML in the next sections.

The application is an e-mail management system that lets users manage messages and contacts. Users have a name and an e-mail address. E-mail messages are

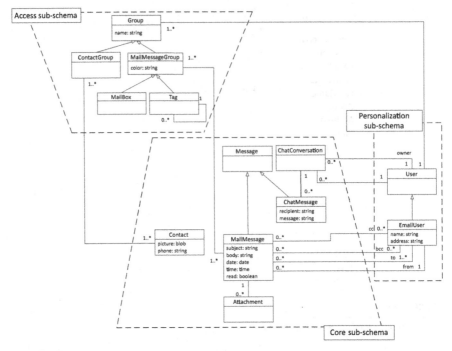

FIGURE 3.25

Domain model of the e-mail management application.

clustered into system- or user-generated mailboxes for easier access. They can also be associated with tags for enabling topic-driven access. Tags themselves can be organized in hierarchies. E-mail messages have a subject, a body, a date and time, a "read" flag, a sender, several recipients (direct, carbon copy, and blind copy), and possibly multiple attachments. Users can be recorded as contacts with additional data such a photo and phone number. Contacts can be clustered in groups for easier access. Users can have chat conversations. A chat conversation consists of several chat messages belonging to the user who produced them.

Figure 3.25 shows the domain model of the e-mail management application. Classes and associations are laid out to highlight the different subschemas:

- Core subschema: contains the classes "Message," "Contact," and "ChatConversation," with their attributes, subclasses, and part-of classes.
- Interconnection subschema: messages are related to their recipient users.
- Access subschema: e-mail messages are categorized by tags and clustered into mail boxes. Contacts are clustered into groups.
- Personalization subschema: the "User" class stores profile data Users are related to the messages, chat conversations, and contacts they possess.

3.13 **SUMMARY OF THE CHAPTER**

This chapter has addressed domain modeling, an activity complementary and highly relevant to interface modeling. Adhering to the principles of simplicity and separation of concerns, IFML does not prescribe a specific domain modelling language but can be interfaced to the notation preferred by designers, provided that it allows expressing the objects and associations of the application domain. For the sake of illustration, we have employed UML class diagrams, and briefly recapped their main features for structural modeling.

To show the interplay of domain and interface modeling, we have discussed design patterns that occur in the domain model, which stem from the joint consideration of data representation and interaction support requirements. The chapter ended with the specification of the domain model of an e-mail application, the running example that we discussed in chapters 4, 5, and 6, devoted to the systematic introduction of the core IFML concepts.

As a final remark, the position of a chapter about domain modeling before those devoted to front-end modeling follows the editorial necessity of sequencing topics, but does not imply a prescription on the order in which things must be done. Discovering the objects and the associations of the domain model benefits from the understanding of the type of interaction that the application must support. The design of the front end equally benefits from the knowledge about the important objects and associations the application deals with. The relative importance and the order in which domain design and front-end design should be executed depend also on the emphasis of the specific application at hand.

3.14 **BIBLIOGRAPHIC NOTES**

Domain modeling dates back to 1976, the year in which the seminal article by Peter Chen, "The Entity–Relationship Model—Toward a Unified View of Data," appeared in the first issue of ACM's *Transactions on Database Systems*. Ever since, conceptual data modeling with the Entity–Relationship model has been the cornerstone information systems development. Conceptual database design is a classic ingredient of data design, described in detail in [BCN92]. A popular book on the subsequent phase of physical database design is [Shasha92].

Domain modeling is also part of object-oriented analysis and design. Classic books on the subject are [BJR98, Booch94, CY90, Jacobson94, RBPEL91, SM88]. In particular, Booch, Jacobson, and Rumbaugh provide an excellent guide to the Unified Modeling Language (UML), by means of an easy-to-understand example-driven approach [BJR98]. A concise reference to UML is Martin Fowler's *UML Distilled* [Fowler03]. The Object Constraint Language official specifications are published in the web site of the OMG (http://www.omg.org/spec/OCL/). The language use is treated extensively in the textbook [WK03].

The idea of using domain modeling in conjunction with web front-end design has been explored by a few web design methods proposed in the research community, including HDM [GPS93], RMM [ISB95], and WebML [BBC03]. These methods have underlined the differences between data modeling for traditional applications and for hypertext-based interfaces. The importance of design patterns in object-oriented design was first been recognized in the milestone book [GBM86]. Design patterns and best practices specific to data design for the web were first discussed in [CFP99].

END NOTES

1. http://www.omg.org/spec/OCL/.

Modeling the composition of the user interface

4

The goal of user interface modeling is the specification of the front end of the application. This activity is performed at a high level, comparable to the conceptual level at which objects and associations are specified in the domain model. In contrast to domain modeling, which rests on a consolidated tradition, interface modeling is a younger discipline based on new concepts and methods.

In this chapter, we describe IFML in detail, commencing with the elements used to specify the general organization of the interface and high-level navigation. In chapter 5, we discuss the IFML primitives for expressing the internal composition of the interface: the published content components and the data entry forms, as well as the interaction mechanisms associated with them. In chapter 6, we focus on the specification of the business actions triggered by user interaction and on their effect on the status of the interface. For a more formal introduction to the elements of IFML and their associations, the reader can refer to chapter 12, where the IFML metamodel is briefly discussed.

4.1 INTERFACE ORGANIZATION

The specification of the interface in IFML is organized hierarchically using modularization constructs called ViewContainers.

> **VIEWCONTAINERS**
>
> A **ViewContainer** is an element of the interface that aggregates other view containers and/or view components displaying content.

In practice, a ViewContainer may represent a physical interface artifact such as a window or a page of a web application. But it can also denote a purely logical aggregation of other view containers, such as a section of a large web portal constituted by several pages dealing with a homogeneous subject.

ViewContainers support navigation, which is the change of focus from one container to another. To specify that a ViewContainer is the source of a navigation command, it is necessary to associate it with an event.

EVENTS

An **Event** is an occurrence that can affect the state of the application by causing navigation and/ or passing parameters. Events may be produced by a user interaction (ViewElementEvent), by an action when it finishes its execution normally or exceptionally (ActionEvent), or by the system in the form of notifications (SystemEvent).

A **ViewElementEvent** is an Event that may be triggered by the user while interacting with ViewContainers, ViewComponents, and parts thereof called ViewComponentParts.

The effect of user interaction—that is, the target ViewContainer displayed after a ViewElementEvent has occurred—is specified by means of a NavigationFlow, denoted as a directed arc connecting the event symbol to the target view container.

NAVIGATIONFLOW

A **NavigationFlow** represents the navigation or the change of the view element in focus, the trig- gering of an Action, or the reaction to a SystemEvent. NavigationFlows are activated when Events are triggered. They connect Events owned by ViewContainers, ViewComponents, ViewComponent- Parts, or Actions with other ViewContainers, ViewComponents, ViewComponentParts, or Actions.

Figure 4.1 shows a very simple IFML model exemplifying these concepts, together with a hypothetical rendition.

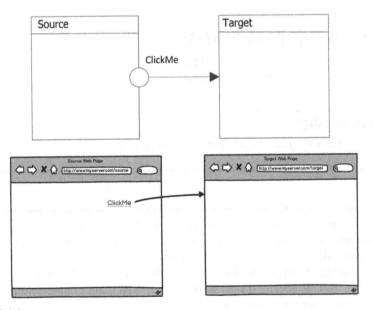

FIGURE 4.1

Model of navigation between view containers expressed with events (top) and the corre- sponding rendition (bottom).

"Source" and "Target" are ViewContainers, denoted as UML classifiers. "ClickMe" is an Event, represented as a circle associated with the owning ViewContainer. The NavigationFlow, denoted by an unlabeled directed arrow, connects the event named "ClickMe" of the "Source" ViewContainer to the "Target" ViewContainer, indicating that the occurrence of the "ClickMe" event causes the display of the "Target" ViewContainer.

Notice that some model features, such as the name of the ViewContainers and of the Event, are purposely shown also in the rendition. This is to highlight that the model features can be employed to create the implementation. For example, the name of the ViewContainer could be used to produce the title of a window or the name and URL of a web page, and the name of an Event could be exploited to create the text of a hyperlink anchor or a button label.

4.2 VIEW CONTAINER NESTING

Most interfaces organize the content and interaction commands presented to the user into a regular structure to enhance usability. For example, many web pages have a central content area and one or two columns for collateral items such as menus, search bars, and ads. Window-based interfaces split the work area into several panels and use tabbing to present alternative views of the work items.

IFML models the structure of the interface by means of nested ViewContainers. Nested ViewContainers express the organization of the interface at a conceptual level but necessarily have an interpretation that depends on the platform where the interface is deployed. Two typical situations arise:

- In window-based platforms, such as Java Swing or Windows.NET, the interface is normally hosted within one top-level container.
- In a pure HTML web application, the interface is normally fragmented across a set of independent page templates, which means that there is no top-level ViewContainer. Rather, one ViewContainer is elected as the one accessed by default (the so-called "Home Page").

The advent of rich Internet applications has blurred the distinction between window-based and page-based interfaces, so it is not uncommon to see interfaces that have an organization that stands in the middle between the two extremes. This is in line with the *single page development* paradigm.

In the rest of this section, we proceed in the explanation of the features of ViewContainers from a platform-independent perspective. We will come back to the influence of platform-dependent features on design when discussing interface design patterns later in this chapter. In chapter 7, we will present some extensions to IFML conceived for desktop, web, and mobile development, which customize the terminology and concepts of IFML to make the language closer to the expectations of developers of these popular classes of solutions.

Nested ViewContainers may be in conjunctive form, which means that they are displayed together, or in disjunctive form, which means that the display of one

ViewContainer replaces another ViewContainer. The property of disjunctiveness is explicitly associated with the enclosing container with the notation shown in Figure 4.2: a XOR label before the name of the ViewContainer. By default, ViewContainers display their inner ViewContainers in conjunctive form.

Figure 4.3 shows an example of disjunctive ViewContainers from the e-mail application used as a running example. The interface consists of a top-level View-Container from which the user can access either the "MailMessages" ViewContainer or the "Contacts" ViewContainer.

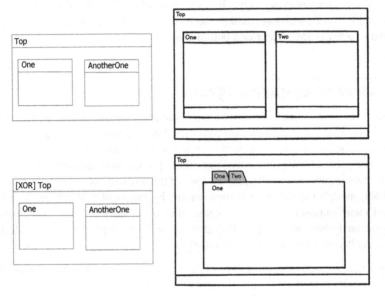

FIGURE 4.2

Cconjunctive and disjunctive nested ViewContainer and a possible rendition.

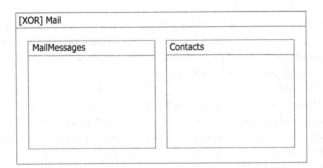

FIGURE 4.3

Example of disjunctive nested ViewContainer in the e-mail application.

4.3 **VIEW CONTAINER NAVIGATION**

ViewContainers support a basic form of navigation, which we call **content-independent navigation** to mark the distinction with the content-dependent navigation described in chapter 5.

Content-independent navigation is expressed by associating a navigation event to a ViewContainer and by specifying the target of the navigation with an Interaction-Flow. An example of this design pattern was illustrated in Figure 4.1.

The meaning of content-independence is that user interaction does not depend on the content of the source and destination ViewContainers. In implementation terms, it is not necessary to associate parameter values with the interaction in order to compute the content of the target ViewContainer. This behavior is in contrast to content-dependent navigation, discussed in chapter 5.

4.4 **VIEW CONTAINER RELEVANCE AND VISIBILITY**

ViewContainers are characterized by some distinguishing properties that highlight their "importance" in the organization of the interface.

DEFAULT VIEWCONTAINERS

The **default property** characterizes the ViewContainer presented by default when its enclosing ViewContainer is accessed.

Default view containers are denoted by a "D" within square brackets placed at the top-left corner of the view container.

LANDMARK VIEWCONTAINERS

The **landmark property** characterizes a ViewContainer that is reachable from all the other View-Containers nested within its enclosing ViewContainer (i.e., from its sibling ViewContainers) and from their subcontainers.

Landmark view containers are denoted by an "L" within square brackets placed at the top-left corner of the view container.

Figure 4.4 shows an example of the landmark and default properties in the e-mail application. When the user starts the application the "Mail" ViewContainer is accessed. The default subcontainer "MailMessages" is displayed, whereas the alternative ViewContainer "Contacts" remains hidden. Both "MailMessages" and "Contacts" are defined as landmarks, which means it is always possible to access the one that is not in view from the one that is in view.

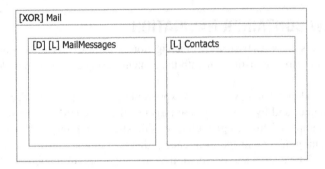

FIGURE 4.4

Use of the landmark and default properties in the e-mail application.

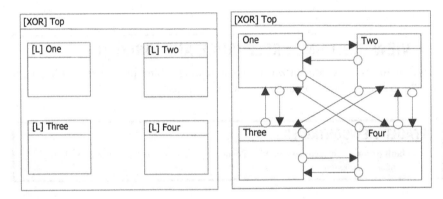

FIGURE 4.5

Landmark ViewContainers (left) and equivalent diagram with explicit events and navigation flows (right).

The landmark property is an example of a construct introduced for model usability. It does not augment the expressive power of IFML, because the access to ViewContainers can be represented explicitly with navigation flows, but reduces the burden of model specification and augments the readability of diagrams. Figure 4.5 illustrates on a small scale example why this is true. It shows two equivalent IFML diagrams. In the diagram on the left, the ViewContainers nested inside the Top ViewContainer are marked as landmarks, which means that every ViewContainer is the target of an implicit navigation flow pointing to it from the sibling ViewContainers. The diagram on the right explicitly shows these navigation flows and the events triggering the navigation. The meaning conveyed by the diagram on the left is that a landmark View-Container can be reached from any other ViewContainer of the enclosing module. If an interface contains many containers, the landmark property significantly reduces the number of events and navigation flows to be drawn and makes the diagram much more readable.

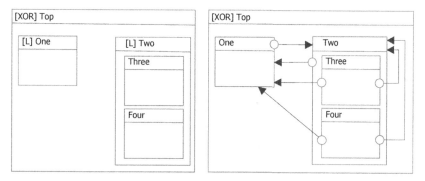

FIGURE 4.6

Landmark ViewContainers with nesting (left) and an equivalent diagram with explicit events and navigation flows (right).

Figure 4.6 shows an example with nested ViewContainers. ViewContainer "One" is landmark and thus accessible from its sibling ViewContainers and their children (i.e., from the ViewContainers "Two," "Three," and "Four"). The same applies to ViewContainer "Two." Again, the use of the landmark property avoids cluttering the diagram with many events and navigation flows.

4.5 WINDOWS

IFML provides a set of specializations of the ViewContainer concept that allow one to represent more precisely the behavior of the container-level navigation.

> **WINDOW**
>
> A **Window** is a specific kind of ViewContainer that represents a window in a user interface. A Window ViewContainer can be tagged as Modal or Modeless depending on its behavior with respect to the user interaction. A **Modal** window opens as a new window and disables the interaction with the background window(s) of the application; a **Modeless** window opens as a new window and still allows interaction with the other pieces of the user interface.

Navigation from a source window to a target window (not tagged as Modal or Modeless) implies that the source window disappears and is replaced by the target. If the target Window is tagged as Modal or Modeless instead, the new window will be superimposed onto the old one and will behave as modal or modeless respectively. Window, Modal, and Modeless specializations can be specified as stereotypes of the ViewContainer classifier, as shown in Figure 4.7.

Navigation between Windows "Step 1" and "Step 2" implies that "Step 2" substitute "Step 1" on the screen. Navigations from "Submission" to "Confirmation" and "ToolsMenu" will open the two new windows in front of the old one and will respectively grant modal and modeless behavior.

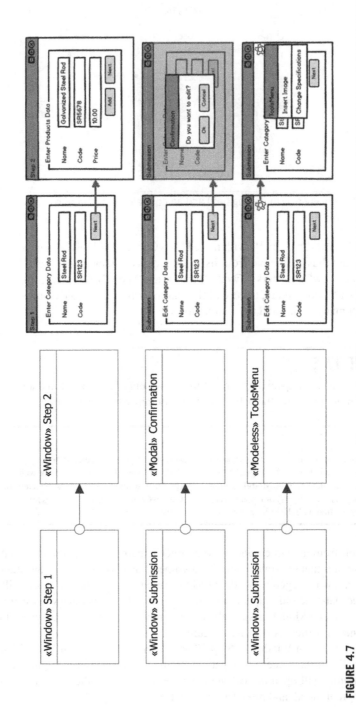

FIGURE 4.7

Examples of window, modal window, and modeless window, and their possible renditions.

4.6 **CONTEXT AND VIEWPOINT**

The composition of the interface is not necessarily a static concept. Many applications update the interface organization and content at runtime, based on information about the context of the user interaction. For example, a mobile application can deliver alerts based on the current position of the user, and a web-based portal may exploit the information of the personalization subschema, introduced in chapter 3, for publishing user profile data and personalized recommendations.

To support the dynamic adaptation of the interface, IFML comprises concepts that capture both the design-time adaptation requirements set by the developer and the runtime values set by the application, which are necessary for deciding which adaptations to apply based on the interaction context of the user. The notion of context provided by IFML is purposely very broad. It may encompass aspects such as the identity, role, geographic position, or device of the user.

CONTEXT AND CONTEXTDIMENSION

The **Context** is a descriptor of the runtime aspects of the system that determine how the user interface is adapted. A **ContextDimension** is a component of the Context.

IFML comes with various predefined extensions of the ContextDimension concept.

USERROLE, DEVICE, AND POSITION

The **UserRole** represents the role currently played by the user in the application. It comprises the attributes that the user's profile should satisfy to enable the context.
Device represents the characteristics that a device possesses.
Position represents the availability of location and orientation information of the device used to access the application.

The predefined Context and ContextDimension elements can be extended to represent finer-grain or other context perspectives, such as network connectivity or temporal aspects.

The requirements for a Context to be active are expressed by OCL expressions, called ActivationExpressions.

ACTIVATIONEXPRESSION

An **ActivationExpression** is a Boolean condition that determines whether the associated Context (or other IFML element) is active (if the condition is true) or inactive (if the condition is false).

Figure 4.8 shows the IFML notation for an ActivationExpression that specifies when a Context is active. The specific context is represented as an instance

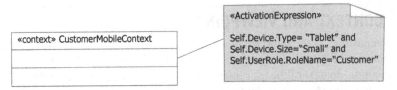

FIGURE 4.8

ActivationExpression specifying the requirements for the Context to be enabled.

("AdminMobileContext") of a classifier stereotyped as «context». The ActivationExpression is expressed as a stereotyped annotation associated to the Context instance.

The example of Figure 4.8 assumes that the "UserRole" ContextDimension has an attribute called "RoleName" that specifies the role that the user should fulfill in a role-based access control (RBAC) system. It also assumes that the "Device" ContextDimension has two attributes. "Type" identifies the class of device, while "Size" indicates the dimensions of the screen. The specification of Figure 4.8 therefore mandates that the "CustomerMobileContext" is enabled when the user's access device is a small screen tablet and the role granted after login is that of a registered customer.

The evaluation of an ActivationExpression associated with a context requires that the values of the relevant ContextDimensions be recorded at runtime. Such runtime values can be represented in IFML as ContextVariables.

CONTEXTVARIABLE

A **ContextVariable** is a runtime variable that holds information about the usage context. It specializes into SimpleContextVariable (of a primitive value type) and DataContextVariable (referencing a DataBinding).

ContextVariables enable a form of fine-grain interface adaption, as we will see in chapters 7, 8, and 9. They can be used in ActivationExpressions associated with ViewElements to condition their visibility based on the situation. Another, coarser-grain form of interface adaptation is achieved by using ViewPoints, which denote whole application designs tailored for a specific context.

VIEWPOINT

A **ViewPoint** is the specification of an entire interface model that is active only when a specific Context is enabled.

The enablement of the ViewPoint is dynamic and governed by the ActivationExpression associated with the Context. When the ActivationExpression is satisfied, the

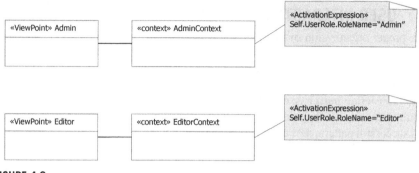

FIGURE 4.9

ActivationExpressions and Contexts enabling different ViewPoints.

Context becomes active and so does the associated ViewPoint with all the ViewElements and Events contained in it.

Figure 4.9 shows an example of ViewPoint specification. Two ViewPoints are defined ("Admin" and "Editor") that contain different interface models for the two distinct roles. They are associated with the contexts that specify the activation requirements of the ViewPoints.

In summary, the ContextDimensions express the enabling dimensions of the Context, and an ActivationExpression can be used to dictate the required values for such ContextDimensions. The actual runtime values for a specific user are represented by ContextVariables. When the relevant runtime values of the ContextVariables match the required values for the ContextDimensions in the ActivationExpression, the Context is enabled. The enabled Context in turn identifies the ViewPoint (i.e., the variant of the interface) to be used. Finer-grain adaptation can be achieved using ContextVariables in ActivationExpressions associated with individual element of the interface.

The values of the ContextVariables can also be used to publish or to put to work the content of the personalization schema

- A ContextVariable holding the user's identity (e.g., the "username" attribute) permits the application to look up the appropriate instance of the "User" class of the personalization subschema, retrieve profile data and personal objects from the database, and publish them in the interface.
- A ContextVariable holding the role of an authenticated user can be used to look up the appropriate instance of the "Group" class in the personalization subschema, retrieve the permissions of the user, and adapt the interface content and actions to such permissions.

In chapter 7, we put these concepts to work in various examples of the adaptation of the interface for web and mobile applications. In chapter 8, we discuss how to set the ContextVariables explicitly based on user interaction (e.g., as the effect of a login Action) and how to use them in applications exploiting the identity and role of the user.

4.7 USER INTERACTION PATTERNS

The proper organization of the interface is paramount for getting a good and user-friendly experience. IFML allows the designer to express such an organization at a conceptual level before committing to the implementation architecture. To support the design of the interface structure, we introduce a set of guidelines based on **user interaction patterns**, reusable models that effectively address a recurrent set of requirements in the design of user interfaces. When most users become accustomed to a successful pattern, new applications tend to implement the same design to reduce the learning curve and induce a sense of familiarity. User interaction patterns are classified into various categories, based on the concern addressed.

We will use a pattern naming convention to help designers immediately identify the purpose of a pattern. The name of a pattern is structured as XY-Z, where:

- X is the category of pattern. For instance, interface organization patterns start with the letter "O."
- D is the deployment platform. For instance, desktop patterns are labeled with "D," web with "W," and mobile with "M." The letter "G" (for "general") is reserved for cross-platform patterns that apply irrespective of the deployment platform.
- Z is a mnemonic label identifying the specific pattern.

For instance, a pattern could be named OD-SWA (as in the first example described in section 4.8.1.1).

4.8 INTERFACE ORGANIZATION PATTERNS AND PRACTICES

An **interface organization pattern** is a user interaction pattern that focuses on the hierarchical structure of the user interface. Different interface organization patterns have emerged for different classes of applications and for the various delivery platforms and access devices. This section reports some of the best-known patterns in this category, classified by platform (desktop, web, and mobile). Other categories of patterns are presented in the next chapters.

4.8.1 DESKTOP INTERFACE ORGANIZATION PATTERNS

In desktop applications—and more recently in single-page rich Internet applications—the entire user interface is hosted within a single topmost ViewContainer, which has an articulated internal structure based on a hierarchy of nested ViewContainers.

4.8.1.1 PATTERN OD-SWA: Simple work area
A typical functional division distinguishes a work area where the main tasks of the application are performed from one or more service areas, including ViewContainers

either hosting commands (e.g., menu bars, tool bars) or supporting auxiliary tasks (e.g., console or error message panels, status bars).

Figure 4.10 shows the IFML model of the simple work area interface organization pattern with an example application (a text editor). The pattern simply comprises a top-level ViewContainer with embedded nested sub-ViewContainers.

4.8.1.2 PATTERN OD-MWA: Multiview work area

When the task supported by the application and the data or the objects to be manipulated grow in complexity, the simple work area organization can be refined. One extension is to allow for multiple alternative views of the object/data/task in the work area, as represented by View1 and View2 in Figure 4.11.

Figure 4.11 shows an example of the multiview work area interface organization. An image editor has a normal view shown by default (called "Home") and a zoom view used for adjusting the zoom level of the image (called "View").

4.8.1.3 PATTERN OD-CWA: Composite work area

An alternative way of breaking down complexity is to split the work area into subregions devoted to different subtasks or perspectives of the object/data/task, presented simultaneously to allow the user to switch without losing the focus on the item under consideration. In such a case, one subregion often hosts the principal representation of the object/data/task and the other regions support collateral properties or subtasks.

Figure 4.12 shows an example of a composite work area interface with an example application: a document editor, featuring the main work area with a set of associated panels plus a set of menu bars.

4.8.1.4 PATTERN OD-MCWA: Multiview composite work area

The decomposition of the work area into alternative perspectives and simultaneous partial views can be combined to achieve a nested structure that best fits the specific requirements of the task supported by the application. For example, the work area could be partitioned into partial views displayed simultaneously, and the main view could be organized into multiple perspectives. Another option could have the work area supporting alternative perspectives, each one composed of several partial views appropriate to a perspective, displayed simultaneously.

Figure 4.13 shows an example of a multiview composite work area: a programming language IDE has an editing and a debug view, the latter composed of several parts.

4.8.2 WEB INTERFACE ORGANIZATION PATTERNS

In web applications, the typical organization of the interface allocates functionality to multiple pages, either produced statically or generated dynamically by page templates or server side scripts. In this case, nested ViewContainers are still useful and can fulfill a twofold role. As with desktop applications, they may express the allocation of content and navigation within regions of a page (e.g., as is possible with

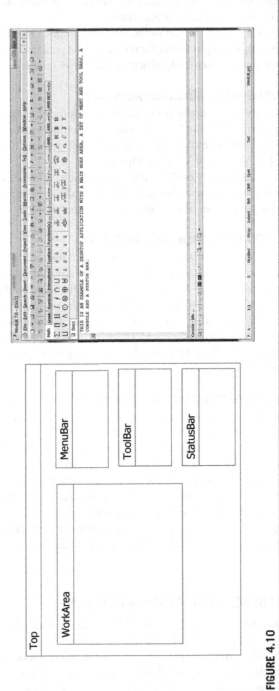

FIGURE 4.10

The simple work area interface organization pattern with an example application (a text editor).

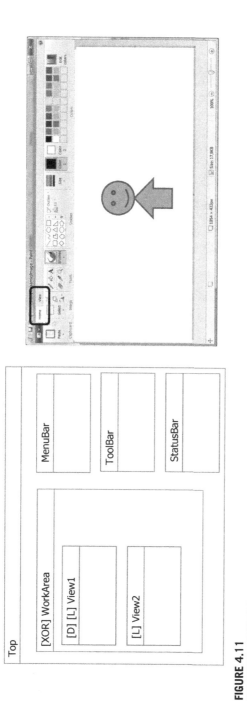

FIGURE 4.11

The multiview work area interface organization pattern with an example application.

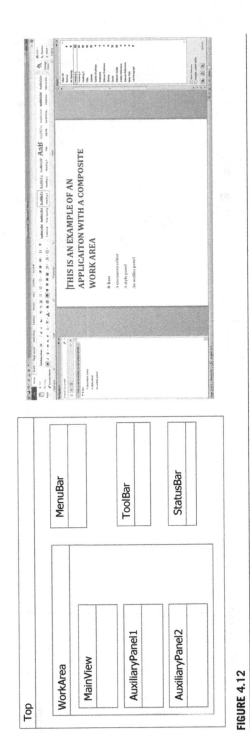

FIGURE 4.12

The composite work area interface composition pattern.

FIGURE 4.13

The multiview composite work area pattern.

HTML frames or through the use of JavaScript). In contrast to desktop applications, they may express the logical clustering of multiple pages that have some common characteristics, for the purpose of modularizing the web application and supporting cross-site navigation mechanisms.

4.8.2.1 PATTERN OW-MFE: Multiple front-ends on the same domain model

In many cases, the web is used as a technical architecture to deliver a set of applications on top of the same data, represented in the domain model. A classical case is that of content management systems (CMS). These applications support two roles, as shown in Figure 4.14: the content editor and the reader, which have different use cases and must be served by distinct front ends acting upon the same data. In such a scenario, the pages constituting the two applications could be clustered into two distinct top-level containers, one for the editor and one for the reader.

Such an organization brings several benefits:

- It expresses a functional modularization of the front end that could be exploited, for example, to partition the implementation effort across different teams.
- It allows ViewContainers to be used as resources in a role-based access control policy. Users with role "editor" will access the pages of the "Editor" ViewContainer, whereas users with role "reader" will access the pages of the "Reader" ViewContainer.
- It enables a better management of the implementation artifacts, including the deployment at different web addresses and the separation of graphic resource files.

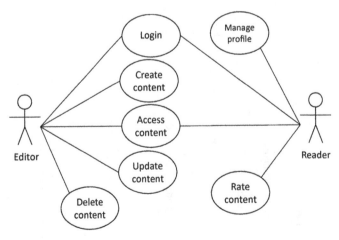

FIGURE 4.14

User roles and use cases in a content management system.

Figure 4.15 shows an example of multiple front ends interface composition pattern applied to a content management application serving the roles and use cases illustrated in Figure 4.14. A top-level ViewContainer "Login" denotes a public page for logging into the application, common to both roles. Then two nested ViewContainers comprise the ViewContainers that denote the web pages specific to the use cases of each role.

The dynamic activation of the appropriate interface after a user request based on his role can be specified using the Context and Viewpoints introduced in chapter 3. For each role, a Context with the appropriate ActivationExpression on the "UserRole" ContextDimension can be defined and associated with a ViewPoint that comprises the ViewContainers of Figure 4.15 appropriate for that role.

4.8.2.2 PATTERN OW-LWSA: Large web sites organized into areas

ViewContainers also come handy for expressing the logical organization of many real-world web applications that exhibit a hierarchical structure whereby the pages of the site are clustered into sections dealing with a homogeneous subject. Nested ViewContainers can play the role of "site areas," recursively structured into other subareas and/or pages. Most real-life web sites exhibit an organization into areas. For example, Figure 4.16 shows an interface fragment taken from a web site whose pages include a navigation bar with anchors pointing to the various areas of the site.

In chapter 7, we will exploit the native extension mechanism of IFML to introduce specializations of the ViewContainer concept that make the specification of web interface organization patterns more expressive.

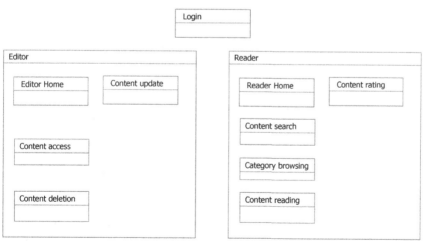

FIGURE 4.15

Example of multiple front ends interface composition pattern applied to a CMS application.

FIGURE 4.16

Popular web sites exhibit an organization into logical areas.

4.8.3 MOBILE INTERFACE ORGANIZATION PATTERNS

Mobile interface organization must account for the reduced screen space of portable devices and for the usage context, whereby users often access the application in unconformable conditions, such as while standing or walking. Therefore, a consistent usage of the scarce screen space is the number one rule of interface organization to reduce the learning curve and minimize the interactions needed to perform tasks. This requirement constrains the top-level organization, which repeats consistently across mobile operating systems and individual applications.

In this section, we introduce only one high-level interface organization pattern. We defer to chapters 7 and 8 the illustration of several other design patters for mobile applications based on the interplay between the organization of the main interface containers and the content components.

4.8.3.1 PATTERN OM-MSL: Mobile screen layout

The basic organization of the interface of mobile applications maps the interface to a top-level grid that contains three regions: the header, the content area, and the footer, as shown in Figure 4.17.

The header is normally used for command menus and notifications. Part of the header may be reserved for operating-system notifications and therefore remains fixed across all applications. The content area normally has a simple layout that limits the use of multiple perspectives and nested panes to a minimum and exploits scrolling along one dimension to accommodate content that overflows the size of the screen. The footer region is normally allocated to system-level commands, such as general or application-specific settings menus.

FIGURE 4.17

Mobile applications organize the interface into header, footer, and content regions.

This essential design pattern can be articulated in a variety of more specific forms depending on the device capacity, the content type, and the application requirements. Chapters 7 and 8 provide many examples of IFML extensions that make the models of mobile applications more expressive and introduce several design patterns that recur in different classes of mobile applications.

4.9 RUNNING EXAMPLE

We return to the running example of the e-mail management application started in chapter 3 to show how to model the organization of the interface.

When the user accesses the application, the interface presents by default the functionality for accessing mailboxes and managing messages, as shown in Figure 4.18.

An equivalent interface is available for contact management, which is accessed upon request. Its organization is shown in Figure 4.19.

The application lets the user always switch from one view to the other by means of a menu, as shown in Figure 4.20.

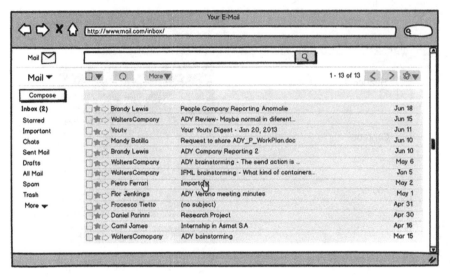

FIGURE 4.18

Mock-up of the initial e-mail message management interface of the e-mail application.

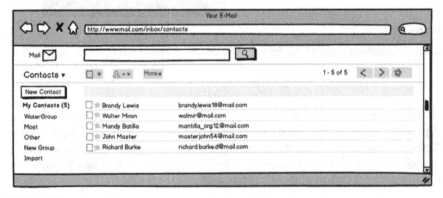

FIGURE 4.19

Mock-up of the contact management interface of the e-mail application.

The message management interface comprises an area for working with mail-boxes and messages. This area is displayed by default, as shown in Figure 4.18. If the user activates the compose command, the mailbox and message area is replaced with a message composer interface, shown in Figure 4.21. Similarly, if the user activates the "Settings" command, a pop-up panel for editing options and preferences is displayed, as shown in Figure 4.22.

The area for working with mailboxes and messages displays a search panel, a toolbar, and a mailbox/message display region, as visible in Figure 4.18. When a

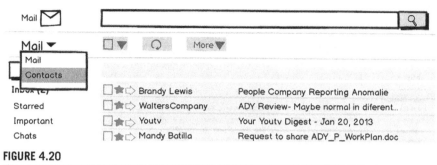

FIGURE 4.20

Mock-up of the view switching menu.

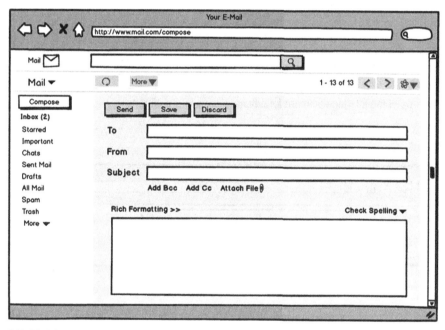

FIGURE 4.21

Mock-up of the interface element for composing message.

message is selected, the message list is replaced with the visualization of the message content, as shown in Figure 4.23.

The message search box alternates between two interfaces for searching: a simple keyword input field, visible in Figure 4.18, and an advanced search form with multiple fields, shown in Figure 4.24.

Figure 4.25 shows an excerpt of the IFML model that specifies the organization of the interface of the e-mail application sketched in Figures 4.18–4.24.

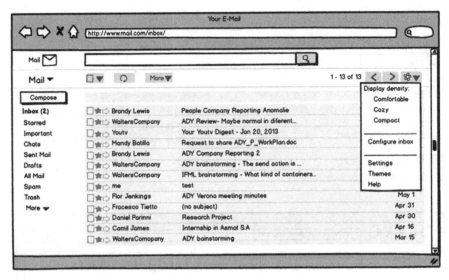

FIGURE 4.22

Mock-up of the interface element for editing options and preferences.

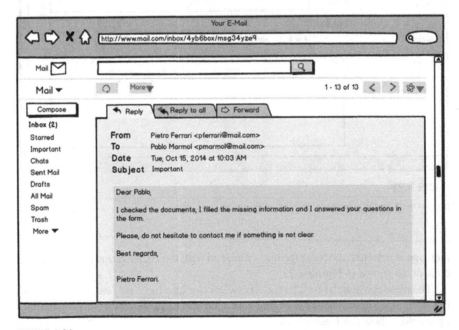

FIGURE 4.23

Mock-up of the interface element for reading a mail message.

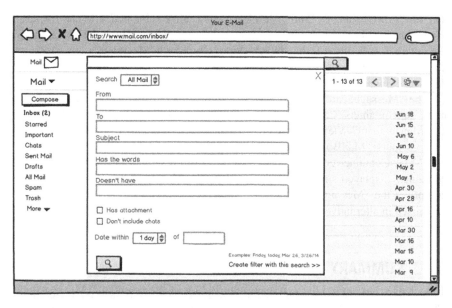

FIGURE 4.24

Mock-up of the interface for advanced searchs.

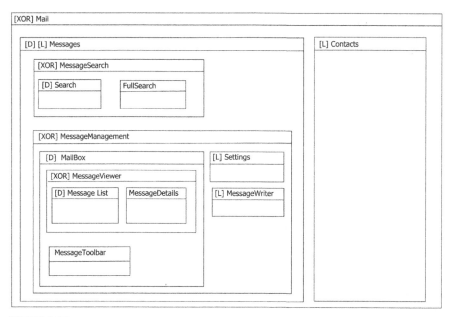

FIGURE 4.25

Fragment of the IFML model specifying the organization of the interface of the e-mail application.

The top ViewContainer ("Mail") hosts two alternative subcontainers: one for message management and one for contact management. For brevity, we illustrate only the internal structure of the default ViewContainer ("Messages"). Its structure comprises two ViewContainers that are displayed together: "MessageSearch" and "MessageManagement."

The "MessageSearch" ViewContainer comprises two mutually exclusive landmark subcontainers: "Search" (shown by default) and "FullSearch." The "MessageManagement" ViewContainer comprises three mutually exclusive landmark subcontainers: "MailBox" (the default), "Settings," and "MessageWriter." The "MailBox" ViewContainer consists of the "Message Toolbar" and the "MessageViewer" containers displayed simultaneously. Finally, the "MessageViewer" ViewContainer comprises the "MessageList" and the "MessageDetails" subcontainers, which are visualized in alternative.

4.10 SUMMARY OF THE CHAPTER

This chapter has started the systematic illustration of the essential IFML concepts, which continues in the next two chapters. We have introduced the IFML constructs for representing the general organization of the interface independently of the content published in the view. Roughly speaking, two types of organizations are possible: one typical of web applications, where multiple peer-level ViewContainers embody the content and navigation of the interface; one typical of desktop, mobile, and rich Internet applications, where the interface is hosted within a top level container with an internal structure of nested subcontainers. We have discussed the concepts of visibility and relevance of ViewContainers and of content-independent navigation. These notions—though very simple—permit the designer to sketch a realistic model of the high-level navigation that can be transformed into a prototype of the interface manually or with the help of tools such as the one described in chapter 11. We have applied the IFML concepts introduced in the chapter to the modeling of various interface organization patterns for web, desktop, and mobile applications, and started the specification of the front end of the running case, which will be completed in chapters 5 and 6.

4.11 BIBLIOGRAPHIC NOTES

Interface composition guidelines are part of usability design, a discipline described in many textbooks, such as the classic work by Ben Shneiderman, recently reedited [Shneiderman10]. Dedicated usability guidelines have also been proposed for web applications that have a specific interaction flavor. An exemplary textbook on the subject is [Nielsen00]. The advent of mobile applications has sparkled interest in the design of usable mobile interfaces. Good textbooks on the subject are [Neil12, NB12]. The first chapter of [HB11] deals with composition patterns for mobile interfaces.

Modeling interface content and navigation

5

Interface composition partitions the user interface into ViewContainers and possibly establishes hierarchical relationships among them. The user interface specification is completed by the definition of the content shown within each ViewContainer and the supported user interaction. The key ingredients of content and navigation modeling are ViewElements, Events, and InteractionFlows.

ViewElements are distinguished in ViewContainers (already treated in chapter 4) and ViewComponents, which are the main subject of this chapter.

Events and InteractionFlows have been already introduced in chapter 4 but acquire a more interesting meaning in content and navigation modeling. They enable the specification **content-dependent navigation**, that is, a form of interaction that exploits the objects of the domain model. The simplest example of content-dependent navigation is the selection of items from a list. The user accesses a ViewComponent that displays a list of objects, selects one, and accesses another ViewComponent that displays detailed information about the chosen object.

On the one hand, content-dependent navigation is similar to content-independent navigation, described in chapter 4:

- It involves a source and a destination element and is expressed by means of an Event and of a NavigationFlow.
- On the other hand, it has important differences: typically the source and target of the navigation are ViewComponents (and not ViewContainers). Furthermore, the target ViewComponent normally depends on some data provided by the source ViewComponent; this dependency is expressed by associating one or more ParameterBinding specifications to the NavigationFlow.

The specification of ViewComponents can be done at different levels of precision:

- At the most abstract level, a ViewComponent is just a "box with a name," as in the preliminary examples introduced in chapter 2 (e.g., see Figure 2.2). Its meaning is conveyed only by the name, without further details except for the optional specification of subcomponents specified with the IFML ViewComponentPart construct. Using this level of abstraction keeps the specification very general and easy to produce but may overlook important information needed for model checking and code generation.
- At an intermediate level of abstraction, IFML allows a standard way of binding ViewComponents to elements of the domain model. This is extremely useful to express, for example, that a ViewComponent "Index of Products" actually

77

derives its content from the instances of a "Product" class of the domain model. This additional knowledge can be used for checking the consistency between the IFML model and the domain model and for automatically generating the data query that extracts the content of the "Index of Products" ViewComponent.

- At the most refined level, the ViewComponent construct can be extended with specialized subclasses to express specific ways in which content is presented or exploited to enable user interaction. For example, a *List* ViewComponent can be defined to represent a specific ViewComponent aimed at publishing an ordered set of objects from which the user can select one item. Extended components may have domain-dependent properties and thus enable deep model checking and full code generation.

In this chapter we discuss both the basic IFML notion of ViewComponent and the extensions already defined in the standard. In chapter 7 we illustrate how the designer can introduce novel extensions, using web and mobile application development as examples.

5.1 WHAT VIEWCONTAINERS CONTAIN: VIEWCOMPONENTS

A ViewContainer may comprise ViewComponents.

VIEWCOMPONENT

A **ViewComponent** is any element that can display content in the user interface or accept input from the user.

Examples of ViewComponents are interface elements for visualizing the data of one object, for displaying a list of objects, data entry forms for accepting user input, and grid controls for displaying and editing data tables. A ViewComponent may have an internal structure consisting of one or more ViewComponentParts.

VIEWCOMPONENTPART

A **ViewComponentPart** is an interface element or a structural property that may not live outside the context of ViewComponent.

The meanings of ViewComponent and of ViewComponentPart are left purposely broad. Their semantics are defined by the designer and conveyed by the component/part name. Figure 5.1 shows the graphic representation of ViewComponents and some exemplary renderings. As can be noted, at the highest level of abstraction only the name of the component is used to suggest the intended meaning.

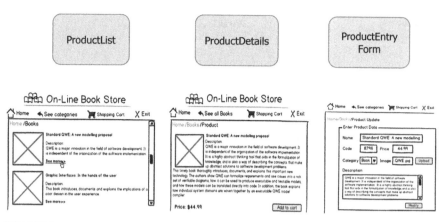

FIGURE 5.1

Examples of ViewComponents and of their rendition.

5.2 EVENTS AND NAVIGATION FLOWS WITH VIEWCOMPONENTS

ViewComponents and ViewComponentParts can support interaction. This capacity is denoted by associating them with Events, which in turn enable NavigationFlows. Figure 5.2 shows an example of an interactive ViewComponent. The "ProductList" ViewComponent is associated with an Event "SelectProduct," which is the source of a NavigationFlow leading to the "ProductDetails" ViewComponent. The meaning of this design pattern is that "ProductList" publishes a list of objects from which the user can select. The selection event triggers an interaction, whose effect is showing the information of the chosen object in the "ProductDetails" ViewComponent.

In content-based navigation, the source and destination ViewComponents can be positioned in different ViewContainers, as shown in Figure 5.2. In this case, the navigation event has the effect of showing the target ViewContainer and of triggering the computation of the ViewComponents present in it. The display of the target ViewContainer may impact the visualization of the source ViewContainer in one of two ways:

- If the source and target ViewContainers are mutually exclusive (either directly or because they are nested within mutually exclusive ViewContainers), the target replaces the source.
- Otherwise the target is displayed in addition to the source.

For example, Figure 5.3 shows the ViewComponents, Event, and NavigationFlow of Figure 5.2, but this time both the source and target ViewComponent are in the same ViewContainer. This indicates that the choice of one product in the list causes the display of the details in the same ViewContainer.

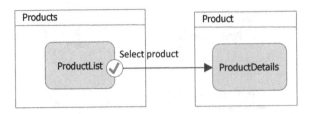

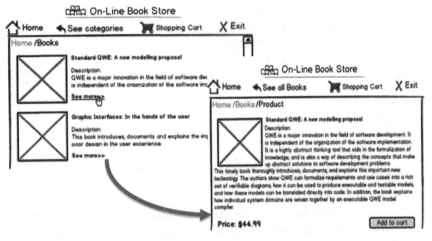

FIGURE 5.2

A basic example of an interactive ViewComponent and a possible rendition.

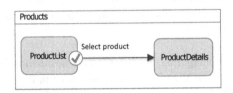

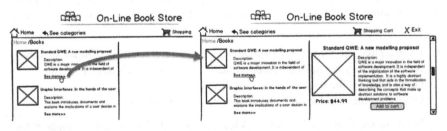

FIGURE 5.3

Content-based navigation within the same ViewContainer.

5.3 CONTENT DEPENDENCIES: DATA BINDING

ViewComponents publish content in the interface. It is therefore necessary to specify the source of the published content. This aspect is represented by means of the ContentBinding specification.

CONTENTBINDING

A **ContentBinding** is a very general representation of the content source of a ViewComponent; its only attribute is the URI of the resource from which the content may be obtained.

Figure 5.4 shows a simple example of ContentBinding: the "FeedReader" ViewComponent is associated with a ContentBinding specification that references the URL of the feed provider.

To represent the common situation in which the content published by a ViewComponent originates from the objects of the domain model or from an external service, the ContentBinding concept is refined in two specializations: DataBinding and DynamicBehavior.

DATABINDING

A **DataBinding** represents the provenance of content from objects of the domain model; it is characterized by features that specify the type of data, the criterion for selecting instances, and the attributes relevant for publication.

More precisely, a DataBinding is associated with:

- a reference to a domain model concept (depending on the type of domain model, the referenced concept can be a UML classifier—which may represent a class in the domain model, an XML file, a table in a database, etc.—or another element);
- a ConditionalExpression, which determines the specific instances to be extracted from the content source;

FIGURE 5.4

Example of ContentBinding.

FIGURE 5.5

A DataBinding with a reference to an entity of the domain model.

FIGURE 5.6

A DataBinding with a reference to an entity of the domain model and an instance selection condition.

- one or more VisualizationAttributes, used by the ViewComponent to locate the data shown in the interface, such as an object attribute, a database column or an XML element or attribute; and
- an optional OrderBy ViewComponentPart, which lists one or more sorting criteria consisting of an attribute name and a sort direction (ASC or DESC for ascending or descending, respectively).

Figure 5.5 shows an example of a simple DataBinding. The "MessageList" View-Component draws its content from the "MailMessage" entity of the domain model. The DataBinding neither specifies which instances are to be published nor the attributes to be visualized, and so these aspects are left unspecified.

Figure 5.6 refines the example of Figure 5.5. The DataBinding contains an OCL ConditionalExpression "self.isRead = false," which specifies that only the instances of the entity "MailMessage" with the attribute "isRead" equal to false should be published. The VisualizationAttributes ViewComponentPart specifies that the attributes "subject" and "date" should be used to display the objects, and the OrderBy ViewComponentPart indicates that they are sorted in descending order of date.

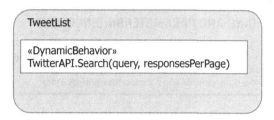

FIGURE 5.7

A DynamicBehavior that specifies the retrieval of content through a call to the API of an external service.

Note that because the conditional expression is defined within the DataBinding ViewComponentPart, the context of the expression is implicitly set to "MailMessage" (i.e., the object referenced by the DataBinding).

The DataBinding represents the association of a ViewComponent to the content elements in a declarative way, which facilitates the generation of the data extraction queries. An alternative way of expressing the content of a ViewComponent is through the DynamicBehavior element.

DYNAMICBEHAVIOR

A **DynamicBehavior** represents the data access of a ViewComponent in an operational way (e.g., through the invocation of a service or method that returns content).

For instance, a DynamicBehavior can be expressed by referencing any UMLBehavior or UMLBehavioralFeature.

Figure 5.7 shows an example of DynamicBehavior used to specify that the "TweetList" ViewComponent exploits the web API of an external service to publish content.

5.4 INPUT-OUTPUT DEPENDENCIES: PARAMETER BINDING

Content-dependent navigation allows expressing the very common situation in which one component displays content that depends on some previous interaction performed by the user. Examples are the display of the data of an object previously selected from a list, the display of the result list of a keyword search, and the drill-down into a hierarchy.

All these situations require expressing an input–output dependency between ViewComponents. The ViewComponent target of the navigation requires input provided by the source ViewComponent for retrieving the content to publish. An input–output dependency is described by means of the ParameterBinding construct.

PARAMETERBINDING AND PARAMETERBINDINGGROUP

A **ParameterBinding** specifies that the value of one parameter, typically the output of some ViewComponent, is associated with that of another parameter, typically the input of another ViewComponent. When the input–output dependency involves several parameters at the same time, ParameterBinding elements are grouped into a **ParameterBindingGroup**.

Figure 5.8 shows an example of an input–output dependency. The "MessageList" ViewComponent displays the messages of the specific mailbox selected by the user in the "MBoxList" ViewComponent. The NavigationFlow is associated with a ParameterBindingGroup that contains the declaration of an input–output dependency: the value of the parameter "SelectedMailBox" (output of the "MBoxList" ViewComponent) is associated with the value of the parameter "MailBox" (input of the "MessageList" ViewComponent). The value of the "MailBox" parameter is used in the ConditionalExpression of the "MessageList" ViewComponent, specified by the following OCL expression:

```
self.MailMessageGroup = MailBox
```

The OCL expression specifies that the instances of "MailMessage" to retrieve are those associated by the relationship role "MailMessageGroup" with the object identified by the value of the parameter "MailBox." The pattern of Figure 5.8 provides an example of a ConditionalExpression that exploits an association in the domain model.

The transfer of parameters necessary for satisfying the input–output dependencies between correlated components does not always requires user intervention.

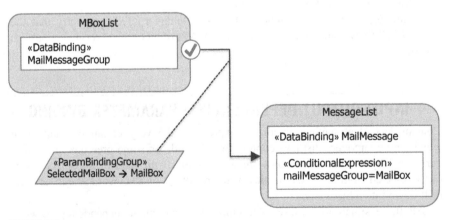

FIGURE 5.8

Example of an input–output dependency expressed with a ParameterBinding and a parametric ConditionalExpression.

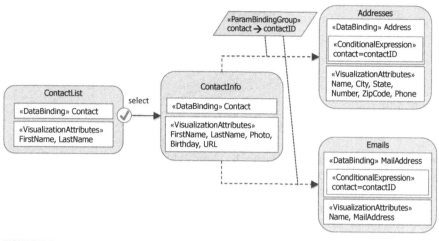

FIGURE 5.9

DataFlows for parameter passing without user interaction.

Figure 5.9 shows an example of such a situation. When one contact is selected in the "ContactList" ViewComponent, the details of the selected object are displayed in the "ContactInfo" ViewComponent. In addition, further information about the same object is displayed, namely, the list of addresses and e-mails in the "Addresses" and "Emails" ViewComponents respectively. These two components are displayed simultaneously with the "ContactInfo" ViewComponent after the selection from the list without any further user interaction. The input parameter needed for computing their content (the ID of the selected contact) is provided by a ParameterBinding associated with the DataFlows from the "ContactInfo" ViewComponent to the "Addresses" and "Emails" ViewComponents.

DATAFLOW

A **DataFlow** is an InteractionFlow that specifies that some parameters are supplied from a source to a target element, without any user's interaction; the involved parameters are specified by means of a ParameterBindingGroup associated with the DataFlow.

DataFlows emanate directly from ViewComponents rather than from Events and are denoted with dashed arrows to distinguish them from NavigationFlows.

5.5 EXTENDING IFML WITH SPECIALIZED VIEWCOMPONENTS AND EVENTS

The examples of the previous sections introduced a rather rudimentary notion of ViewComponent. So far this concept is little more than a box. Its meaning is conveyed only by the name assigned to it by the designer. In this way, however, the

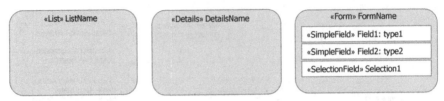

FIGURE 5.10

Extensions of the ViewComponent concept.

model usability and semantics cannot be improved much. If "all boxes are equal," tools could not check the correctness of the models or support the designer with useful inferences and shortcuts.

To allow deeper model checking and improve model usability, IFML supports the extension of the basic ViewComponents with user-defined specializations. Figure 5.10 illustrates the extensions of the base ViewComponent construct already provided in the IFML standard, which are still quite general. More extensions will be introduced in chapter 7 for web and mobile applications.

The List and Details ViewComponents just add a stereotype to the basic ViewComponent concept. The Form ViewComponent also adds novel ViewComponentParts (SimpleField and SelectionField).

5.5.1 DATA PUBLISHING EXTENSIONS

IFML component extensions are represented in the model by stereotypes added to a ViewComponent. For the sake of conformance to the IFML standard, we use textual stereotyping, which is quite cumbersome for ViewComponents, especially when their names are long. However, a tool may replace the textual notation of stereotypes with a more concise representation to save screen space (e.g., small icons, font colors, textures).

LIST VIEWCOMPONENT

A **List** ViewComponent is a ViewComponent used to display a list of objects retrieved through a ContentBinding. When the List ViewComponent is associated with an Event, it means that each object displayed by the component can be used to trigger the Event. Firing the Event causes the passing of the chosen instances as a parameter value to a target IFML element.

DETAILS VIEWCOMPONENT

A **Details** ViewComponent is a ViewComponent used to display the attribute values of one object retrieved through a ContentBinding. When the Details ViewComponent is associated with an Event, it means that the instance displayed by the component can be used to trigger the Event. Firing the Event causes the passing of the displayed instance as a parameter value to a target IFML element.

Figure 5.11 shows an example of List and Details ViewComponents connected with an event and a navigation flow. The "MessageList" publishes the list of all "MailMessage" instances. The "select" event indicates that the "MessageList" ViewComponent supports interaction (i.e., the user can click on one of the displayed object and trigger the event). The firing of the event produces the display of the "Message" Details ViewComponent, which receives as input the chosen "MailMessage" object.

The selection from a list is an event frequently associated with ViewComponents. It thus has a specific representation in IFML as an extension of the base Event concept, shown in Figure 5.11 (and previously in Figures 5.2, 5.3, 5.8, and 5.9).

SELECTEVENT

A **SelectEvent** is a kind of Event that supports the selection of one or more elements from a set. When triggered, it causes the selected value(s) to be passed as a Parameter to the target of its associated NavigationFlow.

In chapter 6 we will introduce another refinement of the Event, the "select all" event, which is used to express an Event that supports the selection of all elements of a set.

Figure 5.12 shows an example that illustrates how adding more semantics to the model via IFML extensions can improve usability. The model representation is more concise than that of Figure 5.11, but the usage of extensions with precise semantics easily allows a tool (or a human reader) to infer that the two models are equivalent. Indeed, the List ViewComponent publishes a set of instances of the "MailMessage" class, the Details ViewComponent publishes one instance of the same class, and the "select" Event actually allows the user to select one item from the source ViewComponent and pass it to the target ViewComponent. Thus the designer could draw the more concise variant of Figure 5.12, sparing the effort of expressing the inferable ParameterBinding and ConditionalExpression.

The selection from a list can also include multiple items, as supported by the multichoice list ViewComponent.

MULTICHOICELIST

The **MultiChoice** List enables the selection and submission of multiple instances. It supports multiple event types. The standard select event expresses the selection of one element of the list, while the **checking** and **unchecking** events express the application or removal of a selection ticker on any element in the list. The **set selection** event denotes the submission of the entire set of objects, and the **submit** event denotes the submission of the currently selected objects.

An example of a multichoice list is shown in Figure 5.31 and in the multiple-object deletion pattern discussed in chapter 8.

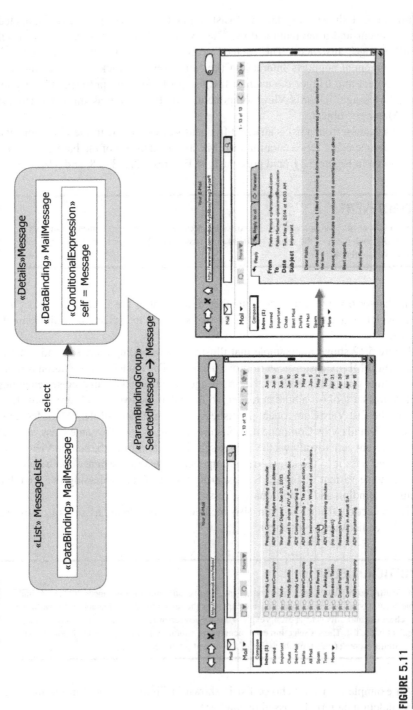

FIGURE 5.11

Example of the List and Details extensions of ViewComponent and their renditions.

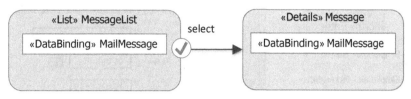

FIGURE 5.12

Concise model representation that a tool can infer as equivalent to that of Figure 5.11.

5.5.2 **DATA ENTRY EXTENSIONS**

Besides content publishing, IFML extensions can also be used to express data entry. This is done using the Form ViewComponent extension.

> **FORM**
>
> A **Form** is a ViewComponent that represents a data entry form.

A form comprises one or more ViewComponentParts that represent input fields (and thus are tagged with the Field stereotype).

> **FIELD**
>
> A **Field** is a subelement of a Form that denotes a typed value acquired from or displayed to the user.

Fields also represent Parameters for passing their values to other IFML elements. There are two kinds of fields: SimpleFields and SelectionFields.

> **SIMPLEFIELD**
>
> A **SimpleField** is a kind of Field that captures a typed value. Such a value is typically entered by the user but can also be designated read-only or even hidden. The value of a SimpleField is an output Parameter that can be passed to other ViewElements or Actions.

As customary in data entry applications, form fields could also allow a quicker and more controlled type of interaction (e.g., the selection of values from a predefined set). This feature is captured by the SelectionField element.

> **SELECTIONFIELD**
>
> A **SelectionField** is a kind of Field that enables the choice of one or more values from a predefined set.

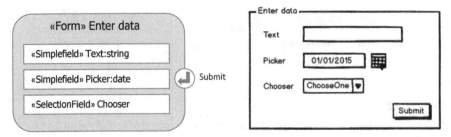

FIGURE 5.13

Form, SimpleField, and SelectionField, and a possible rendition.

Figure 5.13 shows an example of a Form with two SimpleFields and one SelectionField.

The mock-up rendition of Figure 5.13 hints at the fact that the type of the field can be used by the developer or by a code generation tool to produce the most appropriate interaction widget within the form.

Both simple and selection fields can be preloaded with values. Each Field also defines an input parameter of the Form that contains it so that its value can be preloaded with a value supplied by another IFML element. Alternatively, the provenance of the Field content can be expressed with a ContentBinding, if the content is extracted from domain model objects. Preloaded Fields behave as follow: a preloaded SimpleField displays a value to the user, who can overwrite it; a preloaded SelectionField displays multiple values to the user, who can choose the one(s) to submit. Each field also defines an output parameter of the Form that contains it, which assumes as value the entered value (for a SimpleField) or the selected value(s) (for a SelectionField) provided by the user.

Forms support interaction for submitting the content of their Fields. The basic data submission activity of the user can be represented by an extension of the generic Event construct called SubmitEvent.

SUBMITEVENT

A **SubmitEvent** is a kind of event that denotes the submission of one or more values. It triggers the Parameter passing from the ViewComponent owning the event to the ViewComponent or Action target of the NavigationFlow outgoing from the event.

Figure 5.14 shows an example of Form ViewComponent with one SimpleField and one SubmitEvent (note that the SubmitEvent is represented by an "enter button" icon). The "MessageKeywordSearch" Form ViewComponent is associated with the "SearchKey" SimpleField and with the "Search mail" SubmitEvent. The latter triggers an interaction that leads to the display of the "MessageList" ViewComponent, which publishes the messages that contain the search keyword in their

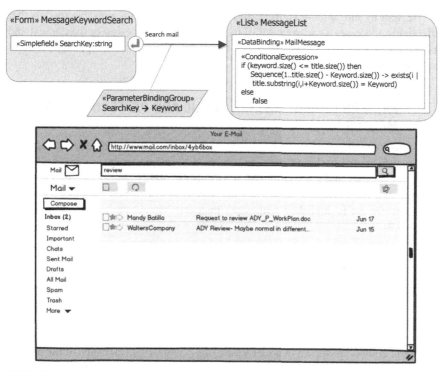

FIGURE 5.14

Example of a Form ViewComponent with one SimpleField and one SelectEvent.

title. The OCL expression that selects the set of instances whose title contains the input keyword is:

```
if (keyword.size() <= title.size()) then
     Sequence(1..title.size()- Keyword.size()) -> exists(i |
title.substring(i,i+Keyword.size()) = Keyword)
   else
     false
```

which checks that the input keyword is a substring of the message title.

5.6 CONTENT AND NAVIGATION PATTERNS AND PRACTICES

As already mentioned in chapter 4, interface design patterns are IFML models that embody the solution to recurrent interface design problems. In the following, we discuss useful patterns that emerge frequently during the design of the content and interactivity of the user interface. The patterns described in this chapter are high level and platform independent. Platform-specific patterns are discussed in chapter 7.

We start by introducing **content and navigation patterns**, reusable models that effectively addresses a recurrent set of requirements in the design of the content and navigation in user interfaces. We prefix the name of platform-independent content and navigation patterns with CN.

5.6.1 PATTERN CN-MD: MASTER DETAIL AND PATTERN CN-MMD: MASTER MULTIDETAIL

The master detail pattern is the simplest data access pattern, already exemplified in Figure 5.11. A List ViewComponent is used to present some instances (the so-called master list), and a selection Event permits the user to access the details of one instance at a time. The master multidetail variant occurs when the object selected in the master list is published with more than one ViewComponents, as shown in Figure 5.9.

5.6.2 PATTERN CN-MLMD: MULTILEVEL MASTER DETAIL

This pattern, sometimes also called "cascaded index," consists of a sequence of List ViewComponents defined over distinct classes, such that each List specifies a change of focus from one object (selected from the index) to the set of objects related to it via an association role. In the end, a single object is shown in a Details ViewComponent, or several objects are shown in a List ViewComponent. A typical usage of the pattern exploits one or more data access classes to build a navigation path to the instances of a core class. For example, Figure 2.2 provides an example of the multilevel master detail pattern exploiting the instances of the "Category" access class to access the instances of the "Product" core class.

5.6.3 PATTERN CN-DEF: DEFAULT SELECTION

A usability principle suggests maximizing the stability of the interface by avoiding abrupt and far reaching changes of the view when they are not necessary. The default selection pattern helps improve the stability of interfaces that show pieces of correlated content and allow the user to make choices.

The basic master detail pattern and the multilevel master detail pattern exhibit possibly unwanted interface instability, as visible in Figure 5.3. When the ViewContainer is initially accessed, the first List ViewComponent is computed and appears rendered in the interface. However, the Details or List ViewComponent, which depends on a parameter value supplied by a user selection, cannot be computed, and thus the interface contains an "empty hole" corresponding to it. When the user selects one item from the list, then the missing parameter value becomes available and the content of the second ViewComponent can be computed, thus filling the hole but producing a possibly unwanted instability of the interface.

The default selection pattern resolves this problem by simulating a user selection at the initial access of the ViewContainer. A default value is chosen from the source

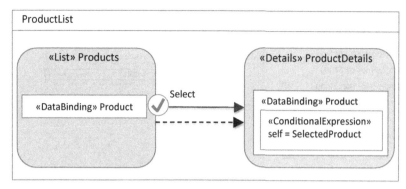

FIGURE 5.15

Default selection pattern.

ViewComponent and used to define the value of the parameter needed for computing the target ViewComponent. In this way, the user sees a stable interface initialized with a system-defined object or list, which the user can subsequently change by using the provided interactive events.

Figure 5.15 shows the notation for expressing the default selection pattern.

Besides the NavigationFlow outgoing from the select event, the pattern also includes a DataFlow, which expresses a parameter passing rule for supplying a default value when the page is accessed, in absence of user interaction.

5.7 DATA ENTRY PATTERNS

Data entry is one of the most important activities supported by the front end and one where usability requirements are most stringent. In the next sections, we illustrate some cross-platform patterns generally applicable to data entry interfaces, based on the usage of Form ViewComponents. We prefix the name of platform-independent data entry patterns with DE.

5.7.1 PATTERN DE-FRM: MULTIFIELD FORMS

The basic data entry pattern consists of a Form ViewComponent with several fields corresponding to such elements as the properties of an object to be created or updated, the criteria for searching a repository, or the parameter values to be sent to an external service.

Figure 5.16 shows an example of multi-field form for composing an e-mail message.

As Figure 5.16 illustrates, assigning a type with the fields adds useful information to the model. For example, a code generator may render a text editing field by means of a rich text editing widget or a Blob field with a file chooser window. Other

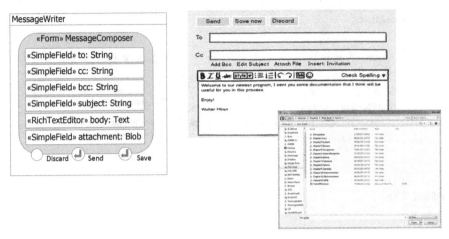

FIGURE 5.16

Multifield form.

examples are Boolean fields rendered as radio buttons and date fields rendered as calendars. We will show how to extend Fields to specify several usability hints in chapter 8.

5.7.2 PATTERN DE-PLDF: PRELOADED FIELD

In many situations, the data entered in a form modify or add to existing information. Examples include updating the description of a product in an online e-commerce web site or changing one's profile in a social network. In each case, preloading fields with content augments the usability of the interface and reduces data entry errors.

Figure 5.17 shows the pattern for preloading a SimpleField and a SelectionField in two different ways. The "Categories" SelectionField incorporates a DataBinding element, which specifies that the values are extracted from the "name" attribute of the "Category" objects of the domain model. Conversely, the "Description" SimpleField is preloaded by means of a ParameterBinding associated with the DataFlow connecting the "ProductDetails" Form and the "UpdateProduct" ViewComponents. In this way, the text of the description attribute of the product object in display is also used to provide an initial value to the homonymous field in the Form.

Figure 5.18 shows another example of field preloading: a form for replying to an existing e-mail message, in which the fields of the new message are partly preloaded with the values of the original message. The "Reply" event associates the subject of the original message to the subject of the new message prefixed with the string "Re: ," copies the recipient of the original message into the sender of the new message, and pulls the body of the original message into the body of the new message.

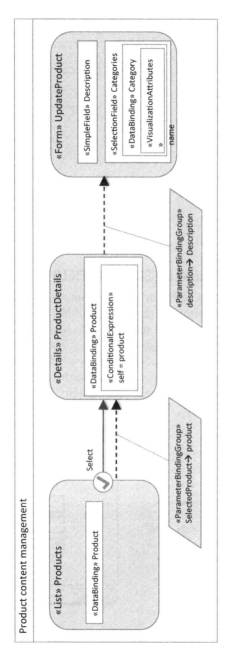

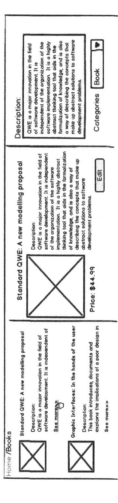

FIGURE 5.17

Form fields preloaded with DataBinding and ParameterBinding.

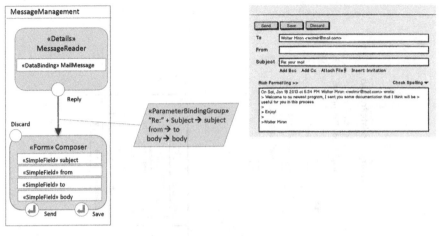

FIGURE 5.18

Form fields preloaded with parameters.

5.7.3 PATTERN DE-PASF: PREASSIGNED SELECTION FIELD

This design pattern helps when the user's selection among a number of different choices can be inferred from available information (e.g., from profile data, previous choices, or the interaction context). In this case, the value of a SelectionField can be initialized with a ParameterBinding, as shown in Figure 5.19.

The "SignUp" ViewContainer shown in Figure 5.19 contains a "UserCountry" Details ViewComponent that retrieves the default country for a user by querying the Locale contextVariable and exposes an OutputParameter UserCountry. Such a piece of information is passed to the form "SignUp" as input parameter CountryPreselect

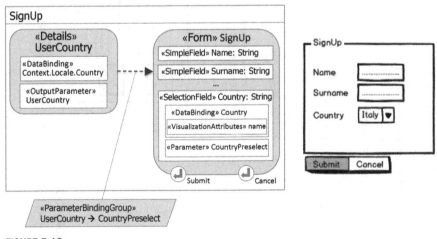

FIGURE 5.19

Preassigned selection field.

to set the value of the "Country" SelectionField. Note the use of a DataFlow from the Details to the Form because no interaction is required except the association of the parameter with the SelectionField parameter value.

5.7.4 PATTERN DE-DLKP: DATA LOOKUP

This design pattern is useful when the data entry task involves a complex form with choices among many options, such as in the case of form filling with large product catalogues. In this case, a SelectionField can be conveniently supported by a data lookup ViewContainer, which contains a data access pattern such as a master details.

Figure 5.20 shows an example of data lookup. The "FillRequest" Form contains a SimpleField "ProductCode" that must be filled with the code of a product.

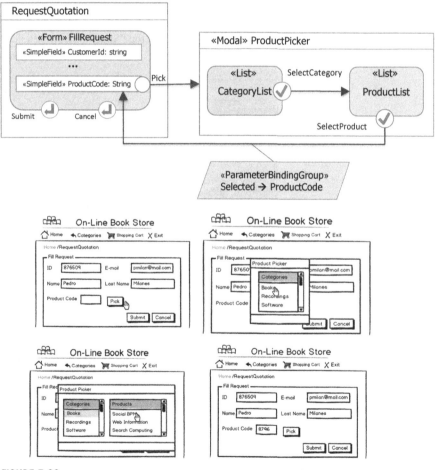

FIGURE 5.20

Selection help.

An event "Pick" opens a ViewContainer (e,g, a modal window) whereby the user can navigate the product taxonomy and select the desired code. The product code chosen with the data lookup is assigned to the SimpleField "ProductCode" using a ParameterBinding.

5.7.5 PATTERN DE-CSF: CASCADE SELECTION FIELDS

The cascade selection field pattern is useful when the data entry task involves entering a set of selections that have some kind of dependency. The typical example is a form for entering user information, where the address is incrementally built by selecting the country, the state or province, and then the city. If this step by step selection is performed within a form with selection fields, the fields need to be dynamically updated according to the selection at the previous step. In this case, the list of states or provinces depends on the selected country, and the list of cities depends on the selected province. Figure 5.21 shows the IFML model that exemplifies this behavior. The selection of an element in the "Country" SelectionField triggers the calculation of the list of associated states to be shown in the "State" SelectionField.

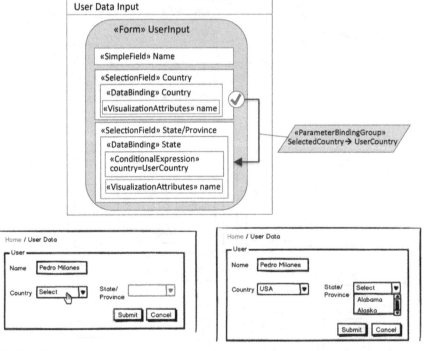

FIGURE 5.21

Cascade selection fields pattern: selecting a country triggers the calculation of the corresponding states or provinces.

5.7.6 **PATTERN DE-WIZ: WIZARD**

The wizard design pattern supports the partition of a data entry procedure into logical steps that must be followed in a predetermined sequence. Depending on the step reached, the user can move forward or backward without losing the partial selections made up to that point. Figure 5.22 shows a three-step wizard.

Notice that at each step the Form ViewComponent shows one Field, the one pertinent to the current step, and caches the values of the inputs of all steps in Parameters. The events and navigation flows for moving from one step to another are associated with a ParameterBinding that carries the current values of all the fields to keep track of interactions performed in previous steps. In this way, the user can go back and forth and—at the end—all the collected values are correctly submitted.

An alternative equivalent design can be that of associating a single copy of all the wizard parameters with the enclosing ViewContainer and updating such global parameters at each previous/next event.

5.8 **SEARCH PATTERNS**

Search patterns address recurrent problems in which user input must be matched against some content to retrieve relevant information. We prefix the name of platform-independent content search patterns with CS.

5.8.1 **PATTERN CS-SRC: BASIC SEARCH**

The basic search pattern has already been exemplified in Figure 5.14, where a Form ViewComponent with one SimpleField is used to input a search key. This key is used as the value of a parameter in the ConditionalExpression of a List ViewComponent that displays all the instances of a class that contain the keyword. A variant of the pattern that searches the keyword in multiple attributes of the target class is obtained using disjunctive subclauses in the ConditionalExpression:

```
if (keyword.size() <= title.size()) then
    Sequence(1..title.size() - Keyword.size()) -> c(i |
title.substring(i, i + Keyword.size()) = Keyword)
  else
false
OR
  if (keyword.size() <= body.size()) then
    Sequence(1..body.size() - Keyword.size()) -> exists(i |
body.substring(i, i + Keyword.size()) = Keyword)
  else
false
```

With the above expression, the keyword is searched in the title or in the body of a message.

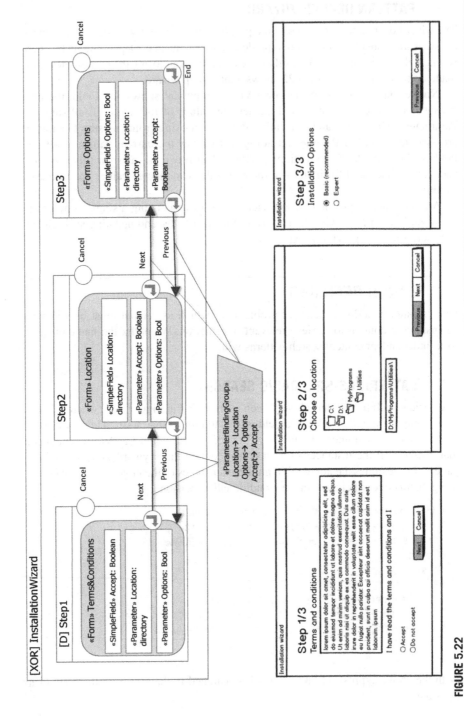

FIGURE 5.22

Three-step wizard.

5.8.2 **PATTERN CS-MCS: MULTICRITERIA SEARCH**

The advanced multicriteria search pattern uses a Form ViewComponent with multiple Fields to express a composite search criterion. Figure 5.23 shows an example of multicriteria search pattern. The "Message full search" Form contains multiple Field elements for the user to fill. A ParameterBindingGroup assigns the field values to the parameters in the ConditionalExpression of the "MessageList" ViewComponent.

5.8.3 **PATTERN CS-FSR: FACETED SEARCH**

Faceted search is a modality of information retrieval particularly well suited to structured multidimensional data. It is used to allow the progressive refinement of the search results by restricting the objects that match the query based on their properties, called *facets*. By selecting one or more values of some of the facets, the result set is narrowed down to only those objects that possess the selected values. Figure 5.24 shows an example of faceted search applied to bibliography information retrieval.

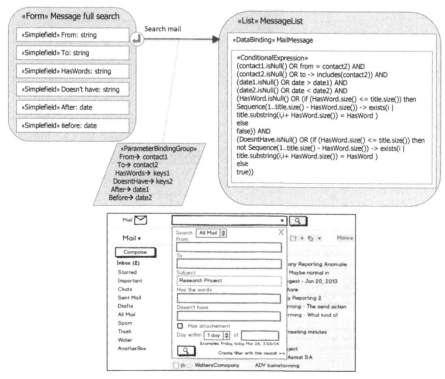

FIGURE 5.23

Multicriteria search pattern.

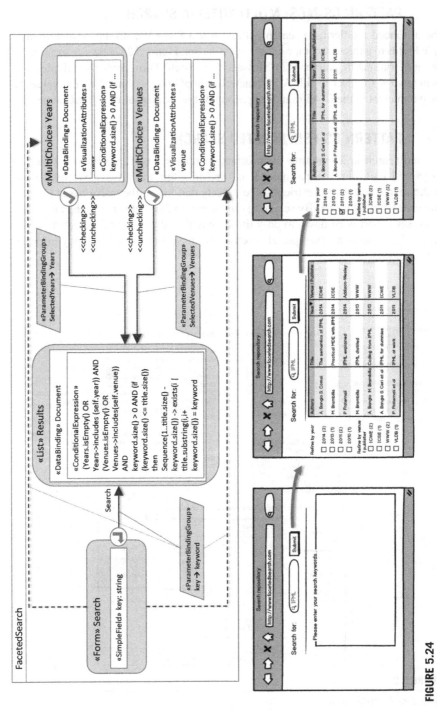

FIGURE 5.24

Faceted search pattern.

The model of Figure 5.24 consists of a ViewContainer ("FacetedSearch"), which comprises a Form for entering the search keywords, a List for showing the query matches ("Results"), and two MultiChoice Lists ("Years" and "Venues") for selecting facet values and restricting the result set. At the first access of the ViewContainer, no keyword has been provided yet by the user, and thus the ConditionalExpression of the "Results" List evaluates to false and the ViewComponent is not displayed. The same holds for the "Years" and "Venues" ViewComponents (their ConditionalExpressions are not entirely shown in Figure 5.24 for space reasons, but they retrieve the documents that match the input keyword). When the user submits a keyword and triggers the "Search" event, the ConditionalExpressions of the "Results," "Years," and "Venues" ViewComponents are evaluated and the content of these ViewComponents is populated with the matching documents. The VisualizationAttributes of the "Years" and "Venues" ViewComponents comprise a single attribute, whose distinct values are displayed as facets[1]. Checking or unchecking the values of the facets triggers the corresponding events shown in Figure 5.24, which causes the binding of the "Years" and "Venues" parameters. As a consequence, the ConditionalExpression of the "Results" ViewComponent is evaluated using thoseparameters, which—if not empty—can lead to the restriction of the result set.

5.9 RUNNING EXAMPLE

As already mentioned in chapter 4, the e-mail application interface consists of a top-level ViewContainer, which is logically divided into two alternative subcontainers: one for managing mail messages (open by default when the application is accessed) and one for managing contacts.

The "Messages" ViewContainer, visible in Figure 5.25, displays the list of the available mailboxes, which is presented in conjunction with the messages contained in a mailbox or with the interface for composing a message or for editing the mail settings. Selecting a mailbox causes the messages it contains to appear in the central part of the interface (the MailBox sub-ViewContainer). Entering the application causes the selection of a default mailbox in accordance with PATTERN CN-DEF: default selection.

Figure 5.26 shows the ViewComponents, Event, and NavigationFlow that model the selection and display of a mailbox.

Access to the messages can also occur through a search functionality displayed together with the mailbox list. An input field supports simple keyword based search. With a click, the user can access an alternative full-search input form that allows the entry of various criteria, as shown in Figure 5.27.

Figure 5.28 shows the model of the two alternate search functions. A modeless ViewContainer is used to denote that the full search form opens in a modeless window, as shown in Figure 5.27. The forms "Message Keyword search" and "Full Search" contain the fields shown in Figure 5.14 and Figure 5.23, respectively. The "Message List" ViewComponent has three ConditionalExpressions. Each expression

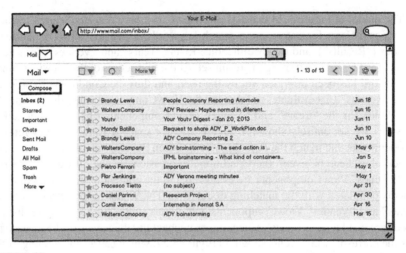

FIGURE 5.25

Mock-up of the top-level ViewContainer of the e-mail application, with the default subcontainer "Messages" in view.

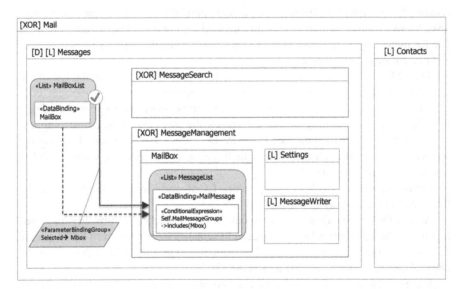

FIGURE 5.26

The ViewComponents, Event, and NavigationFlow that model the selection and display of a mailbox.

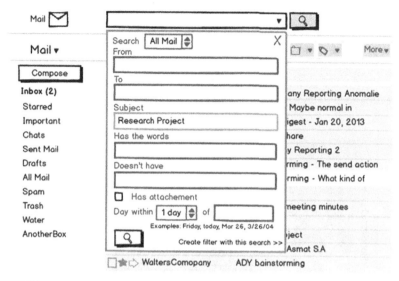

FIGURE 5.27

Mock-up of the full-search input form.

is reached by a navigation flow, one for each of the ways in which it can be accessed. At every user interaction, only the expression that is the target of the current user navigation will be evaluated. The condition expressions are visible in Figure 5.14, Figure 5.23, and Figure 5.26.

For brevity, Figure 5.28 omits representation of the ParameterBindingGroup elements associated with the events "Select Mailbox," "Search mail," and "Search mail full."

Figure 5.28 also shows a refinement of the "MailBox" ViewContainer, which unveils its internal organization into the sub-ViewContainers necessary to alternate between the visualization of a message list and that of a single message. The "MessageList" ViewComponent supports interaction with mail messages individually or in sets. On the entire set of messages, the "MarkAllAsRead" event permits the user to update all the messages in the current MailBox, setting their status to "read" (see Figure 5.29).

As shown in Figure 5.30, the "MessageList" ViewComponent also supports a second kind of interaction, the selection of a subset of messages. When at least one message is selected, a ViewContainer is displayed ("MessageToolbar"), which permits the user to perform several actions on the selected message(s), including archiving, deleting, moving to a MailBox/Tag, and reporting as spam.

When one or more messages are selected in the "MessageList" ViewComponent, the "MessageToolbar" view container appears, which allows the user to perform

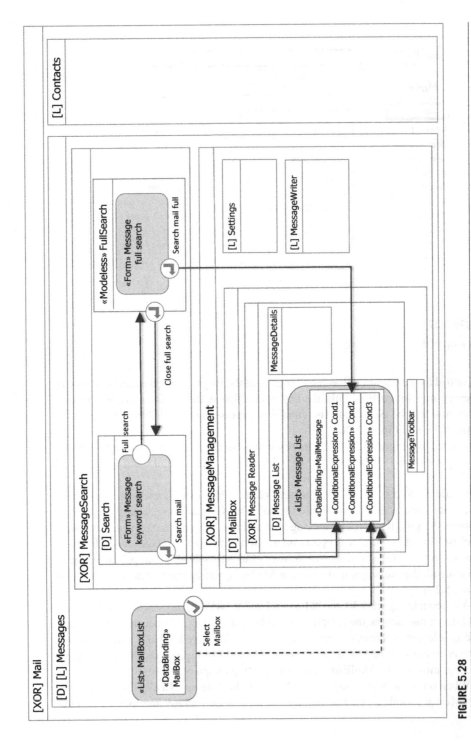

FIGURE 5.28

Refined model of the search functionality, alternating between a basic and a full search form.

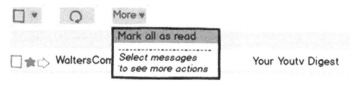

FIGURE 5.29

The "MarkAllAsRead" event marks all messages in the current mailbox as "read."

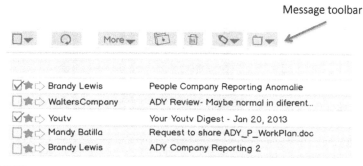

FIGURE 5.30

Behavior of message selection in the "MessageList" ViewComponent.

several actions on the selected messages. If all messages are deselected, such a view container disappears

In summary, the "MessageList" ViewComponent supports three types of interactive events:

1. An event for selecting the entire set of messages and triggering an action upon them, marking all messages as read (Figure 5.29);
2. Two events for checking/unchecking messages (Figure 5.30);
3. An event for selecting an individual message and opening it for reading.

The Events of the "MessageList" ViewComponent are modeled in Figure 5.31 and Figure 5.33.

The "SelectMultiple" checking event marks one or more messages in the current mailbox and produces the display of the "MessageToolbar" ViewContainer, which remains active while at least one message is selected. The "Deselect" unchecking event allows the user to deselect messages, which updates the value of the "MessageSet" parameter. Notice that the checking and unchecking events are triggered every time one element is checked or unchecked in the list. The "SelectMultiple" event has a ParameterBinding, which associates the (possibly empty) set of currently selected messages with an input parameter of the "MessageToolbar" ViewContainer. The "MessageToolbar" ViewContainer is also associated with an ActivationExpression, which verifies that at least one message is selected. The "SelectOne" SelectEvent

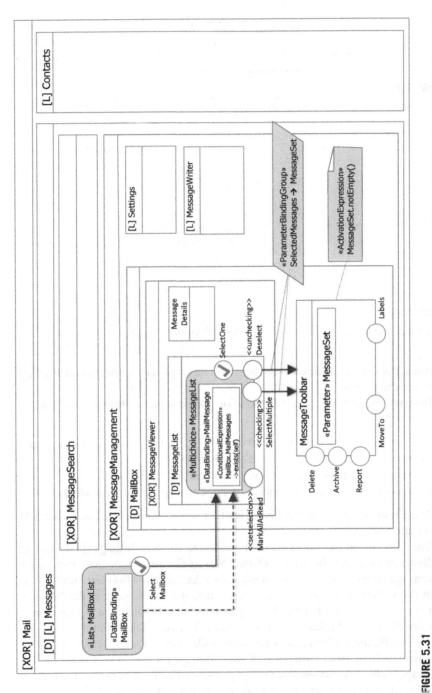

FIGURE 5.31

Model of the behavior of the "SelectMultiple" Event.

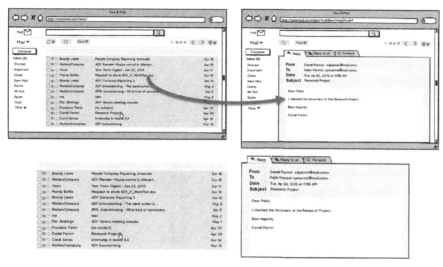

FIGURE 5.32

Mock-up of the selection of a single message, which causes the details of the message to be displayed.

enables the selection of a single message from the mailbox and causes the details of the message to be displayed, as shown in the mock-up of Figure 5.32.

This functionality is modeled in Figure 5.33 with a SelectEvent associated with the "MessageList" ViewComponent, which causes the setting of the "MessageSet" parameter and the display of the "MessageReader" ViewComponent. Such a component permits the user to access one specific message at a time. Its visualization replaces the "MessageList" ViewContainer, as denote by the XOR nesting of the children ViewContainers "MessageList" and "MessageDetails" within "MessageViewer," shown in Figure 5.31 and Figure 5.33.

We conclude this elaborate example with a model of the functionality for composing messages. The interface for composing a message can be accessed in two ways: by clicking on the "Compose" link anywhere in the message management interface (to write a new message) and by selecting one of the various commands available in the message reader interface (for replying to or forwarding an existing message). Consequently, the model should support both the content-independent and the content-dependent navigation to the message composer. Figure 5.34 shows the mock-ups of the two ways for accessing the message composer functionality; notice that the content of the message editing fields and the navigation events available differ in the two cases.

Figure 5.31 and Figure 5.33 show the model of content-independent navigation that permits the user to access the message writing functionality. The "MessageWriter" ViewContainer is marked as landmark, and therefore it is accessible from all the other ViewContainers of the "MessageManagement" ViewContainer. It contains

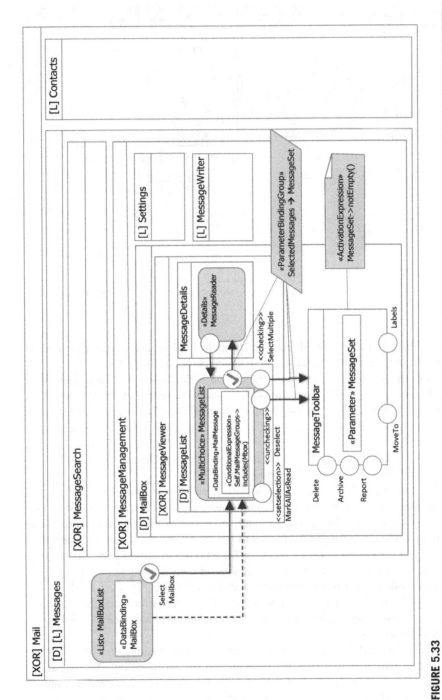

FIGURE 5.33

Model of the events and components for reading a single message.

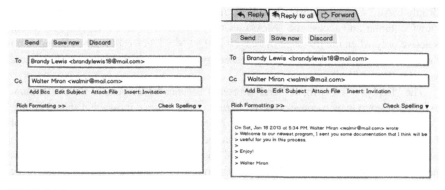

FIGURE 5.34

Mock-up of the interface of the message composer when reached with content-independent navigation (left) and when accessed with content-dependent navigation (right).

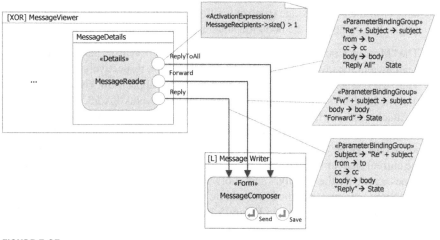

FIGURE 5.35

Model of the content-based navigation to the "MessageWriter" ViewContainer.

the "MessageComposer" ViewComponent, modeled as a form with different fields corresponding to the main attributes and relationships of the domain model class "Message": To, Cc, Bcc, Subject, Body, and Attachment. When the "MessageWriter" ViewComponent is accessed in the content-independent navigation case, the form fields are not preloaded and the user can fill them freely, as shown in the left part of Figure 5.34.

Conversely, Figure 5.35 shows the model expressing the access to the message composer functionality as a consequence of content-dependent navigation. The "MessageReader" ViewComponent is associated with three events ("Reply,"

"ReplyToAll," and "Forward") that allow the user to navigate to the "MessageWriter" ViewContainer and access the "MessageComposer" Form. The "ReplyToAll" event is active only when the message displayed in the "MessageReader" ViewComponent has more than one recipients, as expressed by the activation expression associated with the "ReplyToAll" event.

The "Reply," "ReplyToAll," and "Forward" events are associated with a ParameterBindingGroup, which conveys the properties of the original message displayed in the "MessageReader" ViewComponent. These properties are used to preload the fields of the "MessageComposer" Form as shown in the mock-up in Figure 5.34 (right). Each form field is associated with a parameter of the same name, which takes a value from the proper attribute of the original message as expressed by the ParameterBindingGroup:

- The "Reply" and "ReplyAll" events associate the subject of the original message with the subject of the new message (prefixed with the string "Re: "), the recipient of the original message with the sender of the new message, the body and the cc recipients of the original message to the body and cc recipients of the new message.
- The "Forward" event associates the subject of the original message with the subject of the new message (prefixed with the string "Fw: ") and the body of the original message with the body the new message.

The "MessageComposer" Form supports two SubmitEvents ("Send" and "Save") for sending and for saving without sending the message, respectively.

The "MessageComposer" Form, whose mock-up appears in Figure 5.34, also supports a kind of stateful interaction. Besides the events "AddCc," "AddBcc," "AddAttachment"—which are available irrespective of the kind of response the user is editing—the events "Reply," "ReplyToAll," and "Forward," allow switching the response type. However, only two out the three events are active at a time depending on the current state of the editing. For example, when the user is editing a "ReplyToAll" message, only the "Reply," and "Forward" events are active. This is conveyed by the "State" parameter of the Form and by the three ActivationExpressions associated with the events, as shown in Figure 5.36. The ActivationExpressions check for the value of the parameter "State," which is set appropriately by each of the "Reply," "ReplyToAll," and "Forward" events, so that only the events appropriate to the current editing context are active.

Another example of a conditional event is the "EditSubject" Event. The event for editing the subject field is disabled when the value of the "State" parameter is "Forward."

In chapter 6, we will conclude the e-mail application example by showing how to represent the invocation of the business actions triggered by events, such as sending the message, moving it to another folder, or applying rich formatting to its body.

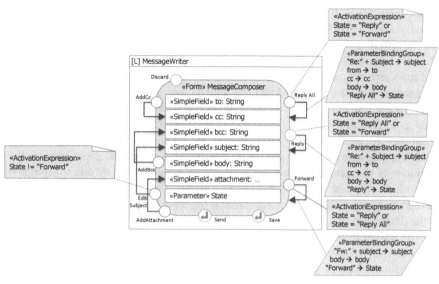

FIGURE 5.36

Model of the stateful interaction supported by the "MessageComposer" Form
ViewComponent.

5.10 SUMMARY OF THE CHAPTER

In this chapter we have delved into the specification of the content and navigation
aspects of the interface and shown how to use ViewContainers, Events, Navigation-
Flows, and DataFlows to describe many configurations. The readability of models is
enhanced by using more specific ViewComponents, such as List and Details, which
make diagram more understandable and amenable to deeper checking and more thor-
ough code generation. We have paid special attention to the input–output dependencies between ViewComponents, which are essential for specifying the runtime
update of interface content induced by user events. The introduced IFML constructs
have been shown at work in the specification of different categories of design pattern for content publication, data entry, and searching. At the end of the chapter, we
resumed the specification of the running case, refining the interface model with the
content publication components and the content-dependent navigation flows.

5.11 BIBLIOGRAPHIC NOTES

Modeling the content of interfaces is a relatively new subject. Its academic roots
can be traced back to a few pioneering design models proposed in the past for
hypermedia applications such as HDM (Hypermedia Design Model) [GPS93],
OOHDM (Object Oriented HDM) [SR95], and RMM (Relationship Management

Methodologies) [ISB95]. The first hypermedia model to gain acceptance was the Dexter Model [HBR94], a model providing a uniform terminology for representing the different primitives offered by hypertext construction systems. In the Dexter Model, components describe the pieces of information that constitute the hypertext, and links represent navigable paths. Many subsequent proposals in the hypermedia field started from the Dexter Model and added more sophisticated modeling primitives, formal semantics, and structured development processes. For example, HDM adds more complex forms of hypertext organization and more powerful navigation primitives to capture the semantics of hypermedia applications. RMM proposes a modeling language built upon the Entity-Relationship model and goes further in the definition of a structured method for hypermedia design. OOHDM takes inspiration from object-oriented modeling by adding specific classes for modeling advanced navigation features. It also exploits classical object-oriented concepts and notations in the design process.

The advent of the web as an application development architecture has sparked new interest in platform-independent modeling of the front end as a means for overcoming the proliferation of the implementation technologies and nonstandard extensions of web languages. The Autoweb system was the first system demonstrating the fully automatic generation of complex web application from a model of the front end [FP00]. Among the several languages and systems proposed in the literature, the Web Modeling Language (WebML) reached industrial maturity, being employed in the development of applications since 2000 [BBC03]. WebML describes the composition of the (web) interface using domain-specific concepts, such as site views, areas, pages, areas, content units, and links. The language includes a set of predefined content publishing components and allows developers to extend the core set with their own components.

END NOTES

1. When the data binding of a List contains objects with duplicate values of the visualization attributes, two options are possible: showing duplicates or distinct values. We assume the latter option as the default. If needed, the alternative option can be specified (e.g., with the «duplicate» stereotype).

Modeling business actions

6

Interactive applications are not only about displaying an interface to the user. The interface is a means for requesting services. These services are performed by the application business logic, possibly with the help of external programs.

Taking the Model–View–Controller pattern as a high-level conceptual description of the way in which an interactive application works, the view allows the user to trigger events, which are handled by the controller. The controller dispatches each event to the proper element in the model, which performs the business action implied by the event. This can result in the update of the application status. At the end of the cycle, the view is updated to display the current status to the user for the next round of interaction. This typical roundtrip is shown in Figure 6.1.

The model could be logically regarded as responsible for two distinct aspects: exposing the business actions that embody the service requested by the user and maintaining the status of the application, which displays in the view.

In chapter 3, we discussed how to construct a domain model that specifies the objects of the application model. In chapter 4, we described how to define the general structure of the application interface. Chapter 5 illustrated how to express the publication of the domain objects in the interface.

The focus of this chapter is on the business logic of the application, be it embedded in methods of the application domain objects, described by suitable UML behavioral diagrams, or delegated to external objects and services.

The goal of IFML is not modeling the internal functioning of the application business logic. Rather the objective is to express the interplay between the interface and the business logic. This is done by:

- Showing that an event triggers a business action, which may imply also the specification of some input–output dependency between the interface and the business logic; and
- Showing that the interface can receive and respond to events generated by "the system," be it a business component of the application or an external service. In this case, IFML also permits the designer to describe the input–output dependency between the information carried by a system event and the affected elements of the interface.

IFML does not replace the behavior specification languages that are normally employed to describe the algorithmic aspects of the business logic. IFML business actions are black boxes that show the minimal amount of information needed to

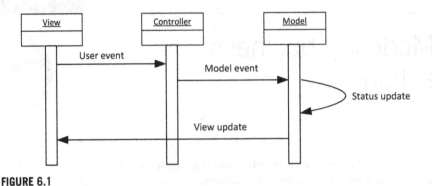

FIGURE 6.1

Sequence diagram describing at a high level the cycle of an interactive application.

specify the abovementioned aspects. The designer is free to focus on such black boxes and describe their internal functioning using the behavioral language of choice. To support this kind of refinement, an action in IFML can reference a behavior in an external model.

6.1 ACTIONS

> **ACTIONS**
>
> An **Action** represents a reference to some business logic triggered by an Event.

Actions may reside on the server or on the client side. The elementary design pattern for triggering actions is represented in Figure 6.2.

The model contains a source ViewContainer and ViewComponent, with an Event connected via an InteractionFlow to an Action (shown as a named hexagon). The Action is itself connected to a target ViewComponent through an outgoing flow by an event typically representing the completion of the Action. ParameterBinding elements are used to denote the input–output dependency between the source ViewComponent and the Action, and between the Action and the target ViewComponent.

For example, the source ViewComponent could be a form for entering a flight request. The Action could be a flight brokering business component that takes as input the form data, checks availability and price at different flight operators, and produces the best offers as output. The target ViewComponent could be a List showing the retrieved options to the user.

The pattern of Figure 6.2 assumes that the action always terminates with the same event, after which the same target ViewContainer is displayed. However, in many situations, invoking a piece of business logic may result in various alternative outcomes lead to different termination events. Therefore, Actions may trigger different

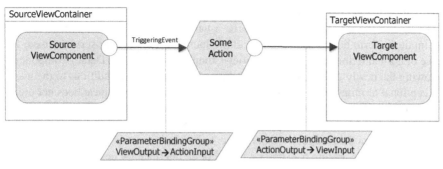

FIGURE 6.2

Elementary model describing the triggering of the action and its effect on the interface.

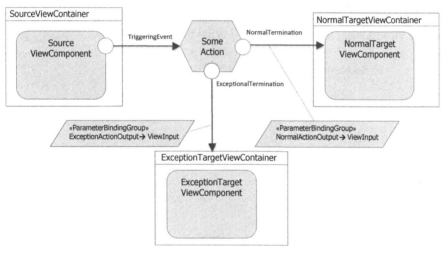

FIGURE 6.3

Model of action invocation with explicit ActionEvent.

Events, called ActionEvents, as the result of the normal termination of computation or to signal the occurrence of exceptions.

ACTIONEVENTS

An **ActionEvent** is an Event that may be produced by an Action to signal normal or exceptional termination.

Figure 6.3 shows the typical usage of multiple ActionEvents. The Action can terminate in normal or exceptional conditions, and the ActionEvents and associated InteractionFlows express the course of action taken in the two cases. For example, the source ViewComponent could be a form for signing up an application to an external service, and the Action could be a validation business component, taking as input the form data, validating it, and producing a limited-time service token. In case of normal termination, the target ViewComponent could be a Details component showing the newly generated token and the service terms and conditions to the user. Exceptional termination may also occur (e.g., when the user's request does not meet the conditions for obtaining an access token). In this case, the target ViewComponent could be a Details component showing the reasons of failure to the user.

The source and the target ViewComponent of an action invocation need not be distinct. For example, Figure 6.4 shows a model of an interface for deleting objects from a list. The source ViewComponent allows the user to select an object for deletion. After the deletion, the same ViewComponent is presented again with its content updated.

Figure 6.4 also shows two shortcuts for simplifying the ActionEvent notation. When no outgoing InteractionFlow and no ActionEvent are associated with the Action, it is assumed that the target is the smallest ViewContainer comprising the source ViewElement from which the Action has been activated.

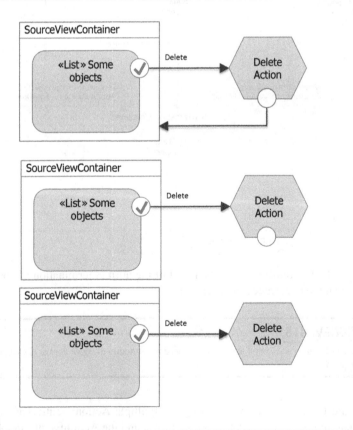

FIGURE 6.4

Model of an interface that redisplays the (updated) source ViewContainer after an action is executed.

6.2 NOTIFICATION

The influence of business logic on the interface manifests not only when the user takes the initiative but also as a consequence of a system-initiated action. This situation requires modeling the notification of an occurrence from the application back end of an external system to the user interface. In this case, the IFML model does not represent the initiation and execution of the action but only its ultimate effect, which is captured by a SystemEvent.

SYSTEMEVENT AND SYSTEMFLOW

A **SystemEvent** is an Event produced by the system that triggers a computation reflected in the user interface. Examples of SystemEvents are time events (which are triggered after an elapsed frame of time), system alerts (such as a database connection loss), or message receipt notifications.

A **SystemFlow** is an InteractionFlow that connects a SystemEvent to a ViewElement to identify the element affected by the occurrence of the SystemEvent.

The cause of a SystemEvent may be left unspecified in the model, although it is also possible to express a condition whose occurrence triggers the SystemEvent. Such a condition is represented by means of a TriggeringExpression.

TRIGGERINGEXPRESSION

A **TriggeringExpression** is an expression that determines when or under what conditions a System-Event should be triggered.

The notification PATTERN A-notif, introduced later in this chapter, contains an example of a SystemEvent, a SystemFlow, and a TriggeringExpression.

6.3 BUSINESS ACTION PATTERNS

Several design patterns embody the solution to recurrent problems in the design of the interplay between the user interface and the business logic. We call such platform-independent patterns **action patterns** and prefix their name with an "A."

6.3.1 CONTENT MANAGEMENT PATTERNS

The most important action patterns relate to the management of the objects of the domain model. Such content management patterns all have a similar structure. They exploit an Action endowed with the input parameters necessary to create, delete, or modify objects and association instances, and with output parameters that characterize the effect of the performed content update. The role of the interface is that of supplying the input and of visualizing the output to the user as a confirmation that the action has been executed and the application state updated.

6.3.2 PATTERN A-OCR: OBJECT CREATION

The object creation pattern enables the creation of a new object. The pattern relies on an Action characterized by:

- a user-defined name;
- a reference to the dynamic behavior that the action must perform; and
- a set of input parameters, used to initialize the attributes of the object to be created.

The input of the Action is typically supplied by a ParameterBindingGroup associated with a NavigationFlow exiting from a Form ViewComponent. The parameter values are used to construct the new object. If some attributes have no associated input value, they are set to null. The only exception is the object identifier (OID), which is normally treated in an ad hoc way: if no value is supplied, a new unique value is generated by the Action. The behavior of the object creation Action typically consists of invoking a class constructor or a factory method in a creator class. The output produced by the Action is the newly created object, comprising its OID and all its attribute values. The output of the Action is defined only when the operation succeeds and thus can be associated as a ParameterBindingGroup only with the InteractionFlow that denotes normal termination. If no ParameterBindingGroup is specified explicitly, a default output ParameterBinding consisting of the OID of the newly created object is assumed as implicitly associated to the normal termination event.

The example of Figure 6.5 shows the typical object creation pattern, which consist of the combination of an entry Form ("EnterProductData") providing input to an Action ("CreateProduct") that creates a new Product by invoking the DynamicBehaviour implemented by a factory method of a creator class. The Form has several fields (e.g., "Code," "Name," and "Price") for entering the respective attribute values. The field values inserted by the user are associated as explicit parameters with the NavigationFlow from the Form to the Action. In the rendition, also shown in Figure 6.5, the SubmitEvent associated with the form is displayed as a submit button, which permits the activation of the Action. The "CreateProduct" Action has two ActionEvents. Normal termination is associated with an InteractionFlow that points to the "NewProductDetails" ViewComponent and with the default output parameter (the OID of the new object). The exceptional termination event is associated with an InteractionFlow that points to a ViewContainer for displaying an error message.

6.3.3 PATTERN A-OACR: OBJECT AND ASSOCIATION CREATION

A variant of the object creation pattern can be used to create a new object and set its associations to other objects. Figure 6.6 shows an example of such an object creation and connection pattern.

The "EnterProductData" Form contains an additional SelectionField, corresponding to the association that must be set, namely the association between Product and Category. The Category SelectionField can be preloaded with all the categories as discussed in chapter 5. The NavigationFlow triggered by the SubmitEvent "CreateNewProduct" has one additional ParameterBinding for the identifier of the selected

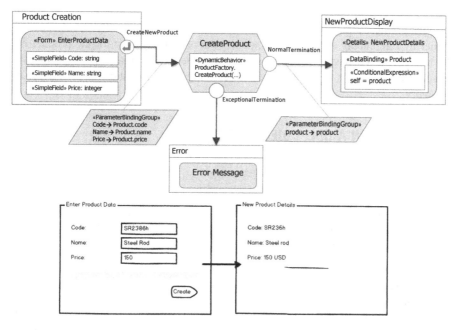

FIGURE 6.5

The object creation pattern and a possible rendition.

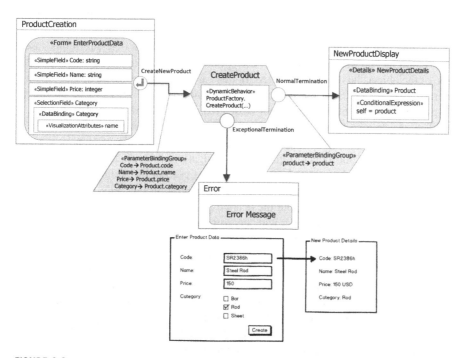

FIGURE 6.6

The object creation and connection pattern.

category, which is passed as input to the Action. The Action itself can be specified either by referencing a constructor that sets the proper category for the product or by referencing a behavioral diagram (e.g., a UML sequence or activity diagram) that describes all the steps to be performed for creating the object and connecting it to a category.

6.3.4 PATTERN A-ODL: OBJECT DELETION

The object deletion pattern is used to eliminate one or more objects of a given class. The pattern requires an Action characterized by:

- a user-defined name;
- a reference to the dynamic behavior that the action must perform, which is typically the invocation of a delete operation of the database; and
- the input parameters necessary to identify the object to delete.

The input to the action is conveyed by a set of ParameterBinding elements. Normally these values are one or more primary keys, although nonkey attribute values can be used as input, and the Action encapsulates the business logic for exploiting such information to retrieve the objects to delete.

At runtime, the user typically chooses either a single object displayed by a Details ViewComponent or selected from a List ViewComponent, or a set of objects chosen from a MultiChoice List ViewComponent. The identifiers of the chosen objects are associated by a ParameterBindingGroup to the NavigationFlow exiting the ViewComponent and pointing to the Action that actually deletes the objects.

Normal termination occurs when all the objects have been deleted. In this case, the Action has no output parameters. Exceptional termination occurs when at least one of the objects has not been deleted. In this case, the Action has an output parameter holding the OIDs of the objects that were not deleted. This can be useful to display the list of items that could not be deleted, together with an error message.

The example of Figure 6.7 illustrates the object deletion pattern applied to a single object. The ViewContainer includes the "ProductsList" ViewComponent connected to the "DeleteProduct" Action. The NavigationFlow has a default parameter holding the OID of the selected product, which is used in the Action. The SelectEvent fires the deletion of the chosen object. If the operation succeeds, the "Products" ViewContainer is redisplayed, but the deleted product no longer appears. In case of failure, a different ViewContainer with an error message is displayed, which may use the information about the object whose deletion failed and any other useful parameter returned by the action (e.g., a human-readable explanation of the failure).

The example of Figure 6.8 shows a variant of the object deletion patterns in which a multichoice list ViewComponent is used to let the user check a set of products and invoke the deletion Action on them. In this case, the default ParameterBinding associated with the "Delete" event of the "ProductList" ViewComponent holds the set of OIDs of the selected objects. These are displayed in the "SelectedProducts" List ViewComponent, which is associated with the "Confirm" event.

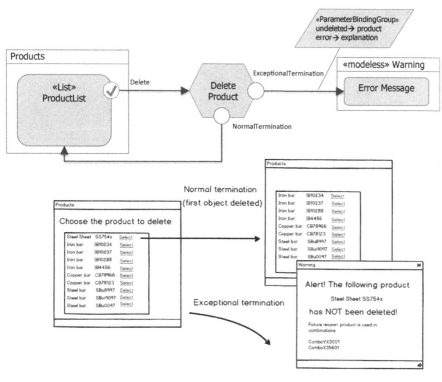

FIGURE 6.7

Basic object deletion pattern.

The NavigationFlow of the Delete set selection event has as default ParameterBinding that includes the entire set of objects output by the source List ViewComponent ("SelectedProducts" in this case) and triggers the "DelectedProduct" action on all the objects bound to the event.

6.3.5 PATTERN A-CODL: CASCADED DELETION

The cascaded deletion pattern allows one to remove a specific object and all the objects associated with it via one or more associations. In this case, the action is implemented by a sequence formed by two or more delete operations, one for removing the main object and the others for removing the related objects (at least one). In particular, cascaded deletion is used to propagate the deletion of an object to other dependent objects, which are connected to it by an association with minimum cardinality of 1, and thus could not exist without the object to which they refer. An example of such a situation is illustrated in Figure 6.9, which shows the use of the pattern for deleting an e-mail message and all its attachment. The "MessageDetails" ViewContainer includes a Details ViewComponent ("Message") showing the message, and a

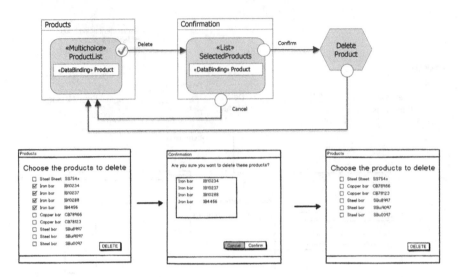

FIGURE 6.8

Multiple objects deletion pattern.

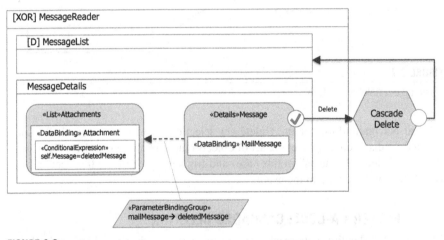

FIGURE 6.9

Cascade delete pattern.

List ViewComponent ("Attachments") displaying its attachments. The "Message" ViewComponent is associated with an event that triggers the "CascadeDelete" Action, which conceptually consists of a sequence of two operations, deleting both the attachment and the e-mail message. The internal structure of the Action is not specified in IFML and can be described by means of a behavioral diagram. For example, Figure 6.10 specifies the cascade deletion using a UML sequence diagram.

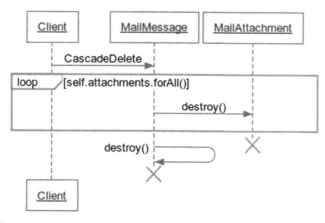

FIGURE 6.10

UML sequence diagram specifying the behavior of the "CascadeDelete" Action.

An alternative Action design could exploit the native referential integrity mechanism of the underlying data store (for example, the ON DELETE CASCADE clause of SQL foreign key constraints) and delete only the message object, leaving to the database the task of cascading the deletion.

The pattern of Figure 6.9 is a good illustration of the intertwining between the business logic and the interface design. The NavigationFlow denoting the normal termination of the "CascadeDelete" Action does not lead back to the source View-Container but instead to the "MessageList" ViewContainer, which is the default subcontainer of the enclosing "MessageDetails" ViewContainer. This is because the object that was displayed in the "MessageDetails" ViewComponent (the deleted message) no longer exists, and it would make no sense to redisplay it. The IFML model is the right place to express this kind of relationship between the semantics of actions and their effect in the interface.

The resulting interaction is shown in the mock-up of Figure 6.11.

6.3.6 PATTERN A-OM: OBJECT MODIFICATION

The object modification pattern is used to update one or more objects of a given class. An object modification pattern uses an Action that is characterized by:

- a user-defined name;
- the reference to the dynamic behavior that the action must perform, which is typically the invocation of a setter method; and
- the input parameters necessary to identify the object(s) to modify and to supply new values to their attributes.

When the user chooses multiple objects at runtime, the same update applies to all the selected objects. The Action must be properly linked to ViewComponents of the interface, to obtain the needed inputs.

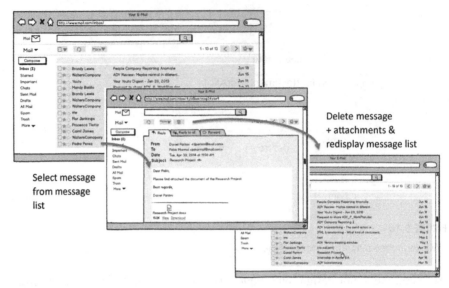

Select message from message list

Delete message + attachments & redisplay message list

FIGURE 6.11

Mock-up of the interaction for deleting a message and its attachments.

- The new attribute values: these are typically defined as a ParameterBinding-Group associated with a NavigationFlow coming from a Form ViewComponent.
- The objects to modify: these are usually specified as a ParameterBindingGroup holding one OID or a set of OIDs.
- As an alternative to the usage of object identifiers as parameters, the objects to modify can be retrieved by the Action based on logical criteria, exploiting the values associated as parameters with InteractionFlows incoming to the Action. In this case, the Action encapsulates the object retrieval business logic.

The normal termination of the Action occurs when all the objects have been successfully modified. In this, case the ActionEvent is associated with a default parameter holding the set of OIDs of the modified objects. An exceptional termination occurs when at least one of the objects could not be modified. In that case, the ActionEvent is associated with a default parameter holding set of OIDs of the objects that were not modified.

The example of Figure 6.12 shows a Form ViewComponent used to supply values to an object modification Action. The "ProductEditor" ViewContainer comprises a Details ViewComponent ("Product"), which shows the name of the product to modify, and a Form ("EnterProductData"), whereby the user can modify the existing product attribute values. A DataFlow from the Details ViewComponent to the Action has a default parameter holding the OID of the product to modify, which is used by the Action to identify the instance to update. The Action is activated by a Submit-Event associated with the Form. The NavigationFlow has a ParameterBindingGroup

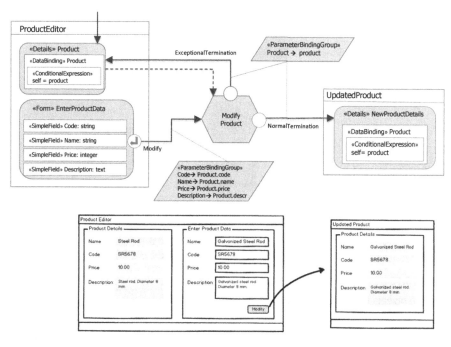

FIGURE 6.12

Single object modification pattern.

element, which associates the value of the fields of the Form with corresponding input parameters of the Action. The normal termination leads to the "UpdatedProduct" ViewContainer, which shows the modified values of the product attributes. The exceptional termination points "back" to the "ProductEditor" ViewContainer, which redisplays the old values.

Note that for classes with many attributes, the specification of the pattern can be cumbersome due to the need to repeat the relevant attributes twice: once as form fields and once in the parameter binding. However, a tool such as the one described in chapter 11 can easily provide a wizard for building the pattern with less effort (e.g., by inserting all the class attributes in the model automatically).

The example of Figure 6.13 illustrates the modification of a set of objects. The "MessageList" multichoice List is associated with a SelectEvent ("MarkAsRead") for updating the status of the chosen messages, marking them as "read." The outgoing NavigationFlow of the event is associated with a ParameterBindingGroup that holds the OIDs of the objects selected in the multichoice list and a constant value ("read") for updating the status of the messages. The operation succeeds if the modification can be applied to all the objects chosen from the list, in which case the normal termination ActionEvent is raised. After this event, the "Messages" ViewContainer is redisplayed, with a notification of the number of marked messages.

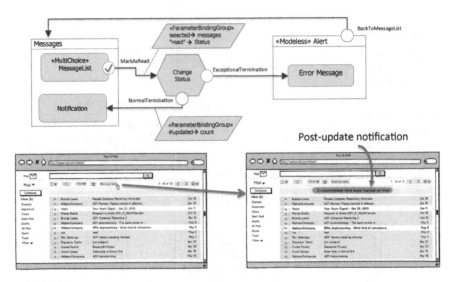

FIGURE 6.13

Multiple objects modification pattern.

The Action fails if the modification cannot be applied to some of the selected messages, which causes the exceptional termination ActionEvent to be raised and an modeless alert window to be displayed.

6.3.7 PATTERN A-AM: ASSOCIATION MANAGEMENT

An association management pattern is about maintaining the instances of associations specified in the domain model. Specifically, it is used to create/replace/delete instances of an association by connecting and/or disconnecting some objects of the source and target classes. The association management pattern exploits an Action characterized by:

- a user-defined name;
- the reference to the dynamic behavior that the action must perform, which is typically the invocation of a setter method acting on the attribute that implements the association in one or in both classes; and
- input parameters for locating the objects of the source class and of the target class.

The Action is triggered by a NavigationFlow and receives as input pairs of objects of the source and target classes, identified by the ParameterBindingGroup of the NavigationFlow. It provides as output the pairs of OIDs corresponding to the objects of the source and of the target class for which an association instance has been created/replaced/deleted. These values can be used to define a ParameterBindingGroup associated with the normal and exceptional termination ActionEvents. The latter is raised when the

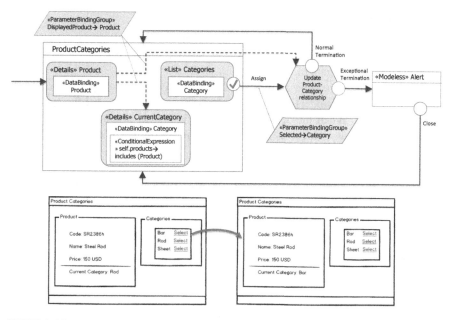

FIGURE 6.14

Association management pattern.

management of at least one association instance fails, whereas the normal termination ActionEvent signals that all the association instances have been managed properly.

Figure 6.14 shows an example of the association management pattern for updating the category of a product, which corresponds to a one-to-many association in the domain model. The "Product" Details ViewComponent in the "ProductCategories" ViewContainer displays a current product, as the result of a previous selection in another ViewContainer (not shown in Figure 6.14). The ViewContainer also includes the "CurrentCategory" Details ViewComponent, which displays the category of the displayed product. The primary key of the displayed product—necessary for determining the actual category in the "CurrentCategory" ViewComponent—is supplied by a ParameterBindingGroup associated with the DataFlow from the "Product" to the "CurrentCategory" ViewComponent.

Finally, the "ProductCategories" ViewContainer comprises a List ViewComponent ("Categories") showing all the categories from which the user can select the desired one and trigger the "Assign" SubmitEvent. This event triggers the Action for updating the relationship instance between the displayed product, whose primary key is supplied by a DataFlow with a ParameterBindingGroup, and the new category selected from the list. The normal termination event of the Action causes the "ProductCategories" ViewContainer to be redisplayed, showing the updated category of the product. In case of abnormal termination, an Alert window is presented before letting the user go back to the original ViewContainer.

6.3.8 PATTERN A-NOTIF: NOTIFICATION

This pattern models the case in which the interface is (typically asynchronously) updated by the occurrence of a system generated event. Figure 6.15 shows an example of the notification pattern.

In the e-mail application, actions on messages (such as sending, deleting, and moving to a different folder) are triggered by an Event and executed by an Action at the server side. When the action terminates, the system produces a completion event and sends an asynchronous notification to the interface. The effect of catching

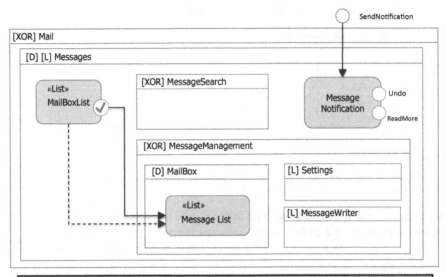

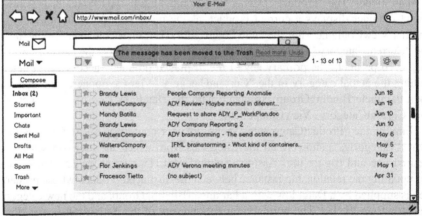

FIGURE 6.15

Notification pattern.

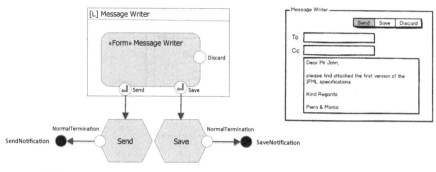

FIGURE 6.16

Model of the production of a SystemEvent that notifies the completion of an action.

a notification event is represented by a SystemEvent, which triggers the display of a "MessageNotification" ViewComponent, as shown in Figure 6.15.

The production of a SystemEvent can be left undetermined, in which case it is assumed that the system sends the event in a completely unspecified manner, or be associated with an Action of the interface model to convey that the notification is connected with the termination of an Action. For example, all the notification events of the e-mail application can be associated with the termination of the respective Action, as shown in Figure 6.16.

6.4 RUNNING EXAMPLE

The e-mail application allows the users to perform a variety of operations on messages, including composing a new message, replying to a received message, and moving a message to a new or to an existing folder. When one or more messages are selected, they can be moved to another folder by means of the "MoveTo" command.

Figure 6.17 shows the mock-up of interface supporting a command. A ViewContainer is displayed in a new window with the list of available MailBox and Tags. The user can select from such a list the destination Folder to which he wants to move the messages. This functionality can be modeled with an instance of PATTERN A-AM: Association management, shown in Figure 6.18: the "MessageToolbar" ViewContainer is associated with the "MoveTo" Event, which causes the display of the "Chooser" modeless window. This ViewContainer comprises a list for selecting the target folder. The selection event triggers the "MoveTo" Action that performs the command and sends a notification event upon termination, which is captured by the "MessageNotification" ViewComponent in the top-level container (as already illustrated in Figure 6.15).

Note that in this example of association management pattern, the messages to move are associated as a ParameterBinding to a DataFlow that connects the "MessageToolbar" ViewContainer to the Action, whereas the OID of the destination folder

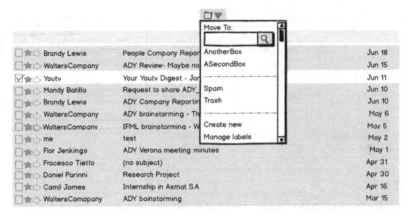

FIGURE 6.17

Mock-up of the "MoveTo" command showing the step for selecting the folder.

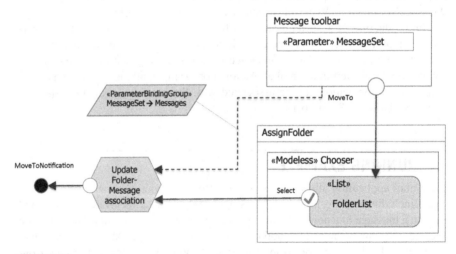

FIGURE 6.18

Model of the interface for moving messages to a folder.

is associated by default with the NavigationFlow of the "Select" Event and thus omitted from the diagram.

As visible in the mock-up of Figure 6.17, the window for choosing the target folder also contains a command for creating a new folder that opens a modal window for entering the name and parent folder of the new folder. Figure 6.19 shows the mock-up of this functionality.

The model including the functionality for moving a message to a newly created folder is shown in Figure 6.20. The "CreateNew" event associated with the "Chooser" ViewContainer opens a modal ViewContainer with the form for entering

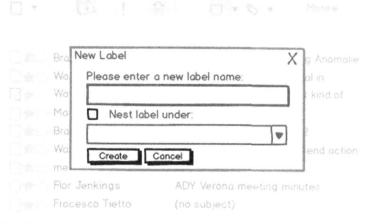

FIGURE 6.19

Mock-up of the modal window for creating a new folder.

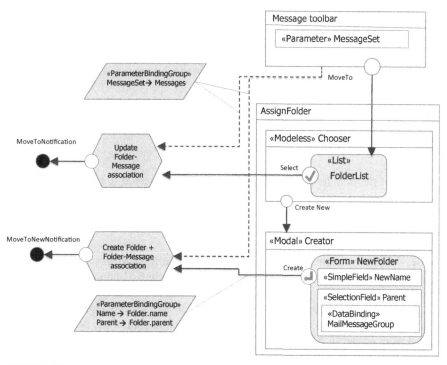

FIGURE 6.20

Complete model of the interface for the "MoveTo" command.

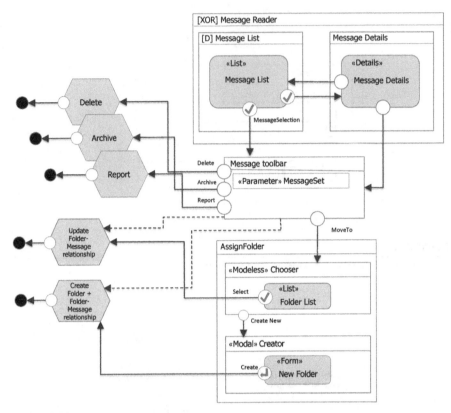

FIGURE 6.21

Complete model of the toolbar commands on messages.

the name of the new folder (using a SimpleField) and selecting the parent folders (using a SelectionField). The "Create" Event in the modal window triggers an Action for creating the new folder and associating it to the specified parent folder and to the messages selected previously. Upon normal termination, the Action emits a notification message.

Besides the commands for moving messages, the toolbar provides functionality for archiving, reporting, and deleting message. Figure 6.21 completes the partial model viewed so far with the remaining Actions.

An additional note concerning the allocation of the business logic to the architectural tiers of the application is needed. So far, the illustration has been purposely neutral as to where an Action is executed within the architecture of the application, because the platform-independent model should not incorporate unnecessary architectural assumptions. However, this does not mean that all actions are executed on the same tier or that only server-side business logic can be modeled. To illustrate this aspect, we conclude the running example with an expansion of the model of the message composition functionality, already described in chapter 5.

The model of the "MessageWriter" ViewComponent can be refined by zooming in inside the "Body" field, which supports client-side business logic (such as rich formatting of the text) and mixed server- and client-side functionality (such as spellchecking). Figure 6.22 shows a mock-up of this functionality.

The embedding of a full-fledged microapplication such as a rich text editor inside a Form ViewComponent can be modeled by replacing the SimpleField with a more complex ViewComponentPart called RichTextEditor, as shown in Figure 6.23. Such

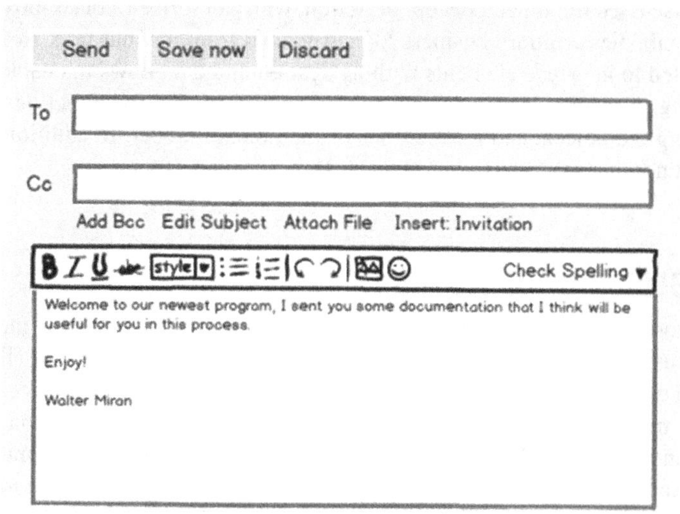

FIGURE 6.22

Mock-up of the "Body" field of the "MessageWriter" ViewComponent.

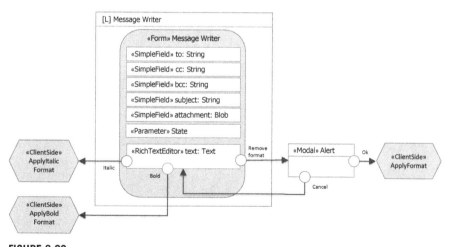

FIGURE 6.23

Model of the rich editing functionality of the "Body" field.

ViewComponentPart could support events and further nested ViewComponentParts as required to express its interface. The execution tier of an Action could also be expressed as a stereotype. For example, Figure 6.23 tags the Actions executed at client side with an appropriate stereotype.

6.5 SUMMARY OF THE CHAPTER

We have discussed the IFML concept of Action, which describes a black-box component that embodies arbitrary business logic triggered from the interface. Actions can be connected to interface elements with navigation and data flows to enable parameter passing. Next we illustrated several design patterns involving actions, mostly for updating the objects and associations of the domain model. In addition, system events and notification have been exemplified.

6.6 BIBLIOGRAPHIC NOTES

Several works have addressed the design of user interfaces and their integration with the business logic based on the MVC paradigm [LR01] [HLS+14]. The work [FCBT10] discusses a model for representing the execution of Rich Internet Applications. The model allows expressing advanced aspects such as the partition of functionality and data across multiple architecture tiers, asynchronous communication patterns, and the selective computation of interface parts after the occurrence of events.

IFML extensions

The IFML standard comes organized as a core set of concepts and a number of extensions that embody general characteristics found in many interactive applications. The extension mechanism applies to all the main concepts of IFML. The extensions included in the standard are:

- ViewContainer extensions: Window
- ViewComponent and ViewComponent Part extensions: Details, Field, Form, List, SelectionField, SimpleField, Slot
- Event extensions: SelectEvent, SubmitEvent, SystemEvent
- ContextDimension extensions: Device, Position, UserRole
- Expression extensions: ValidationRule

Further custom extensions are allowed for the main concepts of IFML: ViewContainers, ViewComponents, ViewComponentParts, Events, and domain and behavior concepts (and their extensions).

The purposes of extensions are manifold:

- Adding expressive power to the modeling language;
- Making the concepts and notation less abstract and closer to the intuition of designers;
- Allowing different specialized concepts to be distinguishable visually, for improved readability of diagrams; and
- Assigning more precise meaning to concepts to enable deeper model checking, formalization of semantics, and executability (through code generation or model interpretation).

Figure 7.1 shows the use of IFML extensions (equipped with customized icons) for making the visual notation more intuitive, enabling model checking, and supporting code generation. This example will be expanded in chapter 11.

The advantages of extensibility persist and even increase when one considers IFML under the perspective of a specific category of applications that exhibit their own interface styles, technological constraints, and sometimes even peculiar terminology or jargon.

This chapter introduces several specializations of IFML that exploit extensibility to capture features found in different classes of applications, including, desktop, web, and mobile applications. The assignment of an extension to a class of application is somewhat arbitrary. The convergence of the implementation languages and platforms makes it impossible to distinguish the features of desktop, web, and mobile

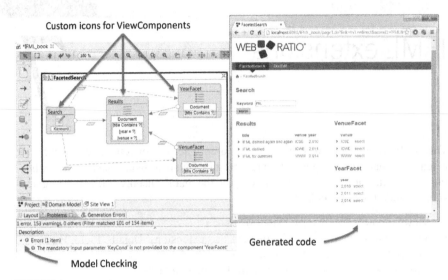

Custom icons for ViewComponents

Generated code

Model Checking

FIGURE 7.1

Use of IFML extensions for visual notation, model checking, and code generation.

application sharply. For a better organization of the chapter, though, we have placed each extension under the category in which it originated or is most often or exclusively used.

7.1 DESKTOP EXTENSIONS

Under the umbrella term of desktop applications we mean applications that allow the most precise control over the user interface, developed with a variety of different technologies, ranging from window-based applications developed in such technologies as Java Swing or Windows Forms to rich Internet applications implemented with JavaScript and HTML 5. Although this equivalence is imprecise from the programming point of view, it is sufficient to identify cross-platform features that are general enough to provide good candidates for IFML extensions.

7.1.1 EVENT EXTENSIONS

Probably, the most relevant capability of desktop applications is the very detailed management of the events that the user can generate in the interface. Therefore, an important area of extensibility of IFML regards the event types supported by desktop interfaces. These events are so numerous as to make it unfeasible to review all of them and the properties to be modeled for creating an IFML extension. Rather, we will discuss what makes an event type worth an extension and the features that

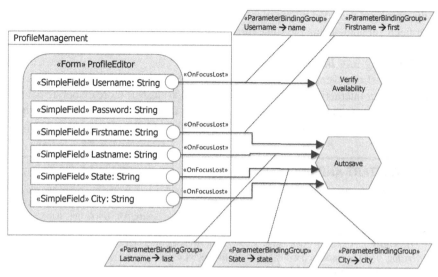

FIGURE 7.2

Example of extended event for Form and SimpleField ViewElements.

should be modeled as additions to the basic notion of Event. When considering a new event type as a candidate for extension, the following questions should be addressed:

- What ViewElements can the event be associated with? ViewContainers, View-Components, ViewComponentParts, a specific extension of such elements, or a mix thereof?
- In there any restriction on the type of ViewElements that can be the target of the InteractionFlow associated with the event?
- What parameters can be associated with the InteractionFlow connected with the event?

Figure 7.2 shows an example of event specialization.

> ## ONFOCUSLOST
>
> The **OnFocusLost** event is an extension of ViewElementEvent that captures the loss of focus of a SimpleField in a Form. The event is triggered when the user moves away from the field (e.g., by using the tab key or by clicking on another field). It can be associated with a SimpleField or with an entire Form. Its outgoing InteractionFlow can have any ViewElement as a target and a ParameterBindingGroup comprising as input parameter the value of the SimpleField or the values of all the SimpleFields of the Form.

Figure 7.2 demonstrates the usage of the OnFocusLost event to invoke Actions. In one case the event is associated with the "Username" field for checking the availability of the username provided by the user. Other OnFocusLost events are associated with other fields for auto-saving the value input by the user when the focus leaves the field.

7.1.1.1 Drag and Drop

The OnFocusLost event and other similar event extensions detect an atomic self-contained user interaction. Desktop applications also support more elaborate behaviors that span a sequence of interactions, such as drag and drop. A drag and drop behavior consists of the correlation of two event types: OnDragStart and OnDrop.

ONDRAGSTART AND ONDROP

The **OnDragStart** event is an extension of ViewElementEvent that captures the beginning of a drag interaction. It can be associated with Details or List ViewComponents (and specializations thereof). It has no outgoing InteractionFlow element. It has a mandatory property "OnDropEvent" that denotes an event of type OnDrop, which is the target of the OnDragStart event.

The **OnDrop** event is an extension of ViewElementEvent that captures the termination of a drop interaction. It can be associated with a Details or List ViewComponent (and specializations thereof). It must appear as the value of the OnDropEvent property of an event of type OnDragStart, which is the source of the OnDrop event. It has one outgoing InteractionFlow element. Such InteractionFlow can have any ViewElement as a target and a DataBindingGroup comprising two input parameters: (1) the value of one or more class instances of the ViewComponent associated with the source OnDragStart event and (2) the value of one or more class instances of the ViewComponent associated with the OnDrop target event.

As shown in Figure 7.3, the drag and drop behavior is modeled with a pair of events: one (OnDragStart) binds to the object(s) that are dragged, and the other (OnDrop) binds to the object(s) on which the dragged item(s) are dropped. These two (sets of) instances can be used as parameter values associated with the InteractionFlow exiting the OnDrop event. In the case of Figure 7.3, one or more messages are dragged from the message list of the currently open mail box and dropped on another mail box. The drop termination event triggers the "MoveTo" Action, which moves the dragged messages to the drop mail box.

7.1.2 COMPONENT EXTENSIONS

Container and component extensions add features to the basic IFML ViewElements.

7.1.2.1 Tree explorer

A "classic" component of desktop interfaces is the Tree component, used to display hierarchical data. Essentially, a tree is a special kind of list that displays not only objects but also their containment associations. Therefore, the data model of a tree component consists of a class, which represents the common type of the objects displayed in the tree, and a recursive association, which represents the hierarchy. In the simplest case, interaction with the tree is done by selecting one node at a time.

TREE VIEWCOMPONENT

A **Tree** is an extension of the List ViewComponent that displays hierarchical data. It owns a DataBinding element that refers to a class of the domain model and a RecursiveNestedDataBinding element that refers to a one-to-many association defined on the instances of the class.

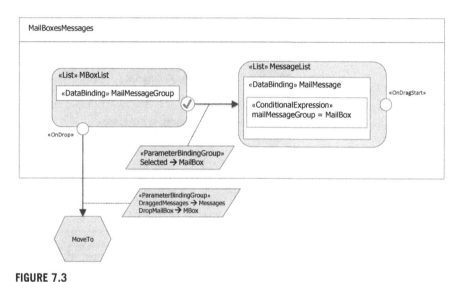

FIGURE 7.3

Extending IFML with drag and drop events.

Figure 7.4 shows an example of the Tree component for publishing a selectable list of nested mailboxes. A Selection event allows the user to select one element in the tree and thus display its details.

7.1.2.2 Table

Another popular component of desktop applications is the table editor, also called a record set editor or data grid. The component displays a table of data and allows the user to add and delete rows and edit cell content. The data model of the component is any piece of tabular data. For simplicity we illustrate the case in which instances of a class are used as data, but alternative data bindings can be defined, as already possible with the standard concept of DataBinding. The only constraint is that the rows of the table should correspond to identifiable objects, if one wants to trap events like row deletion and therefore update the underlying data accordingly.

The Table component can be associated with such events as the update of a cell or the insertion and deletion of a row.

TABLE VIEWCOMPONENT

A **Table** is an extension of ViewComponent that displays tabular data and allows the user to edit them. It has a DataBinding element that typically refers to a class of the domain model. The attributes of the class are mapped to the columns of the table using the ColumnAttribute ViewComponentPart. The Table component can be associated with events of type CellUpdate, RowInsertion, and RowDeletion.

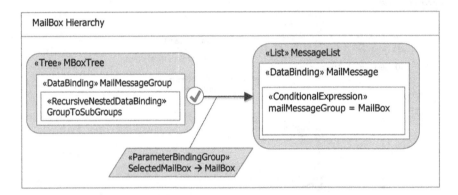

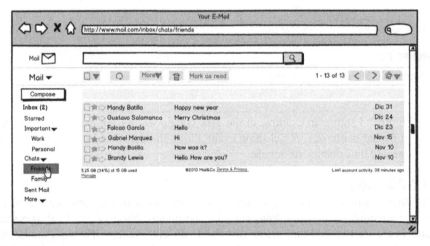

FIGURE 7.4

Example of usage of the Tree ViewComponent

Figure 7.5 shows an example of usage of the Table component for editing a record set of products. At each cell update, a data update Action "SaveProduct" is invoked with a parameter binding that holds the modified field value. The deletion of a row triggers the deletion of the corresponding class instance, identified by a parameter binding corresponding to the object displayed in the affected table row. The creation

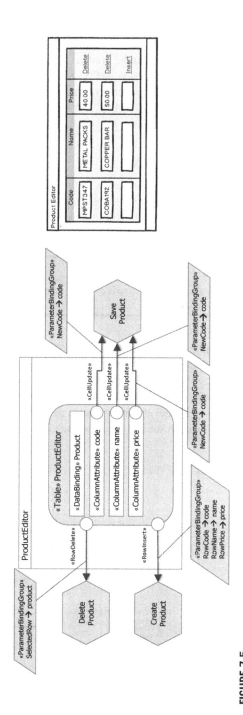

FIGURE 7.5

Example of usage of the Table ViewComponent.

of a row invokes the creation of a new object based on the values entered in the Table row by the user. After the execution of the Actions, the Table is redisplayed with the updated content. (Recall that an InteractionFlow pointing to the source element of the action is assumed by default and thus can be omitted from the diagram).

The basic example discussed in this section can be extended, for example, with event types supporting the explicit synchronization of the table content with the data in the data store, such as "Refresh" and "SaveAll," and with more compact parameters (e.g., representing the content of an entire row or of all the rows of the table).

7.1.3 COMPONENTPART EXTENSIONS

Extensions can also be defined at a finer granularity, such as at the ViewComponentPart level. An example could be an editable selection field that mixes the functionality of SimpleField and SelectionField by allowing the user to edit the value of the input field or choose it from a list of options.

EDITABLESELECTIONFIELD

An **EditableSelectionField** extends the Field element and denotes an input field that is both editable and selectable.

Figure 7.6 shows an example of usage of the EditableSelectionField extension. The "ProductCreator" form contains the "Category" EditableSelectionField that allows the user to pick the category from a list of existing categories or invent a new one. The internal business logic of the "CreateProductAndCategory" Action must distinguish whether the category is new and, if so, create the category in addition to the product. Such a behavior can be described in a separate UML diagram associated with the Action.

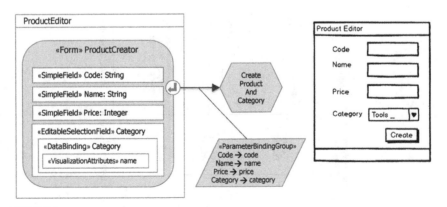

FIGURE 7.6

An example of usage of the EditableSelectionField.

7.2 **WEB EXTENSIONS**

Web applications have brought several new concepts and an almost completely new terminology to user interface development. These are based on the fusion of previously segregated areas such as hypertext, multimedia, and form-based GUIs. The fundamental concepts of a web application are pages and links, which are borrowed from hypertext documents. Both can be viewed as specializations of core IFML concepts.

7.2.1 **CONTAINER EXTENSIONS: PAGES, AREAS, AND SITE VIEWS**

In this section, we introduce IFML extensions that make the specification of the web interface composition patterns introduced in chapter 4 adhere more closely to the terminology and characteristics of web applications. The basic unit of dialogue with the user in a web application is a page, a ViewContainer produced statically by a human editor or generated automatically at the server side by a program (a page template or a server-side script). As user interfaces, pages embed navigation commands; as resources of a document system, they have a human readable address, called uniform resource locator (URL). Web applications offer service to multiple users over a multitier, client-server architecture; therefore they are concerned with the security of data transmission, achieved by delivering the interface over the HTTPS protocol, and with the control of access, achieved by enforcing user's authentication, identification, and permission control.

> **PAGE**
>
> A **page** is an extension of ViewContainer that denotes an addressable web interface unit.

As already mentioned in chapter 4, pages in a large web application can be arranged hierarchically to facilitate user navigation.

> **AREA**
>
> An **Area** is an extension of a disjunctive (XOR) ViewContainer that denotes a collection of pages or other areas, grouped according to an application-specific purpose.

Examples of areas in an e-commerce web application can be products, special deals, shipping rates and conditions, and returns and complaints.

As noted in chapter 4, web applications often offer different viewpoints on the same content to different classes of users. This characteristic can be captured by associating a ViewPoint with a specific type of ViewContainer called SiteView.

> **SITEVIEW**
>
> A **SiteView** is an extension of a disjunctive (XOR) ViewContainer that denotes web application areas and pages grouped together according to an application-specific purpose, typically because they serve the needs of a UserRole.

In summary, a web application can be modeled as a collection of pages logically grouped into Areas and SiteViews. Pages are presented to the user one at a time. This is expressed by the disjunctive form of the enclosing ViewContainer. To express the requirements of a multiuser application, SiteViews, Areas, and Pages can be treated as resources of a role-based access control (RBAC) system. As such they can be associated with a ViewPoint, which in turn is associated with a Context, which is described, for instance, by a UserRole context dimension. The SiteView constitutes the typical item referenced by a ViewPoint. Appropriate activation rules can be defined for specifying that the SiteView is enabled for a given UserRole.

The definition of activation rules upon a SiteView/Area/Page denotes the access permission to that particular object for the specified UserRole. A SiteView/Area/Page not associated with any role is treated as public and can be accessed even when the UserRole is undetermined. In an e-commerce application, for example, different SiteViews could be associated with the UserRoles named "registered customer," "product content manager," and "sales manager." A public SiteView could be addressed to nonregistered customers.

A SiteView/Area/Page has the following characteristics, which extend the standard properties of IFML ViewContainers to cope with specific web application features:

- **URL label**: A string denoting the (fixed part of) the SiteView/Area/Page address. If the page is implemented with a dynamic template, the URL label is typically concatenated with the parameters for the computation of its content. The URLs of a SiteView and of an Area are an alias for the home page of the SiteView and the default page of the Area.
- **Security**: If the property value is "secured," all the pages of the Area or SiteView, or the individual Page, are served under the secure HTTPS protocol.
- **Protection**: If the property value is "protected," all the pages of the Area or SiteView, or the individual Page, are subject to access control. The access control rule is expressed by the association of the SiteView/Area/Page with one or more UserRoles through an ActivationExpression.

Notice that the association of a UserRole with multiple levels of nesting components—such as Pages, Areas, and SiteViews—is purposely redundant and enables the incremental expression of access control rules. For example, access to a SiteView could be granted in general to the UserRoles Role1 and Role2. However, an Area or Page of the SiteView could be associated with a more restrictive ViewPoint that overrides the general one (e.g., to grant access only to Role1).

An important concept in a Web application is that of the **home page**, the page served to a user when accessing the application without requesting a specific resource.

Figure 7.7 reconsiders an example of web application interface organization already specified in chapter 4 using only the standard IFML concepts, and illustrates it with the concrete syntax of the described web extensions. Stereotypes are used to denote SiteViews and Pages and to identify the home page of a SiteView, as well as to determine whether the ViewContainer is Public

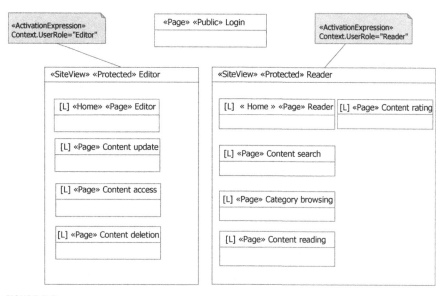

FIGURE 7.7

An IFML model of a typical web application for e-commerce.

or Protected. An ActivationExpression (e.g., Context.UserRole="Editor") is employed to specify that a SiteView is accessible only by a specific UserRole.

7.2.2 EVENT AND INTERACTION FLOW EXTENSIONS

Interaction in web applications occurs in two ways: by submitting the content of a form and by clicking on hypertext anchors. The standard IFML extensions Forms and SubmitEvent already capture the essential characteristics of web forms. The IFML NavigationFlow faithfully mirrors the concept of hypertext link but may be extended to reflect the terminology and properties of web links.

> **LINK**
>
> A **WebNavigationFlow** is an extension of a NavigationFlow that incorporates additional properties specific to hypertext links on the web.

A WebNavigationFlow can be endowed with properties specific to web navigation:

- **Rel**: specifies the relationship between the current document and the linked document; its values are codified by the HTML standard.
- **Target**: specifies where to open the linked document, typically in a browser window; the browser window can be the same one as the original document or a new window.

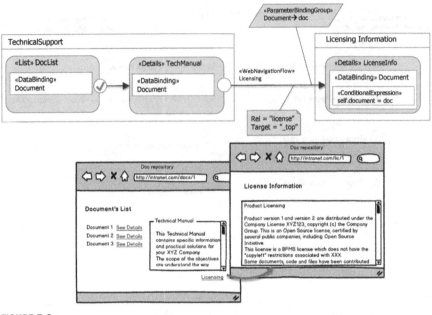

FIGURE 7.8

Example of usage of WebNavigationFlow.

Figure 7.8 shows as example of usage of the WebNavigationFlow extension used to open the licensing information in a new browser window. It also informs search engines of the nature of the linked document via the WebNavigationFlow outgoing from the technical manual to the licensing information.

The WebNavigationFlow extension shows a typical issue in the design of extensions: the tradeoff between platform independence and utility. The Rel and Target properties are clearly dependent on the version of HTML, which is an implementation language. However, a code generator could exploit the additional platform-dependent information to inject the proper attribute values in possibly thousands of automatically generated HTML links, which is an extremely useful feature. An alternative approach would factor out implementation-dependent properties from the model extensions and weave them into the code generator. However, since the values of the properties can be set by each WebNavigation-Flow, in this example we prefer utility over purity and make them definable directly in the model extensions.

7.2.3 COMPONENT EXTENSIONS

The List component in the IFML standard offers a minimalistic functionality that can be extended to support more realistic interfaces.

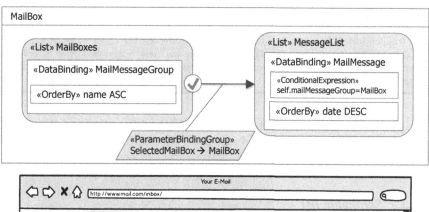

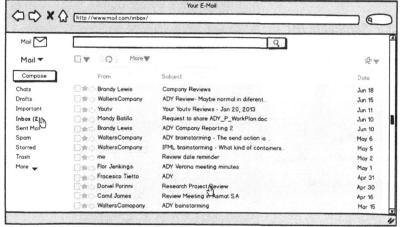

FIGURE 7.9

Example of usage of sorted list.

7.2.3.1 Dynamically-sorted list

As illustrated in chapter 5, the OrderBy ViewComponentPart can be used to enable sorting of the items in a List ViewComponent. This compenent defines the sorting criteria (attribute plus sort direction).

Figure 7.9 shows an example taken from the running case.

The "MailBoxes" List ViewComponent has an OrderBy part that sorts instances by name, whereas the "MessageList" ViewComponent sorts its DataBinding instances by date.

The OrderBy ViewComponentPart is specified at design time and thus does not model a situation in which the user can change the sorting of data at runtime. This additional behavior, popular in both web and desktop applications, can be achieved by introducing an extension of the List ViewComponent called DynamicSortedList.

> **DYNAMICSORTEDLIST**
>
> The **DynamicSortedList** is an extension of the List ViewComponent that allows the user to sort data using visualization attributes. The DynamicSortedList has a one-to-many association, named "SortAttributes," with the metaclass "VisualizationAttribute," which denotes the subset of the visualization attributes usable for sorting.

Figure 7.10 shows a variant of the pattern of Figure 7.9, which uses a Dynamic-SortedList for displaying the list of messages. Note that the default ordering of instances can be defined through an OrderBy ViewComponentPart, which the user can override by exploiting the SortAttributes specified in the component.

7.2.3.2 Scrollable list

A very popular behavior in web applications is the paging of long lists of elements into fixed-size blocks, with commands for scrolling. This is often used, for example,

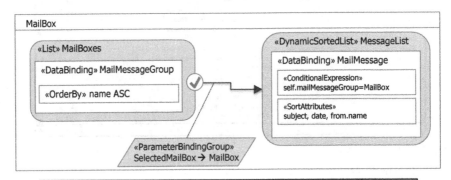

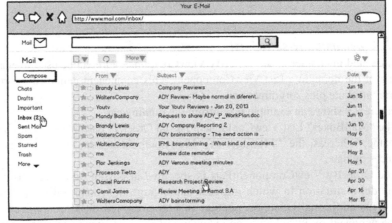

FIGURE 7.10

Example of usage of the DynamicSortedList.

as the base of search engine interfaces. A variant is the scrolling of blocks consisting of individual objects, as found, for instance, in image galleries.

SCROLLABLELIST

The **ScrollableList** is an extension of the List ViewComponent that allows the user access ordered DataBinding instances grouped in blocks. The **ScrollableList** ViewComponent has an attribute called "block size" that specifies how many instances constitute a block. It also has an implicit parameter (named current), which holds the block currently in view, and implicit events for moving to the first, last, i-th, next, and previous block.

Figure 7.11 revises the search pattern introduced in chapter 5 to cater to the scrolling of paged results.

7.2.3.3 Nested list

The multilevel master detail pattern illustrated in chapter 5 can be compacted into a ViewComponent, by nesting one list inside another.

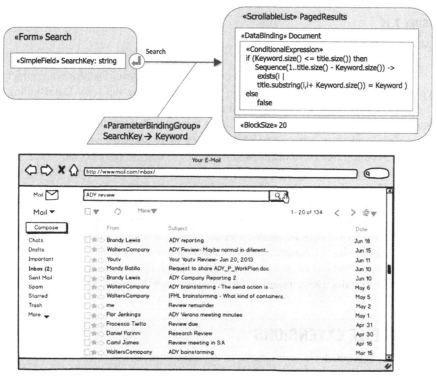

FIGURE 7.11

Example of usage of the ScrollableList.

NESTEDLIST

The **NestedList** is an extension of the List ViewComponent that denotes the nesting of multiple lists, one inside another.

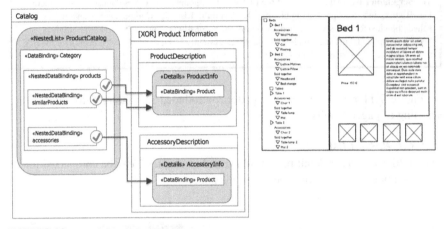

FIGURE 7.12

Example of usage of NestedList.

The data model of the **NestedList** comprises one top-level DataBinding, which typically refers to a class of the domain model. Within the top level DataBinding, one or more first-level NestedDataBindings can be specified that refer to one of the association roles of the class referenced in the top-level DataBinding. Each first-level NestedDataBinding in turn can comprise one or more second-level NestedDataBinding. A second-level NestedDataBinding refers to one of the association roles of the class target of the association role used in the first-level NestedDataBinding. Figure 7.12 shows an example of usage of the NestedList ViewComponent.

The product catalog consists of a three-level nested list. At the top level, categories are displayed. At the next level, the products of each category are listed. At the innermost level, two separate nested lists are presented: the accessories of a product and the other products frequently sold with it. When the user selects a product at the second or third level and an accessory at the third level, the chosen object is displayed either in the "ProductDescription" or in the "AccessoryDescription" ViewContainer.

7.3 MOBILE EXTENSIONS

Mobile applications have rich interfaces that resemble on a smaller scale those of full-fledged desktop applications. Mobility and the availability of sensors, such as cameras and GPS, introduce features that are best captured by providing extensions of the IFML core specialized for mobile application development.

7.3.1 **CONTEXT EXTENSIONS**

The context assumes a particular relevance in mobile applications, which must exploit all the available information to deliver the most efficient interface. Therefore, the context must gather all the dimensions that characterize the user intent, the capacity of the access device and of the communication network, and the environment surrounding the user.

Various dimensions of the context relevant to mobile applications have been catalogued and characterized in several standards and standard proposals, briefly overviewed in the bibliographic notes at the end of this chapter. In this section, we exemplify the most interesting ContextDimensions and ContextVariables that characterize mobile application usage. The illustration is not meant to be exhaustive. Rather, its aim is exemplifying how the contextual features can be represented as IFML extensions and used to model the effect of context on the user interface. The main aspects of the Context are listed below. Some of them have to be considered as ContextDimensions (and thus allow the selection of a Context or another), while other are ContextVariables (thus enabling the use of their value as parameters within the IFML models).

- **Device:** this family of context features can be exploited to specify the adaptation of the interface to different device characteristics, most notably the size and resolution of the screen. These features are usually exploited as ContextDimensions:
  - **DiagonalSize**: the physical size of the screen, measured as the screen's diagonal;
  - **SizeCategory**: for convenience, screen sizes can be grouped in classes that can be treated homogenously (e.g., SMALL, NORMAL, LARGE, EXTRA LARGE); and
  - **DensityCategory**: for convenience, screen density measures can also be grouped in classes treated homogenously (e.g., LOW, MEDIUM, HIGH, EXTRA HIGH).

The following information becomes handy as ContextVariables, so as to calibrate precisely the UI rendering based on some calculation over the size data:

- **PixelSize**: the actual horizontal and vertical size of the screen, measured in pixels;
- **Density**: the quantity of pixels per unit area measured in dpi (dots per inch).

Other characteristics of the device may be considered, such as internal memory size, processing power, and battery status. However, they are less frequently used in the design of applications.

- **Network connectivity:** this dimension can be used to adapt the quantity or quality of content published in the interface, based on the capacity of the network link (e.g., replacing the display of a large media file with a lighter preview when bandwidth is limited). The relevant ContextDimension is

ConnectivityType, which denotes the kind of network available; it can have such values as NONE, BLUETOOTH, NFC, ETHERNET, MOBILE (E, G, 3G, 4G, …), WIFI, and WIMAX;

- **Position:** this family of features can be used to adapt the interface to the presumed activity of the user (e.g., simplifying the interaction commands when the user is moving) or to publish content that depends on the location (e.g., local news or alerts). The ContextDimensions related to position are:
  - **SensorStatus:** denotes the activity status of the position engine of the device. It can have values such as: ACTIVE, INACTIVE.
  - **Activity:** denotes the physical user's activity inferred by the sensor data; possible values are: still, walking, running, cycling, and in-vehicle.

The ContextVariables that can be exploited when the SensorStatus is ACTIVE are:

- **Location:** denotes the position of the device, expressed in latitude and longitude coordinates;
- **Accuracy:** denotes the accuracy of the position.
- **Speed:** denotes the ground speed of the device.
- **Altitude:** denotes the altitude above sea level of the device.

7.3.2 CONTAINERS EXTENSIONS

As shown in chapter 4, the composition of mobile application interfaces can be expressed properly with the core IFML concepts of ViewContainers and ViewComponents. However, a characteristic trait of mobile interfaces—also present in desktop applications although less pervasively—is the utilization of predefined ViewContainers devoted to specific functionalities. These system-level containers provide economy of space and enforce a consistent usage of common features. Examples are the "Notifications" area or the "Settings" panel. These special ViewContainers can be distinguished (e.g., by stereotyping them as «system»).

SYSTEM VIEWCONTAINER

A ViewContainer stereotyped as **«system»** denotes a fixed region of the interface, managed by the operating system or by another interface framework in a cross-application way.

Figure 7.13 shows an example of the usage of system ViewContainers by revisiting the e-mail application running example with a simplified composition of the interface more suited to a small screen. A system-level ViewContainers is employed to deliver notifications, which are typically placed in a fixed position within the header region of the interface. Another system ViewContainer, "Settings," is also used to denote that the standard "Settings" command and window of the operating system are exploited to open the configuration functionality of the e-mail application in the interface region normally devoted to this task for all the applications.

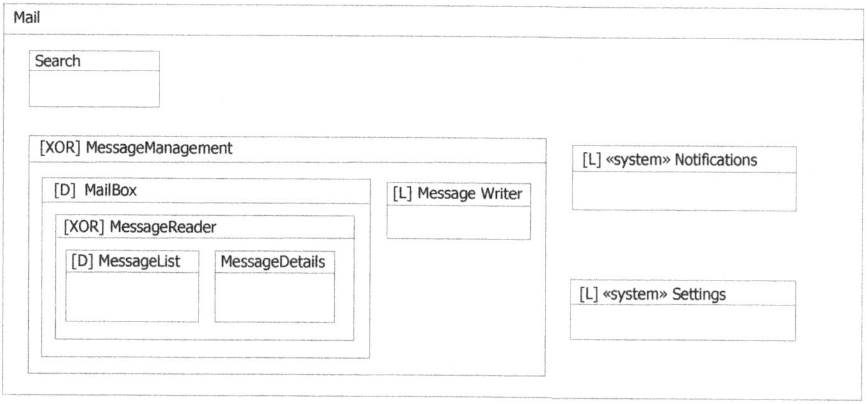

FIGURE 7.13

Example of «system» ViewContainers.

Flexible layouts, another pattern using ViewContainers, are very useful for mobile applications. These are illustrated at the end of this section.

7.3.3 COMPONENT AND EVENT EXTENSIONS

Like ViewContainers, ViewComponents can be predefined in the system as default interface elements that provide basic functionality in a consistent manner to the application developer. An example is the media gallery present in most mobile platforms. The «system» stereotype can be applied also to ViewComponents to highlight that the interface uses the components built into the system.

7.3.4 CAMERAS AND SENSORS

Mobile applications can interact with one or more cameras onboard the device. The basic interaction with the camera requires modeling the ViewContainer for visualizing the camera image and commands, the invocation of an Action for taking the picture, the asynchronous event that notifies that the photo has been taken, and the visualization of the image in the system-level media gallery.

Figure 7.14 shows an example of usage of the camera and of the system-level media gallery. The "PhotoShooter" ViewContainer comprises a system ViewContainer "CameraCanvas," which denotes the camera image viewer. The "Settings" event opens a modal window for editing the camera parameters, and the "Shoot" event permits the user to take a picture. When the image becomes available, a viewer is activated, from which an event permits the user to open the photo in the system media gallery. The internal viewer is modeled as a scrollable list, with block size = 1 to show one image at a time, and an OrderBy ViewComponentPart with a sorting criterion by timestamp to present the most recent photo first.

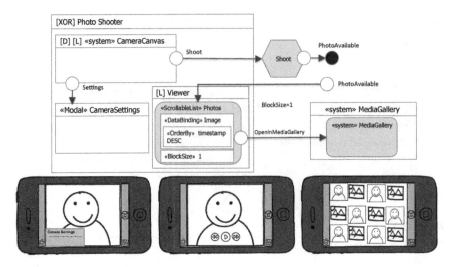

FIGURE 7.14

Example of usage of the camera and media gallery.

7.3.5 COMMUNICATION

Mobile devices communicate in a variety of ways with other fixed or mobile devices that can be discovered dynamically. The aspects of communication that may affect the interface are:

- **Connectivity update notifications:** they signal the change of the available communication channels and can be captured as system events that express an update of one or more ContextDimensions; and
- **Devices in range:** other devices can enter or leave the communication range. This feature can be modeled as a system event that signals the discovery of a device. Data transfer activities can be modeled as Actions that encapsulate the details of the protocol used to manage the conversation.

Figure 7.15 shows an example of communication-enabled interface: the usage of near field communication (NFC) for exchanging the contact details of the user.

The application consists of two parts, a sender and a receiver. The "NFCCard-Sender" interface is minimal, because NFC normally requires the communicating devices to be very close and thus there is little space for user's interaction. The interface presents the personal data to the user who can confirm his intent to make them available to NFC devices in range. The "SendViaNFC" Action abstracts the steps necessary to build up the NFC record and notify the device that it is ready to be dispatched.

The "NFCCardReceiver" ViewContainer models the application on the side of the receiver. The reception of the NFC payload is modeled as an asynchronous event that abstracts the system process of parsing NFC messages and triggering the registered

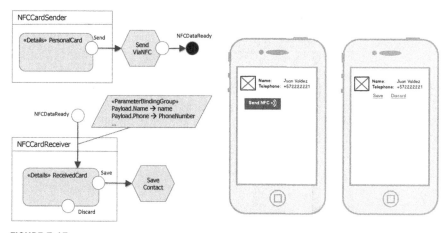

FIGURE 7.15

Example of usage of NFC data exchange

applications that handle them. The interface is again very basic: the user can confirm and save the data or discard the message.

Figure 7.16 shows an example of adaptation of the interface composition to the network type.

The interface for reading a message is implemented in two versions. One version presents a message with all its attachments downloaded automatically. The second interface requires an explicit user command for downloading an attachment, and the attachments are downloaded and shown one at a time using a ScrollableList. The choice of which alternative interface to use is conditioned by means of an Activation-Expression, illustrated in chapter 5, that tests the type of connectivity available based on the ContextVariable ConnectivityType. On-demand attachment visualization is selected when the connection type is "MOBILE" to reduce bandwidth consumption and interface latency.

7.3.6 POSITION

Location awareness enables devices to establish their position so that mobile applications can provide users with location-specific services and information, set alerts when other devices enter or leave a determined region, and adapt the interface to the current user's physical activity, such as walking, running, or driving.

Figure 7.17 shows an example of the usage of the position sensor.

The "Start" event in the "Tracker" ViewContainer allows the user to activate the continuous position tracking system of the device. The Form ViewComponent enables the specification of the position tracking parameters, such as accuracy and frequency, which are communicated to the system service via the "ActivatePosition-Updates" Action. After activating the tracking system, the application starts listening to incoming asynchronous SystemEvents, which provide updates of the current

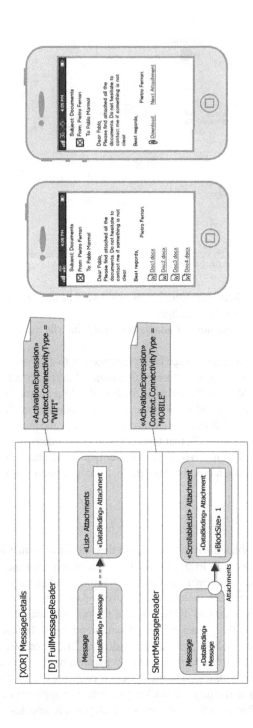

FIGURE 7.16

example of interface adaptation to network capacity

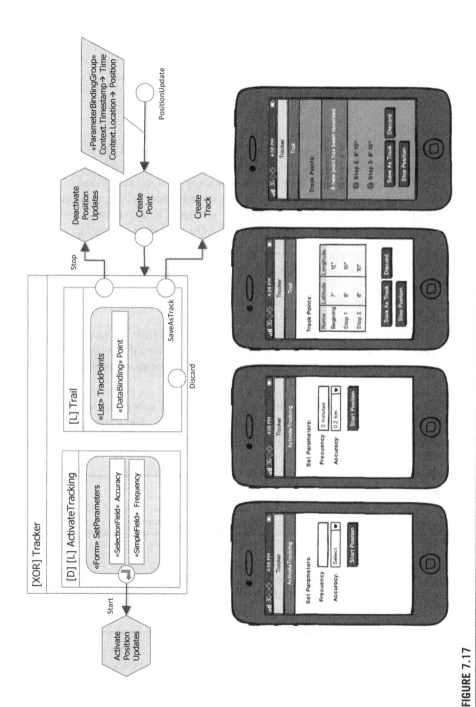

FIGURE 7.17

Example of usage of the position

position at the established frequency. Such events carry parameters indicating the timestamp of the recording and the geographical coordinates, and trigger a background action that stores such data as "Point" objects. The list of recorded points is visualized in the "TrackingPoints" List ViewComponent. At any moment, the user can clear the list of recordings, save the recorded points as a track object, or stop the position tracking system.

7.3.7 MAPS

Maps are a powerful interface over geographic data. The integration of digital maps into user interfaces has become very popular with the advent of the web. Mobile applications add a special flavor to map-based interfaces by combining the dynamic position of the user with the representation of topographic data. Digital maps have become a commodity supported by many proprietary and open-source services. This rich offer boosts the development of map-enabled applications on top of off-the-shelf functionality, for:

- connecting to the mapping service and downloading map tiles for display on the device screen with controls such as pan and zoom for moving the map and zooming in or out;
- setting the map type, choosing among several alternatives, such as normal, satellite, hybrid, and 3D; and
- initializing and changing the viewpoint over the map (also called "camera," to highlight that the map view is modeled as a camera looking down on a flat plane); the rendering of the map is governed by such properties as location, zoom, bearing, and tilt.

A simple way of modeling the map view is to extend the concept of ViewContainer to denote an off-the-shelf map visualization interface. Application-specific content and events can then be added to such an extended ViewContainer as further ViewElements and Events.

MAPVIEW

A **MapView** is an extension of ViewContainer that denotes a map view. It supports the events for panning and zooming and for changing the map type and the camera parameters.

Content—both static and interactive—overlaid on the map can be modeled by extending the ViewComponent concept. For example, the «marker» stereotype can be added to Details and List to denote that the DataBinding instances have a position and are rendered on the map as interactive markers.

MARKER

A **Marker** is an extension of ViewComponent usable in MapView containers that denotes that the underlying DataBinding instances possess a location attribute that is displayable in a map view. It supports the events for selecting, dragging, and dropping.

Another useful way to present an ordered set of locations is the path visualization.

PATH

A **Path** is an extension of the List ViewComponent usable in MapView containers that presents underlying DataBinding instances (that must possess a location attribute) as a polyline in a map view. It supports events for selecting the entire path or a single point on it.

Figure 7.18 elaborates the example of Figure 7.17 to show the usage of the MapView ViewContainer and of the map-specific extensions of the List ViewComponent.

The plain visualization of the tracked points exemplified in Figure 7.17 is replaced by two alternative map-based displays modes. The recorded points are viewable either as a set of markers or as path on the map.

7.3.8 GESTURES

Touch screens enable the use of gestures for the direct manipulation of screen objects. The gestures supported by touch devices include touch, double touch, press, swipe, fling, drag, pinch in and out, and several more. These gestures have well-defined semantics and consolidated conventions to which the interface design must conform to provide a consistent user experience. They can be represented in IFML by extending the core Event concept.

Figure 7.19 shows an example that uses the touch and press events. The distinction between these two gestures allow a finer control over the effect of acting upon the screen objects, much in the same way as mouse click and double click do in desktop applications.

Figure 7.19 revisits the master detail pattern to highlight the usage of touch gestures. The conventions illustrated in the example adhere to the best practices in popular mobile operating systems, such as Android 4. In a master detail interface, the touch gesture activates the default action on the object (in this case, the opening of the details view). The press gesture instead activates the selection mode, whereby one or more objects can be chosen with a touch event, and a toolbar of commands is displayed to act upon the selected object(s). This behavior is represented in Figure 7.19 by using the «press» and «touch» event extensions and by conditioning the effect of the touch event based on the existence of at least one previously selected object. Other gestural conventions can be represented in a similar way.

7.4 MULTISCREEN EXTENSIONS

Single screen applications are conceived to work for a single class of access devices, with homogeneous capabilities. They define the composition of the interface at design time by specifying the hierarchy of ViewContainers and the disjunctive or conjunctive nesting of containers. Multiscreen applications are instead designed to

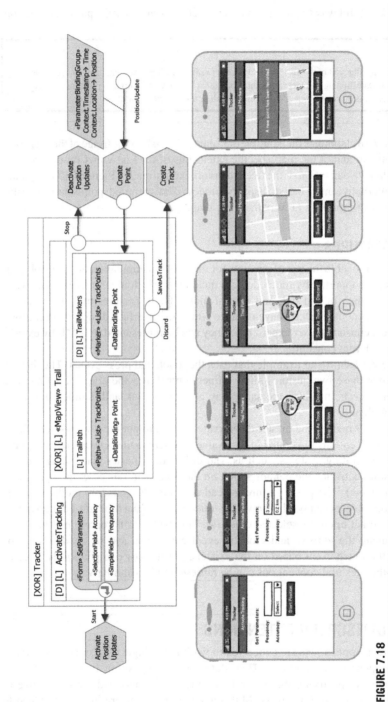

FIGURE 7.18

Example of usage of the MapView ViewContainer.

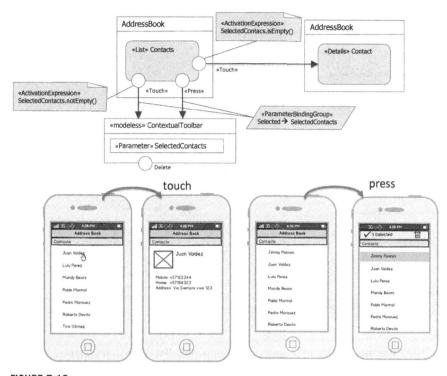

FIGURE 7.19

Example of touch and press event handling.

work on different devices, possibly with different screen characteristics. A goal for their development is to define the interface layout in a flexible way so that it can adapt dynamically to the size, orientation, and density of the screen.

Figure 7.20 shows an application for updating the device settings, designed to adapt to cellular phone small screens and to tablet wider screens. The interface supports two main tasks: picking the desired preference from a list, with the "Preferences" List ViewComponent, and editing its value, with the "PreferenceEditor" Form ViewComponent. The two ViewComponents that address such tasks communicate parameters to the "UpdatePreference" Action through their outgoing Navigation-Flows and the ParameterBindingGroups associated with them.

The flexible interface composition is expressed by means of the "Settings" View-Container, which hosts two distinct subcontainers: "Tablet Settings," in which the two ViewComponents are kept together, and "Phone Settings," in which they are visualized one at a time. The ActivationExpression of the subcontainers ensures that the proper composition pattern is activated based on the device information taken from the Context.

Figure 7.21 shows a mock-up of the interface composition adapted to the type of the screen.

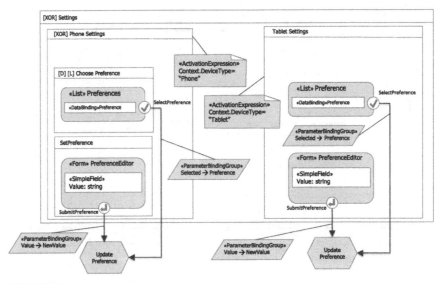

FIGURE 7.20

Example of flexible interface composition.

Note that the model of Figure 7.20 duplicates the ViewComponents, Events, InteractionFlows, and Actions that specify the content and behavior of the interface in the two configurations. This duplication, which puts an unnecessary burden on the designer and may result in misalignment errors, can be avoided with the use of modules (explained in chapter 8).

7.5 SUMMARY OF THE CHAPTER

In this chapter we have illustrated the role of the extension mechanism natively provided by IFML. The basic constructs of the language can be extended to adhere to the terminology and concepts of a specific class of applications and to improve model checking and code generation. We have shown the extension mechanism at work in the definition of several specializations of ViewContainers, ViewComponents, and Events tailored for desktop, web, and mobile applications.

7.6 BIBLIOGRAPHIC NOTES

Example of containers and components for desktop interfaces are found in the libraries of most operating systems and programming languages. For instance, the Java development environment defines the classes for building containers and component in the Package javax.swing [JavaSwing].

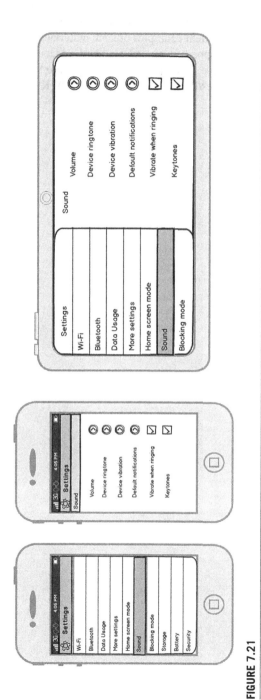

Mock-up of the adaptable composition of Figure 7.20.

Mobile design best practices and patterns are fundamental chapters in the development guidelines of the most popular mobile environments. The iOS and Android developers' sites provide excellent examples of such materials [Android, iOS].

Device properties are mapped in several standard vocabularies and capability models, such as W3C's Device Description Repository Core Vocabulary [Rabin10] and the Composite Capabilities/Preference Profile (CC/PP) [Klyne04, Kiss07].

Modeling patterns

This chapter presents IFML under a problem-oriented perspective and thus complements the construct-oriented perspective of the preceding chapters. It introduces a number of patterns that can be used to tackle typical problems in the design of the interface, with a twofold aim: showing IFML at work in situations of practical use and exemplifying interface design practices in a technology-independent way, so that they can be applied to different development scenarios. The order of presentation is by type of problem, rather than by class of application, because many patters have a general utility that spans more than one type of application. Where appropriate, we will emphasize when a certain pattern is more helpful in desktop, web, or mobile applications.

8.1 INTERFACE ORGANIZATION

In this chapter we complete the discussion about interface organization patterns started in chapter 4 and continued in chapter 7 by illustrating two patterns focused on improving the reuse of submodels within and across projects.

8.1.1 REUSABLE MODULES

In chapter 7, we introduced an example of multiscreen interface design that benefits from the ability of placing the same interface content in different composition layouts to be dynamically adapted at runtime to the screen characteristics. However, as can be seen from the model of figure 7.19, the actual interface content is repeated twice, once for each of the layouts. This solution is unsatisfactory because it forces an unnecessary duplication of model elements and obliges the designer to update each copy after a modification of the requirements.

A better way to organize the model is to factor out the definition of the common part, in the form of a reusable fragment, and reference it from the part of the model where it must be reused. This capability is granted by the notions of Module and Module Definition.

MODULE DEFINITION

A ModuleDefinition is a portion of IFML model, comprising IFML model elements, that may be reused for improving IFML model maintainability.

If needed, ModuleDefinitions can be aggregated in a hierarchical structure of ModulePackages. ModuleDefinitions can exchange Parameters by means of input and output PortDefinitions.

PORTDEFINITION

PortDefinitions represent interaction points with a ModuleDefinition. They hold Parameters for transferring values to and from the ModuleDefinition. An input PortDefinition has outgoing Interaction-Flows to the inside of the ModuleDefinition. An output PortDefinition has incoming Interaction-Flows from the inside of the ModuleDefinition.

ModuleDefinitions can be reused by adding Modules referencing them in IFML models. Modules that reference a ModuleDefinition may comprise Ports, which in turn reference the corresponding PortDefinitions.

MODULE

A **Module** is a named reference to a ModuleDefinition that allows reuse of the model portion specified in the ModuleDefinition.

PORT

A **Port** is an interaction point between a Module and the surrounding model within which it is defined. A Module is associated with a set of Ports, which in turn reference the corresponding PortDefinitions. For every PortDefinition in the ModuleDefinition, each corresponding Module must contain 0 or 1 Ports. An input Port has incoming InteractionFlows from the outside of the Module for receiving input Parameters. An output Port has outgoing InteractionFlows to the outside of the Module for shipping output Parameters.

Figure 8.1 shows the ModuleDefinition "PreferenceSetter" for encapsulating the functionality of updating the value of a preference received in input.

The ModuleDefinition has one input PortDefinition, to acquire the preference object to be updated, and one output PortDefinition. The input PortDefinition is connected to the UpdatePreference Action inside the Module, which permits the actual modification of the value attribute of the preference object based the user's input. Note that this quite trivial example could be made more realistic by modeling different ways to edit the value of a property depending on its nature, as customary in mobile interfaces. Such complex interaction logic would be factored out in the ModuleDefinition and thus would become reusable in multiple projects.

Figure 8.2 shows how to reuse the ModuleDefinition of Figure 8.1 in the multiscreen design pattern discussed in chapter 7, obtained by placing two Modules that reference the ModuleDefinition "PreferenceSetter."

Another example of reusable functionality that can be encapsulated in a module is the payment process of an e-commerce application. After filling a shopping cart, the user proceeds to the check out and payment process, which typically consists of the three steps exemplified in Figure 8.3.

When the user decides to order, a Customer Information Form is displayed, where the user can provide personal information. Next, a Payment Information form lets the user enter the bank account details. Finally, the transaction is executed, and its outcome is presented as a final message.

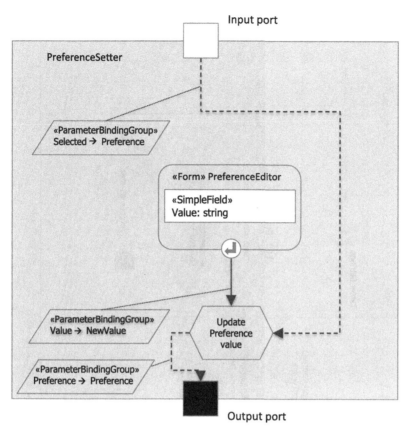

Input port

Output port

FIGURE 8.1

Definition of a module for setting preference values.

This recurrent functionality can be encapsulated in a reusable ModuleDefinition, as shown in Figure 8.4.

ModuleDefinition PaymentExecution can be referenced in the interface model of an e-commerce application by a Module, as shown in Figure 8.5.

8.1.2 MASTER PAGES

Another form of reuse occurs frequently in web applications, where the interface is modeled as a set of independent pages. In this case, it is possible that the various pages of the application share a common section, such as the header, the footer, or a cross-site search form.

Modules do not address this situation properly, because even if the shared content or function is encapsulated within a Module, a reference to the Module must be inserted into each page to denote its repeated appearance.

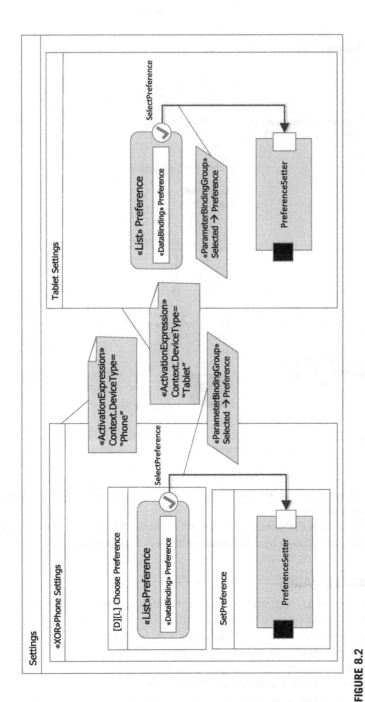

FIGURE 8.2

Multiscreen design pattern reformulated with the help of a reusable module.

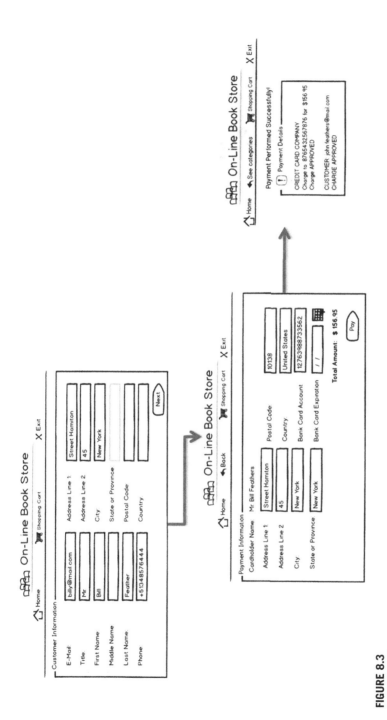

FIGURE 8.3

Mock-up of the checkout process in a typical e-commerce application.

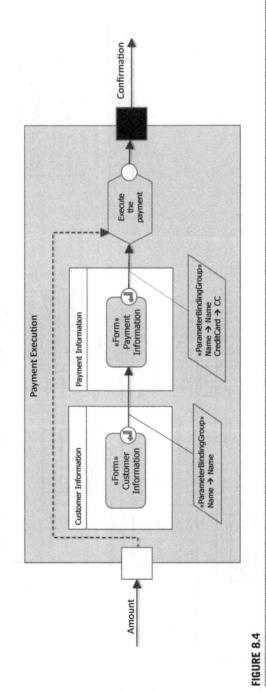

FIGURE 8.4

Reusable module definition encapsulating the payment process.

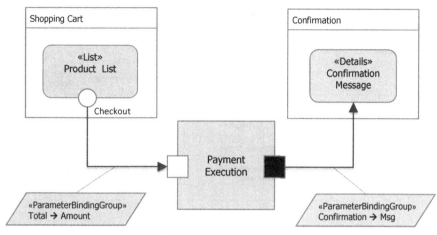

FIGURE 8.5

Module PaymentExecution placed inside the model of an e-commerce application.

A modeling shortcut for avoiding the replication of the reference to the shared functionality relies on the notion of a MasterPage, which further refines the Page ViewContainer extension introduced in chapter 7.

MASTERPAGE

A **MasterPage** extends the Page ViewContainer to denote that its content is replicated in a set of target pages. The target pages of MasterPage are, by default, those contained in the SiteView or Area where the MasterPage belongs.

Figure 8.6 shows an example of MasterPage, which we assume to be defined within the SiteView of a web application offering both public and protected pages. The MasterPage contains the functionality for logging-in and out and for displaying the name of a logged-in user, which repeat identically in all the pages of the Site-View. The use of a MasterPage centralizes the definition of the shared functionality and eases both the initial specification and the evolutive maintenance.

The use of the Login and Logout Actions and of the Context to identify a logged-in user is explained later in this chapter.

8.2 NAVIGATION AND ORIENTATION

Designing an effective access to the application content and functionality is probably one of the most challenging tasks in interface design. The idea is simple: the user should always be able to understand what can be done in the current interaction context and how to "jump" to another context. Next, we discuss some design patterns that have the common goal of helping users find their way in the interface.

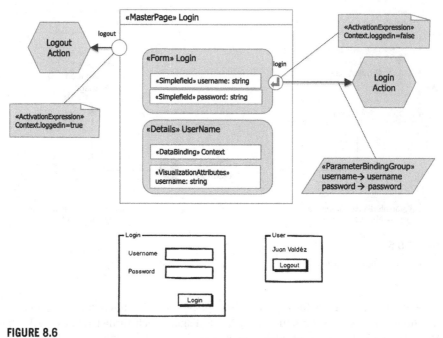

FIGURE 8.6

Example of MasterPage.

8.2.1 TOOLBARS AND MENUS

The standard widgets for orienting the user during navigation are toolbars and menus, used in different flavors in desktop, web, and mobile applications.

Two major categories of toolbars can be distinguished: content-dependent and content-independent. These correspond to the two navigational categories discussed in chapter 4 and 5. Content-dependent toolbars and menus group commands for accessing or acting on objects, whereas content-independent toolbars and menus group commands for navigating from one place to another in the interface.

In IFML, toolbars and menus are modeled as ViewContainers and/or View-Components associated with the events representing the executable navigations and actions.

8.2.1.1 PATTERN CN-SOT: Single object toolbar

Content-dependent toolbars are always modeled explicitly. Their role is to show the user all the actions and navigations that are possible starting from the object(s) in view. The basic case occurs when only a single object is in view.

In a first variant, the toolbar is modeled as a set of events associated directly with the Details ViewComponent that displays the object. In such a realization, the object and the commands for acting on it are displayed together synchronously. This solution is normally employed in web applications, where pop-up menus are used sparingly and the available commands are embedded as hypertext anchors in the page that shows the target object. Figure 8.7a demonstrates an example of this design.

A second variant decouples the appearance of the object from that of the toolbar. An event is shown together with the object, which can be used to display a menu with content-dependent commands. This latter solution is viable when screen space is scarce and the commands numerous, or the object demands all the available space for a better visualization, as in an image or document viewer. Space economy is obviously at the price of an extra interaction, so the tradeoff should be considered carefully. Figure 8.7b shows an example of this solution.

In platforms endowed with multiple ways for selecting objects, such as left, right, and double click, keyboard accelerators, and select and press touch gestures, the basic pattern can be enhanced by assigning some of the Actions to a context menu and some other Actions to dedicated events. Figure 8.7c exemplifies this enhancement, where the right-click event opens a command menu and the double-click event causes the navigation to the full screen view.

Hybrid designs between detached and in situ command placement are also possible, as well as multiple, logically equivalent realizations of the same set of commands. Figure 8.8 shows an extreme case in which the commands for acting on an image are embodied in three ViewContainers: the window menu bar, a toolbar placed below the image, and the menu associated with the right click of the mouse.

Whatever the design pattern adopted—which may depend on the class of the application—the general recommendation of all usability guidelines and textbooks is **consistency**. The adopted interaction scheme should be repeated consistently throughout the application.

IFML allows representing the chosen design patterns at a level higher than the source code. This makes it possible to automatically check the model of a large application for the consistent usage of patterns and even to apply model refactoring automatically to improve uniformity. An example of these techniques is described in [FLMM04].

8.2.1.2 PATTERN CN-MOT: Multiple objects toolbar

To speed up the interaction, commands can be applied to multiple objects (e.g., to move or delete them). In this case, the design of the toolbar must be coordinated with that of the object selection mechanism. Different solutions are possible.

No choice. The commands are applied to all the objects indiscriminately. This may happen, for example, when the set of target objects is identified by a categorical entity, as explained in chapter 3. The toolbar can be modeled as a set of events associated with the categorical object, using any one of the single object patterns discussed before. Particular care should be placed in mixing commands that refer to the categorical object itself (such as renaming a whole photo collection) and commands that apply to the individual members of the set implied by the categorical object (such as setting one image of the collection as the background). A good practice with bulk commands is to provide feedback to the user on the fact that the command is applied to multiple objects (e.g., requiring confirmation or explicitly showing the

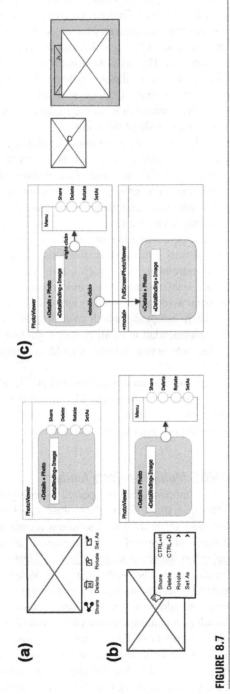

FIGURE 8.7

Content-dependent toolbar for a single object instance.

FIGURE 8.8

Multiple realizations of the content-dependent commands on a single object.

number of objects that will be affected). Figure 8.9 shows an exemplary solution applied to bulk commands for image collections. Each command for acting on *all* the images of a collection is split in two steps: the selection of the target collection, which visualizes the toolbar containing the name and the number of photos that will be acted upon, and the actual bulk commands (RotateAll, MoveAllTo, DeleteAll), which are triggered from the events associated with the toolbar of the "categorical" collection object.

Preselection. The target object(s) are selected first and then the command is applied to them. This pattern is ubiquitous in desktop and web applications, where checkbox lists are used for the purpose. When multiple selections are allowed, the events to be modeled are two: the selection items from the list and the triggering of an Action on the selected objects. If the selection is single, these two events could either be disjoint and asynchronous or collapse into an atomic interaction. Also in the case of preselection, if space restrictions apply and the commands are numerous, the display of the toolbar listing the available commands can be detached from the container allowing the selection of the objects.

Figure 8.10 illustrates these aspects by revisiting the e-mail running example, which contains an instance of the preselection design pattern applied to the "MessageList" ViewComponent. The two event schemes exploited for the selection are clearly visible. On one side, the user can click on the message header, and this interaction immediately opens the "MessageReader" ViewComponent. In this case, the selection and action triggering events coincide. On the other side, ticking a check box only selects an item from the list. This event ("MessageSelection") opens the toolbar, where the actual commands that can be applied to the selected messages become

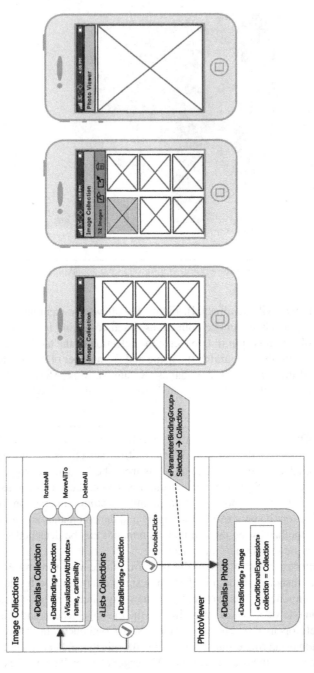

FIGURE 8.9

Content-dependent toolbar for multiple images, associated with the categorical class Collection. When a collection is selected, the number of corresponding images is shown, together with the available actions. A double click on a collection opens the details of the first image.

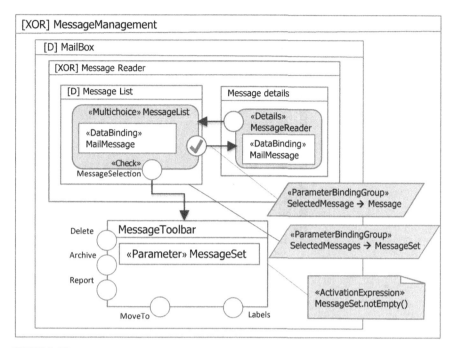

FIGURE 8.10

Content-dependent toolbar for the preselection of instances.

available. In this case, the selection and the action are asynchronous and performed in two separate interactions.

Postselection. The command is selected first, followed by the object(s) to which it must be applied. This pattern is suitable to applications that comprise general purpose commands (such as deletion and sharing), which apply to different classes of objects. Figure 8.11 shows an example of postselection.

8.2.1.3 PATTERN CN-DT: Dynamic toolbars

The commands listed in a toolbar or menu may vary at runtime, based on the status of the interaction. For example, the command "SetAsBackground" could be enabled only when the selected object is an image.

The dynamic addition of commands to a toolbar is modeled in IFML with the ActivationExpression element associated with the events of the toolbar. The ActivationExpression denotes the condition that must be satisfied by the current interaction context for the event that triggers an action to become active.

Figure 8.12 recalls two examples of dynamic toolbar from the e-mail application.

First, the "ReplyToAll" command appears in the toolbar (represented by the events associated with the "MessageReader" ViewComponent) only when the user has selected a message with more than one recipient. Second, the toolbar of the "MessageWriter" ViewComponent (represented by the events associated with the

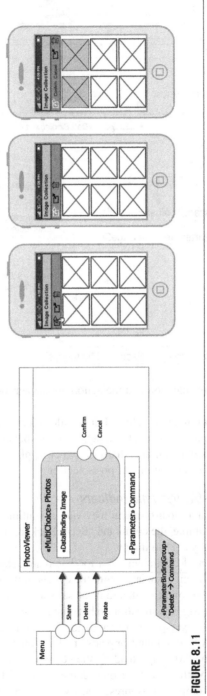

FIGURE 8.11

Content-dependent toolbar for the postselection of instances.

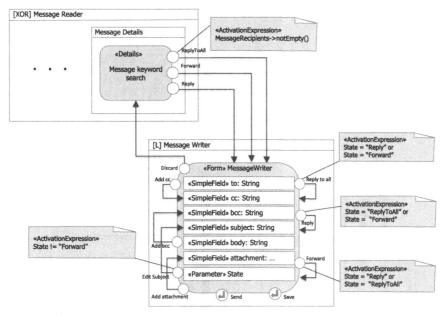

FIGURE 8.12

Dynamic addition of commands to a toolbar.

"MessageWriter" Form) comprises several events dynamically activated based on the status of the interaction. For example, the "EditSubject" command is active only when replying to a message and not when forwarding.

8.2.1.4 PATTERN CN-MSC: Multistep commands

As a corollary to the content-dependent toolbar patterns, we discuss the case of multistep commands, which are often found in toolbars and menus. These commands involve multiple steps. For example, a content sharing command requires the user to select the connection method or application and then the recipient of the shared object.

Figure 8.13 shows the model of a three-step command for sharing a piece of content over a network connection. The command sequence is modeled as a chain of modal windows that can be triggered open when one object is in view. The user is asked to select the network service (e.g., Bluetooth or DLNA) and then to choose among the recipients that are in range.

Note that the interaction is stateful, and thus the user's choice in all the intermediate steps must be represented as parameters associated with the appropriate ViewContainers, as shown in Figure 8.13.

Composite commands can be rather complex—even dynamic—especially in desktop applications, because external applications or plugins can register themselves as providers or recipients of services. To illustrate the case, Figure 8.14 models the command menu (which is a contextual menu) for working with images in the Windows explorer interface.

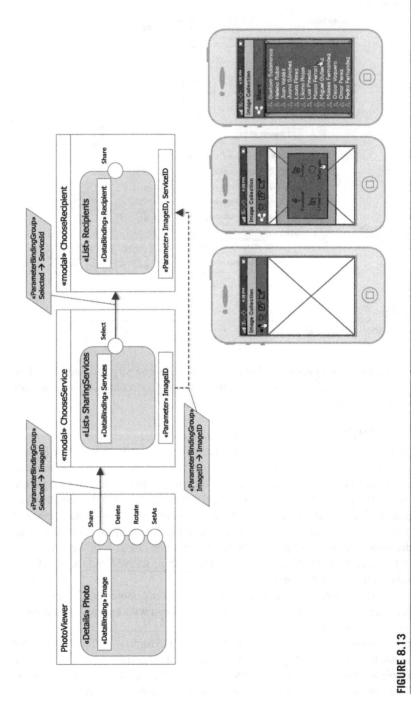

FIGURE 8.13

Three-step command for sharing a file over a network connection.

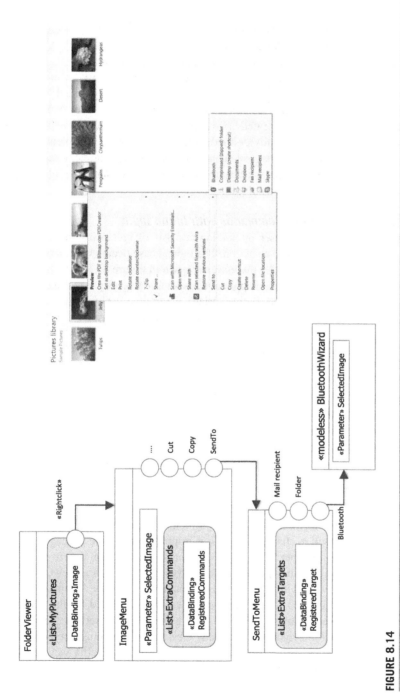

FIGURE 8.14

Command menus for working with images in a typical window-based explorer.

In desktop applications, commands contextual to an object are normally rendered using menus that provide a compact representation and allow the nesting of multistep command chains. Figure 8.14 shows the nested structure of the menu for sending an image to a target destination. A right-click event triggers the display of a ViewContainer that represents the first-level menu (ImageMenu). It contains both statically defined events (SendTo, Cut, Copy) and a List ViewComponent (ExtraCommands), which denotes a further list of commands that are dynamically added by external applications. Selecting the SendTo command from the first-level menu opens a second-level submenu represented as a nested ViewContainer (SendToMenu). This in turn may contain statically defined subcommands (Mail Recipient, Folder, Bluetooth) and dynamically registered subcommands. In the example, selecting the Bluetooth subcommand triggers the display of a window containing a full-fledged microapplication (a wizard) for configuring the transfer.

8.2.1.5 *PATTERN CN-CII: Commands with inline input*

A pattern that helps shorten user interaction consists of collapsing in the toolbar several steps needed to perform an action. The typical case occurs when a command sequence requires a short input by the user, as shown in Figure 8.15.

The search pattern of the e-mail application is revised to collapse the search input box within the command toolbar. In this variant, the toolbar is always in view when messages are accessed. The ActivationExpression associated with the "Delete," "Archive," "Report," and "MoveTo" events makes the command active only when at least one message is selected. Conversely, the keyword input form and its submit event are permanently pinned to the toolbar.

8.2.1.6 *PATTERN CN-CIM&B: Content-independent navigation bars and menus*

Content-independent toolbars, although apparently similar in the rendition to their content-dependent counterparts, express quite a distinct aspect of the interface. They group commands that do not act upon specific objects but shortcut the navigation or help the user go back quickly to the most important view elements, possibly from a deeply nested part of the interface. For this reason, they are often called navigation menus or bars.

In IFML, content-independent navigation menus can be modeled in two ways. The first way, discussed in chapters 4 and 7, is implicit through the concept of landmark. When a ViewContainer is tagged as landmark, a navigation link to it is considered part of an implicit navigation menu ViewContainer. Such a ViewContainer is again implicitly nested within all the ViewContainers where the landmark is visible. In this way, an explicit toolbar does not need to be modeled for the purpose. It is left to the implementation (e.g., to a code generator) to insert the navigation menu with appropriate navigation commands wherever it is appropriate according to the landmark visibility rules. This way of modeling is practical in web application specification, in which the lack of a top-level ViewContainer would force the designer to replicate the same navigation bar in all the pages. Moreover, the implicit

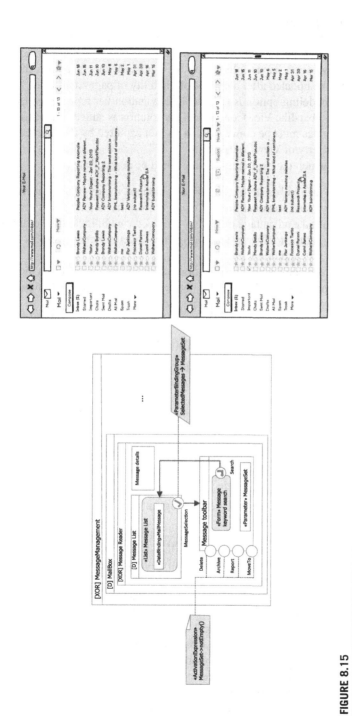

FIGURE 8.15

An input field collapsed with the related command in the toolbar.

representation supported by landmark is also more resilient to changes in the model. If the navigation commands are explicitly listed in the navigation bar, a change in the visibility of areas and pages requires updating the model. Conversely, if the content of the global navigation bar is inferred by the landmark specifications, the model does not need to be updated after a change of visibility of pages and areas.

The second modeling option is to have the navigation bar represented explicitly by means of a toolbar-like ViewContainer. This solution is suited to cases in which some extra semantics must be conveyed that are not captured by the specification of the landmark property of ViewContainers.

Examples in which the explicit modeling could be appropriate are:

- When the navigation bar should exploit a predefined region of the screen, such as a «system» ViewContainer, for enforcing uniformity of navigation across applications or take advantage of system-provided capabilities, such as the automatic splitting of the toolbar or the management of commands overflow based on the screen size and orientation.
- When the content-independent navigation bar should be merged with the content-dependent toolbarfor economy of space or for enforcing a unique placement and style of all the commands, irrespective of their nature.

8.2.2 PATTERN CN-UP AND CN-BACK: UP AND BACK NAVIGATION

The "Up" and "Back" links are classic orientation aids, present in many navigational interfaces, most notably in web and mobile applications. Their semantics are distinct:

- The "Up" link refers to some hierarchical structure associated with the interface; it leads the user to the superior ViewElement in the View hierarchy.
- The "Back" link refers to the chronology of the user's interaction; it leads back in time to the last visited ViewElement. When the previously visited ViewElement coincides with the parent of the current ViewElement, "Back" and "Up" lead to the same target. However, based on the navigation history, the "Back" button can return the user to a screen not logically related to the current one or even to a different application.

The "Up" link can be represented in IFML either implicitly or explicitly. The implicit representation relies on the nesting structure of ViewContainers. Since the parent ViewContainer can be inferred from the composition, there is no need to explicitly represent the "Up" link, and one can delegate its insertion in the interface to the implementation (e.g., to a code generator). However, the "Up" link is not necessarily confined to the content-independent navigation across ViewContainers. Many applications, especially mobile apps where the data navigation patterns are quite repetitive, also associate a meaningful "Up" event to some content-dependent navigation patterns, such as master detail navigation (recall the pattern from chapter 5). In these cases, the implicit representation of the "Up" link requires a clear definition of the content-dependent design pattern where the "Up" link is presumed.

Alternatively, the "Up" link can be represented explicit by means of an Event and a NavigationFlow. For example, Figure 8.16 reconsiders the master detail design pattern of chapter 5 and makes evident the "Up" nature of the link from the detail to the master.

UP

The **Up** Event extends the Event to denote navigation upward in a hierarchy.

Using an extension to qualify the event, as done in Figure 8.16, helps in the implementation. For example, a code generator could produce code where both the content-independent and the content-dependent "Up" NavigationFlows are rendered homogeneously.

A word of caution is warrented for situations in which a ViewContainer can be accessed using multiple navigation paths. Such a situation is frequent in both web and mobile applications. For example, a web page with the details of a product could be reached both by a direct link from the home page, where some products are highlighted for promotion, or at the end of a sequence of navigations traversing the category–product hierarchy. In these cases, the semantics of the "Up" command is not well defined, and most usability guidelines suggest to give the "Up" link the semantics of "Back" or even to disable it to avoid confusion.

The "Back" navigation can be represented in IFML with a stereotyped event, as shown in Figure 8.17.

BACK

The **Back** Event extends the Event to denote navigation in reverse chronological order.

The extension is necessary because the event has extra semantics that cannot be inferred from the rest of the model. The destination ViewElement is not specified by means of an InteractionFlow but is defined as the last accessed ViewElement in reverse chronological order.

8.2.3 PATTERN CN-BREAD: BREADCRUMBS

A breadcrumb (or breadcrumb trail) is a navigation aid that shows the user's location in the application interface. The term derives from the Hansel and Gretel fairytale in which the two children drop breadcrumbs to mark the trail back to their home. Breadcrumb navigation is used especially in large web applications endowed with a hierarchical organization of pages or content items (e.g., in e-commerce websites where products are structured hierarchically).

Three types of breadcrumb navigation can be distinguished:

- **Topological**: the trail represents the position of the current ViewContainer within the static hierarchy of the ViewContainers. With reference to the e-mail application use case, when the user is composing a message, the trail could be something like "Email>Messages>MessageComposer."

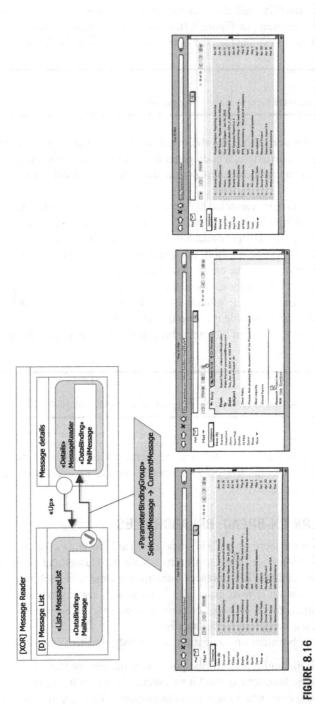

FIGURE 8.16

Master detail pattern with "Up" navigation.

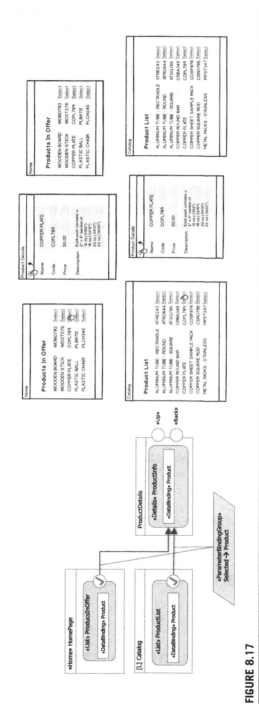

FIGURE 8.17

Example of ViewContainer with multiple access paths and "Up" and "Back" navigation.

- **Content-based**: the trail represents a path of access classes that index the core object currently in view. For example, in a online computer hardware shop, the trail appearing in the page of a product could look like "Products>Laptops>Aspi re>AspireE."
- **Dynamic**: in applications that do not provide a notion of a "Back" link, history-based navigation is sometimes provided by a breadcrumb trail constructed by chaining the last few visited ViewContainers. This variant should be used sparingly, because it overlaps with the usual "Back" navigation and may confuse users accustomed to the structural interpretation of this navigation aid.

Breadcrumb links can be modeled in IFML in different ways depending on their nature. Topological breadcrumbs can be inferred from the composition of the interface, so in principle they could be left implicit in the model and their insertion could be delegated to the implementation. Content-based breadcrumbs, by contrast, cannot be inferred from the model because the designer must specify the path of access classes and the core class to use for their construction. For homogeneity of design, it may thus be convenient to extend the ViewComponent concept to denote the insertion of the breadcrumb links trail in a ViewContainer.

BREADCRUMB

The **Breadcrumb** is an extension of ViewComponent that denotes a breadcrumb trail. It has a property **type**, which can have the values **Topological** and **Content-based**. If the type is Content-based, the Breadcrumb incorporates nested DataBinding elements that specify the path of classes and association roles that support the creation of the content-based trail.

Figure 8.18 shows an example of content-based breadcrumb navigation, situated in the "ProductCatalog" Area of a web application.

The "Catalog" Breadcrumb specifies the path of association roles that support the construction of the trail: from the access class "Category" to the access class "Family," and from "Family" to the core class "Product." Note that the ViewComponent is placed inside a MasterPage within the Area container, which is equivalent to repeating the Breadcrumb ViewComponent inside all the pages of the Area.

8.3 CONTENT PUBLISHING, SCROLLING, AND PREVIEWING

In this section, we illustrate a few more patterns to complete the gallery of content and navigation patterns started in chapter 5.

8.3.1 PATTERN CN-MMD: MASTER MULTIDETAIL

The master multidetail pattern is an extension of the basic master detail pattern introduced in chapter 5. It occurs when the class providing the detail is internally

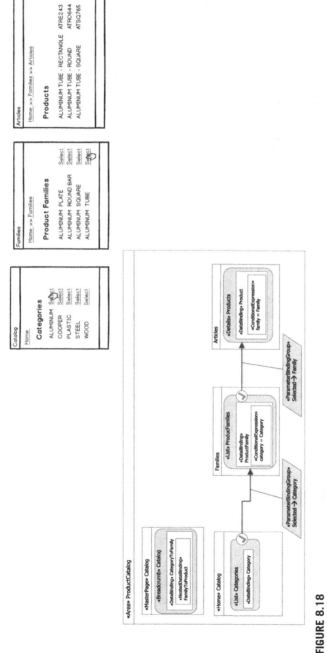

FIGURE 8.18

Content-based breadcrumb navigation.

substructured with further components and associations. The pattern provides a compact representation of the salient aspects of the core class and of its internal organization.

Figure 8.19 shows an example of master multidetail pattern.

Notice the use of DataFlows to provide the Product OID to the ViewComponents that publish the accessories and the guarantee, which constitute the multidetail parts together with the product information.

8.3.2 PATTERN CN-PG: PAGING

Another pattern of content publication occurs when multiple objects form a sequence that has a meaningful sense to the user (e.g., they are sorted by date or by relevance) and the screen space is too limited for displaying all the objects simultaneously. The paging pattern displays a block of objects at a time and allows the user to scroll rapidly back and forth in the collection.

A popular instance of this pattern is provided by the "swipe view" of mobile applications: one object is shown, and the swipe gesture is used to scroll over the collection. Figure 8.20 shows an example of the paging pattern applied to a collection of multimedia objects.

Notice that the pattern specifies the ParameterBinding associated with the gesture events explicitly, because the choice of the left (right) swipe for accessing the previous (next) object cannot be inferred from the model. The "next" and "previous" parameters are shortcuts for the previous and next block with respect to the current one, which is a default parameter of the ScrollableList ViewComponent (see chapter 7).

The pattern is adequate when the objects to display cannot be easily summarized, and thus the display of one exemplary instance is a good way to start user interaction. However, the pattern requires the collection to contain objects grouped according to a meaningful criterion (e.g., images pertaining to the same photo album) sorted in a way that anticipates user intention (such as sorting by date). The next pattern provides a way to highlight the context of the current object within the collection to which it belongs.

8.3.3 PATTERN CN-PR: COLLECTION PREVIEW

When the paging pattern is used to show one object at a time, the user may lose the notion of the logical placement of the object in the collection to which it belongs. Having a preview of the object's position in the sequence and of what comes before and after it may greatly help the user locate the content of interest quickly. This functionality is granted by the collection preview pattern, shown in Figure 8.21, which is essentially the synchronization of two ScrollableList ViewComponents: one for scrolling one object at a time (represented by the Photos ViewComponent) and one for having a preview of the objects that are close in the collection to the one in view (represented by the Blocks ViewComponent).

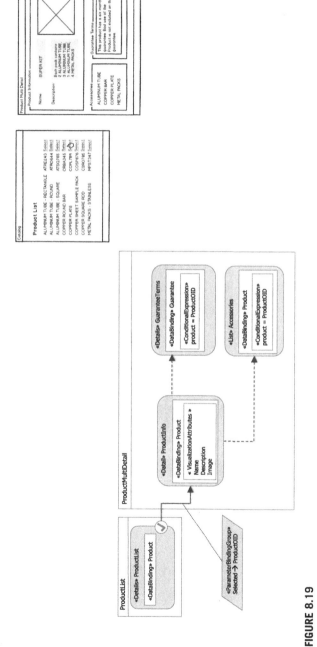

FIGURE 8.19

Example of master multidetail pattern.

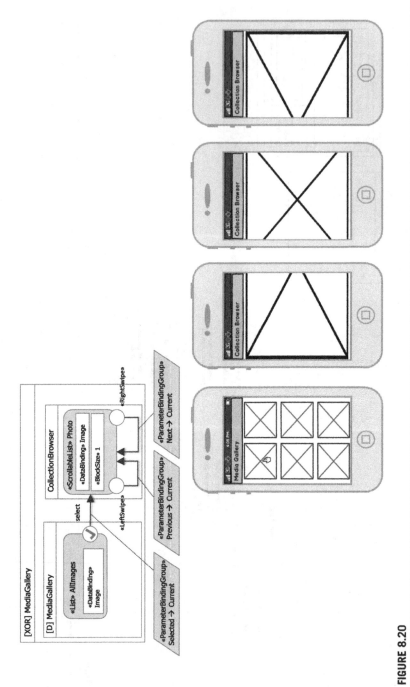

FIGURE 8.20

Example of paging pattern.

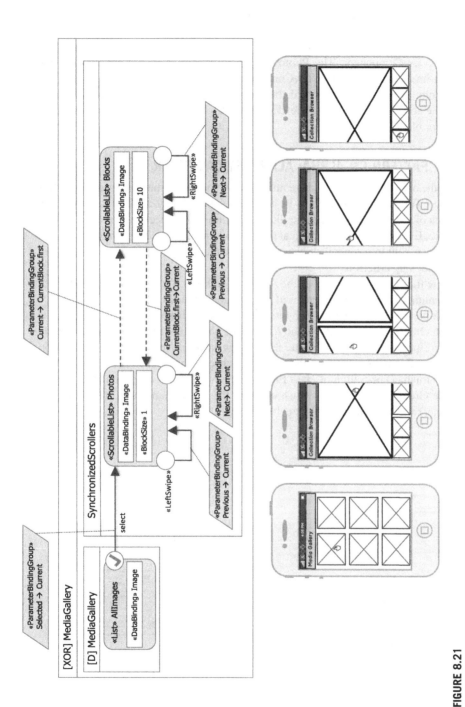

FIGURE 8.21

Example of the collection preview pattern.

Notice that two DataFlows are used to communicate the value of the current block and current image between the two ScrollableList ViewComponents. The Blocks ViewComponent communicates the first object of the current block to the Photos ViewComponent. The Photos ViewComponent in turn communicates the current image to the Blocks ViewComponent. When one gesture event occurs, the ViewComponent that has changed the value of its "current" parameter communicates the new value to the other ViewComponent, which may in turn synchronize the object or block in view.

8.3.4 PATTERN CN-ALPHA: ALPHABETICAL FILTER

When the objects to be accessed are numerous but possess a meaningful attribute (for instance, Title) that allows them to be accessed alphabetically, a useful access pattern consists of providing an alphabetic filter to partition the collection into chunks. Figure 8.22: Example of the alphabetical filter shows an example. The personnel list of a company is split into subcollections using the first letter of the surname of employees as the indexing criterion.

Note that the DataBinding of the AlphabeticalFilter ViewComponent is defined as an enumeration of all the letters of the alphabet (called LettersOfAlphabet).

The pattern can be improved by making the filter display the number of objects in each chunk. This also allows the removal of characters from the display that do not correspond to any object. Figure 8.23 shows the improved pattern, which exploit a DynamicBehavior content binding: the reference to the Employees::getGroupCountsBySurname() operation of class Employee, which returns a collection of objects of type GroupCount, each of which contains the group name (i.e., one alphabetic character) and a count of the objects in the group.

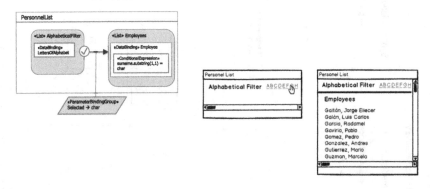

FIGURE 8.22

Example of the alphabetical filter pattern.

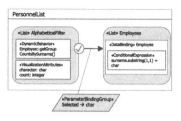  

FIGURE 8.23

Example of alphabetical filter with preview of the number of objects.

8.4 DATA ENTRY

IFML is not meant to express the purely visual or platform-dependent properties of ViewComponents and their parts, which are better delegated to the implementation, be it manual or tool supported. However, the designer may want to adorn the IFML diagram with stereotypes that provide hints to the implementation about fundamental usability issues to ensure that the final application will incorporate the best inter-action practices. Data entry is surely an aspect of the application where usability concerns are prominent. Entering data is a cumbersome procedure. Facilitating the user's task is a key factor in ensuring the acceptance and success of the application. In the following, we extend the list of data entry patterns initiated in chapter 5 with more examples that can be used to improve the usability of form-based application interfaces.

8.4.1 PATTERN DE-TDFP: TYPE-DEPENDENT FIELD PROPERTIES

Best-of-breed desktop, web, and mobile applications exploit a wealth of widgets and techniques for accelerating user input. These can be suggested in the IFML model by adequately stereotyping the Field element. Table 1 exemplifies a number of fre-quently used data entry facilitation patterns. The list is by no means exhaustive but aims at illustrating the kind of model extensions that are worth expressing to address data entry usability requirements in the IFML model.

shows an example of a form for uploading and captioning an image that exploits a Field of type image enhanced with the capabilities to drag and preview the file to be submitted Figure 8.24.

8.4.2 PATTERN DE-RTE: RICH TEXT EDITING

As shown in chapter 6, the editing of text could be specified in an even more detailed way by modeling a microapplication that embodies the commands applicable to the text. The model of such a microapplication could be encapsulated within a Module and be reused. Figure 8.25 shows the definition of such a Module.

Table 1 Stereotypes for Type-Dependent Field Properties.

Type	Stereotype / Input parameters	Behavior
Date	«Calendar»	The user can pick a date from a perennial calendar
Date	«ConstrainedCalendar» startDate, endDate	Choice is restricted to dates in a given calendar interval
Date range	«DateRange»	choice of a start date and an end date to represent a range of dates.
String	«Password»	Input is masked
Boolean	«ToggleButton»	The user can toggle a two-states button, a checkbox or a two-options radio button
Text	«FormattedText»	Text is displayed with format (e.g., CCS-style properties)
Text	«RichTextEditor»	Text is displayed with format that can be changed in the editor
Blob	«Draggable»	A blob can be dragged onto the input field
Blob/Image	«Preview»	Image is previewed before submission
Blob/Image	«Crop»	Image is previewed and can be cropped
Blob/Image	«RichImageEditor»	Image is previewed and can be edited with a rich image editor

8.4.3 PATTERN DE-AUTO: INPUT AUTO-COMPLETION

Auto-completion is the procedure of automatically providing suggestions for completing input based on what the user has already typed in a field. Functionally, the pattern is similar to a SelectionField, but its ubiquitous presence in data entry and search applications make it worth a dedicated pattern and an extension of the SelectionField ViewElement.

AUTOCOMPLETION

AutoCompletion is an extension of SelectionField that denotes the dynamic formation of a suggestion list from the attribute values of objects. It has a parameter **UserInput**, which denotes the input progressively inserted by the user. The property ConditionalExpression is used for retrieving the DataBinding instances to match the user's input. The property VisualizationAttributes identifies the attributes of the matching DataBinding instances used to construct the selection list.

The auto-completion design pattern is preferred over a simple form with a SelectionField when the list of values from which the user should select is very long.

Figure 8.26 shows an example of the auto-completion pattern.

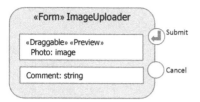

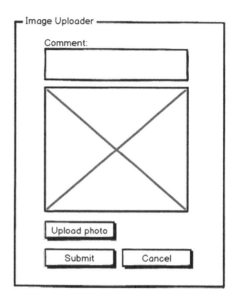

FIGURE 8.24

Example of image uploader with preview. The "upload photo" button and the image preview represent the rendition of the type-dependent field "Photo."

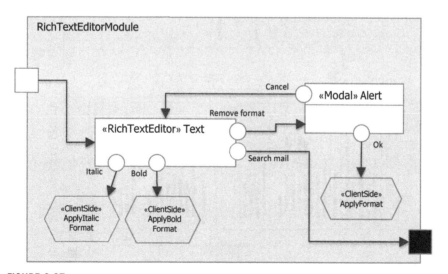

FIGURE 8.25

A Module encapsulating a rich text editing microapplication.

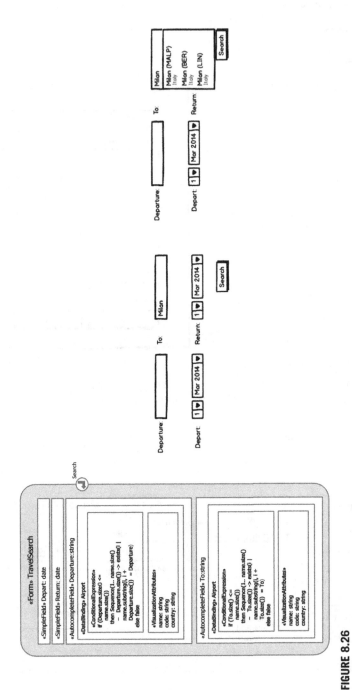

FIGURE 8.26

Example of auto-completion pattern.

8.4.4 PATTER DE-DYN: DYNAMIC SELECTION FIELDS

Dynamic selection fields are used when the application requires the user to input data that have dependencies. In this case, the choice of one object in a Selection-Field may affect the options available for filling another SelectionField. The typical case occurs with hierarchical data. For example, when filling one's address, the choice of the country determines the list of available states or provinces, which in turn determines the list of available cities. Figure 8.27 shows a form with three SelectionField elements. The first one, Country, is preloaded from the database, as shown by the DataBinding associated with it. It displays the list of country names extracted from the Country entity. The second SelectionField, StateProvince, is dynamic; it extracts the state or province names *related to the currently chosen country*. The dependency is expressed by the parametric ConditionalExpression, which exploits the *country* relationship role between class Country and StateProvince. The parameter is supplied to the dynamic SelectionField by means of a Data-Flow associated with the appropriate ParameterBinding element. When the country is not selected, the Selected parameter is undefined and thus the StateProvince SelectionField has an empty list of options. After a user's selection in the Country SelectionField, the parameter becomes defined and the StateProvince Selection-Field displays the provinces or states of the selected country. The third Selection-Field (City) is also dynamic and has a behavior similar to that of the StateProvince SelectionField.

8.4.5 PATTERN DE-INPL: IN-PLACE EDITING

In-place editing allows the user to edit content without abandoning the current view to access a data entry form. The pattern is useful when the user only needs to specify a few values in a simple format, such as a text string or a selection from a list of options. It is applicable when authentication is not necessary or the user is already authenticated. In-place content editing requires extending the VisualizationAttribute ViewComponentPart, to denote a piece of content that is displayed and edited.

EDITABLEVISUALIZATIONATTRIBUTE

EditableVisualizationAttribute extends VisualizationAttribute to denote a piece of content that is at the same time displayed and edited. To capture the termination of the editing, the element can be associated with events triggered by the completion of the editing, such as OnFocusLost.

Figure 8.28 shows an example of the in-place editing pattern. The Photo View-Component displays an image, with its timestamp, name, and description. These two latter attributes are also editable in-place.

In this way, the user can quickly update the title or the description of an image while looking at it and without the need of being redirected to an edit form.

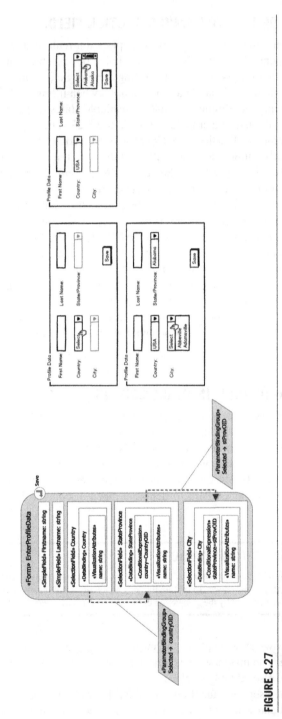

FIGURE 8.27

Example of dynamic selection field.

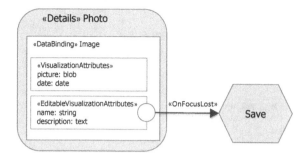

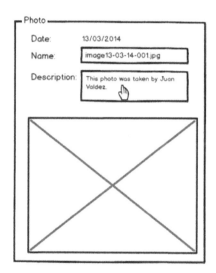

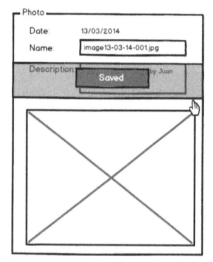

FIGURE 8.28

Example of in-place editing pattern.

8.4.6 PATTERN DE-VAL: INPUT DATA VALIDATION

A recurrent pattern associated with data entry is the validation of the input provided by the user to ensure that it meets the application requirements. When the data are submitted to a business operation, a simple way to model this functionality is to exploit the termination events of the Action to signal the receipt of incorrect data from the user. Alternatively, data validation can be modeled explicitly as an Action. This solution is shown in Figure 8.29.

The "DocuSearch" Form includes three search fields for retrieving documents. A constraint requires that at least one of the three values is supplied. This is checked by the "Validate" Action. If the "Validate" Action terminates normally, it forwards the input to the "Results" ViewComponent, which shows the results of the search. It the Action terminates abnormally, this signals a validation error, which can be displayed in the "Search Documents" ViewContainer to instruct the user about the missing

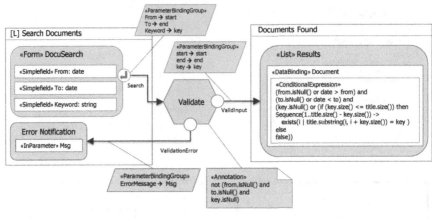

FIGURE 8.29

Example of input data validation.

values. For better readability of the model, an annotation is associated with the "Validate" action, expressing the constraint that must be respected by the input values.

8.5 SEARCH

The basic search patterns illustrated in chapter 5 can be refined with further functionality to improve the effectiveness of information retrieval.

8.5.1 PATTERN CS-RSRC: RESTRICTED SEARCH

Search over large collections of objects can be made more efficient by restricting the focus to specific subcollections. This can be done by a mixed pattern that exploits both content search and access categories. Figure 8.30 shows an example of the restricted search pattern.

The user can search the product repository by providing a keyword and selecting a product category. The search keyword is only matched to the name and description of the products of the specified category.

8.5.2 PATTERN CS-SRCS: SEARCH SUGGESTIONS

The use of popular search engines has made it customary for users to expect search hints in the form of suggested keywords that complete the partial input they provide. The search suggestion pattern exploits the autocomplete pattern and requires the logging of keywords previously inserted by the user along with their frequency. The log data can then be used to construct a list of matching keywords, sorted by frequency, as shown in Figure 8.31.

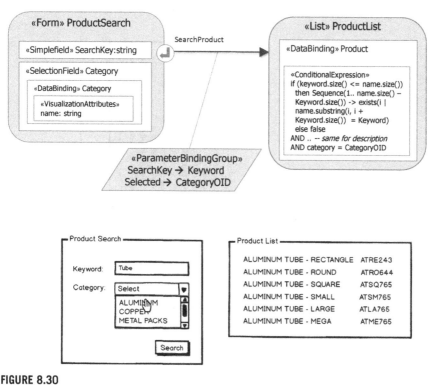

FIGURE 8.30

Example of restricted search pattern.

8.6 CONTENT MANAGEMENT

Content management patterns allow the user to manipulate the objects of the application. They were overviewed in chapter 5 when introducing Actions. Content management patterns require a mix of data publication to ensure the user is always aware of the object(s) being manipulated and of data entry, which enables the insertion of new or replacement data. After the completion of a content update action, the user should be given a confirmation of the action's effects, which can be achieved by displaying the modified status of the affected object(s).

8.6.1 PATTERN CM-CBCM: CLASS-BASED CONTENT MANAGEMENT

A typical content management pattern addresses the creation, modification, and deletion of an object and its association instances. Figure 8.32 shows an example of the content management pattern in a situation in which the user is requested to manage the entire lifecycle of instances, including creation, modification, and deletion. The illustrated design allocates the content management commands in as few ViewContainers as possible and strives to keep the context of the ongoing modification always in view.

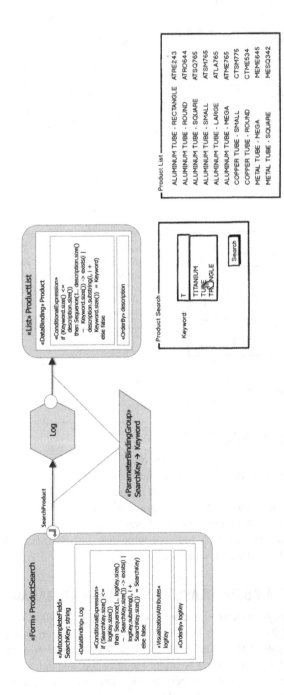

FIGURE 8.31

Example of search suggestions.

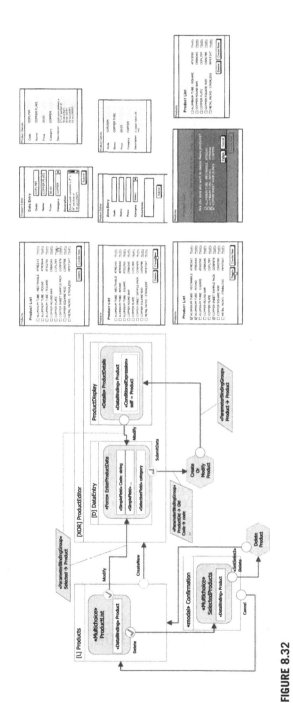

FIGURE 8.32

Example of class-based content management pattern.

The pattern displays the objects to be managed in the "ProductList" ViewComponent, where the user can select multiple instances for deletion. The "Choose" event causes a modal confirmation window to appear, which previews the objects to delete and giving the user the option either to trigger or to cancel the delete action. The "CreateNew" event starts a content-independent navigation that accesses the "ProductEditor" ViewContainer, which by default displays the "DataEntry" ViewContainer. The user can enter the data for a new product in the Form and submit them to the "CreateOrModifyProduct" Action, which creates a new object (if no OID is supplied) or modifies an existing object (if an OID is provided in input). Upon successful termination, the new product's details are displayed in the "ProductDetails" ViewComponent to confirm the effect of the action to the user. The two "Modify" events available in the "Products" ViewContainer (for selecting the product to update from the list) and in the "ProductDisplay" ViewContainer (for updating the specific product in view) allow the user to edit the data of a product. Note the ParameterBinding Oid→ProductOid associated with the InteractionFlow emanating from both the "Modify" events, which makes the identity of the product available in the Form to enable the preloading of the fields with existing attribute values of the identified object (not shown for brevity; refer to chapter 5). For simplicity, Figure 8.32 omits the specification of the error page displayed when any of the invoked actions fails.

8.6.2 PATTERN CM-PBCM: PAGE-BASED CONTENT MANAGEMENT

Another popular content management pattern occurs in blogs and page-based content management systems. These applications have a fixed schema consisting of a hierarchical collection of pages and offer the user an intuitive interface for adding pages, editing their content, organizing pages in hierarchies, defining the pages' order in menus, and setting the graphical properties and visibility of pages.

Figure 8.33 shows a simplified example inspired by a popular blog platform. The "AllPages" ViewContainer shows all the existing pages and supports an event ("Trash") for deleting one or more pages. The "Edit" and "AddNew" events open the "PageEditor" ViewContainer, where a form allows the user to define all the attributes of the page: the title, the body content (created with a rich text editor), the parent page in the hierarchy, the menu order, the visibility and publication status, and the graphic template. The temporary modifications can be previewed in the "PageView" ViewContainer or made persistent with the "Save" event. The basic example of Figure 8.33 can be enriched with more functionality, such as the addition of widgets, the creation of a new page from a clone of an existing page, and the management of the revision history.

8.7 PERSONALIZATION, IDENTIFICATION, AND AUTHORIZATION

Personalization is the adaptation of the interface to the user's characteristics. It may assume an elementary form, such as the insertion of the user's name into a welcome page, or employ sophisticated patterns such as the display of content that depends on

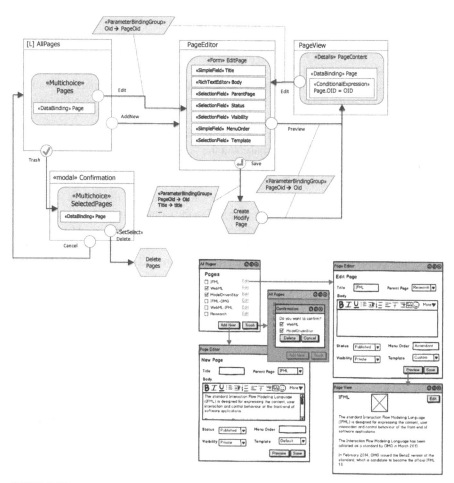

FIGURE 8.33

Example of page based content management pattern.

the user's context. The personalization of the interface requires the user to be identified, so the personalization patterns are treated together with the identification and authentication ones. In chapter 3, we discussed the Context and UserRole classes and showed examples of the personalization domain model, which allow the designer to represent the information needed for adapting the interface to the individual user. In this chapter, we show how to exploit such features to build interface models that take into account the user's identity and role. The patterns in this category are identified by the acronym IA (Identification and Authorization).

8.7.1 PATTERN IA-LOGIN: LOGIN

The identification and authentication of the user are the procedures whereby the application recognizes and checks a user-provided identity for validity. The most common means to achieve this functionality is the login process. The user enters credentials using a Form in a public access ViewContainer, and such input is verified against the content of an identity repository. Upon success, the «NormalTermination» ActionEvent is raised by the login Action, the user is authenticated, and this information is preserved in the Context. Upon failure, the «ExceptionalTermination» ActionEvent is raised, which can be trapped by the application to give the user an appropriate warning message.

Figure 8.34 illustrates the simplest login pattern. The "Login" form models the mask for entering the user's credentials, and the "Login" Action triggered by the submit event denotes the process of identification and authentication, which has two possible outcomes. Upon the successful completion of the Action, the Context object becomes initialized with the identity of the user, represented by the unique username. As we will see, this information allows exploiting the Context to build several personalization patterns. Figure 8.34 shows a basic one in which the source ViewContainer— reaccessed after a successful login—displays the username of the authenticated user. Upon unsuccessful termination, the pattern of Figure 8.34 simply redisplays the source ViewContainer. This time, however, the identity information of the Context is undefined, and thus the "UserName" ViewComponent displays no content.

8.7.2 PATTERN IA-LOGOUT: LOGOUT

The information about the user's authenticated identity preserved in the Context can be cleared by the initiative of the user by means of a "Logout" Action, as shown in Figure 8.35.

The typical pattern comprises an event that triggers the "Logout" Action, which normally terminates without exceptions. In Figure 8.35, after the Logout Action is completed, the user is shown the same source ViewContainer, but, as a side effect of the logout process, the identity information in the Context is no longer defined, and thus the "UserName" ViewComponent has no content.

8.7.3 PATTERN IA-CEX: CONTEXT EXPIRATION NOTIFICATION

The Context information holding the authenticated identity of the user can also be cleared by the system (e.g., for security reasons). This pattern is frequently used in web applications where storage of the Context information associated with an authenticated user is implemented by means of a session object in the server. Irrespective of how the Context is implemented, the update of the interface after the expiry of the authentication information can be modeled with a system event, as shown in Figure 8.36. In this pattern, the interface is notified by the "expiration" system event, which causes the redisplay of the "SourceViewContainer," expunged of the content that depends on the Context.

Note that the Context is more abstract than the Session object of a web application, which is implementation level. The example implies no commitment as to the way in which the Context is preserved. It could be stored in the data-tier or in the

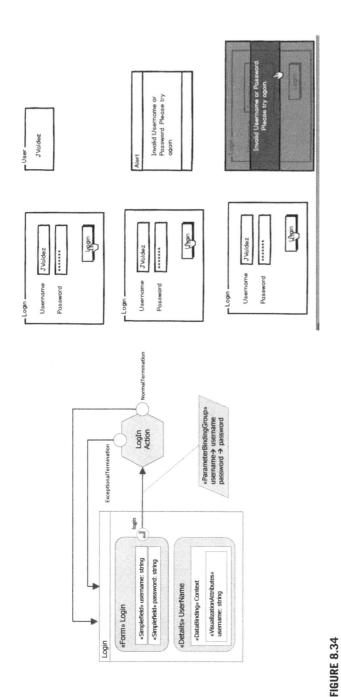

FIGURE 8.34

Example of the login pattern.

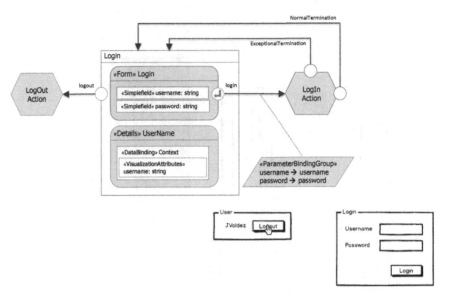

FIGURE 8.35

Example of the logout pattern.

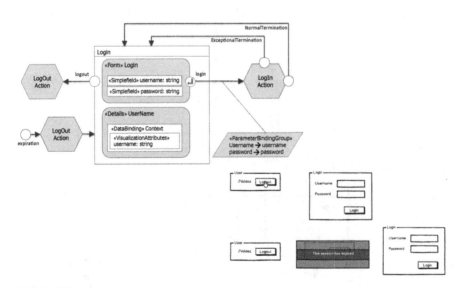

FIGURE 8.36

Example of the authentication expiration pattern.

middle-tier of a web application, in the model objects of a desktop application, or in a "fat" client of a mobile or rich Internet application.

8.7.4 PATTERN IA-SPLOG: LOGIN TO A SPECIFIC VIEWCONTAINER

The examples of Figure 8.34 and Figure 8.35 assume that the login and logout actions redisplay to the user the same source ViewContainer from which the action has been triggered. This is not always the case, because in many applications—especially on the web—the authentication is performed in one ViewContainer to obtain access to another ViewContainer. This is the case, for example, in a web content management system, where the authentication is provided in a public page, and then the authenticated user accesses the collection of private pages. A simple model that represents such a situation is shown in Figure 8.37.

The "Login" and "Logout" Actions now have an explicit InteractionFlow that specifies the destination ViewContainers.

8.7.5 PATTERN IA-ROLE: USER ROLE DISPLAY AND SWITCHING

As discussed in chapter 3, the role played by the user in a role-based access control system can be modeled with the UserRole extension of the Context. The Login pattern has a second side effect in addition to identification: if users are classified in roles, the Login Action defines the default role of the logged-in user by initializing the content of the UserRole object. Again, notice that the Login Action is an abstract concept, which can be implemented in several ways (e.g., using RBAC data stored in

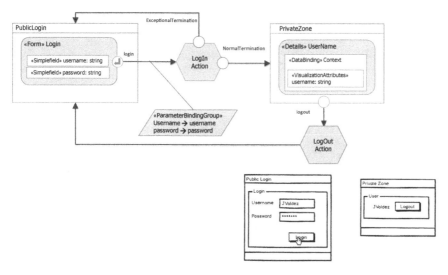

FIGURE 8.37

Example of the login pattern with an explicit destination ViewContainer.

a relational database with a directory service such as LDAP). For IFML, its essence of the Action is the authentication of the user and the assignment of a default role (if defined) to the verified identity.

Figure 8.38 illustrates the publication of the role information in addition to the username after a successful login.

Figure 8.38 shows also an example of the role switching pattern, usable in RBAC systems that enable users to embody multiple roles (e.g., a conference management system where the user could be both an author or a reviewer).

The "CurrentRole" ViewComponent has a DataBinding to the UserRole object, the extension of the Context object that stores the current role impersonated by the authenticated user. The list of potential rules is instead displayed by the "PossibleRoles" List ViewComponent. This component determines the list of allowed roles for the user thanks to a ParamaterBinding that makes available the identity of the logged-in user held in the "CurrentUser" ViewComponent.

Notice that the ConditionalExpression `users.username->exists(name)` exploits the "users" association end of the "Membership" association between the User and the Group classes, introduced in chapter 3. The content of the "PossibleRoles" List ViewComponent could be determined in other ways (e.g., with a Dynamic-Behavior element denoting the call to a role lookup method of an RBAC system).

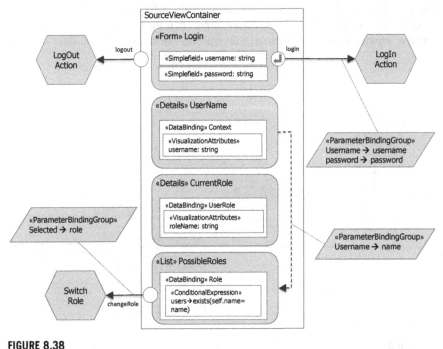

FIGURE 8.38

Example of role switching pattern.

The SelectionEvent associated with the "PossibleRoles" List ViewComponent triggers the "SwitchRole" Action, which assigns to the user the role specified in input. After the successful completion of the Action, the source ViewContainer is reaccessed (by default) and the updated role is displayed in the "CurrentRole" ViewComponent.

8.7.6 PATTERN IA-RBP: ROLE-BASED PERMISSIONS FOR VIEW ELEMENTS

When the user is authenticated, the Context information can be used to implement access permissions that depend on the user's role. The access control rules presented here should not be confused with those implemented at the back end to control the access to the data by applications. We use the term "access control rules" with a slight extension to denote the interface design pattern that shows in the interface only the ViewElements that the user is entitled to see or the objects the user can see and manipulate. However, bypassing the user interface to access the data tier is possible in multitier applications, and thus the access control rules embodied in the front end descend from, reinforce, and do not substitute for those specified in the role-based access control policies and implemented in the back-end tiers.

Access control at the level of ViewElements is typical of web applications, where the interface is split into distinct pages. Since pages are addressable and their address could be "forged," they should be treated as resources under role-based access control. As noted in chapter 7, the level of accessibility of pages can be expressed in the interface model with the «protected» stereotype to distinguish pages that require user authentication from public pages that are freely accessible. The «protected» access requirement can be associated also with logical containers such as Area and SiteView, with the meaning that the property applies recursively to all the contained ViewElements.

The ViewPoint concept, which identifies a set of interrelated InteractionFlowModelElements defining a functional portion of the system, can be used to express the access rights to protected resources. Role X is associated with ViewPoint Y to denote that users in the role X are authorized to access the resources of the ViewPoint Y. In practice, web user roles are associated—through ViewPoints—with SiteViews. For example, an authenticated user with content manager role would be granted permission to access the protected SiteView containing the content management pages. Figure 8.39 shows an example of RBAC applied to the SiteViews of a web application. The Login Action has multiple termination events, one for each defined UserRole. An ActivationCondition associated with each event tests the default role of the authenticated user and activates the corresponding NavigationFlow, which specifies the SiteView to be accessed. Notice that specifying the NavigationFlow is equivalent to associating the destination SiteView with the ViewPoint of the UserRole mentioned in the event's ActivationCondition (e.g., SiteViewRole1 with the ViewPoint of the UserRole named "role1" and SiteViewRole2 with the ViewPoint of the UserRole named "role2").

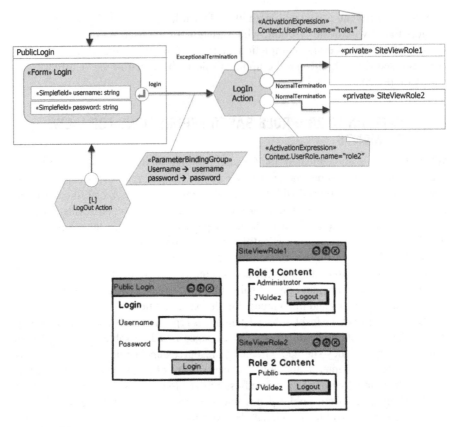

FIGURE 8.39

Example of the role-based access control pattern applied to the pages of a web application.

Notice that the "Logout" action invalidates the authentication and thus clears the permissions to access a protected resource, which entails that the SiteView accessed after its successful completion should be public. If the "Logout" Action can be triggered from any page of the application, as customary in web applications, it can be denoted as landmark, as shown in Figure 8.39.

8.7.7 PATTERN IA-NRBP: NEGATIVE ROLE-BASED PERMISSIONS FOR VIEW ELEMENTS

When the access rights for a role are a subset of those of another role, separating the ViewPoints in two segregated SiteView is improper because it results in SiteViews sharing most of their ViewElements, with consequent design and maintenance inefficiency. In this case, an alternative design pattern may be more adequate: designing a unique SiteView for both roles and enforcing "negative" permissions (denials) for

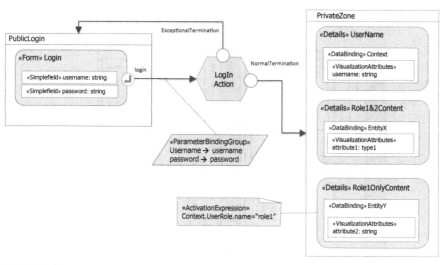

FIGURE 8.40

Role-based access control over ViewElements with denial conditions.

the role with stricter access rules. Figure 8.40 shows how to express the pattern using ActivationConditions.

After the successful login, the "PrivateZone" ViewContainer is accessed. The "UserName" and "Role1&2 Content" ViewComponents are visible to users with both "role1" and "role2." The ActivationCondition UserRole.roleName="role1" expresses an access restriction: the ViewComponent is displayed only to users of "role1." This clause is actually a denial of access for all roles different from "role1."

8.7.8 PATTERN IA-OBP: OBJECT-BASED PERMISSIONS

Another complementary kind of access control is expressed over the content objects using the concept of personalization associations introduced in chapter 3.

The "MyBlog" ViewContainer displays the user's identity and the list of his blog articles, determined by means of the personalization association end "author." One article can be selected for modification, or a new article can be edited, using the "ArticleEditor" Form. Submitting the form data triggers the "CreateOrModifyArticle" Action, which either creates a new article and associates it with the authenticated user or updates an existing article **owned by the user**. Therefore, the "author" association end acts as a kind of permission, which dictates the articles that a specific user is entitle to update.Figure 8.41

8.7.9 PATTERN IA-PRO: USER PROFILE DISPLAY AND MANAGEMENT

The user profile is the application-dependent information associated with the identity of an authenticated user. Such information can be represented explicitly in the data

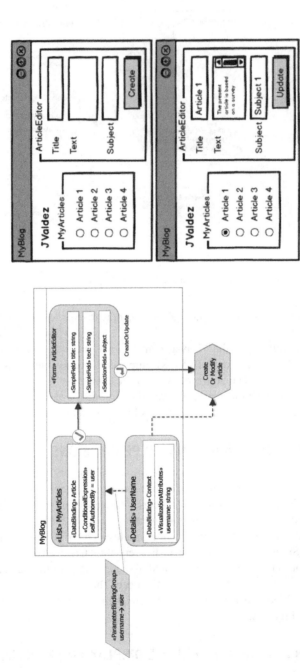

FIGURE 8.41

Example of the access control pattern applied to content objects.

model, as shown in chapter 3. The key to personalization is associating the identity of the authenticated user with the attributes in the user profile. This can be achieved simply by using the same identifier (e.g., the unique username or e-mail address) as a key attribute both in the Context object and in the User class that stores the profile information. Figure 8.42 shows a very simple pattern for displaying the user profile and changing its data.

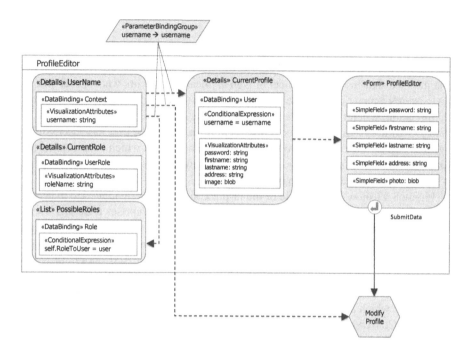

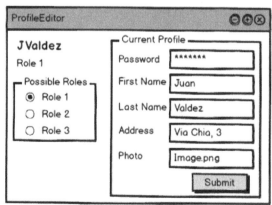

FIGURE 8.42

Example of profile display and editing.

Figure 8.42 applies the class-based content management pattern to the profile information. The "ProfileEditor" ViewContainer displays the essential context information (the user's identity and current role) and retrieves the list of available roles. The identity information (username) is propagated to the ViewComponents and Action through appropriate DataBinding elements to enable the display of the profile attributes in the "CurrentProfile" ViewComponent, the preloading of field values in the "ProfileEditor" Form, and the identification of the object to modify in the "ModifyProfile" Action.

8.7.10 PATTERN IA-IPSI: IN-PLACE SIGN-IN

The in-place sign-in pattern, typical of web applications, occurs when a user who is not currently authenticated in the application wants to perform an action that requires identification. When the user attempts to trigger the action, he must be warned of the need to sign in first and be routed to the login form. When the user has successfully signed in, he must be returned to the interface element from which he requested the initial action. When handling the submission of information, any data entered prior to the login procedure must also be preserved.

Figure 8.43 shows an example of the in-place sign-in pattern applied to the comment section of a blog article. The Blog ViewContainer comprises a Details ViewComponent displaying the article's text, a list of comments, and a form for entering a new comment. When an unauthenticated user submits a comment, the NavigationFlow guarded by the `Context.username.oclIsUndefined()` ActivationExpression is followed, which causes the display of the InPlaceLogin modal windows whereby the user can enter credentials. Upon submission, the Login&CreateCommand Action is executed, which authenticates the user and creates the comment (if the credentials are valid). Conversely, when an already authenticated user submits a comment, the NavigationFlow guarded by the `NOT Context.username.oclIsUndefined()` ActivationExpression is followed, which simply creates the comment.

8.8 SESSION DATA

Session data management is an issue arising in some online applications, whereby users can produce temporary information lasting only for the duration of their interaction with the system. The interface model of an application that exploits session data is similar to that of a general purpose content management application. IFML is neutral with respect to policies for managing data and thus does not represent the way information is preserved or aligned between different architecture tiers. This is apparent from the initial example of chapter 2, where we introduced the model of the bookstore toy application, which dealt with a shopping trolley, a data structure typically endowed with session duration. The "AddToCart" Action of Figure 8.2.16 encapsulates the business logic for inserting an item into the trolley at an abstract level that hides the actual data management policy.

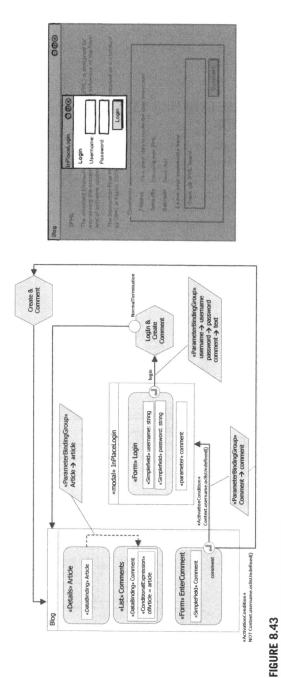

FIGURE 8.43

Example of the in-place sign-in pattern.

One aspect in which session data management interfaces differ from generic data management is in the necessity of handling the asynchronous invalidation of the session by the system. In this case, the interface must handle a user request referring to session data in a safe way by showing alternative content with respect to what is no longer available. Another aspect is the possibility for the user to change the duration of session data by making it persistent.

8.8.1 PATTERN SES-CR: CREATING SESSION DATA FROM PERSISTENT DATA

Figure 8.44 shows an example of session data creation from persistent information. The "FlightSearch" form allows the user to enter the usual flight selection criteria. The submit event triggers the "RetrieveFlight" Action, encapsulates the business logic for extracting the flights that match the user's need, and uses

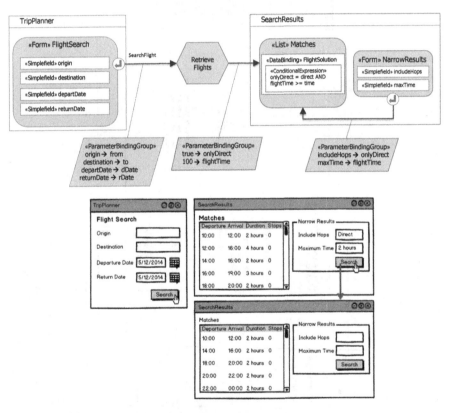

FIGURE 8.44

Example of session data creation from persistent data.

such data to create instances of the FlightSolution class in the session. The session objects are displayed in the "Matches" List ViewComponent, which initially shows all objects. Another form in the SearchResult ViewContainer allows the user to narrow the displayed session objects based on further restrictive conditions.

8.8.2 PATTERN SES-PER: PERSISTING SESSION DATA

Figure 8.45 exemplifies a pattern that is the reverse of that of Figure 8.44: the creation of persistent data from session data. From the "Matches" List ViewComponent, the user can pick one flight option and activate the book event. This triggers the CreateBooking Action, which inserts the data of the booking into the persistent store. To complete the example, the in-place sign-in pattern could be added to have the user login prior to creating the persistent booking.

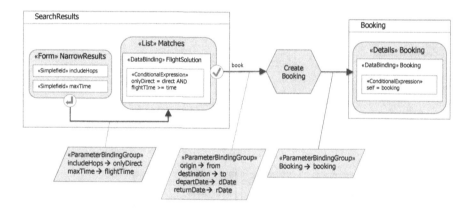

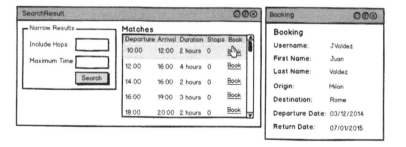

FIGURE 8.45

Example of the pattern for persisting session data.

8.8.3 PATTERN SES-EXC: SESSION DATA EXPIRATION CATCHING

PATTERN IA-CEX, discussed earlier in this chapter, handles the asynchronous notification of the expiry of the Context to the user interface by causing an automatic refresh of the content that expunges the parts that depend on the Context object (e.g., the user's identity). We now show an alternative way of handling the expiration of the Context or of the session data based on a "lazy" policy. Instead of refreshing the interface based on a system event, the pattern conditions the effect of a user-generated event on the validity of the Context object, which is assumed to be silently invalidated by the expiration of the session.

Figure 8.46 shows that ActivationConditions trapping the invalidation of the session are added to the NavigationFlows associated with the events of the View-Container publishing session data. If the Context is still valid, the interaction proceeds normally; otherwise, the effect of the events is redefined (e.g., to display a page that does not contain session-dependent data).

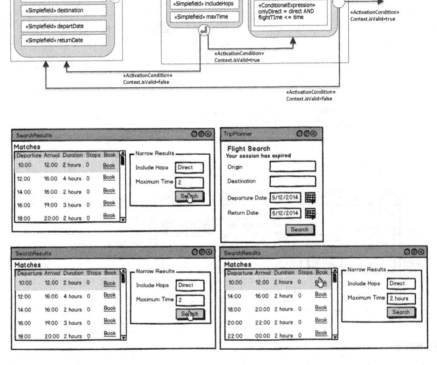

FIGURE 8.46

Example of lazy management of session expiration.

8.9 SOCIAL FUNCTIONS

Social networks are applications popular with both web and mobile users. They focus on the social activity performed by users, such as posting, rating, liking, commenting, and sharing. Such activities are made visible to a specific user based on friendship connections and the privacy rules set by the originator.

8.9.1 PATTERN SOC-AW: ACTIVITY WALL

Figure 8.47 shows the pattern for modeling the log of social activity typical of a social network platform. The interface model corresponds to a protected application, which entails that the user's identity is known and accessible via the Context object. The "PersonalActivityWall" ViewContainer models the interface for accessing the log of the social activities in the user's circles. The log is split into two ViewComponents. The "AllVisible" ViewComponent displays the complete stream of activities that are visible to the user via a compact visualization: only the author's username and the activity description are shown. A system event "activityNotification" signals the arrival of a new activity, which causes the ViewComponent to refresh its content. The "onMouseOver" event associated with the "AllVisible" List allows the user to see a preview of the full details of each activity in a modal ViewContainer. The "Activity" Details ViewComponent shows all the attributes of the activity, the comments made about it by other users, and the likes received. The likes are displayed differently depending on their number, using two separate «NestedDataBinding» elements. If only one like is present (as specified by the ActivationCondition `likes->size()=1`), the VisualizationAttributes comprise the name of the user who liked the activity (not shown in Figure 8.47 for simplicity); otherwise, only the number of likes is displayed (againm Figure 8.47 omits the VisualizationAttributes ViewComponentPart, for space reasons).

The events "comment," "like," and "share" associated with each activity allow the user to perform the corresponding social action on one activity. The "like" event is also associated with each comment of the activity.

The "Selected" NestedList ViewComponent displays only the activities flagged as highlighted for the user. For each activity, the username of the author, image, and description are shown. Also in the "Selected" ViewComponent, each activity is accompanied by the list of comments and likes and by several events that allow the user to act on both the activities and their comments. Finally, the "PersonalActivity-Wall" ViewContainer also contains a Form whereby the user can post status updates and media elements, such as images or a videos.

The "post," "comment," "like," and "share events all create activity instances that are then displayed on the walls of other users based on the visibility rules set by the author and on the social network platform internal activity highlighting algorithm.

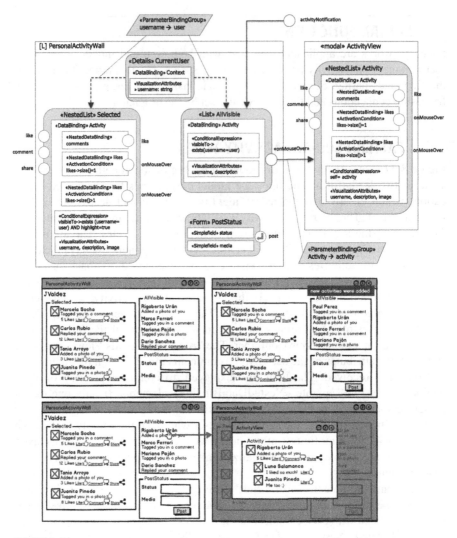

FIGURE 8.47

Example of the activity wall pattern.

8.9.2 PATTERN SOC-SH: SHARING, LIKING, AND COMMENTING

The activity stream typical of social networks is the result of the user's interactions, such as posting, commenting, liking, and sharing content produced by other community members.

Figure 8.48 exemplifies the design pattern for the sharing action. Posting, commenting, and liking are similar.

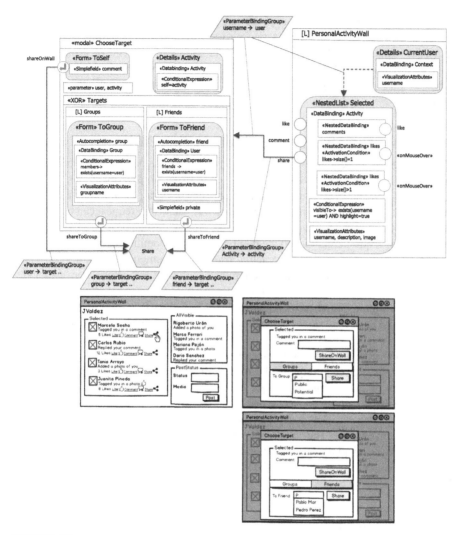

FIGURE 8.48

Example of the sharing pattern.

The "share" event in the "PersonalActivityWall" causes the opening of the "ChooseTarget" modal ViewContainer. This container preserves as parameters the identity of the authenticated user and contains a summary of the content to be shared in the "Activity" Details ViewComponent, as well as a Form for inserting a comment. The user can choose among three modalities of sharing: the "shareOnWall" event causes the activity to be shared as if it were a post by the user; the "shareToFriend" and "shareToGroup" events cause the activity to be shared on the activity wall of a selected friend or group, respectively.

For supporting the selection of the target friend or group, the "ChooseTarget" modal ViewContainer comprises two nested alternative subcontainers, which in turn host two Forms. Each form enables the choice of a friend or group with an auto-completion field. When the user selects a friend, he can also decide to share the content as a private message (using the "private" SimpleField of the "ToFriend" Form).

8.9.3 PATTERN SOC-FR: FRIENDSHIP MANAGEMENT

The dynamics of social networks revolve around the links between members, which descend from asymmetric (follow) or symmetric (friendship) associations.

Figure 8.49 shows an example of a pattern for managing a symmetric association between users by means of friendship requests. A friendship request can be modeled as an object connecting a requestor to a target user, with such properties as the timestamp of the request creation and the number of friends common to both the requestor and the target of the request. The actual friends in common between the requestor and the target of the request can be computed with the OCL expression: `request.requestor.friends->intersection(request.target.friends)`. Accordingly, the (derived) attribute "numberOfCommonFriends" of class Request can be computed with the OCL expression: request.requestor.friends->intersection(request.target.friends)-> size().

The "Friends" ViewContainer displays the list of the friendship requests of the logged-in user. For each request, the timestamp and number of friends in common between the requestor and the target user are shown. A nested data binding also allows the display of the username and a photo of the requestor. The user can accept or decline the request. The "accept" event creates an instance of friendship connecting the two involved users. The "decline" event deletes the request. The "onMouseOver" event causes the display of a modal window that lists the names of the friends in common between the current user and the requestor.

8.10 GEO PATTERNS

We conclude this chapter with a last a design pattern, which exploits the geographical position of the user embodied in the Context object.

8.10.1 PATTERN GEO-LAS: LOCATION-AWARE SEARCH

Figure 8.50 exemplifies a location-aware geo-search pattern. The "ProximitySearch" ViewContainer contains a form for specifying the restaurant requirements and a ViewComponent with the position of the user taken from the context. Submitting the form retrieves the restaurants in range and displays them on the map as markers. A selection event allows the user to see a window with the restaurant's essential details.

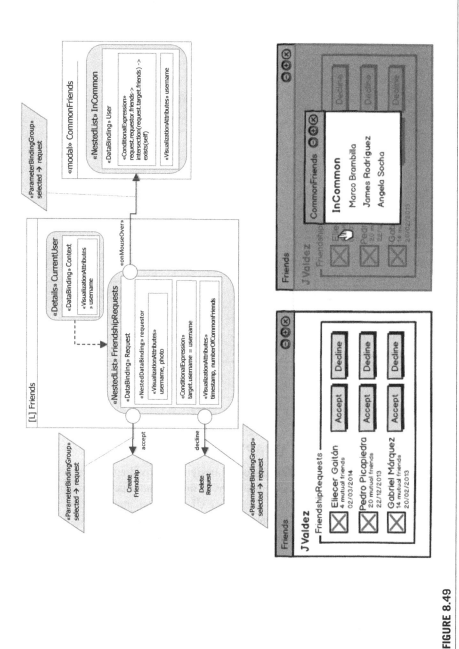

FIGURE 8.49

Example of the friendship management pattern.

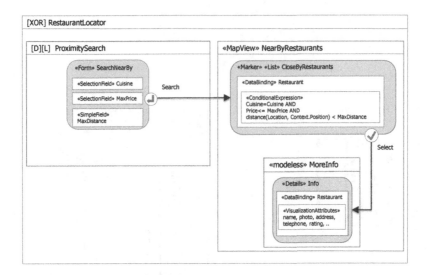

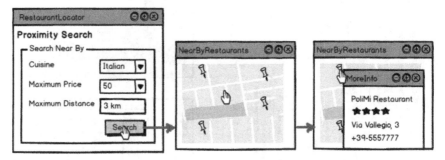

FIGURE 8.50

The location-aware search pattern.

8.11 SUMMARY OF THE CHAPTER

This chapter addressed typical problems of UI design by providing a reasoned categorization of classical user interaction patterns in modern interfaces. Each pattern was described by the IFML model, an exemplary UI rendering, and a textual explanation of its behavior. Some of the patterns described here will be shown at work in chapter 9, where realistic examples of applications are presented.

8.12 BIBLIOGRAPHIC NOTES

Pattern-based design is a typical way of addressing user experience problems and software engineering problems at large. Patterns can be exploited in a generative way (as in [VM10]), where portions of existing models are identified and reinstantiated in new problem settings. Usability guidelines themselves can be considered design patterns. A specific workshop on UI patterns has been held at CHI 2003 [FFG+03]. Many different sources of UI design patterns exist today [Borchers01, Erickson14, Fincher14] and a Pattern Language Markup Language (PLML) has been specified too [FFG+03]. Some efforts to bridge software engineering patterns and user interaction patterns are also ongoing [FVB06]. Social network patterns have also been investigated [Brambilla11].

IFML by examples

9

Chapter 8 illustrated a gallery of IFML design patterns that occur frequently in applications. In this chapter, we take the reverse approach, considering how a sample of realistic applications—inspired by popular real-world ones—can be modeled in IFML with the help of the language constructs and design patterns introduced so far.

9.1 MEDIA SHARING APP

The first example we consider is a mobile app for smartphones providing an online photo- and video-sharing service. The service allows people to take pictures and videos, to apply digital effects to them, and to share them on several social networks.

Figure 9.1 shows the initial screen of the app, which permits the user to register or sign in.

9.1.1 DOMAIN MODEL

The main assets of the application are users, comments, media object (images and videos), and tags, which can be represented with their associations as shown in the domain model of Figure 9.2.

The "Media" entity includes attributes describing an image or a video: a textual description, the upload timestamp, the location, and the media type, which can be video or photo. Attribute "numLikes" is calculated as the sum of all "likes" cast by users.

Users have a number of profile attributes and can be connected with other users, with the association characterized by the "follower" and "followedBy" 0..* roles. Users can be associated with "Media" and "Comment." The association with roles "posting"/"postedBy" represents the ownership of a media asset by a user. The association with roles "like"/"likedBy" records the expression of preference for a media asset by a user. The association "mention"/"taggedIn" denotes that a user has been tagged in a media item.

Comments are produced by users (associated with roles "publisher"/"publishedBy"), refer to a media asset (associated with roles "comment"/"attachedTo"), and can mention other users (associated with roles "mention"/"taggedIn"). Comments can be associated with a tag, which denotes that the text actually contains the tag (associated with roles "taggedBy"/"comprisedIn"). A tag can also qualify a media object to help retrieve objects of interest (associated with roles "annotation"/"taggedBy").

FIGURE 9.1

Initial screen of the media sharing app.

Some activities (e.g., posting and liking an object) are logged: entity "Activity" records, with the time of occurrence, the operations performed by the user (association with roles "performer"/"action"), which may optionally refer to a media asset (association with roles "performedUpon"/"action").

Finally, the attribute "numLikes" of the media object is derived. Its value is the sum of the preferences received from the users (i.e., the number of users connected by the "likedBy" association role). Similarly, the "Comment" entity contains another derived attribute, "userName," which enriches the comment with the name of its author.

9.1.2 **IFML MODEL**

We now proceed to modeling the interface of the media sharing app, following a few usage scenarios that demonstrate the main functions. Figure 9.1 shows the start ViewContainer of the application, displayed when the application is accessed by the user or when a session is closed. The interface offers two options: a new user can sign up, while an already registered user can sign in. The IFML model of the start ViewContainer and of the events it supports is shown in Figure 9.3.

The IFML model for registering a new user exploits a common object creation pattern (such as the PATTERN AG-OCR discussed in chapter 6), and thus is not further elaborated. The "Sign In" ViewContainer follows the PATTERN IA-LOGIN, shown in chapter 8. When a registered user logs in successfully, the "Media Sharing Top" ViewContainer is displayed. Yhis is the principal interface container, which comprises five landmark subcontainers embodying the main functionalities shown in alternative but always reachable by the user. This general organization of the interface is represented by the IFML model of Figure 9.4.

The Landmark stereotype on the "Home," "Explore," "Take Picture," "News" and "Profile" subcontainers models the main menu (shown in Figure 9.5), which is visible in all the pages of the application. The "Home" ViewContainer is also marked

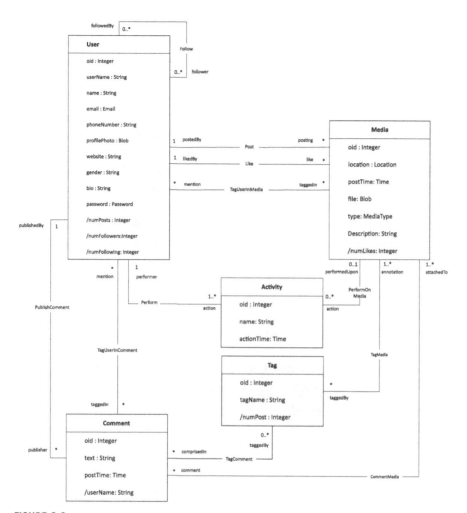

FIGURE 9.2

Domain model of the media sharing app.

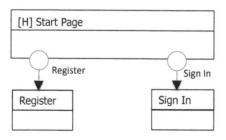

FIGURE 9.3

IFML model of the start page.

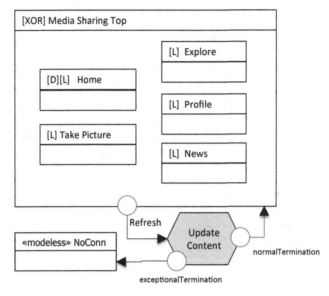

FIGURE 9.4

General organization of the interface of media sharing app.

FIGURE 9.5

Menu for Landmark navigation.

as Default to specify that is the one displayed when entering the "Media SharingTop" ViewContainer.

The model of Figure 9.4 also contains the "Refresh" event, which triggers an action for updating the content of the application. In the interface, the event is fired by touching the icon in the top-right corner of the screen (shown in Figure 9.8). The event is associated with the top-level container because it is always visible to the user. When the user tries to reload the page without having the connection, the Action "UpdatePage" triggers a modeless window that signals the failure of the action, as shown in Figure 9.6.

Introducing the "Media Sharing Top" View Container makes the model more concise and avoids repeating common elements, such as the "Refresh" event, in multiple ViewContainers. For the sake of illustration, Figure 9.7 contrasts the model with and without the "Media SharingTop" ViewContainer.

The "Home" ViewContainer, displayed when the user enters the application, contains a vertically scrollable list of the recent photos and videos posted by users,

FIGURE 9.6

Modeless window showing the message for connection failure.

ordered by time of publication. For each media object, the interface displays the name and photo of the author, the content, upload timestamp, location, users who "like" the object, and the associated comments, as shown in Figure 9.8.

9.1.2.1 MediaViewer module

The presentation of media objects in the "Home" ViewContainer appears identically in several other places of the interface. It is therefore convenient to represent it as a module definition ("MediaViewer," shown in Figure 9.9). The module definition can be referenced in the interface model whenever the same presentation is reused. The input port of the "MediaViewer" module definition is associated with a dataflow carrying a ParameterBindingGroup denoting the collection of identifiers of the media objects to display ("MediaOIDs"). When the input collection contains multiple objects, the data of each instance are presented sequentially in a vertical scrollable layout. When the input consists of only one object, one photo or video is shown with its associated data.

Since the content displayed in the module belongs to multiple entities connected hierarchically, a «NestedList» ViewComponent is used. Each photo or a video acts as a top-level item in the list, and several nested levels specify the data of the objects depending on it, such as the user who posted it, referenced users, comments, and tags with the users mentioned in them.

The three-level "MediaViewer" «NestedList» comprises at the top level a DataBinding that refers to the "Media" entity and displays the "postTime," "location," and "file" attributes. A conditional expression filters the data binding instances to display only the object(s) whose identifiers are passed in input to the module: `MediaOIDs->includes (oid)`. Instances are ordered by time of posting according to the clause «OrderBy» postTime DESC.

A nested data binding, built on the association role "postedBy," visualizes the "profilePhoto" and the "userName" of the user who posted the video or photo.

The "numLikes" visualization attribute of the media objects is modeled separately, because the number of "likes" is visible only when greater than ten, as

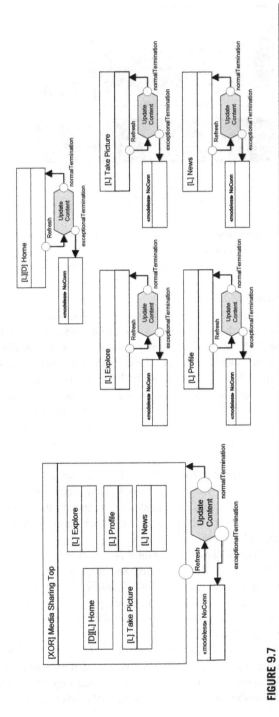

FIGURE 9.7

(a) ViewContainers nested within a XOR top-level ViewContainer. (b) Model with independent ViewContainers.

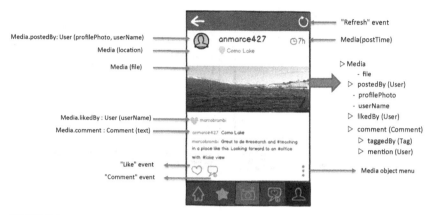

FIGURE 9.8

Content shown on the home page.

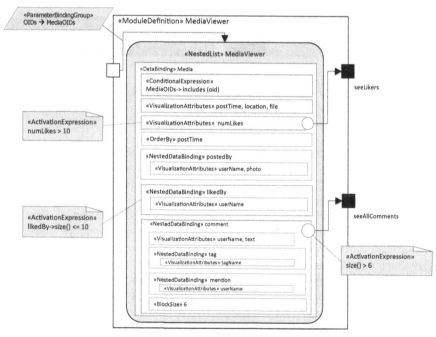

FIGURE 9.9

Initial model of the "MediaViewer" module.

expressed by the «ActivationExpression» numLikes > 10. In this case, the user can trigger the "SeeLikers" event by clicking on the number of "likes," which displays a separate ViewContainer showing the list of all the users who "like" the photo or video. Conversely, the NestedDataBinding built on the association role "likedBy,"

FIGURE 9.10

Visualization of the likers and of the number of likers. Interface when likers are fewer than 11 (left) and greater than 10 (right).

which displays the usernames of the people that like the media asset, is shown only when number of "likes" is fewer than eleven, as expressed by the «ActivationExpression» `likedBy->size() < 11`. These different forms of visualization and interaction are contrasted in Figure 9.10.

The "MediaViewer" NestedList also displays the received comments (as shown in Figure 9.10) modeled as NestedDataBinding built on the association role "contains." This displays a maximum number of objects (six, in this case) as denoted by the «block» ViewComponentPart associated with the NestedDataBinding. If the object has more comments than the maximum number displayable, an event is activated that lets the user access all the comments in a separate ViewContainer. This is expressed by the "see-AllComments" event and by the `size()>6` «ActivationExpression» associated with it.[1]

The NestedDataBinding that displays the comments has another nested level, built on the association role "comprises," which displays the names of the tags found in a comment. Note than this nested level is rendered in a specific way, because the tags are actually embedded within the text comment (see Figure 9.11). Similarly, another NestedDataBinding, built on the association role "mentions," displays the names of the users mentioned in a comment.

Each object in the "MediaViewer" nested list supports a rich set of interaction events, summarized in the refined model of Figure 9.12.

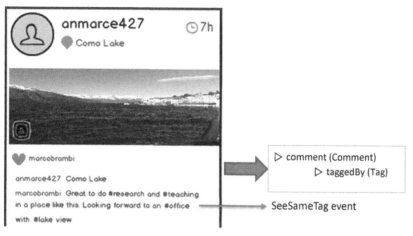

FIGURE 9.11

Visualization of the tags as clickable anchors within the text of the comment.

Most events cause the display of a distinct interface. For convenience, we encapsulate each interface into a separate reusable module, as shown by the «Module» elements in Figure 9.12.

From the "MediaViewer" NestedList, one can access the profile of the user who uploaded, liked, commented on, or was mentioned in one of the comments. All these interactions are represented by multiple "SeeUser" events, triggered by clicking on the username or photo of the owner of the media element currently under view or on the username of the author of a comment, the person who cast a like, or a person mentioned in a comment. All these options are visible in Figure 9.8 and modeled by the "SeeUser" events in Figure 9.12.

The "See Location" event corresponds to selecting the location of a media object (visible in Figure 9.8) and permits one to access a separate module with a map showing the place where the photo or video was shot, together with the positions of other photos or videos nearby.

As shown in Figure 9.11, tags in a comment are rendered as navigation anchors. By clicking on one of them, users can see other videos or photos with the same tag. The "SeeSameTag" event of the "MediaViewer" NestedList shown in Figure 9.12 models this interaction.

Two icons (highlighted in Figure 9.13) let the user post a comment and toggle appreciation (liking and unliking an object). A double touch on the media object is equivalent to casting a like. These interactions are represented by the "TogglePreference," «DoubleTouch» "Like," and "Comment" events in the model of Figure 9.12.

When the media object is a video, a single touch toggles the play/pause status. When it is a photo, the single touch shows the list of tagged uses, if any. The corresponding events appear in Figure 9.12.

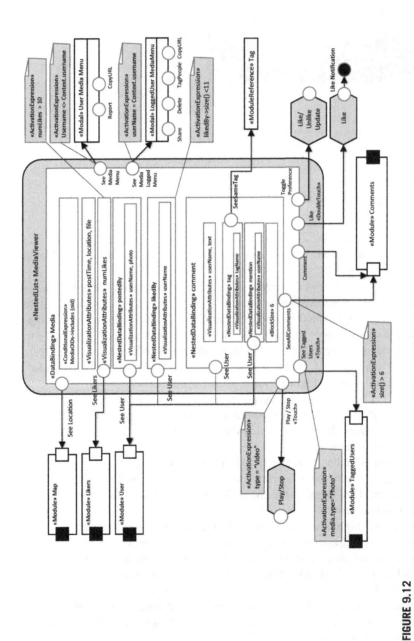

FIGURE 9.12

Refined model of the content and interactions of the "MediaViewer" module.

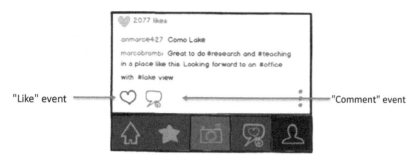

"Like" event ←——————→ ⟶ "Comment" event

FIGURE 9.13

Command for toggling the "like" status and commenting. A double touch on the object casts a like on it.

Finally, each media object has a menu of further actions that apply to it. The menu differs if the photo or video belongs to the logged-in user or to another user. This behavior is represented in Figure 9.12 with two distinct events ("SeeMediaMenu" and "SeeMediaLoggedMenu"). Such events are activated alternatively thanks to two mutually exclusive ActivationExpressions that test if the owner of the media object is the logged-in user, using a pattern similar to the object-based permission (PATTERN IA-OBP) discussed in chapter 8.[2] The condition exploits the fact that the identity of the logged-in user is preserved in the Context object (userName = Context. username).

9.1.2.2 Comments module

The "Comments" module, accessed from the "SeeAllComments" and "Comment" events of the "MediaViewer" ViewComponent of Figure 9.12, specifies the interface elements for managing the comments of a media object. The interface contains a simple list of comments, shown in Figure 9.14.

The model of the "Comments" module is shown in Figure 9.15. The input to the module is the identifier of the media object to which the comments belong, as specified by the ParameterBindingGroup. The content of the module is a «NestedList» ViewComponent ("Comments"), bound to the instances of the Comment entity associated with the media object passed in input, as represented by the ConditionalExpression belongsTo = media.

As in the "MediaViewer" module, the "SeeUser" events can be triggered to display the profile of users who posted or are mentioned in a comment. Also, clicking a tag name triggers the "SeeSameTag" event, which allows one to see other media objects qualified by that Tag.

The "Comments" module also contains a Form ViewComponent with a Simple-Field ("text") and an event "CreateComment " for adding a comment to the media object. The action triggered by the event saves the comment, creates the association instance with the media object, and possibly extracts the tags and mentioned users and links them to the comment.

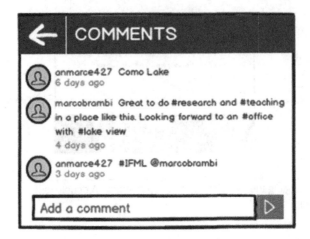

FIGURE 9.14

Interface for accessing and manipulating comments of a media object.

Selecting an entry in the "Comments" NestedList displays a menu, based on the owner of the comment and of the media object, as illustrated in Figure 9.16.

If the comment belongs to the logged user (independently of the owner of the media object to which the comment refers), the menu comprises the "DeleteComment," "ViewProfile," and "CopyText" events. If the media object belongs to the logged user and the comment belongs to a different user, the menu comprises the "DeleteComment," "Delete&Report," "ViewProfile," and "Copy-Text" events. Finally, if both the media object and the comment belong to another user, the menu comprises the "Report," "ViewProfile," and "CopyText" events. These different menu configurations are modeled in Figure 9.15 by means of ActivationExpressions that condition the activation of the event to the relationship between the comment, the media, and the user objects.

As visible in the screenshot of Figure 9.17, the Action that copies the text of the comment ends with a notification event, displayed in a pop-up window. This is modeled by the "CopyNotification" ViewContainer of Figure 9.15.

9.1.2.3 User module

The "SeeUser" and "ViewProfile" events, available in such modules as the "Media-Viewer" and "Comments," trigger the display of an interface with the essential data of a user. Such an interface is used in various situations: to show the profile of the logged user, of the author of a post, or of the person mentioned in a comment. Figure 9.18 shows how the user profile appears for a logged-in user and for a generic one.

The interface comprises an upper section showing the essential user's data, with a menu in the upper right corner enabling various actions on the user's profile, and a lower section dedicated to the posts. Four icons below the user's profile data supports commands for displaying media objects with a tiled layout, displaying media objects

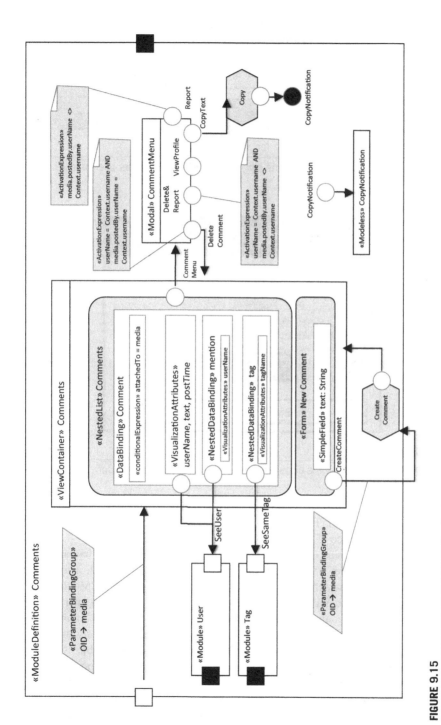

FIGURE 9.15

Model of the interface for accessing and manipulating comments of a media object.

FIGURE 9.16

Menu when the comment belongs to the logged user (left) or to another user (middle, right).

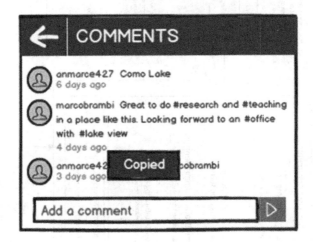

FIGURE 9.17

Pop-up window triggered by the system event for the notification of the "CopyText" Action.

with a vertical layout, displaying media objects on a map, and showing images where the user has been tagged. The latter two commands open separate ViewContainers that take the entire space of the screen, as visible in Figure 9.19.

Figure 9.20 illustrates the model. The "User" module definition has an input parameter (the identifier of the user) and organizes the interface with a top-level XOR ViewContainer, which alternatively displays the "ProfileData," "MediaMap," or "PhotosOfUser" sub-ViewContainers. The "ProfileData" ViewContainer is presented by default and comprises a Details ViewComponent ("UserInfo") publishing the essential user's data (photo, name, bio, web site, and social and activity statistics) and a sub-ViewContainer ("UserPosts"), which displays the media objects, either tiled or scrollable vertically. The two alternative visualizations are supported by the "MediaViewer" and "MediaTiled" modules. The former has been already described in Figure 9.12. The latter has a simpler and more compact structure consisting of a List ViewComponent publishing only the "file" attribute of the media objects with

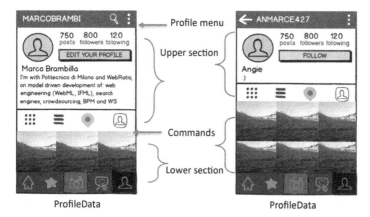

FIGURE 9.18

Interface of the user profile: logged-in (left) and not logged-in (right).

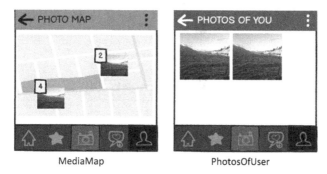

FIGURE 9.19

Full-screen display of the posts on the map (left) and of the media objects where the user has been tagged (right).

a "Select" event for accessing a separate full-screen instance of the "MediaViewer" module (see Figure 9.21). Note that the "PostOIDs" List ViewComponents in the "UserPosts" ViewContainer has no VisualizationAttributes. It simply extracts the identifiers of the relevant media and supplies them as parameters to the "MediaTiled" and "MediaViewer" reusable modules. In this way, the modules do not depend on the objects extraction criterion and can be employed wherever the interface displays a set of photos or videos.

The bottom part of Figure 9.20 represents the reuse of the module "User" and its integration within the rest of the application model.

Clicking on the number of followers and following users triggers the "SeeFollowers" and "SeeFollowing" events, which cause the display of separate ViewContainers. Clicking on the number of posts hides the "UserInfo" ViewComponent and allocates

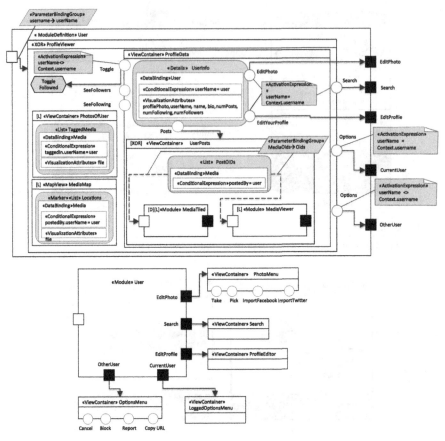

FIGURE 9.20

Specification of the "User" ModuleDefinition and its reuse as "User" Module.

all the screen space to the default ViewContainer of "UserPosts" (the tiled collection of posts).[3]

When the interface shows the logged-in user, it permits the editing of the profile data. The events "EditPhoto" (activated touching the user's picture) and "Edit Your Profile" (triggered with the button visible in the screen on the left of Figure 9.22) open two ViewContainers for setting the image options and for editing the profile data, respectively. When the interface shows a generic user, the profile editing events are not active. Instead, an event "Toggle" allows one to toggle the status of the "follow" relationship with the user on display.

A global menu, reachable by clicking on the vertical dots icon in the upper-right corner of the interface (see Figure 9.22Figure 9.18), gives access to several profile management options. The available events and actions differ when the interface displays the logged-in user or a generic user. This dual behavior is represented by the "Options" events and their ActivationExpressions in the model of Figure 9.20.

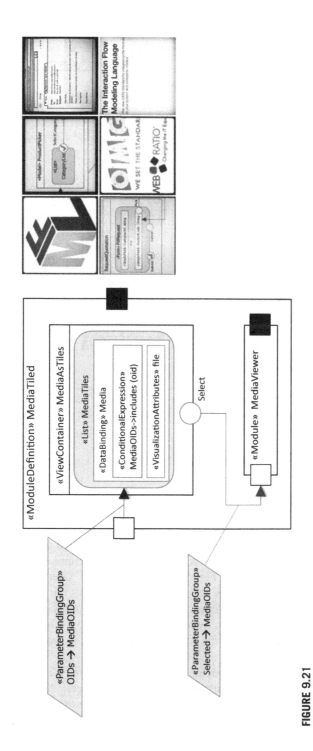

FIGURE 9.21

Model of the "MediaTiled" module showing a compact representation of a set of media objects.

FIGURE 9.22

Alternative commands when the interface displays the logged-in or a generic user.

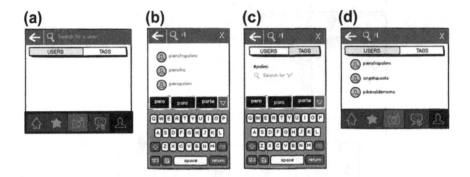

FIGURE 9.23

Interface for people and tag searchs: empty search for users (a); suggested users matching the input (b); suggested tags matching the same characters (c); and the result of the search for users (d).

9.1.2.4 Search users and tags

The magnifying lens icon in the upper-right corner of the interface, visible in Figure 9.22 when the profile belongs to the logged-in user, allows one to open a "Search" interface, shown in Figure 9.23 and modeled in Figure 9.24.

The search function consists of an input form with the usual submit button, but the target of the search can be either a user or a tag. This is implemented by means of the tabbed interface visible in Figure 9.23. Selecting the "User" tab matches the input keyword to user names. Opening the "Tag" tab matches it to the tags. When a user types in the string to be searched, the application presents a list of suggestions matching the inserted characters. Switching from the "User" tab to the "Tag" tab preserves the input but modifies the suggestions displayed, as well as the target of the search.

The search interface is modeled as shown in Figure 9.24. The "Search" XOR View Container comprises two sub-ViewContainers: "UserSearch" and "TagSearch." The former is the default, shown when the user opens the search

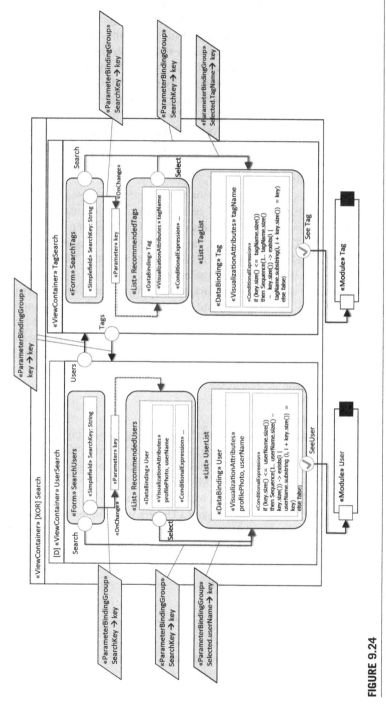

FIGURE 9.24

Model of the search interface for users and tags.

interface. Both ViewContainers repeat the same pattern: an input form permits the user to insert the keyword to match. The «onChange» event reacts to the insertion of each character, saves the current input into the "key" Parameter, and displays a list of suggestions (users or tags) that match the current input. The value of the "key" parameter is made available to the "RecommendedUsers" and "RecommendedTags" List ViewComponents by means of a DataFlow. For brevity, we omit the formula of the ConditionalExpression needed for retrieving the recommendations. The data extraction query filters the users and tags that have been accessed recently and match the value of the "key" Parameter. The "Select" events in the "RecommendedUsers" and "RecommendedTags" List ViewComponents allow the user to pick a search keyword from the recommended ones and perform the search with that.

The user can bypass the recommendations and perform the search directly by submitting a keyword using the "Search" event. In this case, the entered keyword is used to extract the full list of matching users (or tags) displayed in a List ViewComponent ("UserList" or "TagList"). From the "UserList" and "TagList" ViewComponents, the user can select an item and access its details in the "User" and "Tag" modules, depending on the type of object selected.

Note that the value of the "key" parameter is remembered when one switches from the "User" tab to the "Tag" tab and vice versa. This behavior is supported by two NavigationFlows between the XOR sub-ViewContainers associated with a ParameterBindingGroup that represents the explicit transfer of the parameter value. This design replaces the use of landmarks, which cannot express the fact that the value of the "key" Parameter is passed from one ViewContainer to the other at every switch of the search target.

9.1.2.5 Tag module
The Tag module displays the media objects annotated by a given tag. It can be activated from various places in the interface, such as the "Home," "Comments," and "Search" ViewContainers. Figure 9.25 shows the interface presented after selecting a tag and Figure 9.26 the corresponding IFML model.

The "Tag" ModuleDefinition takes as input parameter the tag name. It comprises a XOR ViewContainer ("TaggedMedia") and a Details ViewComponent ("TagInfo") displaying the name of the tag and the number of posts associated with it. The "MediaOIDs" List ViewComponent extracts the identifiers of the media objects to display. These are passed in as input by a DataFlow to the "MediaTiled" and "MediaViewer" modules, which are displayed in alternative.

9.2 ONLINE AUCTIONS
As a second example, we illustrate the interface of an online auction site inspired by some popular web applications where people and businesses buy and sell a broad variety of goods and services from all around the world. Auctions are also held where

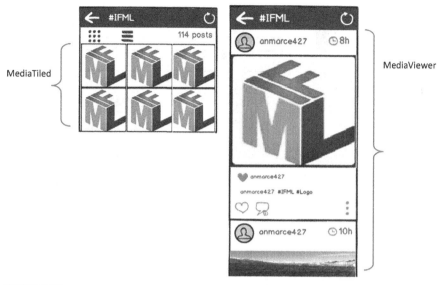

FIGURE 9.25

Interface for the media objects qualified by a tag: tiled (left) and vertically scrolled display (right).

buyers can get bargains on a wide variety of items or even find rare items. This example complements the media sharing app case with the modeling of an interfact with a different organization.

9.2.1 DOMAIN MODEL

The domain model is illustrated in the class diagram of Figure 9.27. The application deals with three principal assets: listings, users, and bids. Listings are the central objects. As such they are correlated by a number of attributes: an identifier ("id"), a title ("title"), the description of the condition of the item on sale ("itemCondition"), a descriptive text ("description"), the validity period of ("startDate" and "endDate"), the number of articles available ("availability"), the acceptance of returns ("returnsAccepted"), the location of the item ("location"), delivery options ("shipping"), sales currency ("currency"), and the guarantee terms ("guarantee"). A listing may be sold directly at a value set by the seller (entity "DirectSale" and association roles "selling" and "soldIn"). Alternatively, it may be associated with an auction (entity "Auction" and association roles "selling" and "soldIn"), characterized by an initial price ("startPrice") and the minimum price accepted by the seller ("reservePrice"). The listing belongs to a user (association roles "sales" and "seller"), can be bought or watched by another user (association roles "purchases" and "buyer," "watches" and "watchedBy"), and can be illustrated with one or more photos or videos (association roles "illustrations" and "listings").

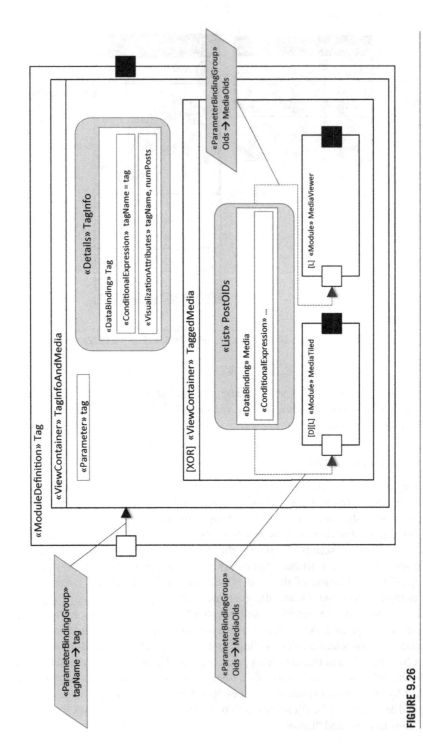

FIGURE 9.26

Model of the interface for accessing the media objects qualified by a tag.

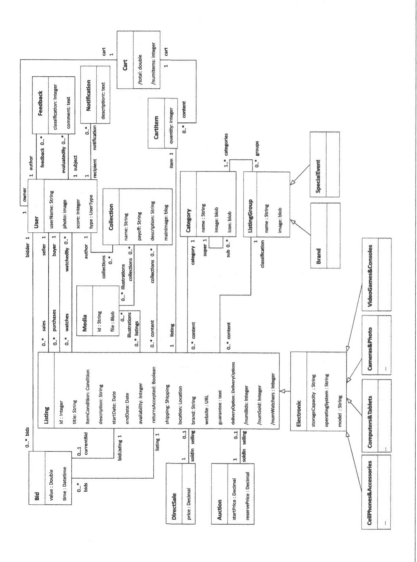

FIGURE 9.27

Domain model of the online auctions application.

Users create bids (association roles "bids" and "bidder"). Each bid has a value ("value"), is published at a given point in time ("time"), and refers to a listing (association roles "currentBid" and "listing"). Users have some profile variables (e.g., "userName" and "photo"), can publish feedback about other users— characterized by a graded mark ("classification") and a commentary ("comment")—and receive notifications (entity "Notification" with association roles "notification," and "recipient"). They are assigned a feedback score ("score"), which represent their trust as buyers or sellers.

A "Cart" entity represents the shopping trolley of a user (association roles "cart" and "owner") with its content (associations roles "content" and "cart"). Listings are classified by category (association roles "category" and "content") and have specific attributes depending on the category to which they belong. Categories are organized into a hierarchy of subcategories. They are also organized by other taxonomies, such as by brands and by special sale events. Finally, listings can be grouped into collections (association roles "content" and "category"), characterized by a name and a description, created by users (association roles "collections" and "author"), and illustrated with one or more photos or videos (association roles "illustrations" and "collections").

9.2.2 IFML MODEL

We model the online auctions web interface with the help of the IFML web extensions introduced in Chapter 7. For space reasons, we limit the example to a few significant elements of the SiteView: the home page, the search functionality, and the most important listing pages. For the search and product pages, we focus on the electronic and fashion categories and only model the most relevant interactions.

The general organization of the front end is captured by a SiteView, which comprises several pages clustered within areas. Figure 9.28 shows the "Home" page, which acts as the entry point to the application. The content-independent navigation among the pages of the front end is supported by the menus present in the header and footer of pages, partially visible in Figure 9.28 and highlighted in Figure 9.29. Such menus allow the navigation to the landmark areas and pages shown in Figure 9.30.[4]

Each link in the menu bar leads either to an individual page (e.g., "Home," "DailyDeals") or to the default page of a group of correlated pages (e.g., "Customer-Support"). Correspondingly, in the IFML model of Figure 9.30, landmarks are either individual pages or areas (i.e., groups of correlated pages). Navigating to a landmark area leads to the default page of that area. As an example, Figure 9.30 expands the content of the "Sell" area and shows the three wizard-like pages contained in it, of which the default one is the "Tell us what you're selling" page. The "Home" page of the SiteView is marked with the [H] qualifier to express that it is displayed by default when the application is accessed using its top-level address.

The SiteView also contains the "Listing Categories & Collections" area, which clusters the most important pages of the application for searching and navigating the database of listings. This area is not defined as a landmark because its pages are

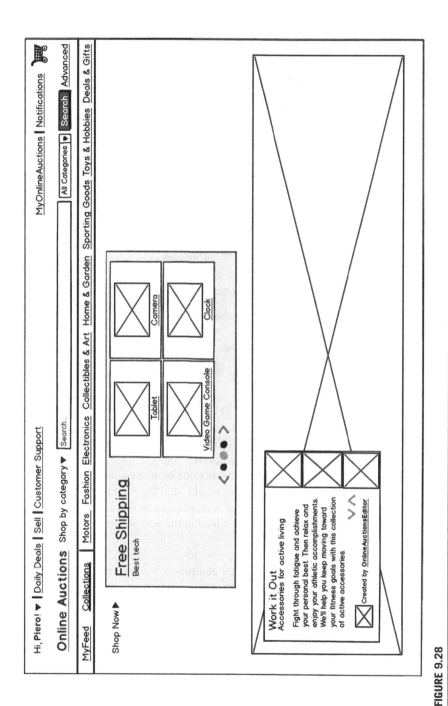

FIGURE 9.28

Home page of the online auctions web application, with landmark links and repeated view elements.

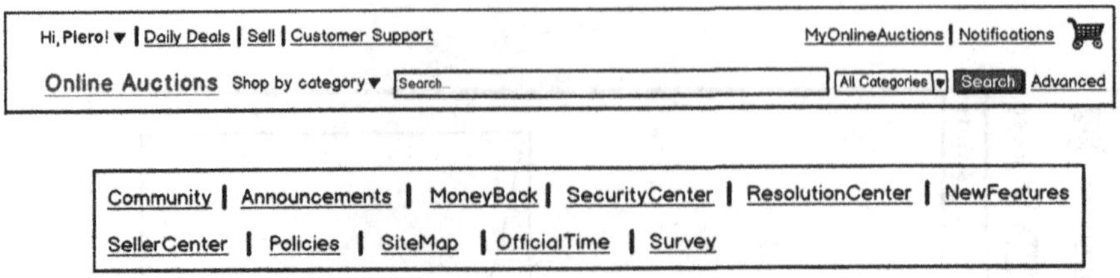

FIGURE 9.29

Landmark menus in the header (top) and footer (bottom) of the online auctions web application pages.

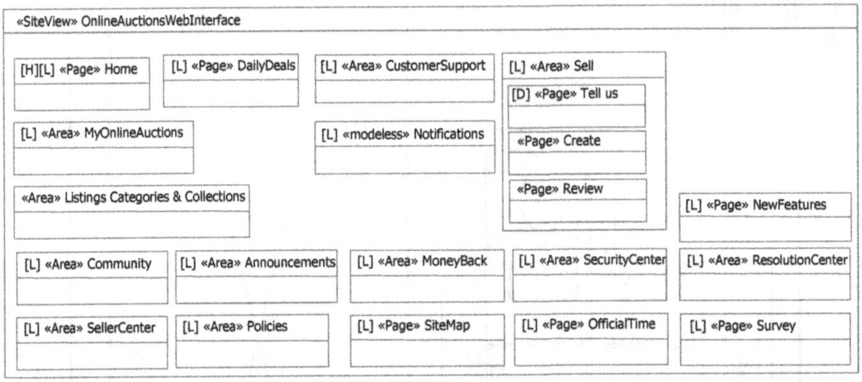

FIGURE 9.30

SiteView of the online auctions web interface, with top level landmark areas and pages.

accessed only with content-dependent navigation, either by searching or by browsing the hierarchy of goods and the available collections.

Note that the header shown in Figure 9.29 contains more elements: the personalized welcome message, the sign-in and register links, and the summary of the shopping cart content. Such view elements are not plain navigation flows but have a more elaborate behavior. They are modeled as explained in the next section.

9.2.2.1 Repeated content element

Figure 9.28 shows the "Home" page, which comprises both specific content and some view elements that appear identically in multiple pages of the SiteView. These are visible in Figure 9.29: the search bar, the sign-in and register links, the personalized welcome message, and the shopping cart item count. Such recurring elements add up to the landmark links in the navigation bar in the footer of the pages.

To avoid duplicating the model of the common view elements in all the pages where they appear, we exploit the concept of a Master Page, discussed in Chapter 8. The Master Page models the view elements common to a set of other pages

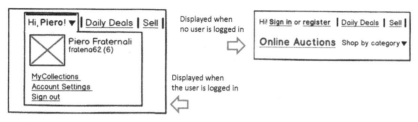

FIGURE 9.31

Personalized message, with an event opening a window of commands (left), versus sign-in and register links (right).

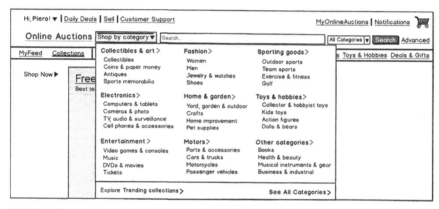

FIGURE 9.32

Modeless window opened with the "Shop by category" link.

(by default, the pages of the same Area or SiteView where the Master Page belongs). Such elements are implicitly assumed to be included in the model of each page associated with the Master Page. The recurring view elements are included in the Master Page model of Figure 9.35.

The register and sign-in links are displayed in alternative to the user's personalized welcome message. The two options are contrasted in Figure 9.31.

The personalized welcome message displays the name of the user and provides a link that opens a window with the user's name, feedback score, and photo, and links to sign out, edit account settings, and access the personal collections. The sign-in and register links, displayed when no user is logged in, lead to separate ViewContainers where the user can provide login credentials or register for the online auctions web application. The cart summary shows the number of items currently present in the trolley of a logged-in user or a fixed message if the cart is empty or the user is unknown. The header also contains a "Shop by category" link to facilitate access to the listings. It opens a window with the first two levels of the category hierarchy, visible in Figure 9.32.

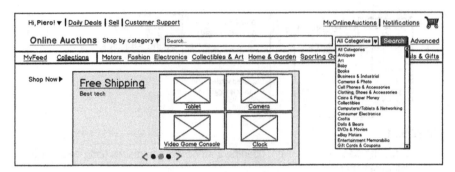

FIGURE 9.33

The category selection functionality of the search bar.

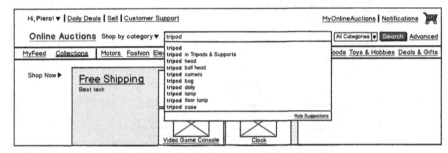

FIGURE 9.34

The auto-completion functionality of the search bar.

Listings can also be accessed by searching. The header presents a search bar enriched with an auto-completion function, which can be switched on and off explicitly, and a drop down list of categories to restrict the search to the chosen category (respectively PATTERN CS-SRCS: Search suggestions and PATTERN CS-RSRC: Restricted search, both discussed in chapter 8). These two usability widgets are shown in Figure 9.33 and in Figure 9.34.

The model of the Master Page, with all the described common features present in the header of multiple web application pages, is represented in Figure 9.35.

The personalized welcome message is modeled as a Details ViewComponent ("UserName"), which exploits the Context object recording the identity of the logged-in user (as exemplified in the PATTERN IA-LOGIN discussed in Chapter 8). The ViewComponent is visible only when the user is logged in, as expressed by the ActivationExpression associated with it. An "onMouseOver" event opens a ViewContainer with the "Sign out," "Settings," and "MyCollection" events. The "Sign out" event supports the user's logout, modeled according to PATTERN IA-LOGOUT explained in Chapter 8.

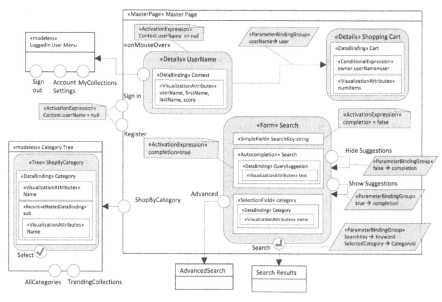

FIGURE 9.35

The model of the Master Page, representing the content that appears on multiple pages.

A DataFlow binds the identity of the user to the "Shopping Cart" Details View-Component, which displays the number of items in the user's trolley. The ConditionalExpression of the ViewComponent exploits the "owner" association role between entity User and Cart (see the domain model of Figure 9.27).

9.2.2.2 Home page

Besides the common content elements modeled in the Master Page, the Home page—shown in Figure 9.28—also contains specific view elements. These are a list of the most important categories (shown in Figure 9.36), the links to collections and feeds (also visible in Figure 9.36), the advertisement of special features (shown in Figure 9.37), a top collection (visible in Figure 9.38), a list of promoted collections, and a second list of "trending" collections (shown in Figure 9.39).

The features published on the home page are special objects. They may advertise a set of listings of a certain product or brand (e.g., Apple iPads), a limited-time sale (e.g., today's deals), or even content explaining some important aspect of the business (e.g., a money back guarantee). As visible in Figure 9.37, a feature may group several subfeatures (e.g., several groups of correlated listings). In the domain model, features can be represented as composite objects, as shown in Figure 9.40.

The domain model specifies that a feature is a composite object with one or more subfeatures (the minimum cardinality of the association role "components" is one).

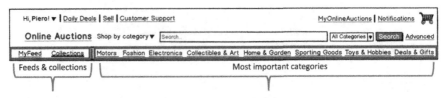

FIGURE 9.36

The list of most important categories in the home page and the links to feeds and collections.

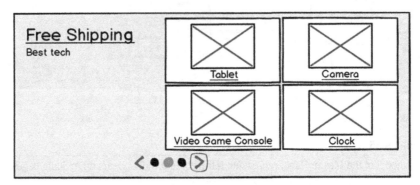

FIGURE 9.37

Special features, shown in a scrollable list.

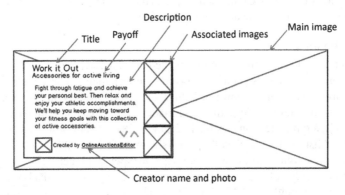

FIGURE 9.38

Top collection of the day, shown individually.

Each feature (and subfeature) has an image, a title, a description, and a link storing the address of the web page where the content of the feature is published.

Figure 9.41 shows the IFML model of the home page. This is a typical example of the use of the access subschema of the domain model for indexing the content of

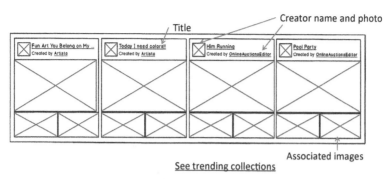

FIGURE 9.39

Home page collections, shown as a list, and a link to access all the trending collections (bottom).

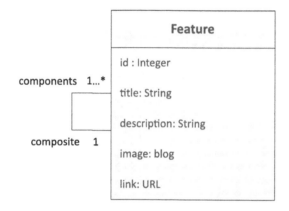

FIGURE 9.40

Domain model extended to represent features.

a large application (discussed in chapter 3). The home page essentially contains view elements that publish the content of categorizing classes and specialized subclasses. The "MainCategories" List ViewComponent models the menu of the most important categories (visible in Figure 9.36). This is the starting point of a hierarchical navigation toward the listings of interest, which are described next. The home page also contains three sub-ViewContainers ("Top collection," "Promoted Collections," and "Trending Collections"), each containing an instance of the "Collections" reusable module (modeled in Figure 9.42).

The "Collections" module publishes the essential information about one or more collections. It is instantiated in the home page with three distinct parameter bindings that identify different groups of collections. The "type" attribute of the "Collection" entity defines a subclass consisting of all the objects with a given value of the attribute. The module is also reused with another parameter binding in the "AllTrending"

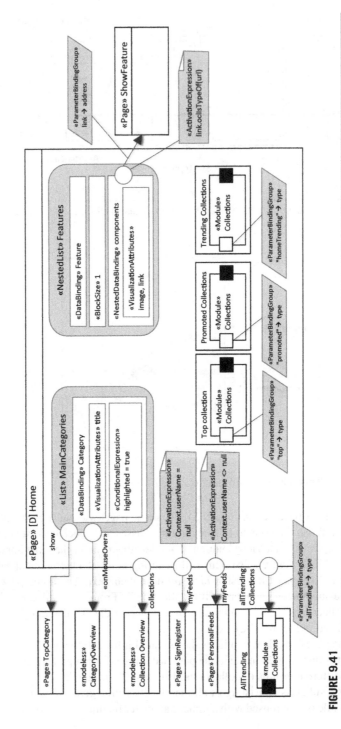

FIGURE 9.41

IFML model of the home page.

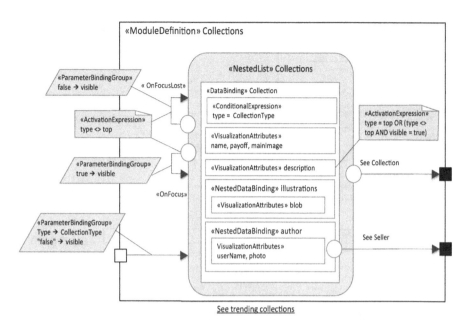

FIGURE 9.42

The "Collections" reusable module.

ViewContainer, which is accessed by means of the "allTrendingCollection" event, implemented as the link visible at the bottom of Figure 9.39.

The model of the "Collections" module is illustrated in Figure 9.42. It comprises a NestedList ViewComponent bound to the entity "Collection." The actual objects displayed depend on the input parameter "type," which is used in the ActivationExpression of the NestedList to select one or more collections of the given type. For each matching collection, the name, payoff, and main image are shown. Two nested data bindings also publish the name and photo of the creator and the other images associated with the collection (see the rendition of one collection in Figure 9.38 and of multiple collections in Figure 9.39). When the type is "top," which identifies only one collection, the description is also displayed. Otherwise, two events («onFocus» and «OnFocusLost») toggle the visibility of the description.

9.2.2.3 Category pages

On the home page, the menu of the most important categories (shown in Figure 9.36) allows two different hierarchical navigation paths toward the listings of interest.

When the user hovers on a category name in the home page menu of Figure 9.36, a modeless window ("CategoryOverview") appears (see Figure 9.43), which offers an overview of that category.

The "CategoryOverview" ViewContainer displays an illustrative image and two lists of significant subcategories of the selected category (labeled "Top categories" and "Shop for" in Figure 9.43). Selecting one subcategory leads to the page of that

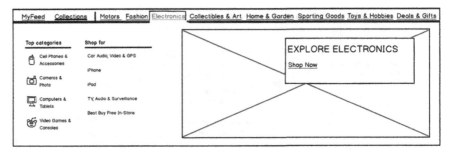

FIGURE 9.43

The top category overview page.

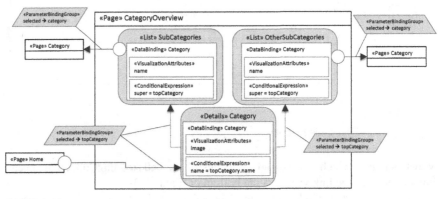

FIGURE 9.44

Model of the top category overview page.

category. Figure 9.44 shows the model of the "CategoryOverview" page, accessed from the "MainCategories" List ViewComponent in the home page.

The second navigation path is activated by clicking on the category name in the home page menu. This event causes the display of the page of the selected category, as exemplified in Figure 9.45.

The model of the "Category" page is shown in Figure 9.46.

The model comprises a Details ViewComponent for displaying the category name, accompanied by a number of List ViewComponents that publish content depending on the current category. Selecting an item from one of the lists permits the user to proceed with the navigation within the category by focusing on its events, brands, special features, subcategories, and listing groups. By contrast, the "PeerCategories" ViewComponent allows the exploitation of other "sibling" categories (i.e., children of the same super-category of the one displayed). Finally, the "Category" page also contains an instance of the PATTERN CN-BREAD discussed in chapter 8: a bread-crumb ViewComponent "Categories" is defined over the (recursive) association between categories and subcategories, which is rendered as the trail of breadcrumb links visible in Figure 9.45.

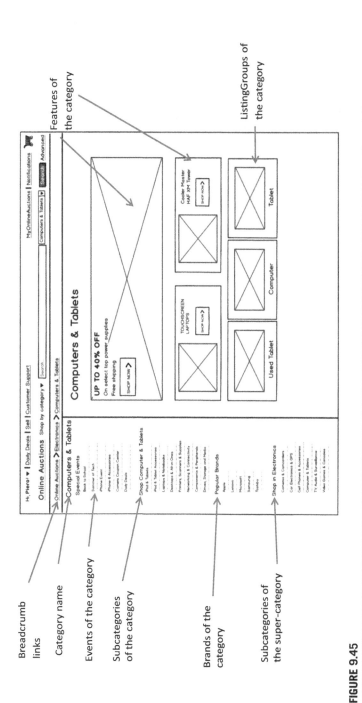

FIGURE 9.45

Category page for computers and tablets.

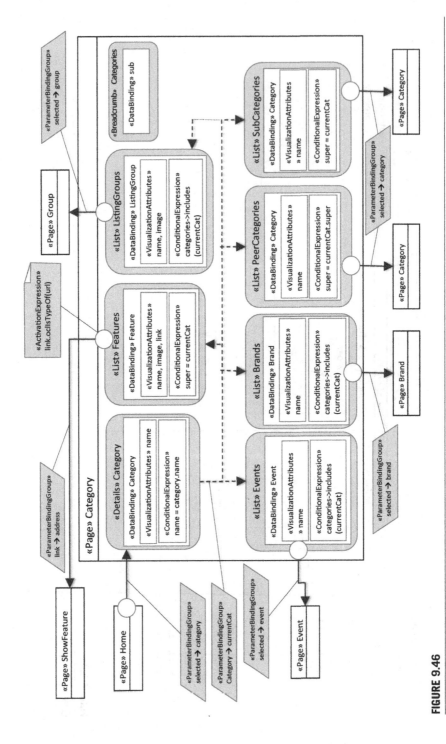

FIGURE 9.46

Model of the "Category" page.

9.2.2.4 Search results

As an alternative to the hierarchical navigation along the category taxonomy, the user can locate a listing by performing a keyword search using the input box at the top of the home page. After submitting the keyword(s), the listings with a matching name or description are presented, as shown in Figure 9.47.

The search result page contains the listings returned in response to the query. The list of results is dynamically sortable according to multiple criteria (relevance, price, distance, and expiry).

The page contains an instance of the faceted search pattern (PATTERN CS-FSR: faceted search), discussed in chapter 8. The left column and the three links at the top of the result list present a set of facets that the user can select to restrict the result list. The facets include the hierarchy of the categories where the matched listings belong, the price range, the sale formats (displayed in the left column and in the links above the list), the locations, the delivery options, and other refinements. The count of the relevant results is displayed, both for the entire result set and for the number of objects that possess a given value of each facet. The search suggestions pattern (PATTERN CS-SRCS: search suggestions) is also exploited, using a variant in which the suggested keywords are listed as links below the search box rather than used to build

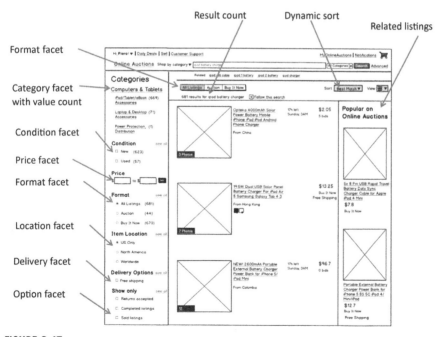

FIGURE 9.47

Search result page for the keywords "iPad battery recharger."

an input auto-completion pattern. The page also contains a number of recommended listings related to the user's query.

For brevity, we do not model some of the other features of the search result page, including the switch between the list view of Figure 9.47 and a tiled view, and the customization of the result display options (number of objects per page, shown attributes).

Figure 9.48 shows the model of the "Search Results" page. The design is based on the faceted search pattern, which relies on the retrieval and caching of the search results and of collateral information about them, such as the result count, the values of the facets (in this case, the attribute values of the found listings and the associated object count), and the queries correlated to the current search keywords. The results of the query are represented by a set of additional entities in the domain model. The entity "ListingResult" identifies the instances of the "Listing" entity that satisfy the query. It has a "count" static attribute that represents the number of matching result. Entities "CategoryResult," "Format," "Condition," "Location," Delivery," and "Options" represents the values of attributes or the associated category objects that are found in the relevant listings, which can be used as facets. Each value of a facet is accompanied by the attribute count of the objects that possess that value. Entity "RelatedQuery" displays queries (i.e., set of keywords) that are similar to the submitted query.

The facets are published on the page thought suitable ViewComponents that let the user select or input values and thus restrict the visualized results to those that match the specified constraints.

The faceted search pattern is at the core of the model in Figure 9.48. The "Listing" ViewComponent displays the result set. It is a dynamically sorted, scrollable list (these extensions are illustrated in chapter 7) that shows the listings that match the user's query and satisfy the current restrictions. The block size is variable, with a default of fifty, which can be overridden by the user activating the "View options" event and its associated window (not shown).

The restrictions are specified by selecting the facet values from the List View-Components "Format" (values: "AllListings," "Auction," "BuyItNow"), "Condition" (values: "New," "Used"), "Location" (values: "onlineauctions.com" and geographical areas), "Delivery" (value: "free shipping"), and "Options" (values: "Returns accepted," "Completed," "Sold"). The price facet is represented by a Form ViewComponent because the user can input any value rather than selecting from a list of precomputed values. For brevity, we show the DataBinding and the VisualizationAttributes for only the "Format" component. The other List View-Components are similar, and the "Form" view component comprises two Simple-Field elements.

The categories to which the results belong along with their nesting are represented by the "Categories" Tree ViewComponent (described in chapter 7), which has a DataBinding with the "CategoryResult" entity and the "sub" association describing the recursive nesting between a category and its subcategories.

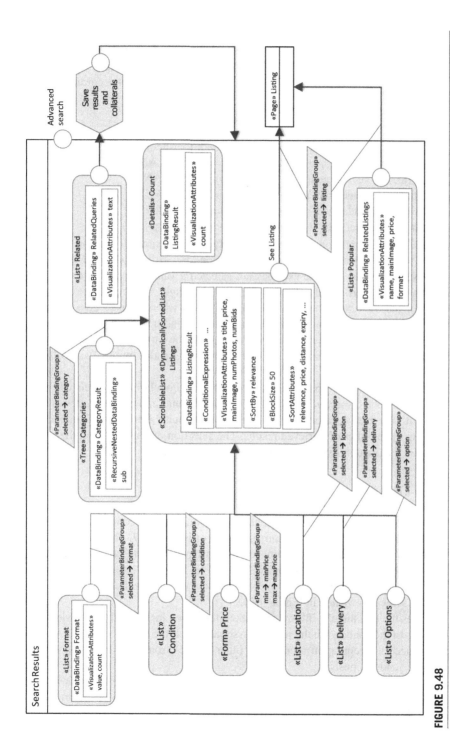

FIGURE 9.48

Model of the "Search Result" page.

The DataBinding of the "Listing" ViewComponent specifies that the component publishes content from the entity that represents the original query results ("Listing-Result"). The ConditionalExpression exploits the facet values provided by the user and restricts the instances shown in the "Listing" ViewComponent accordingly. The condition is:

(category.oclIsUndefined() OR self.category=category) AND
(format="AllListings" OR self.PurchaseFormat=format) AND
(itemCond.oclIsUndefined() OR self.itemCondition=itemCond) AND
(maxPrice.oclIsUndefined() OR self.price<=maxPrice) AND
(minPrice.oclIsUndefined() OR self.price>=minPrice) AND
(location.oclIsUndefined() OR self.location=location) AND
(delivery.oclIsUndefined() OR self.delivery=delivery) AND
(option.oclIsUndefined() OR self->options->includes(option))

The ConditionalExpression tests for the nullity of each parameter or for the facet value to be equal to or included in the corresponding attribute value of the result listing. Nullity means that the user has not selected a value for the facet. The sale format is handled differently. The explicit "All Listings" value expresses the "no choice" of the user instead of the null value implied when the user does not provide a constraint. The parameters mentioned in the ConditionalExpression are conveyed by the DataBinding associated with the navigation from the ViewComponents "Format," "Condition," "Price," "Location," "Delivery," and "Options," as visible in Figure 9.48.

The "Search Results" page also comprises the "Popular" and "Related" List ViewComponents, respectively displaying popular listings and previous queries correlated with the user's search. It also includes the "Count" Detail ViewComponent, publishing the number of retrieved results. The selection of a listing from the result set or from the popular listings yields to the "Listing" page.

9.2.2.5 Listings

When the user selects a listing, the page shown in Figure 9.49 is displayed. The page content is centered on the information about the listing, which comprises the values of the attributes mentioned in the domain model of Figure 9.27. The article is illustrated by an interactive gallery of images. Hovering with the mouse on one image thumbnail changes the currently highlighted image. Hovering on the current image zooms in, and clicking on it opens a modal window with the entire gallery enlarged to the full screen, as visible in Figure 9.50.

Besides the list, there is information about the seller, including links to view the full details of the vendor, see the reputation score, access the history of user feedback that produced the reputation score, view other articles from the same vendor, and follow the vendor's posts.

If the sale format is an auction, the current bid is put in evidence and a form with a single input field allows the user to enter an offer (as in the case of the article in Figure 9.49).

Breadcrumbs

Current bid

Bid input

Back link

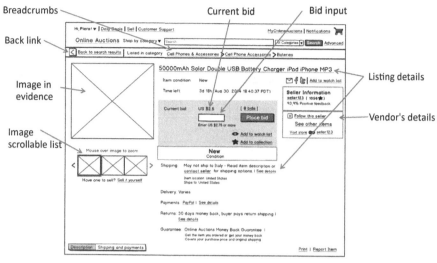

Listing details

Image in evidence

Vendor's details

Image scrollable list

FIGURE 9.49

The "Listing" page.

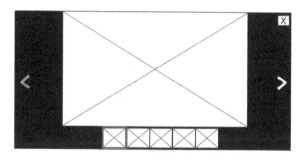

FIGURE 9.50

Enlarged image gallery.

If the sale format is "BuyItNow," the page publishes the direct sale price instead of the current bid and a form with an input field with two buttons: one for adding the item to the shopping cart and one for proceeding immediately to the purchase. Instances when both formats are associated with the same listing are also possible. In such cases, both types of forms are displayed. Figure 9.51 contrasts the interfaces for the three cases.

The model of the "Listing" page is shown in Figure 9.52.

The central element of the page is the "Listing" Details ViewComponent, which receives the identity of the listing to display as an input parameter ("currentListing") associated with the NavigationFlow used to access the page (e.g., the one coming from the result set of the search, modeled in Figure 9.48).

Auction format

Direct sale format

Mixed format

FIGURE 9.51

The three different sale formats: auction, direct sale ("BuyItNow"), and mixed.

The "Listing" Details ViewComponent has a set of VisualizationAttributes that includes the most relevant properties of the listing, which are identified in the domain model of Figure 9.27. In addition to the generic attributes available for each type of listing, the page also publishes time-specific information that depends on the category of listing. For brevity, we omit this feature, which can be represented with a set of Details ViewComponents (one for each category that requires specific attributes) and suitable ActivationExpressions that condition the display of the Details View-Components to the actual category of the listing.

The "Vendor" Details ViewComponent displays the information about the seller of the listing, identified with the ParameterBinding id→currentListing and the ConditionalExpression built on the "sales" association role between the "User" and the "Listing" entities: Self.sales->includes(currentListing). Suitable events permit the user to access further information on the seller on separate pages or to subscribe to the vendor's posts.

The purchase of the item is supported by the "Buy" Form, the "LastBid" and "SalePrice" ViewComponents ,and their associated fields, visualization attributes, and events. Two ActivationExpressions are used to discriminate the sale format and enable only the fields, attributes, and events relevant for the sale type.

The images of the article on sale are published in a scrollable list of thumbnails, five by five. The PATTERN CN-DEF: default selection, introduced in chapter 5, is exploited. It anticipates the interaction of the user (i.e., moving the mouse over one of the thumbnails) and displays one default image (see Figure 9.49). An event

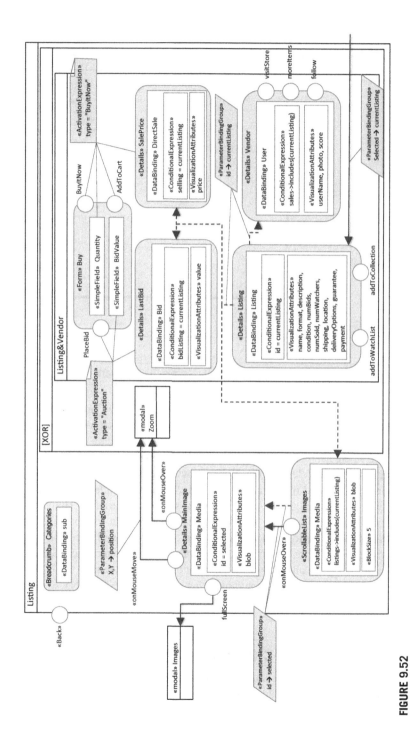

FIGURE 9.52

Model of the "listing" page.

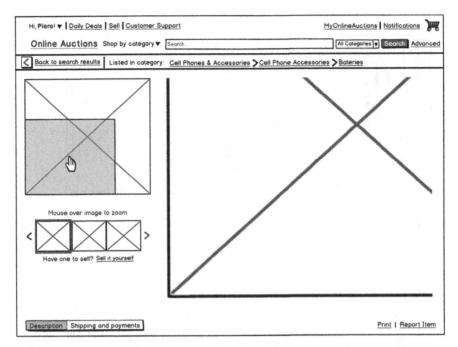

FIGURE 9.53

Overlay of the image zoom onto the page area that displays the listing and vendor details.

("fullScreen"), activated with a click from the "MainImage" ViewComponent, opens the full-screen image gallery shown in Figure 9.50. The "onMouseOver" event in the main image opens a zoom and pan window, which is superimposed on the same region of the interface where the listing and vendor details are shown, as visible in Figure 9.53.

This behavior is modeled by the XOR ViewContainer, which includes sub-ViewContainers visualized in alternative. "Listing&Vendor" displays the details of the listing and of the seller, as well as the form for submitting an offer. The "Zoom" ViewContainer comprises a single ViewComponent (not shown for space reasons) bound to the "Media" entity, which displays the enlargement of the image. The "onMouseMove" event in the "MainImage" ViewComponent communicates the current position of the mouse and allows the panning of the zoom area.

Finally, the "Listing" page also contains an instance of the PATTERN CN-UP: up navigation and of PATTERN CN-BREAD: breadcrumbs (introduced in chapter 7).

9.3 SUMMARY OF THE CHAPTER

In this chapter we provided two samples of realistic applications, inspired from real-world popular applications, and describes how they can be modeled in using IFML. More precisely, the chapter covered two large modeling examples: a mobile app tailored to smartphones, providing an online photo and video-sharing service that allows people to take pictures and videos, apply digital effects to them, and share them on several social networks; the second one illustrates an online auction site, inspired by some very popular web applications, where people and businesses buy and sell a broad variety of goods and even services from all around the world. Both cases are thoroughly modeled with IFML. Design patterns are applied.

END NOTES

1. More precisely, if more than six comments exist, the first and last five comments are shown. This can be modeled with two NestedDataBindings with appropriate block factors and sorting criteria.
2. The ActivationExpression in Figure 9.12 uses the "Context" variable name as a shortcut notation for accessing the properties of the Context object. PATTERN IA-OBP uses a Detail ViewComponent bound to the Context object.
3. The effect of the "Posts" event to hide the user's details can be represented as follows: a Boolean parameter ("UserInfoVisible"), defaulting to true, is associated with the "User-Info" ViewComponent with the ActivationExpression (UserInfoVisible=true); the NavigationFlow of the "Posts" event sets the parameter to false, thus invalidating the condition and hiding the component.
4. Some links in the footer refer to separate applications and are not modeled as part of the SiteView (e.g., "About us," which leads to the corporation's site).

Implementation of applications specified with IFML

10

The usefulness of modeling an application at a high level is directly proportional to the ease of implementing the specifications. In this chapter, we discuss a few exemplary roadmaps for implementing an application specified in IFML on top of several technical platforms. The aim is to show that having a high-level model of the front end helps in the manual coding phase too, because it allows the developer to reason about the implementation strategy in a systematic way based on the abstract interface computation semantics illustrated in chapter 6.

Given the platform-independence of IFML, implementation could be illustrated for any software architecture that supports user interactivity. For space reasons, this chapter restricts the illustration to four main categories of platforms that represent a good sample of the current status of the practice: pure HTML with a template-based approach, pure HTML with a presentation framework, rich Internet applications, and mobile applications. To be concrete, the illustration is based on four specific platforms listed in Table 1.

- PHP and MySQL represent the most widespread web site development platform, hosted on so-called LAMP (Linux, Apache, MySQL, PHP) environments; we use them to illustrate the template based approach to pure HTML front-end implementation.
- Spring is one of the most popular web presentation frameworks, which allows us to illustrate a different organization of the pure HTML front end, based on the Model-View-Controller pattern.
- JavaScript is instrumental to the illustration of rich Internet applications, which evolve pure HTML front ends towards the handling of more advanced user's interactions. Specifically, we discuss the use of Asynchronous JavaScript and XML (AJAX) for managing partial interface updates and system events and JQuery for simplifying several recurrent interface programming tasks.
- Android is chosen as a representative of mobile application development with a native approach. Other approaches are also possible, including browser-based approaches (similar to the one for rich Internet applications) and cross-platform approaches (supported by such mobile development frameworks as Phonegap and Appcelerator Titanium).

Although the illustration is necessarily limited and focused on specific technologies, the general line of reasoning for mapping IFML constructs to code artifacts can be regarded as quite general. The techniques presented in this chapter could

Table 1 Summary of the Model to Implementation Mapping for Four Exemplary Platforms.

Platform Type	Template Based Pure HTML	Web Presentation Framework	Rich Internet Application	Native Mobile
Exemplary platform Application	PHP, MySQL Set of PHP templates and scripts	Spring Controller classes, model objects, business services, view templates	AJAX, jQuery HTML5 document, JavaScript functions, server-side business logic components	Android Java classes, XML configuration files, resources
ViewContainer	PHP template	Controller class, request mapping, model objects, business service, view template	HTML document	XML layout description, activity class
Nested View Container	PHP template, with HTML iframes	View template with HTML iframes and separate controllers	Nested <div> elements refreshed independently	Nested layout, with View and ViewGroup elements
Nested XOR ViewContainer	PHP template with conditional content production	ViewContainer service and View with conditional content extraction/visualization	Nested <div> elements made visible on demand	Visibility setting of view elements
Landmark	HTML (static) anchors in PHP template	HTML (static) anchors in view template	HTML anchors or JavaScript menu	Activity with intent filter for dispatching
List, Details, DataBinding, VisualizationAttributes	Select SQL query plus printout of the markup	ViewComponent service, model objects, JSP/JSTL bean content extraction tags	JavaScript function for content rendering and server-side component for data extraction	Java component extracting content and creating view elements
Form	HTML form	HTML form with Spring custom tags	HTML form	Layout with nested view elements

Select Event	HTTP GET request	HTTP GET request	HTML DOM event, processed at the client or dispatched to the server	Event and event listener
Submit event	HTTP POST request	HTTP POST request	HTML DOM event and asynchronous server request	Event and event listener
System event	Not available	Not available	WebSocket or WebRTC callback	Broadcast intent
NavigationFlow	HTML anchor or button	HTML anchor or button	JavaScript function execution after event	Intent, event listener
DataFlow	Request parameter propagation to query or other template	Request parameter propagation in ViewContainer or Action service class	Parameter passing to JavaScript function	Parameter passing from event to listener or within an intent
ParameterBinding	Request parameter propagation to query or other template	Request parameter binding to parameters of controller methods	Parameter passing to event handling JavaScript function	Data stored inside an intent object
Action	PHP script	Controller, business service	JavaScript function calling asynchronously server-side action component	Java class called by an activity
Context	Session variables	Session-scoped model objects	JavaScript global variables at the client side	Activity state variables on the client

be reformulated for other platforms of the same type. Table 1 summarizes how the essential IFML modeling concepts are mapped into the artifacts of the four platforms selected for illustration.

10.1 IMPLEMENTATION OF THE FRONT END FOR URE-HTML PAGE TEMPLATES

Dynamic web sites are a popular type of interactive application in which the front end allows users to browse content dynamically extracted from a database and perform such actions as uploading content and sending e-mails. In the simplest case, the interface browsed by the user consists of a pure HTML document, dynamically generated by a server-side program.

As an exemplary platform for illustrating pure HTML web development, we adopt the PHP server-side scripting language, which is natively coupled to the MySQL relational database. The PHP code is interpreted by a processor integrated in the web server. Most frequently, the Apache open source system is used as the HTTP engine.

The basic artifact in PHP is the *page template*, which is a document, typically encoded in HTML, with embedded instructions for extracting content dynamically from a data source and publishing it in the interface.

10.1.1 OVERVIEW OF THE VIEWCONTAINER COMPUTATION STEPS

The typical structure of a PHP web site consists of multiple page templates and corresponds in IFML to a set of independent, interlinked ViewContainers comprising ViewComponents for dynamic data publication and data entry. The computation of a ViewContainer is triggered by the user, who sends an HTTP request to the server hosting the application. Responding to the user's request entails processing a dynamic page template according to the execution steps illustrated in Figure 10.1.

In the first step, the HTTP request is analyzed to extract possible parameters, typically the values to be used in the content extraction queries. In the second step, the page template establishes a direct connection to the database and assembles and submits the queries for retrieving the content needed to populate the interface. The execution of a query may compute some parameter values needed to instantiate another query. Therefore, query processing is iterated until all the queries needed to retrieve the content are executed. Finally, when all the necessary pieces of content have been retrieved, the output is produced and returned as the HTTP response. Specifically, the dynamic content of the page typically consists of texts, images, and other elements, and hypertext links expressed as HTML anchor tags.

The translation of IFML ViewContainers and ViewComponents into PHP produces dynamic page templates with the general structure shown in Figure 10.2.

- The first step extracts from the HTTP request the parameters for computing the ViewComponents. Such parameters represent either the "fresh" values produced by the user's interaction or "history" values used to preserve past choices made by the user in previous navigations.

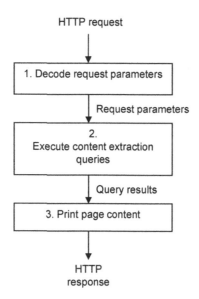

FIGURE 10.1

Computation of a dynamic page template from database content.

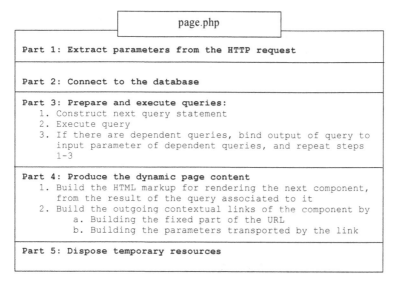

FIGURE 10.2

General schema of the PHP template implementing a page.

- The second step addresses the connection to the database, preliminary to the execution of the data binding queries necessary to fetch the content of ViewComponents. PHP has a native interface to the MySQL database and an ODBC-mediated interface to any other data store compliant to such interconnection standard.
- The third step embodies the ViewContainer execution semantics illustrated in chapter 12. It processes all the computable ViewComponents, based on the way the ViewContainer has been accessed, which corresponds to a specific parameter configuration in the HTTP request. First, the initially computable ViewComponents are determined by means of a suitable conditional statement checking the values of the request parameters, and ViewComponents data binding queries are evaluated. The output of such queries the is used as input for executing the query of other dependent ViewComponents. This part of the template must also resolve conflicts caused by ViewComponents with multiple alternative input parameter values. This requires further conditional statements for discriminating the most specific values based on the chosen conflict resolution strategy. At the end of this part of the template, all the data binding queries of the computable ViewComponents have been performed, and their results are stored in appropriate data structures from which they can be extracted to produce the dynamic portion of the HTML markup.
- The fourth step builds the HTML content of each ViewComponent, mixing the dynamically generated content with the static HTML markup to achieve the desired page layout. The construction of the ViewComponents' markup addresses two aspects: the rendition of the content and the construction of the anchors and buttons for triggering events. The latter issue requires the definition of the URL associated with the HTML hypertext reference, which typically consists of a fixed part, depending on the target ViewContainer, and a variable part with the necessary output parameters. The relevant parameters passed on the link are determined according to the navigation history preservation criteria discussed in chapter 12.
- Finally, the last step simply disposes the temporary objects used in the previous phases.

We now show progressive examples of PHP dynamic templates built according to this general scheme.

To show concretely the computation steps of Figure 10.2, we use the master detail pattern based on the domain model classes shown in Figure 10.3. For convenience, the figure also shows the mapping of the "NewsCategory" and "NewsItem" classes into persistent relational tables.

10.1.2 STANDALONE VIEWCONTAINER

Figure 10.4 shows the simplest case of a ViewContainer with dynamic content, which contains a single nonparametric ViewComponent, the "NewsCategories" List, which publishes all the news categories. In the example, we assume that each news category is denoted simply by the category name and the List is ordered by ascending category name.

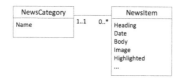

NEWSCATEGORY		
OID	NAME	DESCRIPTION

NEWSITEM							
OID	HEADING	DATE	BODY	IMAGE	HIGHLIGHTED	...	CATID

FIGURE 10.3

News and news categories domain model and equivalent relational tables.

FIGURE 10.4

ViewContainer with a single List ViewComponent.

Figure 10.5 shows the PHP page template implementing the ViewContainer of Figure 10.4.[1]

With respect to the general schema of Figure 10.2, the extraction of the parameters from the HTTP request is not needed because the "NewsCategories" List ViewComponent has no incoming NavigationFlow. Only the data binding content extraction and the production of the ViewComponent interface markup are relevant.

The page template starts by creating the connection with the MySQL database (lines 3–7). This code will remain the same in all the subsequent examples. The reference to the database connection is assigned to the PHP variable $con, which is then used for submitting the ViewComponents data binding queries. In the present example, this task is particularly simple because there is a single ViewComponent and the code of its associated query is fixed and without input parameters. Obviously, parameter propagation does not occur inside the ViewContainer, because there is only one ViewComponent. At line 9, the mysqli_query function is invoked to submit the query to the database. The function takes as argument the database connection and the SQL code of the query, and returns the query result in the form of a record set. In this example, the query is a simple SELECT statement, and the result is assigned to the PHP variable named $result. Note that no ConditionalExpression is specified in

```
1  <?php
2  // DATABASE CONNECTION
3  $con=mysqli_connect("example.com","user","pwd","my_db");
4  if (mysqli_connect_errno())
5  {
6  echo "Failed to connect to MySQL: " . mysqli_connect_error();
7  }
8  // QUERY EXECUTION
9  $result = mysqli_query($con,"SELECT NAME FROM NEWSCATEGORY ORDER BY NAME");
10 // CONTENT PRODUCTION
11 echo "<html>";
12 echo "<head>";
13 echo "<title>News Categories</title>";
14 echo "</head>";
15 echo "<body>";
16 // ViewComponent markup production
17 echo "<table>";
18 while($row = mysqli_fetch_array($result))
19 {
20  echo "<tr><td>" . $row['NAME'];
21  echo "</td></tr>";
22 }
23 echo "</table>";
24 echo "</body>";
25 echo "</html>";
26 // connection disposal
27 mysqli_close($con);
28 ?>
```

FIGURE 10.5

PHP implementation of NewsCategories page.

the List ViewComponent, and thus the SELECT statement does not include the WHERE condition and extracts from the NEWSCATEGORY table all the existing rows. The SELECT statement has an attribute list containing the NAME column, which corresponds to the VisualizationAttributes clause of the List ViewComponent, and an ORDER BY clause, which mirrors the sorting criterion (ascending by NAME) of the ViewComponent.

The production of the HTML markup starts at line 11. After some static HTML (lines 11–17), the page template contains the section for computing the dynamic content of the List ViewComponent (lines 18–22). This portion builds an HTML table with one row and one cell for each record in the result set. To construct the table, a while loop is used (lines 18–22), which halts when the mysqli_fetch_array() function returns false, meaning that there are no more rows to process. Inside the loop, an HTML row and cell are created containing the value of the NAME attribute of the current row, extracted from the PHP variable $row with the expression $row['Name']. Therefore, executing the loop produces as many HTML rows as the number of rows in the NEWSCATEGORY table. Finally, the last part of the PHP template simply prints the remaining static markup (lines 23–25) and closes the connection with the database (line 27).

The example can be generalized to ViewComponents with ConditionalExpressions. If the ViewComponent has a ConditionalExpressions, the SQL statement of the data binding query includes an appropriate WHERE clause. For example, the List ViewComponent shown in Figure 10.6 has an attribute-based ConditionalExpression,

FIGURE 10.6

List with attribute-based selector.

which retrieves only the news categories with attribute "approvalStatus" equal to 1, and corresponds to the following SQL query:

```
SELECT NAME FROM NEWSCATEGORY WHERE APPROVALSTATUS = 1 ORDER BY
NAME
```

10.1.3 NAVIGATION ACROSS VIEWCONTAINERS

The next example shows the implementation of Events and NavigationFlows, which raises two issues:

- The production of the HTML rendition of the Event triggering the Navigation-Flow in the source ViewContainer.
- The retrieval of the parameters associated with the NavigationFlow and the assignment of their values as the input of ViewComponents in the destination ViewContainer.

Figure 10.7 shows an IFML model extending the example of Figure 10.4 to a master detail pattern. The List ViewComponent is now connected to a Details View-Component defined on class "NewsCategory," placed in a distinct ViewContainer so that the selection of one element in the List opens the "CategoryDetails" ViewContainer on the selected object.

The implementation is extended in two ways. A PHP template for the "CategoryDetails" ViewContainer is introduced. This template is called by means of an HTTP request holding the identifier of the news category object to show. The template uses this parameter in the SQL query associated with the "Category" ViewComponent. The PHP template for the "Categories" ViewContainer is extended by adding one HTML anchor for each row of the dynamically built list of categories. The href attribute of each anchor tag contains a different URL, concatenating the name of the

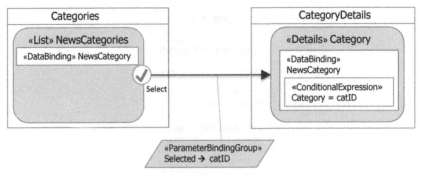

FIGURE 10.7

Two ViewContainers connected by a NavigationFlow.

```
 1  <?php
 2  // Database connection
 3  $con=mysqli_connect("example.com","user","pwd","my_db");
 4  if (mysqli_connect_errno())
 5  {
 6  echo "Failed to connect to MySQL: " . mysqli_connect_error();
 7  }
 8  // QUERY EXECUTION
 9  $result = mysqli_query($con,"SELECT NAME, OID FROM NEWSCATEGORY ORDER BY NAME");
10  // CONTENT PRODUCTION
11  echo "<html>";
12  echo "<head>";
13  echo "<title>News Categories</title>";
14  echo "</head>";
15  echo "<body>";
16  // ViewComponent markup production
17  echo "<table>";
18  while($row = mysqli_fetch_array($result))
19  {
20   echo "<tr><td><a href=\"categoryDetails.php?category=".$row['OID']."\">";
21   echo $row['NAME']."</a></td></tr>";
22  }
23  echo "</table>";
24  echo "</body>";
25  echo "</html>";
26  // connection disposal
27  mysqli_close($con);
28  ?>
```

FIGURE 10.8

PHP implementation of the "Categories" ViewContainer.

template implementing the "CategoryDetails" ViewContainer and a request parameter transporting the primary key of the object in the current row of the list.

Figure 10.8 shows the PHP template of the "Categories" ViewContainer. As a first extension, the SQL query at line 9 has been augmented to retrieve also the OID column of table NEWSCATEGORY. The OID is used at lines 20 to construct the URL associated with each row by wrapping the name of each category inside an HTML anchor (`<a>...</a>`) tag. For each row, the HTML anchor tag includes an href

```
1  <?php
2  // REQUEST PARAMETER EXTRACTION
3  $category = $_GET['category'];
4  // DATABASE CONNECTION
5  $con=mysqli_connect("example.com","user","pwd","my_db");
6  if (mysqli_connect_errno())
7  {
8  echo "Failed to connect to MySQL: " . mysqli_connect_error();
9  }
10  // QUERY PREPARATION AND EXECUTION
11 $stmt = $con->prepare('SELECT NAME,DESCRIPTION FROM NEWSCATEGORY WHERE OID=?');
12 $stmt->bind_param("i",$category);
13 $stmt->execute();
14 $result = $stmt->get_result();
15 // CONTENT PRODUCTION
16 echo "<html>";
17 echo "<head>";
18 echo "<title>News Category Details</title>";
19 echo "</head>";
20 echo "<body>";
21 // DETAILS VIEWCOMPONENT MARKUP PRODUCTION
22 echo "<table>";
23 if($row = mysqli_fetch_array($result))
24  {
25  echo "<tr><td>".$row['NAME']"</td></tr>";
26  echo "<tr><td>".$row['DESCRIPTION']"</td></tr>";
27  }
28 echo "</table>";
29 echo "</body>";
30 echo "</html>";
31 // CONNECTION DISPOSAL
32 mysqli_close($con);
33 ?>
```

FIGURE 10.9

PHP implementation of the "CategoryDetails" ViewContainer.

attribute consisting of a fixed part (categoryDetails.php?category=) and a variable part ($row['OID']). The fixed part is the file name of the template associated with the destination page (categoryDetails.php) followed by the constant part of the query string, which contains the name of the parameter (category). The variable part of the URL is built from the value of the OID column of the current row of the NEWSCATEGORY table, retrieved from the query result. Executing the template produces a table of news categories, but this time each category name is also the anchor of an HTML link.

Figure 10.9 shows the JSP code for page CategoryDetails, stored in the file named categoryDetails.php. The template demonstrates the extraction of parameters from the HTTP request and the construction of a parametric data binding query. At line 3, the value of the parameter named category is extracted from the global PHP variable named $_GET, which represents the content of a GET HTTP request, and stored in the $category PHP variable. The value fetched from the request is exactly the one appended to the URL constructed in the "Categories" ViewContainer, as shown by line 20 of Figure 10.8.

The value of the $category variable is used to prepare the data retrieval query for the "Category" Details ViewComponent. The source code of the SQL query is not fixed, as in the previous examples, because the value of the OID to use in the WHERE clause may vary depending on the selection of the user, which determines the value stored in the HTTP request. Therefore, a different technique is necessary to build the query, as shown in lines 11–14. At line 11, the connection object is used to create a so-called "prepared statement," which is a partially instantiated SQL query. In particular, the SQL query "SELECT NAME, DESCRIPTION FROM NEWSCATEGORY WHERE OID = ?" is prepared, which extracts the name and description of the news category identified by the OID passed as a parameter to the query. The value of the OID is represented by the question mark in the source code of the query. The prepared statement is incomplete and must be bound to an actual parameter value before execution. This is done at line 12, where the instruction $stmt->bind_param("i",$category) supplies the prepared statement object $stmt with the value of the $category variable, as a parameter of type integer ("i"). After this instruction, the prepared statement is ready to execute. This is done at line 13, and its result is bound to variable $result at line 14.

The rest of the code is devoted to content production. The result of the query is the single news category having the specified OID, which is used at lines 22–28 to insert the category name and description into an HTML table. Note that a real example would include error-checking code, such as code to cope with HTTP requests that do not provide a value for the OID parameter or with the failure of the SQL query. For brevity, we will skip error-checking and exception-handling code in the examples discussed in this chapter.

10.1.4 NAVIGATION WITHIN THE SAME VIEWCONTAINER

The next example shows the implementation of a ViewContainer containing multiple ViewComponents connected by NavigationFlows.

Figure 10.10 shows a master detail pattern in a single ViewContainer, which comprises a List ViewComponent connected to a Details ViewComponent by a

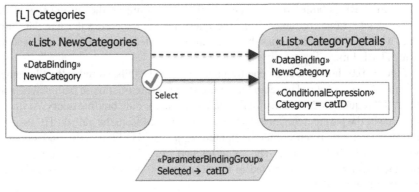

FIGURE 10.10

Master detail pattern contained within a single ViewContainer.

NavigationFlow and by a DataFlow that expresses the CN-DEF default selection pattern. The presence of intra-ViewContainer NavigationFlows impacts the implementation in three ways:

- The ViewContainer can be accessed in more than one way: by a noncontextual navigation [2] and by using an intra-ViewContainer contextual NavigationFlow. This implies that the ViewContainer can be called with different HTTP requests that include different parameters. The template must extract the parameters from the request and check their values to understand which ViewComponents are initially computable. Computation propagation then proceeds (as explained in chapter 12) from the initially computable ViewComponents to their dependent ones.
- The destination ViewComponent of the NavigationFlow may be computed with alternative input values, either from a fresh value transported in the HTTP request by the navigation of the intra-ViewContainer NavigationFlow, or from the default value supplied by the ViewComponent linked to it. The template must contain a suitable conditional statement for deciding which input to use.
- To cope with the fact that the HTTP request refreshes the entire content of the page, the HTML construction part must build the anchor tag for an intra-ViewContainer NavigationFlow by appending to it all the parameters required to recompute the ViewContainer, which may comprise both the fresh values determined by the user's selection and the "history" values necessary to restore the content of some ViewComponent to the value preceding the navigation.

The PHP template of Figure 10.11 starts from the decoding of the HTTP request parameter, which is the OID of the category required by the Category Details View-Component. At line 6, the `category` parameter is extracted from the request and assigned to the variable named `$category`. In contrast to the previous example, this variable may contain either a null value or a valid object identifier, depending on the way the page is accessed. If the page is accessed noncontextually, the parameter is null. If the page is accessed by navigating the intra-ViewContainer flow, the parameter stores the identifier of the selected news category to be displayed in the Details ViewComponent.

In this example, the interaction with the database is implemented using the PHP Data Object (PDO) interface, an alternative higher-level interface designed to support better portability across different relational systems.

The List ViewComponent is nonparametric, and its query can be executed irrespective of any input, whereas the Details ViewComponent depends on the user's selection or on the default value of the list. Therefore, the query for the List View-Component is executed first, and the query of the Details ViewComponent follows.

At lines 17–20, the template contains the preparation and execution of the query for extracting the data binding instances of the List ViewComponent. In contrast to the previous examples, all rows are fetched at once into an array (line 20). This is required because the first row of the result set of the List ViewComponent may be accessed twice: once for getting the OID to be used as default input for the Details

```
1  <?php
2  // REQUEST PARAMETER EXTRACTION
3  $category = null;
4  if (isset($_GET['category']))
5  {
6    $category = $_GET['category'];
7  }
8  // Database connection
9  try {
10     $con=new PDO('mysql:host=localhost;dbname=my_db', 'root', 'root');
11 }
12 catch (PDOException $e)
13 {
14 echo "Failed to connect to MySQL: " . $e->getMessage();
15 }
16 // CONTENT EXTRACTION: LIST VIEW COMPONENT
17 $q1 = 'SELECT OID, NAME FROM NEWSCATEGORY ORDER BY NAME';
18 $stmt = $con->prepare($q1, array(PDO::ATTR_CURSOR => PDO::CURSOR_SCROLL));
19 $stmt->execute();
20 $cats = $stmt->fetchAll();
21 // CONTEXT PROPAGATION TO DATA UNIT QUERY
22 if ($category == null) { // NO USER'S CHOICE, NONCONTEXTUAL ACCESS
23   $category = $cats[0]['OID']; // FETCH ALL ROWS INTO AN ARRAY
24 }
25 // CONTENT EXTRACTION: DETAILS VIEW COMPONENT
26 $q2 = 'SELECT NAME, DESCRIPTION FROM NEWSCATEGORY WHERE OID = ?';
27 $stmt2 = $con->prepare($q2);
28 $stmt2->bindParam(1,$category,PDO::PARAM_INT);
29 $stmt2->execute();
30 // CONTENT PRODUCTION
31 echo "<html>";
32 echo "<head>";
33 echo "<title>News Categories</title>";
34 echo "</head>";
35 echo "<body>";
36 // LIST VIEWCOMPONENT MARKUP PRODUCTION
37 echo "<table>";
38 foreach($cats as $cat)
39 {
40   echo "<tr><td>".$cat['NAME']."</td></tr>";
41 }
42 echo "</table>";
43 // DETAILS VIEWCOMPONENT MARKUP PRODUCTION
44 echo "<table>";
45 $row2 = $stmt2->fetch();
46 echo "<tr><td>".$row2['NAME']."</td></tr>";
47 echo "<tr><td>".$row2['DESCRIPTION']."</td></tr>";
48 echo "</table>";
49 echo "</body>";
50 echo "</html>";
51 // connection disposal
52 $con=null;
53 ?>
```

FIGURE 10.11

PHP implementation of page "Categories" and "NewsDetails" ViewComponents in a single ViewContainer.

ViewComponent (line 23) and once for printing the HTML rendition of the List ViewComponent (lines 37–42).

After the List ViewComponent query is executed, it is the turn of the Details View-Component. Before preparing the query, the test at line 22 is performed to ensure that the most specific value is used to build the component. If the ViewContainer has been accessed noncontextually, the value of $category variable is null and default parameter propagation from the List to the Details must take place: the first row of the result of the List is extracted from the array to get a default input, and the value of the OID column is assigned to the $category variable (line 23). If the ViewContainer has been accessed by navigating the intra-ViewContainer flow, the value of the $category variable is not null, and the default context propagation is skipped. In this case, the OID value that comes from the HTTP request is used. After this test, the Details query is executed, using as parameter the most specific value stored in the $category variable (line 26–29).

The HTML code is then built using the results of the two queries. For simplicity, we construct just two tables: one for the List and one for the Details. In a real example, extra HTML formatting would be needed to obtain a more aesthetic result.

The code of Figure 10.11 can also be adapted to cope with an intra-ViewContainer NavigationFlow without a default object selection policy. In this case, default param-eter propagation does not apply. As a consequence, when the ViewContainer is accessed noncontextually, the Details query is not executed nor its content is shown. To skip the construction of the Details ViewComponent, it is sufficient to condition the execution of the query at lines 26–29 and the production of the HTML code at lines 44–48 with the following test: if ($category != null), which ensures that the intra-ViewContainer flow has been navigated.

10.1.5 **FORMS**

The search pattern shown in Figure 10.12 help illustrate the implementation of Form ViewComponents and demonstrates a second way of building NavigationFlows based on HTML forms and on the HTTP POST method.

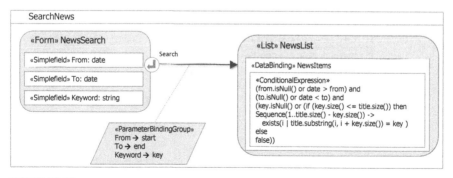

FIGURE 10.12

Search pattern.

Forms are different from List and Details ViewComponent for two reasons:

- They do not have an associated content retrieval query but are directly translated into an HTML form in the body of the template[3].
- Their outgoing NavigationFlow, which transports as parameters the values entered by users, is implemented using the action attribute and submit button of an HTML form instead of an anchor tag. The parameters transported by the NavigationFlow are typically submitted using the HTTP POST method instead of the default GET method. The predefined HTTP $post variable can be exploited to extract input parameters from the POST request.

The code implementing the search pattern of Figure 10.12 is shown in Figure 10.13. At lines 2–6, the PHP $_POST variable is exploited to extract the values entered by the user, which are communicated from the front end as a POST request submitted

```
1  <?php
2  $keyword = null;
3  if (isset($_POST['keyword']))
4  // REQUEST PARAMETER EXTRACTION
5  {
6    $keyword = $_POST['keyword'];
7  }
8  $con = mysqli_connect("example.com","user","pwd","my_db");
9  // DATABASE CONNECTION
10 if (mysqli_connect_errno())
11 {
12   echo "Failed to connect to MySQL: " . mysqli_connect_error();
13 }
14 if (($keyword != null) && $keyword!=""){
15 // PARAMETER PROPAGATION AND QUERY EXECUTION
16     $stmt = $con->prepare(
17         'SELECT HEADING, BODY FROM NEWSITEM WHERE BODY LIKE ?');
18 $keyword_like = "%".$keyword."%";
19 $stmt->bind_param("s",$keyword_like);
20 $stmt->execute();
21 $result = $stmt->get_result();
22 }
23 echo "<html>";
24 echo "<head>";
25 echo "<title>News Search</title>";
26 echo "</head>";
27 echo "<body>";
28 echo "Enter a search keyword: </br>";
29 // CONTENT PRODUCTION: FORM
30 echo "<form method=\"POST\" action=\"searchNews.php\">";
31 echo "Keyword: <input type=\"text\" name=\"keyword\">";
32 echo "</br>";
33 echo "<input type=\"submit\" name=\"submit\">";
34 echo "</form>";
35 // CONTENT PRODUCTION: LIST
36 if (($keyword != null) && $keyword != "") {
37   echo "<table>";
38   while (($row = mysqli_fetch_array($result)) {
39     echo "<tr>";
40     echo "<td>".$row['HEADING']."</td>";
41     echo "<td>".$row['BODY']."</td>";
42     echo "</tr>";
43   }
44   echo "</table>";
45 }
46 echo "</body>";
47 echo "</html>";
48 // CONNECTION DISPOSAL
49 mysqli_close($con);
50 ?>
```

FIGURE 10.13

PHP implementation of the basic search pattern.

with an HTML form. The subsequent part of the template contains the query preparation and execution code. The only ViewComponent requiring a data binding query is the List, which has a ConditionalExpression with one input parameter. The code at lines 12–19 wraps the data binding query with a test for checking if the ViewComponent is computable: the test verifies that there is a keyword submitted by the user and is not the empty string. If the test succeeds, the List data binding query is instantiated and executed. If the ViewContainer has been accessed noncontextually or the user has left the input field blank, the test fails and the query is skipped.

The content production part follows. First, the Form is rendered as an HTML form (lines 27–31), which contains an `<input>` tag of type text, named `keyword`. The SubmitEvent and the outgoing NavigationFlow of the Form are implemented as the form's `action` attribute (line 27), which specifies the destination of the Navigation-Flow, and as an `<input>` tag of type `submit` (line 30), which is rendered as a confirmation button and implements the SubmitEvent. When the user presses the button, the input of the keyword field is packaged as a request parameter named `keyword`, and the ViewContainer is reinvoked. After the HTML form is the code for constructing the markup of the List ViewComponent from the results of the corresponding SQL query. Note that the loop for constructing the HTML table is not entered if the page has been accessed noncontextually or with a null keyword, because in such case no query was executed and there are no results to display. In a real example, a further test would be needed in the HTML production part to distinguish the case in which the query is executed but no results are found. An appropriate message would then be shown to the user.

The extension to more complex search forms and ConditionalExpressions is straightforward. The HTML form is extended with as many fields as required, and the `WHERE` clause of the SQL query of the List ViewComponent is expanded with suitable subclauses using the values of the input fields in comparison predicates.

10.1.6 LANDMARKS AND NESTED VIEWCONTAINERS

Landmarks do not impact implementation in a substantial way because they are merely devices for noncontextual navigation. In practice, the references to landmarks are implemented simply by inserting the appropriate noncontextual links in each template of the front end, using HTML anchor tags.

Conjunctive sub-ViewContainers show various pieces of content *in different regions of the interface* and can be realized with HTML inline frames. The PHP page template is divided into as many independent files as the number of conjunctive subpages. Then a master template is built, to put the frames together.

Disjunctive sub-ViewContainers show alternative pieces of content *in the same region of the interface*, which requires the PHP template code to enable alternative portions of content selectively. As an example, consider the page of Figure 10.14, in which the "Category" Details ViewComponent displays a news category, from which it is possible to visualize either the list of all news of the category or a list of only the most recent news but with the full details of each piece of news. The "RecentNews"

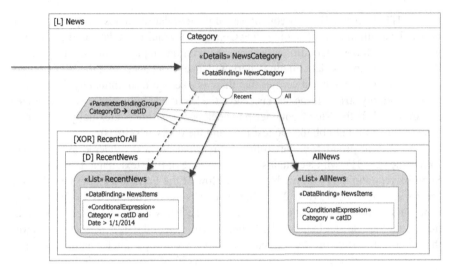

FIGURE 10.14

Example of disjunctive ViewContainers.

sub-ViewContainer is the default one, shown when the "News" ViewContainer is accessed for the first time. Implementing this pattern requires a conditional statement in the template code to establish which sub-ViewContainer must be processed. The ViewContainer to display is the default one if the enclosing ViewContainer is accessed from another part of the interface. Otherwise, the one targeted by the flow explicitly navigated by the user is shown. To ease the implementation of such conditional statements, every NavigationFlow pointing to an alternative ViewContainer may comprise one extra URL parameter (e.g., `target`) that explicitly carries the name of the alternative ViewContainer to display.

The code in Figure 10.15 shows this implementation technique at work.

At lines 3–4, the HTTP request is analyzed to extract the two possible parameters: the OID of the category to display and the name of the ViewContainer that has been accessed. Then, after connecting to the database and performing the SQL query for the Details ViewComponent (line 5–16), a test determines which alternative View-Container is required (line 18). If the nondefault alternative page ("AllNews") is requested, a SQL query is composed to retrieve the content of the "AllNews" List, that is (i.e., the headings of all the news items of the input category [lines 19–20]). Otherwise, a SQL query is composed to retrieve the content of the "RecentNews" List (i.e., the heading and body of the news items issued after 1/1/2014 [lines 21–22]). The query is executed at lines 23–24.

In the HTML production part of the template, first the Details markup is built from the result of the SQL query (lines 28–38). After the name and the description of the category, one HTML anchor is inserted for each of the alternative ViewContainers, distinguished by the value of the `target` parameter, which can be `all` or `recent` (lines 33–36).

```php
1   <?php
2   // REQUEST PARAMETER EXTRACTION
3   $category = $_GET['category'];
4   $target = $_GET['target'];
5   // DATABASE CONNECTION
6   $con=mysqli_connect("example.com","user","pwd","my_db");
7   if (mysqli_connect_errno())
8   {
9     echo "Failed to connect to MySQL: " . mysqli_connect_error();
10  }
11  // QUERY PREPARATION AND EXECUTION: DETAILS
12  $stmt = con->prepare(
13      'SELECT NAME, DESCRIPTION, OID FROM NEWSCATEGORY WHERE OID = ?');
14  $stmt->bind_param("i",$category);
15  $stmt->execute();
16  $result = $stmt->get_result();
17  // CONDITIONAL QUERY PREPARATION AND EXECUTION
18  if ($target = "all")
19      $stmt2 = con->prepare(
20      'SELECT HEADING FROM NEWSITEM WHERE CATEGORYOID = ? ');
21  else $stmt2 = con->prepare('SELECT HEADING, BODY FROM
22      NEWSITEM WHERE NEWSDATE > '1/1/2014' AND CATEGORYOID = ? ');
23  $stmt2->bind_param("i",$category);
24  $result2 = $stmt2->get_result();
25  echo "<html>"; // CONTENT PRODUCTION
26  echo "<head> <title>News </title> </head>";
27  echo "<body>";
28  if ($row = mysqli_fetch_array($result)) { //CONTENT PRODUCTION: DETAILS
29  echo "<table>";
30  echo  "<tr><td> Name </td><td>".$row['Name']."</td></tr>";
31  echo  "<tr><td> Description </td> <td>".$row['Description']."</td></tr>";
32  echo  "<tr><td colspan="2"><a href=\"
33          newsPage.php?target=recent&category=".$row['OID']."\">";
34  echo                      "Recent News</a></td></tr>";
35  echo  "<tr><td colspan="2"><a href=\"
36          newsPage.php?target=all&category=".$row['OID']."\">"
37  echo                      "All News</a></td></tr>";
38  echo "</table>"; }
39  if ($target="all"){
40    echo "<table>";   // CONTENT PRODUCTION: ALL NEWS
41    while ($row2 = mysqli_fetch_array($result2)) {
42      echo "<tr><td>".$row2["HEADING"]."</td></tr>";
43    }
44    echo "</table>";
45  }
46  else {
47    echo "<table>"; //CONTENT PRODUCTION: RECENT NEWS
48    while ($row2 = mysqli_fetch_array($result2)) {
49      echo "<tr><td>".$row2["HEADING"]."</td></tr>";
50      echo "<tr><td>".$row2["BODY"]."</td></tr>";
51    }
52    echo "</table>";
53  }
54  echo "</body></html>";
55  // connection disposal
56  mysqli_close($con);
57  ?>
```

FIGURE 10.15

PHP implementation of disjunctive ViewContainers.

Prior to creating the markup of the list of news, the `target` request parameter is tested to determine which ViewContainer must be rendered (lines 39 and 46). If the parameter's value is equal to `all`, the content of the "AllNews" ViewComponent is produced (lines 40–45). Otherwise the content of the of the "RecentNews" View-Component is built (lines 47–53).

10.1.7 ACTIONS

IFML does not model the internal organization of Actions but only their interplay with the user interface. In a PHP pure-HTML architecture, Actions are implemented by server-side scripts, which may access external systems through suitable APIs, such as the `mysqli` interface used in the examples of ViewContainer computation.

An Action is inserted in an IFML diagram by establishing an Event and a NavigationFlow between a ViewElement and the Action, with the meaning that the event triggers the Action targeted by the NavigationFlow. This basic configuration can be extended by drawing additional DataFlows from the ViewContainer whereby the Action is activated, transporting further parameters to the Action. Therefore, the implementation of an Action deals with how to realize the business logic (not treated in this book) and how to implement the Event and NavigationFlow that activate it. In PHP, Actions are implemented by means of a server-side script with the general structure shown in Figure 10.16.

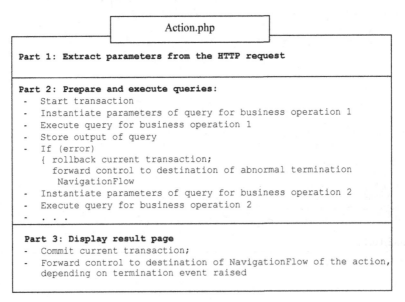

FIGURE 10.16

General schema of an Action server-side script.

The first part of the script deals with request parameters fetching, as in the case of a ViewContainer template. The parameters transported by the NavigationFlow must be extracted from the request to be used in the execution of the business operations.

The second part of the script deals with execution of the business logic. If the Action consists of a single operation, the script simply initializes the component with the input parameters, executes it, and checks the result to determine if the normal or exceptional termination event must be raised and which NavigationFlow must be followed. If the Action consists of a workflow of operations, the script must address the execution of the operations in the proper order, the passage of parameters between operations, and—if needed—the atomicity of execution.

The implementation of the Action also affects the coding of the template whereby the Action is activated. In particular, the HTML implementation of the Navigation-Flows outgoing from the ViewContainer and pointing to Actions must obey the following rules:

- Besides the parameters explicitly associated with it, the activating Navigation-Flow must also carry all the parameters transported by DataFlows reaching the Action. This can be done in two ways:
  - If the NavigationFlow is implemented as an anchor tag, appropriate parameters can be added to the query string of its URL.
  - If the NavigationFlow is implemented as the submit button of an HTML form, input fields of type hidden can be added to the HTML FORM element.
- The activating NavigationFlow must also transport the extra parameters needed to "remember" the history of user choices—as explained in chapter 12—if any of the outgoing flows of the Action points back to the ViewContainer whereby the Action is activated.

10.1.8 CONTEXT

Context information requires maintaining information across multiple user interactions. In a pure HTML architecture, this feature is normally implemented at the server side by means of a transient session data structure. Retention of information at the client side is also possible with cookies. Cookies, however, support only a limited storage capacity. Next, we exemplify the most basic usage of the Context: the storage of the identity and the authentication status of a user. Other Context information can be implemented following the same approach. We do so by discussing the implementation of the Login pattern presented in chapter 6. The login Action verifies the credentials of the user, forwards the user to the proper ViewContainer if the credentials are verified or to an error page if verification fails. The Actions also sets the Context information about the authenticated identity of the user. In RBAC systems, the default role the user is preserved as part of the context.

Context information, such as the identity of the currently logged-in user and his default role, can be implemented exploiting the PHP session variables. The PHP session is created either automatically upon the first request of the user or by means of an explicit script instruction executed at a specific point of the interaction.

The session is maintained for specified amount of time and is associated with a unique ID used to identify subsequent HTTP requests pertaining to it. It terminates either when the application invalidates it explicitly or when a time out defined in the server's configuration occurs. Upon termination, all the information stored in the session is lost. If session information must persist beyond the life of the session object or survive a server failure, it must be transferred into persistent storage at the server side.

The script of Figure 10.17 implements the login Action invoked by an HTML form containing two input fields, one for the username and one for the password. For the sake of simplicity, the script assumes the user's credentials are unique and stored in the database. The user's session is created automatically upon the user's first access to the ViewContainer with the login Form (line 2). The script retrieves the value of the username and password from the POST HTTP request (lines 3–4). It then connects to the database and uses these values to instantiate the prepared statement shown at lines 11–15. The SQL statement verifies that the given username and password do exist in the USER table and retrieves the OID of the user associated to the credentials and the OID of his default group. The outcome of credential verification is examined at line 17. If the SQL query did not find any object matching the username and password, the connection is closed and control is transferred (using the PHP header instruction) to the page template loginError.php, which may request the username and password again.

```
1   <?php
2   session_start();
3   $uname= $_POST["username"];
4   $pwd= $_POST["password"];
5   $con=mysqli_connect("example.com","user","pwd","my_db");
6   if (mysqli_connect_errno())
7   {
8   echo "Failed to connect to MySQL: " . mysqli_connect_error();
9   die();
10  }
11  $stmt = $con->prepare(
12  "SELECT OID, GROUPOID
13     FROM USER WHERE USERNAME = ? AND PASSWORD = ?");
14  $stmt->bind_param("ss",$uname, $pwd);
15  $stmt->execute();
16  $result = $stmt->get_result();
17  if (!($row = mysqli_fetch_array($result))) { // NO VALID USER DATA FOUND
18  mysqli_close($con);
19  header("location: loginError.php");     // REDIRECT TO ERROR VIEWCONTAINER
20  } else {                                 // VALID USER DATA FOUND
21  $_SESSION["uname"]=$row['OID'];          // REGISTER CONTEXT INFO
22  $_SESSION["urole"]=$row['GROUPOID'];     // IN THE SESSION
23  mysqli_close($con);
24  header("location: home.php");  // REDIRECT TO APPROPRIATE VIEWCONTAINER
25  }
26  ?>
```

FIGURE 10.17

PHP implementation of the login Action, which sets Context information.

If verification succeeds, the OID of the user and group are stored in two session variables, `uname` and `urole`, (lines 21–22), and control is forwarded to the proper ViewContainer.

Note that the simple script of Figure 10.17 can be made more realistic and secure by adding code for checking that the session exists, for regenerating it at each login to avoid session fixation attacks, and for managing clients such as robots that do not respect the redirect HTTP directive. In addition, transmission of the user's password via a secure protocol such as HTTPS would ensure better protection at no extra programming effort because the Secure HTTP protocol is transparent to the programmer.

The Context information can be cleared by the logout Action, which amounts to invalidating the session and forwarding control a proper ViewContainer.

10.2 IMPLEMENTATION OF THE FRONT END FOR PRESENTATION FRAMEWORKS

In the last decade, web programming has been supported by several software frameworks, which are partially instantiated architectures used for accelerating the development of enterprise class applications. These systems exploit an internal organization of the components that promotes modularization of the code through separation of concerns, so that each module addresses only one specific aspect, such as data access, business logic, interaction handling, or presentation.

10.2.1 MODEL-VIEW-CONTROLLER AND ITS ADAPTATION TO THE WEB

One of the most widespread software architectures for interface development is the so-called *Model-View-Controller* pattern (MVC for short). The MVC is conceived to separate the three essential parts of an interactive application: the domain objects and business logic of the application (*the model*), the rendition of the interface for the user (*the view*), and the decision about what to do in response to the user's interactions (*the controller*).

In the MVC architecture, the typical flow of control is the one represented in Figure 10.18.

The computation is activated by a user's request for some content or service, addressed through a controller. The controller dispatches a request for action to the suitable component of the model. The model incorporates the business logic for performing the action and executes such logic, which updates the state of the application and produces a result to be communicated to the user. The change in the model is observed by the interface view components. The affected view components thus update their presentation status and display the outcome to the user, who can then

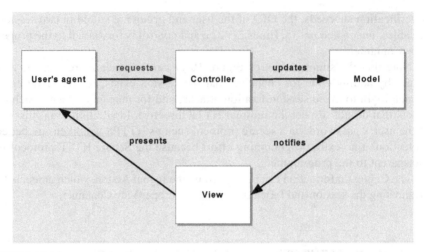

FIGURE 10.18

Model View Controller (MVC) architecture.

prosecute the interaction. The MVC assigns distinct responsibilities to the three types of components:

- The **model** encapsulates the business actions required for answering a user's request and keeps the state of the application. It ignores the format in which requests are issued and responses are presented to the user.
- The **view** embodies the presentation of the user interface. An application may have a single view or multiple views, and a view may be composed of subviews, relevant to different types of results. The view ignores how its content has been prepared.
- The **controller** interprets the user's request, produces the appropriate request for action, examines the result of each action, and decides what to do next. An application may have a single controller or multiple controllers, one for each request type or view. A controller is unaware of the business logic of the actions and of the presentation of the view.

In recent times, the MVC architecture has been exploited for organizing the architecture of web applications. Examples of web frameworks that take inspiration from the MVC pattern are the *Struts* project of the Apache Software Foundation (http ://jakarta.apache.org/struts/) and the *Spring MVC Framework* (http://spring.io/), part of a larger tool suite for the development of enterprise applications. Both projects feature an implementation of the MVC pattern realized on top of the Java platform.

In the web context, the original MVC scheme is adapted to take into account the specificity of HTTP as a client–server protocol, especially the lack of mechanisms for maintaining the state of the interaction at the client side and for the server to notify the client of events. Figure 10.19 shows the adaptation of the classical MVC

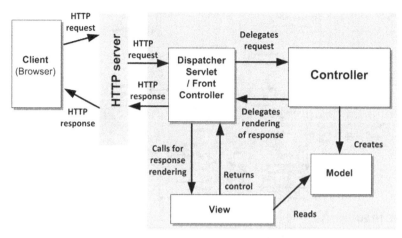

FIGURE 10.19

The MVC architecture applied to web applications.

architecture to the web context, using Java as a reference platform. The illustrated scheme is sometimes called MVC Model 2 (MVC2, for short), to contrast it with the Model 1 approach, which merges the view and the controller roles in the page template, similar to the approach in the PHP examples discussed in the section 10.1.

The emitter of requests in the MVC2 architecture is the web browser. The HTTP requests of the client are mapped to a single entry point—in Java implemented as a servlet—acting as the front controller (also called dispatcher). The front controller delegates the user's request to a specific controller in charge of deciding the actual course of action necessary to service the user's request. The specific controller creates the model objects necessary to perform the business actions implied by the user's request. Examples of actions could be the execution of a database query, the sending of e-mail, or the authentication of the user. Model objects also record the state of the application until the request is serviced or even between consecutive requests. For example, they may store the trolley items of the user or the result of a data binding query. After completion, the specific controller returns the control and the updated model objects to the front controller. In the typical flow of a web MVC application, after an action completes the front controller invokes a view—in Java implemented as a JSP page template—responsible for presenting the updated state of the application to the user. For doing so, the view template accesses the model objects, where the current state of the application is stored, and builds the HTML page sent back to the front controller and then to the browser. Examples of views could be the display of the result of a database query, the notification that an e-mail has been sent, and the home page of the web site after the successful login of the user.

In a concrete implementation of the MVC2, such as the Spring MVC framework, further technical components and mechanisms contribute to the architecture. These components are illustrated in Figure 10.20.

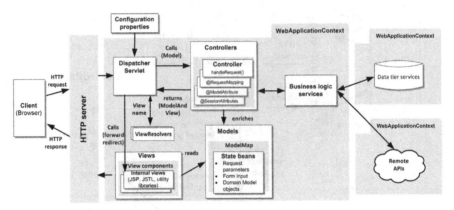

FIGURE 10.20

Spring MVC Framework components.

The entry point of the Spring Architecture is the dispatcher servlet, which is the orchestrator of the workflow for serving the incoming requests. It maps the client requests to the controllers that handle them. The controllers are Java classes with methods for handling the flow of actions implied by a specific request, such as creating the model objects to display in a view, accepting input, and updating the status of the application. The request-to-controller mapping logic can be expressed in several ways: by means of annotations (@RequestMapping) on the classes and methods of the controller, through encoding in an XML configuration file made available to the dispatcher servlet, or even by inference from naming rules with a "convention over configuration approach." The invocation of the controller by the dispatcher servlet has also the side effect of initializing the model. Spring implements a default model as a Java map indexed by symbolic attributes that can be used to store the Java objects that embody the model content. The dispatcher servlet and its helper classes initialize the default model map with the user's input and the request parameters, which are thus available to the controller. Also, the annotation @ModelAttribute can be attached to controllers' methods or to individual parameters in their signature, which causes the tagged method to be invoked before the actual handling of the request and causes their return value or parameter values to be added to the default model. These methods normally prepare additional model objects (e.g., by extracting content from the data tier). Some of the model objects can be made persistent across multiple requests by storing them in the session. This requirement can be expressed declaratively by annotating the signature of a controller's methods (with @SessionAttribute).

The controller can interact with back-end services deployed in one or more packages (called WebContexts) connected with the main WebContext that contains the MVC components. These services can support data access, such as through object relational mappings of the domain model onto relational data sources and integration with remote services (e.g., access to REST APIs on the web).

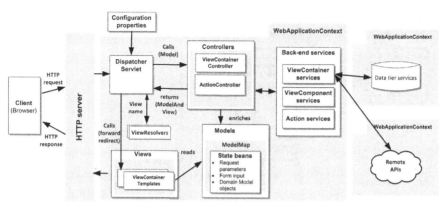

FIGURE 10.21

Mapping IFML concepts to the MVC architecture.

The methods of the controller invoked to handle an incoming request may return to the dispatcher servlet the indication of the model object (if different from the default one) and of the view to display next. Spring supports a variety of mechanisms and defaults for specifying the view to call. In the base mechanism, the controller simply returns a string denoting the symbolic name of the pertinent view, which is translated by a ViewResolver utility object into the physical address of the component implementing the view.

The view components can be realized in a variety of ways, including the delegation to external programs or the display of static resources. The typical implementation employs Java Server Pages (JSP) or JSP Standard Template Library (JSTL) components. Spring offers utility libraries that can be used in the view to facilitate the access to the model objects, including the retrieval of form input data associated with the request and of the errors produced by the server-side validation of such data.

10.2.2 MAPPING IFML TO THE SPRING MVC FRAMEWORK

The mapping of an IFML application onto the Spring architecture is illustrated in Figure 10.21, which fills the generic "boxes" of Figure 10.20 with IFML-specific elements.

In the rest of this section, we discuss how the implementation of the fundamental IFML primitives (ViewContainers, ViewComponents, InteractionFlows, and Actions) exploits the components appearing in Figure 10.21. As an example, we show the implementation of the IFML model illustrated in Figure 10.22, which includes one ViewContainer with a master detail pattern consisting of two List ViewComponents and two ViewContainers for a basic search pattern with data entry validation.

10.2.3 MAPPING VIEWCONTAINERS TO SPRING MVC

Each ViewContainer is mapped onto four elements: (1) a ViewContainer controller, (2) a ViewContainer service in the business tier, (3) a ViewContainer template in

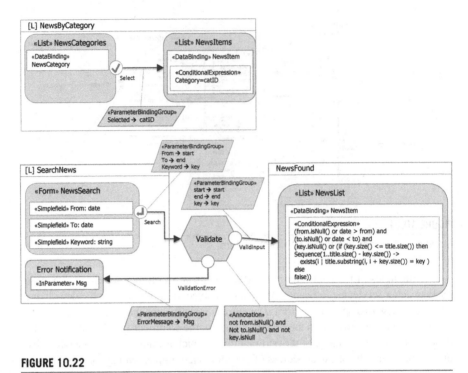

FIGURE 10.22

Example of an IFML model implemented using Spring MVC.

the View, and (4) a @RequestMapping annotation on the responder methods of the ViewContainer controller—or alternatively a handler mapping specification in the dispatcher servlet configuration file.

The ViewContainer controller is a Java class. It exposes a "handleRequest" method that extracts the input from the HTTP request and calls the ViewContainer service in the business tier, passing to it a reference to the model. When the service terminates, the ViewContainer controller analyses the outcome and returns the specification of the View to display to the dispatcher servlet.

The ViewContainer service is a business function that orchestrates the parameter propagation and ViewComponent execution process illustrated in chapter 12. The ViewContainer service invokes in the proper order the ViewComponent services, which embody the business logic of the ViewComponents embedded in the View-Container. Typically, a ViewComponent service implements the data binding logic of the component, which extracts the content from the data source and stores it in the model. At the end of the ViewContainer service execution, all the model objects holding the result of the content binding queries of the ViewComponents are available to the view, together with the request parameters and form input stored in the model by the dispatcher servlet. Finally, the ViewContainer template in the view computes the HTML page to be sent to the user based on the content of the model. It contains the

```
1   @Controller
2   public class NewsByCategoryController {
3
4     @Autowired
5     private ApplicationContext appContext;
6
7     @RequestMapping(value = "NewsByCategory")
8     public final Object handleRequest(@RequestParam(required = false)
9                       String catId, Model model) throws Exception {
10      model.addAttribute("catId", catId);
11      NewsByCategoryViewContainerService s =
12          appContext.getBean(NewsByCategoryViewContainerService.class);
13        s.computeViewContainer(model);
14        return "NewsByCategory";
15    }
16  }
```

FIGURE 10.23

Spring controller for the "Categories" ViewContainer.

static HTML needed to define the layout where the ViewComponents are positioned and custom tags or scripts implementing the dynamic rendition of ViewComponents.

We now illustrate these artifacts in detail, using the "NewsByCategory" ViewContainer of Figure 10.22. Figure 10.23 shows the code of the ViewContainer Controller that implements the response to requests for the NewsCategories ViewContainer. We assume that the implementation of the ViewContainers uses the same names as the IFML model ("NewsByCategory," "SearchNews," and "NewsFound") and that parameters are passed in the query string[4]. Therefore, the requests for the "NewsBy-Category" ViewContainer are formulated with the following URI template:[5]

http://www.myserver.com/newsByCategory.do&catID=X

If the "catID" parameter is missing, the URI denotes the request for the content of the "NewsCategories" ViewComponent only. Otherwise, it represents the request for the news associated with the selected category ("X" in the example). The IFML model and the Spring implementation can be easily modified to handle the display of the news of the default category in the "NewsCategories" ViewComponent when the "catID" parameter is not present.

The controller is implemented by a Java class ("NewsByCategoryController") annotated with the @Controller tag (lines 1–2). The controller class declares a private member "appContext," annotated with @Autowired (lines 4–5). As a result, an object of type "ApplicationContext" is automatically created by Spring and injected into the controller. Such an object provides access to configuration information and to the bean factory used for creating or retrieving the application services. The controller "handleRequest" method (lines 7–9) is marked with @RequestMapping(value ="newsByCategory") to associate it with the incoming requests matching the specified URI template. The signature of the method comprises the optional parameter catID and the default model object. If the request actually contains the ID of a category, the value is exploited to initialize the method parameter, as specified by the @ RequestParam annotation.

```
1 public class NewsByCategoryViewContainerService {
2
3     @Autowired
4     private ApplicationContext appContext;
5
6     // Compute the ViewContainer
7     public void computeViewContainer(Model model) throws Exception {
8         // execute services of ViewComponents
9         NewsCategoriesService viewComponentService1 =
10        appContext.getBean(NewsCategoriesService.class);
11        viewComponentService1.execute(model);
12        // computes the category details in case a newsCategory has been selected
13        if (model.asMap().get("catID") != null)){
14         NewsItemsService viewComponentService2 =
15         appContext.getBean(NewsItemsService.class);
16         viewComponentService2.execute(model);
17        }
18    }
19}
```

FIGURE 10.24

ViewContainer service for the "NewsCategories" ViewContainer.

The method first stores the (optional) request parameter in the model under the name "catId" (line 10). It then looks up the application context to retrieve a Java bean that implements the service for the "NewsByCategory" ViewContainer (lines 11–12). Next, it executes such the service by calling its "computeViewContainer" method (line 13). The method takes as input the model map, which at the end of the computation will contain the data binding instances of all the ViewComponents of the ViewContainer. The "handleRequest" method concludes by returning a string with the symbolic name of the view to the dispatcher servlet (line 14).[6]

The ViewContainer service invoked by Controller is illustrated in Figure 10.24. It addresses the execution of ViewComponents and the propagation of parameters. The service is a Java class ("NewsByCategoryViewContainerService") that implements the method "computeViewContainer" called by the Controller (line 7). That method takes as input the model map object and creates an instance of the ViewComponent services according to the order of computation and parameter passing rules explained in section 6. First, it creates an instance of the service for the "NewsCategories" List (line 9–10), and calls its "execute" method (line 11), which computes the content of the list. In such invocation, the model object is passed to the method to store the result of the data binding query. Then, the method checks the presence of the "catID" parameter in the model (line 13) and, if a value is present, instantiates and calls the service for the "NewsItems" List (lines 14–16)[7].

The symbolic name returned by the Controller (in our case, "NewsByCategory") is translated by a ViewResolver component of the Spring MVC framework into the physical name of a View template (e.g., NewsByCategory.jsp).

The implementation of the "NewsByCategory" View template is exemplified in Figure 10.25. The template starts with the inclusion of the JSTL tag library and the declaration of the content type and character encoding of the HTTP response (line 1–3). The template then contains regular HTML markup for the static part of the page, including the hypertext links that implement the implicit navigation to the

```
1 <!DOCTYPE html>
2 <%@ taglib prefix="c" uri="http://java.sun.com/jsp/jstl/core" %>
3 <%@ page contentType="text/html; charset=UTF-8"%>
4 <html>
5 <head>
6     <title>News by Categories</title>
7     <link rel="stylesheet" type="text/css" href="style.css">
8 </head>
9 <body>
10  <div>
11    <h2><a href="NewsByCategory.do">News By Category</a> |
12        <a href="SearchNews.do">Search News</a></h2>
13  </div>
14    <div style="float: left;">
15      <h3>News Categories</h3>
16      <c:forEach var="nc" items="${newsCategories}">
17        <li><a href="NewsByCategory.do?catID=${nc.id}">
18               <c:out value="${nc.name}"/></a></li>
19      </c:forEach>
20    </div>
21    <c:if test="${not empty(newsItems)}">
22      <div style="float: left;">
23        <h3>News Items</h3>
24        <c:forEach var="ni" items="${newsItems}">
25          <div><strong><c:out value="${ni.heading}"/></strong></div>
26          <div><small>Date: <c:out value="${ni.date}"/></small></div>
27          <div><c:out value="${ni.body}"/></div>
28        <br/>
29        </c:forEach>
30      </div>
31    </c:if>
32
33  </body>
34</html>
```

FIGURE 10.25

View template of page NewsCategories, using a custom tag library.

landmark ViewContainers (lines 4–13). Next the content of the "NewsCategories"
List ViewComponent is rendered using the JSTL foreach iterator tag (lines 16–19).
The iteration is performed over the list of news category objects created by the List
ViewComponent service—described next—and stored in the model, bound to the
JSTL variable items. At every iteration, the name of the category is printed, sur-
rounded by an HTML anchor tag pointing back to the same ViewContainer. The URI
of the anchor tag contains as a parameter the identity of the current category. The
ViewContainer template continues with the (optional) rendition of the second View-
Component. If the content of the "NewsItems" ViewComponent is found (checked
with the test at line 21 for the bean variable newsItems), the template prints the
List ViewComponent (lines 22–30). If the content is not found—meaning that no
category has been selected—the rendition of the "NewsItems" ViewComponent is
omitted.

In the simple example of Figure 10.25, the production of the markup code of the
List ViewComponent is directly embedded within the template of the ViewContainer.

In a more elaborate example of a ViewContainer comprising multiple ViewComponents of different types, a more modular approach would be that of separately coding the view template of each ViewComponent and then assembling the various fragments into the template of the ViewContainer (e.g., using the dynamic inclusion mechanism provided by JSP).

10.2.4 MAPPING VIEWCOMPONENTS TO SPRING MVC

ViewComponents are associated with a ViewComponent service, which implements the business logic and populates the model with state information. Details and List ViewComponents contribute a data bean and a list of data beans, respectively. IFML Forms are associated in the model with a *command object* (also called a *form bean*) constructed by the framework to maintain the values entered by the user. Data beans and command objects both help the construction of the view but differ in the origin of their content. Data come from the data layer in the case of data beans and from user input in the case of command objects.

List and details View components and their extensions map onto Java service classes for extracting the data binding content and creating one or more JavaBeans, filled with such content.

Figure 10.26 shows the service for the "NewsCategories" List ViewComponent, which retrieves the list of all the category objects.

The service class shown in Figure 10.26 encapsulates the business logic for computing the content of the List. It has a private member ("appContext") storing a reference to the bean factory, injected by the Spring MVC framework. The "execute" method exploits the application context to create a data access object (DAO)—an instance of class "NewsCategoryRepository"—and then invokes the "findAll" finder method of the DAO to retrieve all the categories. The collection returned by the finder method is stored in the model under an attribute named "NewsCategories," where it is retrieved by the view template shown in Figure 10.25.

The DAO can be implemented in Spring using various technologies, such as Java DataBase Connectivity (JDBC), Java Persistence API (JPA), and Hibernate. Figure 10.27 and Figure 10.28 show the JPA entity declaration implementing the object

```
1 public class NewsCategoriesService {
2
3   @Autowired
4   private ApplicationContext appContext;
5
6   public void execute(Model model) throws Exception {
7       model.addAttribute("newsCategories",
8         appContext.getBean(NewsCategoryRepository.class).findAll());
9   }
10}
```

FIGURE 10.26

Business service for a List ViewComponent.

```
1 @Entity
2 public class NewsCategory {
3
4   @Id
5   @GeneratedValue(strategy = GenerationType.AUTO)
6    private Long id;
7    private String name;
8   @OneToMany(targetEntity = NewsItem.class, mappedBy = "category")
9   private Set<NewsItem> newsItems = new LinkedHashSet<NewsItem>();
10
11   protected NewsCategory() {
12   }
13
14   public NewsCategory(String name) {
15       this.name = name;
16   }
17
18   public Long getId() {
19       return id;
20   }
21
22   public void setId(Long id) {
23       this.id = id;
24   }
25
26   public String getName() {
27       return name;
28   }
29
30   public void setName(String name) {
31       this.name = name;
32   }
33
34   public Set<NewsItem> getNewsItems() {
35       return newsItems;
36   }
37
38   public void setNewsItems(Set<NewsItem> newsItems) {
39       this.newsItems = newsItems;
40   }
41
42   @Override
43   public String toString() {
44       return String.format("NewsCategory[id=%d, name='%s']", id, name);
45   }
46}
```

FIGURE 10.27

Entity declaration for news category.

```
1 public interface NewsCategoryRepository extends CrudRepository<NewsCategory, Long>
{
2    List<NewsCategory> findAll();
3 }
```

FIGURE 10.28

Data access interface for news categories.

relational mapping for class "NewsCategory" of the domain model and the DAO interface for retrieving the news categories from the persistent store.

Class "NewsCategory" is a JPA entity bean, which defines the object-oriented counterpart of the relational tables storing the "NewsCategory" instances and of the relationship between "NewsCategory" and "NewsItem." The entity declares data members corresponding to the columns of the relational attributes. The relationship between "NewsCategory" and "NewsItem" is mapped to the "newsItems" member of class "NewsCategory" and to the inverse "category" member of class "News-Item," using the @OneToMany JPA annotation (lines 8–9).

Figure 10.28 shows the DAO interface for retrieving news categories.

The interface extends the "CrudRepository" Spring Data JPA system interface, which permits the framework to automatically generate an implementation of the data access methods. Inside the repository interface the "findAll" method retrieves all the instances of the entity. These data retrieval methods, called "dynamic finder methods," are implemented and resolved automatically by the framework using naming conventions.

10.2.5 MAPPING FORMS TO SPRING MVC

Form ViewComponents are implemented differently from other components because they do not require a data retrieval service but accept user input. This function is normally supported by HTML forms, with a number of limitations. For example, an HTML form neither buffers the user's input nor supports validation and error messages. An implementation with Spring may exploit the automatic binding of input data to command objects and custom tags, easing the retrieval of user input and of possible validation errors in the view. As an example, we consider the search pattern illustrated in Figure 10.22 with the constraints that the search keyword, start date, and end date must be all supplied by the user.

The JSP template of Figure 10.19, named SearchNews.jsp, implements the View for the "SearchNews" ViewContainer, using the Spring form tag library.

The template initially declares a custom tag library named "form" (line 2). All tags of the included library have the form: prefix, which distinguishes them from the regular HTML tags. Following the markup for landmark navigation, the HTML body of the template includes a form for submitting the search criteria (lines 16–27). Custom tags replace the HTML <form> and <input> tags (lines 16, 18, 21, and 24). The form action attribute specifies that the form input is submitted to the component responding at the "SearchNews" URI template, and the "commandName" attribute specifies the name of the model attribute under which the form object is exposed, which is "SearchInput" in the example (line 16). The form object is created by the framework and stored in the model for both validation and retrieval by the view template.

The "path" attribute of the input element (lines 18, 21, and 24) identifies the property of the command object used for data binding. If specified, the content of the input field is stored with the attribute of the command object and can be fetched by the view to redisplay the data previously entered by the user.

The `<form:errors>` tags placed after the keyword and date input elements (lines 19, 22, and 25) implement the display of notifications present in the model of Figure 10.22. Each tag retrieves and prints the error message produced by the submission of a void field. The URI template invoked by the form ("SearchNews") is mapped to the controller illustrated in Figure 10.30.

The Controller class exposes the "handleGet" method (lines 3–8), which is mapped to the HTTP GET request that implements the landmark navigation to the "SearchNews" ViewContainer. This request does not need a business service for extracting content from the data source, and thus the "handleGet" method just returns the symbolic name of the view to show, which is resolved by the framework to the template of Figure 10.29. The `@ModelAttribute` annotation on the method causes the framework to create and insert into the model an empty form bean under the model attribute named "SearchInput." This object is filled with the user's input when the form in the template of Figure 10.29 is submitted.

The controller class also exposes the "handlePost" method (line 10–21), mapped to POST requests addressed to the "SearchNews" URI template. Such requests are emitted upon the submission of the form illustrated in Figure 10.29. The signature of the method comprises the default model object ("model"), the command object storing the form input ("formBean"), the framework object holding the result of the validation of the input data ("result"), and a special argument ("redirectAttributes")

```
1 <!DOCTYPE html>
2 <%@ taglib prefix="form" uri="http://www.springframework.org/tags/form" %>
3 <%@ page contentType="text/html; charset=UTF-8"%>
4 <html>
5 <head>
6    <title>Search News</title>
7    <link rel="stylesheet" type="text/css" href="style.css">
8 </head>
9 <body>
10   <div>
11   <h2><a href="NewsByCategory.do">News By Category</a> |
12       <a href="SearchNews.do">Search News</a></h2>
13   </div>
14   <div>
15    <h3>Input Search Criteria</h3>
16      <form:form action="SearchNews.do" commandName="SearchInput">
17        <div>Keyword</div>
18        <div><form:input id="keyword" path="keyword" size="100"/></div>
19        <div><form:errors path="keyword" /></div>
20        <div>From</div>
21        <div><form:input id="from" type="date" path="from" /></div>
22        <div><form:errors path="from" /></div>
23        <div>To</div>
24        <div><form:input id="to" type="date" path="to" /></div>
25        <div><form:errors path="to" /></div>
26        <div><input id="submit" title="Search" type="submit" value="Search"></div>
27      </form:form>
28</div>
29</body>
30</html>
```

FIGURE 10.29

View template for the "SearchNews" ViewContainer.

```
1  @Controller
2  public class SearchNewsViewContainerController {
3    @RequestMapping(value = "SearchNews", method = RequestMethod.GET)
4    public final Object handleGet(@ModelAttribute("SearchInput")
5     SearchFormBean formBean, BindingResult result, Model model)
6         throws Exception {
7      return "SearchNews";
8    }
9
10   @RequestMapping(value = "SearchNews", method = RequestMethod.POST)
11   public final Object handlePost(@Valid @ModelAttribute("SearchInput")
12     SearchFormBean formBean, BindingResult result,
13         Model model, RedirectAttributes redirectAttributes) throws Exception {
14     if (result.hasErrors()) {
15         // input errors! Back to search form
16         return "SearchNews";
17     }
18     // redirect to news items view preserving search parameters
19     redirectAttributes.addAllAttributes(formBean.asMap());
20     return "redirect:NewsFound.do";
21   }
22 }
```

FIGURE 10.30

Controller for the "SearchNews" ViewContainer.

used to exercise fine grain control over the information to be communicated in the redirection of the request.

The annotation @ModelAttribute("SearchInput") specifies that the command object containing the user's input is stored in the model under the same attribute ("SearchInput") used in the <form:form> element of the view template of Figure 10.29 and in the "handleGet" method.

The controller first tests for the presence of validation errors in the submitted input (line 14). If such errors are found, the controller returns the symbolic name of the view to display, which in this case is the same JSP template from which the request was emitted ("SearchNews"). If no errors are found, the controller stores the command object in the redirect attributes (line 19), to ensure that the user's input is preserved, and returns the symbolic name of the view corresponding to the "News-Found" ViewContainer. The return statement prefixes the view name with redirect: so that the framework transfers the control through a redirect mechanism rather than a forward. This ensures that the browser emits a new request for the specified view template, so that if the user refreshes the page with the list of news, the browser does not resend the POST data.

Figure 10.31 show the controller that responds to the request addressed to the "NewsFound" URI template.

The "handleRequest" method extracts from the request the values of the "keyword," "from," and "to" model attributes (lines 8–10), instantiates the ViewContainer service needed to extract the content from the data source (line 14), calls its "computeViewContainer" method—passing to it the model object filled with the parameter values extracted from the request—and returns the name of the view to display.

The Controller of Figure 10.30 exemplifies also the support offered by Spring for validating the input of the form. The @Valid annotation before the "searchBean"

```
1   @Controller
2   public class NewsFoundViewContainerController {
3
4       @Autowired
5       private ApplicationContext appContext;
6
7       @RequestMapping(value = "NewsFound")
8       public final Object handleRequest(@RequestParam(required = false) String keyword,
9           @RequestParam(required = false) @DateTimeFormat(pattern = "yyyy-MM-dd") Date from,
10          @RequestParam(required = false) @DateTimeFormat(pattern = "yyyy-MM-dd") Date to,
11          Model model) throws Exception {
12          model.addAttribute("keyword", keyword).
13            addAttribute("from", from).addAttribute("to", to);
14          NewsFoundViewContainerService containerService =
15            appContext.getBean(NewsFoundViewContainerService.class);
16            containerService.computeViewContainer(model);
17            return "NewsFound";
18      }
19  }
```

FIGURE 10.31

Controller for the "NewsItems" ViewContainer.

```
1   public class SearchBean {
2
3       @NotNull
4       private String keyword;
5       @NotNull
6       private Date from;
7       @NotNull
8       private Date to;
9
10  // setters and getters
11      ..
12  }
```

FIGURE 10.32

Definition of the SearchBean command object class.

parameter specifies that the command object is subjected to declarative field validation using the Bean Validation standard (also known as JSR-303). For this type of declarative validation to occur, the definition of the command object must be enriched with JSR-303 compliant annotations, as shown in Figure 10.32.

The @NotNull annotation at lines 3, 5, and 7 causes the command object to be checked after creation and an error message to be inserted in the "BindingResult" object associated with the form bean if a field is null.

10.2.6 MAPPING OPERATIONS TO THE MVC ARCHITECTURE

IFML actions are mapped to Spring MVC similarly to ViewContainers. Each action requires an action controller and a service. The action controller is analogous to the ViewContainer controller. It exposes methods that are mapped to the requests that trigger the action, such as the post of data from a form or the triggering of a NavigationFlow. The controller possibly prepares the content of the model and then instantiates the proper action service in a way similar to that for ViewContainers (as explained above). The action service implements the business logic. It may produce and consume the content of the model and terminate with different outcomes corresponding to the termination events specified in the IFML model. The controller detects the outcome of action service termination and returns the appropriate view specification based on it, thus implementing the different flows that connect the action termination events to the target ViewContainers.

10.3 IMPLEMENTATION OF THE FRONT END FOR RICH INTERNET APPLICATIONS

The term rich Internet application (RIA) was first introduced in 2002 by Jeremy Allaire in a white paper [Allaire02] to describe a novel generation of online applications that exploit several technologies to provide a sophisticated user experience on top of the open architectural standards of the Internet. The most noticeable innovation of RIAs lies in the powerful interaction mechanisms of the interface (such as native multimedia support, transition effects, animations, widgets, drag and drop, etc.) coupled to a flexible partition of work between the client and the server, comparable to that of preweb client-server applications. The twofold nature (part client-side, part server-side) of RIAs is one of the main reasons for their success: using the web as a back-end retains all the advantages of an open, low-cost, installation-free architecture, while increasing the computation power of the client ensures the quality of interaction that modern desktop applications and operating systems can offer. The basic architecture of a RIA is shown in Figure 10.33 and consists of a web application server connected with applications running on client machines. These applications are implemented inside the browser using a variety of technologies, such as HTML 5, JavaScript, JSON, and XML. Communication between the application tiers exploits multiple paths: synchronous client-server with HTTP, asynchronous client-server with AJAX or WebSocket, and peer-to-peer with Web Real Time Communication (WebRTC).

Having an application runtime environment at the client-side grants novel opportunities with respect to the pure HTML and HTTP architecture: (1) the control logic can be implemented either at the client or at the server; (2) the business logic can be partitioned between the client and the server opportunistically; (3) data can be stored at both tiers; (4) communication can be more flexible: client to server, server to client, and client to client; and (5) the client-side can work also when disconnected from the server.

From the developers' perspective, RIAs introduce a spectrum of new architectural patterns, design decisions, and implementation languages. In essence, any event (raised by the user or notified by the server or by another client) can be handled locally at the client, delegated to the server, or treated at both tiers. In summary, the new RIA architecture enables novel and more efficient web applications, where data and business logic are distributed between the client and the server and where

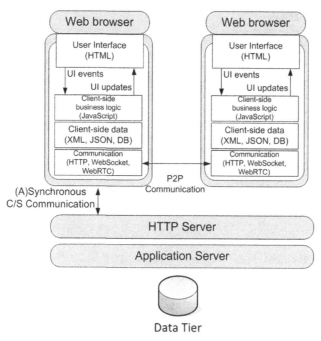

FIGURE 10.33

Rich Internet application architecture.

the client and the server can communicate in both directions. The downside is the increased complexity of the software and the proliferation of languages, data formats, and communication protocols, which make the model-driven development of RIAs an interesting possibility.

10.3.1 MAPPING IFML TO THE RIA ARCHITECTURE

The mapping of IFML constructs to the RIA architecture is based on the principle of separating the management of user events from the invocation of the business services implementing the ViewComponents. The implementation of the IFML constructs exploits HTML DOM events for ensuring a richer user experience, the JavaScript language for event handling, and the XMLHttpRequest object for asynchronous communication and data exchange with the server.

For space reasons, we limit the illustration to the master detail example of Figure 10.34, under the assumption that the application works online. More specifically, the management of events and the display of the view are performed at the client side, whereas the data binding logic of ViewComponents is executed (asynchronously) at the server side.

Although in recent times there has been a proliferation of libraries and frameworks for organizing the client-side functionality—including complete MVC frameworks

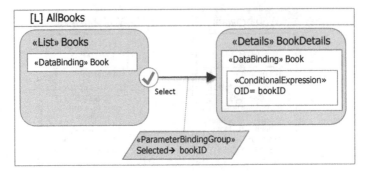

FIGURE 10.34

Master detail pattern.

```
1  <!DOCTYPE html>
2  <html>
3 <head>
4        <title>All Books </title>
5        <link rel="stylesheet" type="text/css" href="style.css">
6        <script src="https://code.jquery.com/jquery.min.js"></script>
7        <script src="books.js"></script>
8 </head>
9 <body>
10          <h2>Books Sample</h2>
11          <div class="book-list"></div>
12          <div class="book-details"></div>
13      </body>
14  </html>
```

FIGURE 10.35

JSP template of the "AllBooks" ViewContainer.

implemented in the browser through JavaScript—in the following we exploit only public or otherwise widely used standards (most notably the jQuery JavaScript library) to avoid dependency on still not-so-consolidated toolkits.

The mapping of IFML concepts to the RIA architecture assigns a server-side page template to each ViewContainer. In most cases, the IFML model of a RIA application comprises one top-level ViewContainer partitioned into several subcontainers displayed either in parallel or in alternation.

Figure 10.35 shows the template of the "AllBooks" ViewContainer encoded in JSP (the PHP implementation would be almost identical).

The head of the template references the JavaScript utility libraries (line 6) and the JavaScript program that implement the client-side logics of the ViewContainer (line 7). The body contains one empty HTML `<div>` element for each ViewComponent. These elements are filled dynamically by the client-side logic, which asynchronously calls the server-side service for ViewComponent data binding.

```
1 jQuery(document).ready(function($) {
2
3    function loadBookList() {
4      $.ajax({
5          type: "GET",
6          url: "book-list.jsp",
7          dataType: "xml",
8          success: function (xml) {
9              createBookList(xml);
10                 }
11            });
12
13    function createBookList(data) {
14        var $list = $("<ul/>");
15        $.each($("book", data), function (index, book) {
16          var $book = $("<li>" + $("title", book).text()
17        + "</li>").data("id", $("id", book).text());
18            $book.click(function (e) {
19                loadBookDetails(this);
20            }).appendTo($list);
21        });
22        $(".book-list").html($list);
23    }
...
46        loadBookList(); // INVOKED WHEN THE DOCUMENT LOADING HAS COMPLETED
47 }); // END OF THE "ON READY" FUNCTION
```

FIGURE 10.36

JavaScript functions implementing the business logic of the "AllBooks" ViewContainer.

Figure 10.36 shows part of the JavaScript code contained in the "books.js" external script, which exploits the jQuery library for simplifying the coding of the View-Container computation.

The JavaScript code declares the business logic methods within a top-level function associated with the document ready event (line 1). This practice avoids running any code before the document is completely loaded. When the document is ready, function "loadBookList" is executed (line 46), which computes the content of the "Books" ViewComponent as prescribed by the ViewContainer computation procedure explained in chapter 12. Notice that—in contrast to the server-side implementations in PHP and Spring—the ViewContainer computation algorithm is embodied within JavaScript code executed at the client side.

The "loadBookList" function performs an asynchronous call through the $.ajax() method. The target of the call is the server-side JSP template book-list.jsp, which contains the data extraction logic of the "BookList" ViewComponent. The server-side script returns a presentation-independent encoding of the data in XML, which is then transformed into HTLM markup at the client-side. For this purpose, the "loadBookList" function associates with the successful completion of the AJAX request a presentation function called "createBookList" (lines 8–9). This function (lines 13–23) receives as a parameter the data binding content of the ViewComponent and creates the corresponding HTML markup for the view.

For example, the data binding content of the "BookList" ViewComponent could be represented by the following XML document:

```
<books>
<book>
<id>1</id>
<title>Head First Design Patterns</title>
</book>
<book>
<id>2</id>
<title>Programming Ruby: The Pragmatic Programmers' Guide, Second
Edition</title>
</book>
<book>
<id>3</id>
<title>CSS Mastery: Advanced Web Standards Solutions</title>
</book>
<book>
<id>4</id>
<title>Beginning PHP 5 and MySQL: From Novice to Professional
</title>
</book>
</books>
```

The "createBookList" function constructs an initially empty HTML unordered list (line 14). Next, a loop (lines 15–21) iterates through all the <book> elements present in the input data. At each iteration, a function is executed that constructs a list item from the title and the id of the book data (lines 16–17) and appends it to the unordered list. For each list item constructed, a function is associated with the user's selection event (line 18). The click event triggers the invocation of the "loadBook-Details" function, with input equal to the selected book element. After each iteration, the book item is appended to the unordered list (line 20), and at the end of the loop the entire list is inserted into the ViewContainer as the HTML content of the <div> element of class "book-list" (line 22).

Notice that in a RIA implementation, the creation of view element for producing an event and the handling of the event itself are performed at the client side. Conversely, in a PHP or Spring implementation, the view element representing the event is generated at the server side by producing an HTML anchor tag when the view is rendered. The event handling is also delegated to the server because the navigation of an HTML hyperlink implies a call to a web server.

The computation of the "BookDetails" ViewComponent proceeds in a similar manner, using the JavaScript function illustrated in Figure 10.37.

Note that the "createBookDetails" function (lines 37–43) is invoked every time the user selects a book. Therefore, it starts by emptying the HTML <div> element that hosted the content of the previously selected book (line 38) before creating and inserting the content of the newly selected one (lines 39–42).

```
24   function loadBookDetails(book) {
25       var bookId = $(book).data("id");
26       $.ajax({
27           type: "GET",
28           url: "book-details.jsp",
29           data: {id: bookId},
30           dataType: "xml",
31           success: function (xml) {
32               createBookDetails(xml);
33           }
34       });
35   }
36
37   function createBookDetails(book) {
38       $(".book-details").empty()
39           .append($("<h3>").text($("title", book).text()))
40           .append($("<div>").html("Authors: " + $("authors", book).text()))
41           .append($("<div>").html("Publisher: " + $("publisher", book).text()))
42           .append($("<div>").text($("description", book).text()));
43   }
44   ..
```

FIGURE 10.37

JavaScript functions implementing the computation of the "BookDetails" ViewComponent.

10.4 IMPLEMENTATION OF THE FRONT END FOR MOBILE APPLICATIONS

Mobile application development is the perfect playground for the model-driven specification and implementation of the interface. On the one hand, mobile apps require an extremely effective user interface, given the interaction constraints imposed by the usage context and by the device limitations. On the other hand, they should be deployed across a variety of devices with very different capabilities. Mobile app development faces the dilemma "native versus browser-based versus cross-platform." Native app development uses the programming framework of the operating system (e.g., Android, iOS, or Windows), which grants a better exploitation of the device capabilities and a deeper fine tuning of the interface at the cost of more effort for portability. Browser-based development resorts to web standards for improving device- and platform-independence and exploits the same technologies used for RIAs (HTML5, CSS, JavaScript). The resulting applications are more portable but are less integrated with the device hardware (e.g., sensors, camera) and cannot be deployed in the mainstream native app stores. Cross-platform frameworks, such as Phonegap and Appcelerator Titanium, exhibit a variety of architectures and approaches, all aimed at bridging the gap between native and browser-based development. They allow the programmer to use one development environment and then port the code to diverse native systems, either by cross-compiling the source code for the target operating system or by equipping the operating system with a runtime interpreter.

For space limitations, we illustrate only one approach for mapping IFML to mobile app code: the development of a native Android app. The browser-based approach is similar to that of RIAs, whereas cross-platform frameworks are a hybrid between native and HTML-based development.

10.4.1 THE ANDROID DEVELOPMENT ENVIRONMENT

Android is an open-source software stack that includes the operating system, middleware, and built-in mobile applications based on a modified version of Linux that device vendors can further customize to differentiate their products.

Figure 10.38 summarizes the main elements of the Android architecture. The operating system kernel handles low-level hardware operations, including drivers and memory management, with special attention to power optimization. The Android runtime supports applications written in Java, executed within a custom virtual machine. It includes the core Android libraries and incorporates most

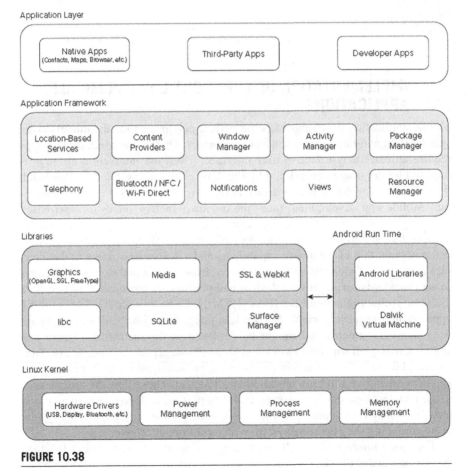

FIGURE 10.38

The Android architecture.

of the Java Standard Edition functionality. The runtime mediates the access to such basic libraries as WebKit, SSL, and OpenGL. The application framework interacts with the libraries indirectly through the virtual machine and exposes high level APIs that developers can use in their applications for window management, location management, data storage, communication, sensing, and more. The application layer comprises the standard apps that ship with the Android devices, such as the phone dialer, the SMS messenger, the contact manager, and the music player, as well as proprietary apps bundled with the device, such as app stores and e-mail clients.

Programming an Android application involves writing the business logic code, supplying the multimedia assets needed by the application, and providing the resources required for the user interface, such as the layout specification expressed declaratively in XML, the icons, and the localization strings.

The main concepts that constitute an Android application are:

- **Activities**: an activity is a basic user task, such as entering a contact in the agenda or taking a photo.
- **Views and View Groups**: a view is an interface widget, such as a button or a text input; views are grouped into view groups, which represent hierarchical organizations of the layout and content.
- **Intents**: an intent is the specification of a request for action. Intents allow communication between activities, either explicitly, by naming the activity the intent is targeting, or implicitly, by naming the desired action to which activities capable of performing it can be bound at runtime. Implicit intents are resolved by associating activities to **intent filters**, which are conditions that specify the actions an activity can perform. Intents are also used to send and receive broadcast messages, which notify system or applications event. Intents can also contain data to enable parameter passing among activities.
- **Events and event listeners**: an event is an intra-activity occurrence, which can be handled directly by a business method hardwired to the view element that produced the event. Alternatively, an event can be published so that registered business methods (called listeners) can intervene.

10.4.2 MAPPING IFML TO NATIVE ANDROID CODE

For the sake of illustration, in the following we discuss how to implement in Android a simple "ToDo" app, whose IFML model is shown in Figure 10.39. The app supports a simple interaction for managing to-do lists and alarms.

The application contains two landmark ViewContainers. The "ToDoList" is shown by default when the application is launched, whereby the user can access the to-do list for viewing and deleting items. The "AddToDo" container allows the user to enter a new to-do. Upon creation, a to-do can be enriched with an alarm (date and time), in which case a pop-up message is displayed when the deadline occurs. The firing of the alarm pops up another ViewContainer for clearing the alarm.

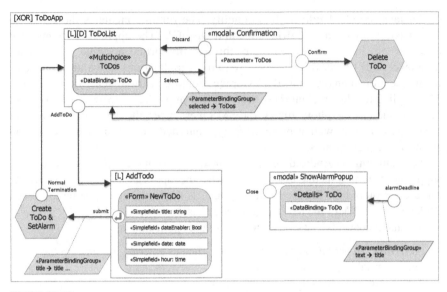

FIGURE 10.39

The "ToDo" Android app.

Each nonmodal ViewContainer is mapped to an activity. The noncontextual NavigationFlow between the "ToDoList" and the "AddToDo" ViewContainers is mapped to an explicit intent because it denotes a direct communication path between distinct activities. The system event that triggers the alarm pop-up is mapped to a broadcast intent, which is received by an alarm handling activity. The IFML events and navigation flows internal to the boundaries of an activity, such as the selection of a to-do in the "ToDos" ViewComponent, are mapped into Android events handled by suitable event listeners.

Figure 10.40 shows the XML manifest file of the "ToDo" app, which contains the declaration of the principal components and resources.

After a preamble (lines 1–8), the <application> element contains the declaration of the main components of the application: three activities ("ToDoListActivity," "AddToDoActivity," and "ShowAlarmPopupActivity") and one broadcast intent receiver ("AlarmReceiver"). The "ToDoListActivity" contains an intent filter (lines 18–21), which specifies that it responds to the implicit intent associated with a system action called MAIN (i.e., the launch of the app by the user).

Each activity is associated with an XML resource file, which dictates the interface layout of the activity's ViewContainer. Figure 10.41 shows the layout specification of the "ToDoListActivity."

The ViewContainer of the activity is mapped into a <ScrollView> element containing a vertical <LinearLayout> subelement; this defines an elementary screen configuration consisting of a vertical scrollable pane where items can be placed. The XML layout also specifies the static elements that implement the

```
1 <?xml version="1.0" encoding="utf-8"?>
2 <manifest xmlns:android="http://schemas.android.com/apk/res/android"
3    package="it.polimi.todo"
4    android:versionCode="1"
5    android:versionName="1.0" >
6    <uses-sdk
7        android:minSdkVersion="8"
8        android:targetSdkVersion="17" />
9    <application
10       android:allowBackup="true"
11       android:icon="@drawable/ic_launcher"
12       android:label="@string/app_name"
13       android:theme="@style/AppTheme" >
14       <activity
15           android:name="it.polimi.todo.activities.ToDoListActivity"
16           android:label="@string/app_name"
17           android:launchMode="singleTop" >
18           <intent-filter>
19               <action android:name="android.intent.action.MAIN" />
20               <category android:name="android.intent.category.LAUNCHER" />
21           </intent-filter>
22       </activity>
23       <activity
24           android:name="it.polimi.todo.activities.AddToDoActivity"
25           android:label="@string/title_activity_add_to_do" >
26       </activity>
27       <receiver
28           android:name="it.polimi.todo.receivers.AlarmReceiver"
29           android:label="@string/title_activity_alarm" >
30       </receiver>
31       <activity
32           android:name="it.polimi.todo.activities.ShowAlarmPopupActivity"
33           android:label="@string/title_activity_show_alarm_popup" >
34       </activity>
35   </application>
36</manifest>
```

FIGURE 10.40

The manifest file of the ToDo Android app.

```
1 <ScrollView xmlns:android="http://schemas.android.com/apk/res/android"
2     xmlns:tools="http://schemas.android.com/tools"
3     android:layout_width="fill_parent"
4     android:layout_height="fill_parent"
5     tools:context=".ToDoListActivity">
6     <LinearLayout android:id="@+id/checkBoxContainer"
7         android:layout_width="fill_parent"
8         android:layout_height="wrap_content"
9         android:orientation="vertical">
10        <Button android:layout_width="wrap_content"
11         android:layout_height="wrap_content"
12         android:text="@string/button_requireAdd"
13         android:onClick="requireNewToDo"/>
14     </LinearLayout>
15 </ScrollView>
```

FIGURE 10.41

The layout specification of the "ToDoListActivity" mapping the "ToDoList" ViewContainer.

content-independent navigation: the "AddToDo" NavigationFlow is mapped to a <Button> element (lines 10–13). The event triggering the NavigationFlow is mapped into the "onClick" attribute of the <Button> element, which specifies the activity target of the NavigationFlow[8].

The business logic for building the dynamic content of the ViewContainer maps onto the implementation code of the activity. The general schema for such a mapping is as follows:

- The ViewContainer is mapped to an activity class (i.e., a Java class that extends Activity).
- Each ViewComponent is mapped to a helper class, which supports data extraction and content rendering for the component. The helper class is also responsible of creating the listeners for the events associated with the ViewComponent.
- The standard "onCreate" method of the activity class implements the business logic for populating the activity interface after a noncontextual access. The method orchestrates the invocation of the ViewComponent helper classes, according to the execution sequence discussed in chapter 6.
- The activity class contains one method implementing the refresh of the ViewContainer after the navigation of a flow triggered by another activity. The method extracts the possible parameter values associated with the NavigationFlow, implemented as data associated with the intent, and orchestrates the invocation of the ViewComponent helper classes, according to the execution sequence discussed in chapter 6.
- The activity class contains one method for each NavigationFlow of the corresponding ViewContainer that triggers the navigation to a distinct ViewContainer. This method creates an explicit intent, stores in it the data corresponding to the parameters associated with the NavigationFlow, and fires the intent to start the target activity.

Figure 10.42 shows the code of the "ToDoListActivity" class. Since the "ToDoList" ViewContainer contains only one component (the <<MultiChoice>> List ViewComponent), the "ToDoListActivity" class exploits only one helper class (the private data member of class "ToDoListService," at line 4) for dynamic data retrieval and rendering. The code of the "ToDoListService" helper class is shown in Figure 10.43. The "ToDoListActivity" class comprises: the "onCreate" method for populating the content of the ViewContainer after a noncontextual access (lines 7–14); the "requireNewToDo" method for triggering the "AddToDo" activity (lines 17–20); and the "onActivityResult" method, for refreshing the content of the ViewContainer after the completion of the "AddToDo" activity (lines 23–29).

Note that the "requireNewToDo" method initializes the intent with the REQUIRE_NEW_TODO request code (line 19). The "onActivityResult" method then checks the "requestCode" and "resultCode" fields of the triggering intent (line 26) to verify that it has been activated by the normal termination of the previously triggered activity. This mechanism realizes the point-to-point asynchronous communication between activities.

```
1 public class ToDoListActivity extends Activity {
2   public static final int REQUIRE_NEW_TODO = 0;
3   private DatabaseHandler databaseHandler;
4   private ToDoListService toDoList;
5   // Initial content creation
6   @Override
7   protected void onCreate(Bundle savedInstanceState) {
8     super.onCreate(savedInstanceState);
9     setContentView(R.layout.activity_to_do_list);
10    this.databaseHandler = new DatabaseHandler(this);
11    LinearLayout linearLayout = (LinearLayout)findViewById(R.id.checkBoxContainer);
12    toDoList = new ToDoListService(this);
13    toDoList.loadAndRender(databaseHandler,linearLayout);
14  }
15
16  //Implements the AddToDo event of the ToDOList ViewContainer
17  public void requireNewToDo(View view) {
18    Intent intent = new Intent(this, AddToDoActivity.class);
19    startActivityForResult(intent, REQUIRE_NEW_TODO);
20  }
21
22  //Answers to the completion of the AddToDo activity
23  @Override
24  public void onActivityResult(int requestCode, int resultCode, Intent intent) {
25    super.onActivityResult(requestCode, resultCode, intent);
26    if (requestCode == REQUIRE_NEW_TODO && resultCode == RESULT_OK)
27      if (intent != null)
28        toDoList.loadAndRender(databaseHandler,linearLayout);
29  }
30 }
```

FIGURE 10.42

Implementation of the "ToDoListActivity" class.

Figure 10.43 shows the code of the "ToDoListService" helper class, which wraps the business logic for implementing the data binding and the rendition of the "ToDoList" multichoice ViewComponent. The "LoadAndRender" method (lines 9–22) extracts from the database the list of to-dos, creates one check box GUI element for each to-do, associates a listener method with each check box, and inserts the check box into the GUI layout. Note that the "onCheckBoxClicked" method implementing the select event in the "ToDos" ViewComponent (lines 25–37) supports the navigation to the "Confirmation" modal ViewContainer and implements also the construction and rendition of that ViewContainer; specifically, the method creates the alertDialog object corresponding to the modal ViewContainer (line 30) and attaches the event listeners corresponding to the "discard" and "confirm" events to it (lines 33–34).

The "LoadAndRender" method exploits the "databaseHandler" utility object (line 10), which wraps the connection with the data store. For brevity, we omit the illustration of the code implementing the persistence of the to-do list; we only mention that it can be realized quite simply using the SQLite engine natively supported by the Android framework and extending the library class "SQLiteOpenHelper" to obtain a "DatabaseHandler" class exposing the classical CRUD methods.

Figure 10.44 shows the implementation of the listeners for the "confirm" (lines 1–19) and "discard" (lines 21–35) events associated with the "Confirmation" modal ViewContainer.

```
 1 public class ToDoListService {
 2  private Activity activity;
 3
 4  public void ToDoListService (Activity activity){
 5    this.activity=activity;
 6  }
 7
 8  //Implements the data binding and rendition of the ToDoList
 9  public void loadAndRender(DatabaseHandler databaseHandler,LinearLayout
linearLayout) {
10    List<ToDo> toDos = databaseHandler.getAllToDos();
11    for (int i = 0; i < toDos.size(); i++) {
12      CheckBox checkBox = new CheckBox(this);
13      checkBox.setText(toDos.get(i).getText());
14      checkBox.setId(toDos.get(i).getId());
15      checkBox.setOnClickListener(new View.OnClickListener() {
16        @Override
17        public void onClick(View v) {
18          onCheckBoxClicked(v);
19        }
20      linearLayout.addView(checkBox);
21    }
22  }
23
24  // Implements the select event and NavigationFLow on the ToDoList
25  public void onCheckBoxClicked(View view) {
26    Resources resources = getResources();
27    ConfirmDialogListener confirmListener = new
28                      ConfirmDialogListener(view, databaseHandler);
29    DiscardDialogListener discardListener = new DiscardDialogListener(view);
30    AlertDialog alertDialog = new AlertDialog.Builder(ToDoListActivity.this)
31      .setTitle(resources.getString(R.string.confirmTitle))
32      .setMessage(resources.getString(R.string.confirmText))
33      .setPositiveButton(resources.getString(R.string.confirmButton),
confirmListener)
34      .setNegativeButton(resources.getString(R.string.discardButton),
discardListener)
35      .create();
36    alertDialog.show();
37  }
38 }
```

FIGURE 10.43

Implementation of the "ToDoListService" helper class for the "TodoList" ViewComponent.

The "ConfirmDialogListener" implements an "onClick" method (lines 11–19), which extracts from the clicked checkbox the text of the to-do and passes it to the "deleteToDo" method of the "databaseHandler" class as the identifier of the object to delete (line 14). The method also updates the GUI of the ToDoList ViewContainer by accessing the parent view's layout and removing the deleted to-do from it (lines 15–16). The "DiscardDialogListener" "onClick" method simply unchecks the view element corresponding to the selected to-do (lines 29–34).

Note that updating the content of the target "ToDoList" ViewContainer directly in the "onClick" event handling method, as done at lines 15–16, is convenient only is simple cases.If the ViewContainer comprises multiple interconnected View-Components, it is better to delegate the refresh of its content to a method of the ViewContainer's activity class, similar to the "onActivityResult" method used for inter-activity NavigationFlows.

The "AddToDo" ViewContainer is mapped onto an activity whose layout specification is shown in Figure 10.45

```
 1 public class ConfirmDialogListener implements OnClickListener {
 2   private View clickedView;
 3   private DatabaseHandler databaseHandler;
 4
 5   public ConfirmDialogListener(View clickedView, DatabaseHandler databaseHandler)
{
 6     this.clickedView = clickedView;
 7     this.databaseHandler = databaseHandler;
 8   }
 9
10  @Override
11  public void onClick(DialogInterface dialog, int which) {
12    CheckBox checkBox = (CheckBox) clickedView;
13    ToDo toDo = new ToDo(checkBox.getId(), (String) checkBox.getText());
14    databaseHandler.deleteToDo(toDo);
15    LinearLayout layout = (LinearLayout)clickedView.getParent();
16    layout.removeView(clickedView);
17    }
18
19 }
20
21 public class DiscardDialogListener implements OnClickListener {
22   private View clickedView;
23
24   public DiscardDialogListener(View clickedView) {
25         this.clickedView = clickedView;
26     }
27
28  @Override
29  public void onClick(DialogInterface dialog, int which) {
30         if (clickedView.getClass() == CheckBox.class) {
31             CheckBox checkBox = (CheckBox)clickedView;
32             checkBox.setChecked(false);
33         }
34     }
35 }
```

FIGURE 10.44

Implementation of the listeners for the "confirm" and "discard" events.

The layout is a simple vertical scrollable pane that contains four widgets corresponding to the field of the "NewToDo" Form ViewComponent and one button implementing the submit event.

Figure 10.46 shows the activity class implementing the "AddToDo" ViewContainer.

The "onCreate" method (lines 6–32) constructs and initialized the objects corresponding to the GUI widgets. In particular, the "dateEnabler" check box is enriched with an "onClick" event handler that toggles the state of the date and time picker widgets so that they become visible when the checkbox is selected (lines 18–26).

The "addToDoToList" method (lines 35–54) implements the submit event. It creates an intent (line 36), extracts the relevant information from the GUI widgets (lines 37–50), executes the "CreateToDoAndSetAlarm" action (line 51) implemented as a private method of the activity class, stores the result of the execution in the intent (line 52), and finishes. The "CreateToDoAndSetAlarm" method also schedules an alert for the new to-do when the user has provided a deadline. This requires creating another intent (line 61), targeted to an alarm receiver class, storing in it the identifier of the to-do, and registering a pending intent with the system alarm manager (lines 67–69).

```
 1 <ScrollView xmlns:android="http://schemas.android.com/apk/res/android"
 2          xmlns:tools="http://schemas.android.com/tools"
 3          android:layout_width="fill_parent"
 4          android:layout_height="fill_parent">
 5     <LinearLayout
 6          android:id="@+id/newToDoLayout"
 7          android:layout_width="fill_parent"
 8          android:layout_height="wrap_content"
 9          android:orientation="vertical">
10      <EditText android:id="@+id/toDoContent"
11            android:layout_width="match_parent"
12            android:layout_height="wrap_content"
13            android:hint="@string/defaultToDo"
14            android:inputType="text"/>
15      <CheckBox android:id="@+id/dateEnabler"
16            android:layout_width="match_parent"
17            android:layout_height="wrap_content"
18            android:text="@string/insertDate"/>
19      <DatePicker android:id="@+id/toDoAlarmDatePicker"
20             android:layout_width="match_parent"
21             android:layout_height="wrap_content"/>
22      <TimePicker android:id="@+id/toDoAlarmTimePicker"
23             android:layout_width="match_parent"
24             android:layout_height="wrap_content"/>
25     <Button android:layout_width="wrap_content"
26        android:layout_height="wrap_content"
27        android:text="@string/button_addToList"
28        android:onClick="addToDoToList"/>
29     </LinearLayout>
30</ScrollView>
```

FIGURE 10.45

Layout specification of activity mapping the AddToDo ViewContainer.

Figure 10.47 shows the class implementing the alarm receiver, which maps the "alarmDeadline" system event and the "ShowAlarmPopup" ViewContainer of Figure 10.39.

The "AlarmReceiver" class implements the "onReceive" method (lines 6–16), which extracts from the broadcast intent the message and the identifier of the to-do, checks if the to-do exists in the database, and creates an intent to start the "ShowAlarmPopup" activity. Note that setting the FLAG_ACTIVITY_NEW_TASK flag for the intent causes the pop up alert to be brought to the front of the screen with the state it was last in.

Finally, Figure 10.48 shows the layout and Figure 10.49 shows the activity class mapping the "ShowAlarmPopup" ViewContainer.

The layout definition uses a <RelativeLayout> element and the flexible "match_parent" size qualifier (lines 1–4), to let the pop-up window take all the space occupied by the parent activity, which is the entire screen.

The activity class implements the "onCreate" method, which extracts from the triggering intent the alarm message and creates a dialog box with one confirmation button associated with the "ReturnToListListener" class, implementing the outgoing NavigationFlow of the "ShowAlarmPopup" ViewContainer. This listener, shown in Figure 10.50, simply declares the termination of the calling activity.

```
 1 public class AddToDoActivity extends Activity {
 2   public final static String  TODO_CONTENT = "it.polimi.todo.TODO_CONTENT";
 3   public final static String  TODO_DATE = "it.polimi.todo.TODO_DATE";
 4
 5   @Override
 6   protected void onCreate(Bundle savedInstanceState) {
 7     super.onCreate(savedInstanceState);
 8     setContentView(R.layout.activity_add_to_do);
 9
10     CheckBox dateEnabler = (CheckBox) findViewById(R.id.dateEnabler);
11     dateEnabler.setOnClickListener(new View.OnClickListener() {
12       @Override
13       public void onClick(View v) {
14         CheckBox c = (CheckBox) v;
15         TimePicker t = (TimePicker) findViewById(R.id.toDoAlarmTimePicker);
16         DatePicker d = (DatePicker) findViewById(R.id.toDoAlarmDatePicker);
17
18         if (c.isChecked()) {
19           t.setEnabled(true);
20           d.setEnabled(true);
21         }
22         else {
23           t.setEnabled(false);
24           d.setEnabled(false);
25         }
26       }
27     });
28     TimePicker t = (TimePicker) findViewById(R.id.toDoAlarmTimePicker);
29     DatePicker d = (DatePicker) findViewById(R.id.toDoAlarmDatePicker);
30     t.setEnabled(false);
31     d.setEnabled(false);
32   }
33
34   // Implements the submit event and NavigationFLow of NewToDo
35   public void addToDoToList(View view) {
36     Intent intent = new Intent();
37     EditText editText = (EditText) findViewById(R.id.toDoContent);
38     String newContent = editText.getText().toString();
39     CheckBox dateEnabler = (CheckBox) findViewById(R.id.dateEnabler);
40     if (dateEnabler.isChecked()) {
41       DatePicker datePicker = (DatePicker) findViewById(R.id.toDoAlarmDatePicker);
42       int day = datePicker.getDayOfMonth();
43       int month = datePicker.getMonth();
44       int year = datePicker.getYear();
45       TimePicker timePicker = (TimePicker) findViewById(R.id.toDoAlarmTimePicker);
46       int hour = timePicker.getCurrentHour();
47       int minute = timePicker.getCurrentMinute();
48       GregorianCalendar pickedDate = new
49                   GregorianCalendar(year, month, day, hour, minute);
50     }
51     createToDoSetAlarm(newContent, pickedDate);
52     setResult(RESULT_OK, intent);
53     finish();
54   }
55
56   private void createToDoSetAlarm(String message, GregorianCalendar alarmDate) {
57     if (!message.isEmpty()) {
58       ToDo toDo = new ToDo(message, alarmDate);
59       long id = databaseHandler.addToDo(toDo);
60       if (alarmDate != null) {
61         Intent intent = new Intent(this, AlarmReceiver.class);
62         intent.putExtra(AlarmReceiver.ALARM_MESSAGE, message);
63         intent.putExtra("toDoId", id);
64         PendingIntent pendingIntent = PendingIntent.getBroadcast(this, 0,
65                     intent,
66                     PendingIntent.FLAG_UPDATE_CURRENT);
67         AlarmManager alarmManager = (AlarmManager) getSystemService(ALARM_SERVICE);
68         alarmManager.set(AlarmManager.RTC_WAKEUP, alarmDate.getTimeInMillis(),
69         pendingIntent);       }
70   }
71 }
```

FIGURE 10.46

Implementation of the listeners for the "confirm" and "discard" events.

```
1 public class AlarmReceiver extends BroadcastReceiver {
2   public final static String ALARM_MESSAGE = "it.polimi.todo.ALARM_MESSAGE";
3   public final static int ALARM_REQUEST = 2;
4
5   @Override
6   public void onReceive(Context context, Intent intent) {
7     String message = intent.getStringExtra(ALARM_MESSAGE);
8     long toDoId = intent.getLongExtra("toDoId",0L);
9     DatabaseHandler dbHandler = new DatabaseHandler(context);
10    if (dbHandler.retrieveToDo(toDoId) != null) {
11      Intent startPopupIntent = new Intent(context, ShowAlarmPopupActivity.class);
12      startPopupIntent.putExtra(ALARM_MESSAGE, message);
13      startPopupIntent.setFlags(Intent.FLAG_ACTIVITY_NEW_TASK);
14      context.startActivity(startPopupIntent);
15    }
16  }
17 }
```

FIGURE 10.47

Implementation of the receiver for the to-do alarm.

```
1 <RelativeLayout xmlns:android="http://schemas.android.com/apk/res/android"
2   xmlns:tools="http://schemas.android.com/tools"
3   android:layout_width="match_parent"
4   android:layout_height="match_parent"
5   android:paddingBottom="@dimen/activity_vertical_margin"
6   android:paddingLeft="@dimen/activity_horizontal_margin"
7   android:paddingRight="@dimen/activity_horizontal_margin"
8   android:paddingTop="@dimen/activity_vertical_margin"
9   tools:context=".ShowAlarmPopupActivity" >
10</RelativeLayout>
```

FIGURE 10.48

Layout specification of the "ShowAlarmPopup" ViewContainer.

```
1 public class ShowAlarmPopupActivity extends Activity {
2   @Override
3   protected void onCreate(Bundle savedInstanceState) {
4     super.onCreate(savedInstanceState);
5     setContentView(R.layout.activity_show_alarm_popup);
6     Intent intent = getIntent();
7     if (intent.getExtras() != null) {
8       String message = intent.getStringExtra(AlarmReceiver.ALARM_MESSAGE);
9       Resources resources = getResources();
10      AlertDialog dialog = new AlertDialog.Builder(this)
11        .setMessage(message)
12        .setPositiveButton(resources.getString(R.string.confirmButton),
13          new CloseListener(this)).create();
14      dialog.show();
15    }
16  }
17 }
```

FIGURE 10.49

Implementation of the "ShowAlarmPopup" activity class.

```
1 public class CloseListener implements OnClickListener {
2   private Activity        contextActivity;
3
4   public CloseListener(ShowAlarmPopupActivity contextActivity) {
5     this.contextActivity = contextActivity;
6   }
7
8   @Override
9   public void onClick(DialogInterface dialog, int which) {
10    contextActivity.finish();
11      }
12 }
```

FIGURE 10.50

Implementation of the "CloseListener."

10.5 SUMMARY OF THE CHAPTER

This chapter discussed on how to map the platform-independent IFML models into specific technological platforms and provided a set of guidelines on how to generate running code from IFML diagrams. Ideally, the mapping to the implementation layer could be illustrated for any software architecture that supports user's interactivity. For space reasons, this chapter illustrated four main categories of platforms that represent a good sample of the current status of the practice: pure HTML with a template based approach (specifically, on so-called LAMP environments comprising Linux, Apache, MySQL and PHP), pure HTML with a presentation a framework (namely, Spring, one of the most popular web presentation frameworks based on the Model-View-Controller pattern), rich internet (specifically, Asynchronous JavaScript and XML - AJAX), and mobile applications (Android is chosen as a representative of native mobile application development).

10.6 BIBLIOGRAPHIC NOTES

Web programming is a very popular subject for which there are lots of online references and textbooks. A popular online resource for beginners is the W3schools web site (http://www.w3schools.com/), which publishes tutorials and self-evaluation exercises on the most relevant web technologies.

The programming of web applications with the LAMP architecture is also the subject of innumerable textbooks ad online resources. The book by Robin Nixon [Nixon2012] is a good start on the subject. The PHP reference web site (http://www.php.net/) is a hub for language documentation.

Spring-based development requires a background in Java servlets and possibly in Java Enterprise Edition (JEE). The official reference for JEE is Oracle's web site (http://docs.oracle.com/javaee/), which offers both a tutorial and the reference documentation of the platform APIs. The official web site of the Spring Project (http://spring.io/) publishes online reference documentation, getting started guides, and advanced tutorials, introducing the reader to several Spring tasks. Among the many textbooks, Spring in Action by Craig Walls [Walls11] and Spring in Practice by Willie Wheeler and Joshua White [WW13] offer a comprehensive overview.

Rich Internet applications are developed with a mix of technologies and approaches, including HTML5, JavaScript, CSS, AJAX, and jQuery. Quick tutorials on all of these are published in the already mentioned W3School web site. The book HTML5: Designing Rich Internet Applications (Visualizing the Web) by Matthew David [David13] addresses RIA development with HTML, from the tag structure of HTML5 to its multimedia capabilities, and programming with JavaScript and advanced AJAX patterns. An official introduction to HTML5 is published by the W3C (http://www.w3.org/TR/html5/introduction.html).

Extensive coverage of jQuery and JavaScript programming can be found in the Learning jQuery book by Jonathan Chaffer and Karl Swedberg [CS13].

Native, web-based, and cross-platform mobile application development approaches are discussed and contrasted in [CL11, RB12, PSC12]. The Android developers' web site (http://developer.android.com/) is the official source of materials for Android training, featuring the APIs references and development guides. A popular text on Android development is Professional Android 4 Application Development by Reto Meier [Meier12].

END NOTES

1. For brevity, the examples do not show PHP security practices such as storing sensitive data in separate include files, masking error logs, interrupting the script upon database connection failure, etc. See http://www.php.net/manual/en/security.php for an introduction to PHP security.
2. Noncontextual navigation can be based on an explicit InteractionFlow from another ViewContainer or on an implicit one if the target ViewContainer is a landmark.
3. Forms with preloaded fields may have one or more data retrieval queries. In this case, each preloaded field is treated as a List (preload cardinality = many) or Details (preload cardinality = 1).
4. An alternative is to use REST-style parameter concatenation in the URI template.
5. The .do suffix is commonly used in Java web frameworks to distinguish requests addressed to the dispatcher.
6. For simplicity, we do not consider failures in the computation of ViewContainers.
7. The display of the news of the default category requires the extraction of the default value from the "NewsCategoriesService" and its storage in the model before invoking the "NewsItemsSearchService."
8. In the sequel, we sometimes use the terms activity and ViewContainer interchangeably to denote the activity that maps a ViewContainer and vice versa.

Tools for model-driven development of interactive applications

11

The modeling notations, the development process, and the implementation techniques for building interactive applications with IFML have been overviewed in previous chapters independent of any specific tool. As shown in chapter 10, the domain model and the IFML models can be manually mapped to executable programs and structures, such as a relational database and a set of JSP templates and components of the MVC architecture. The guidelines provided in the previous chapters can help engineers produce a working application using the coding environment and deployment platform of their choice. However, when a well-defined software engineering method is in place, development can be assisted by rapid application development tools, supporting and documenting the design and automating in part the production of the implementation code.

To make this discussion concrete, this chapter exemplifies the support to IFML model-driven development with the help of a specific tool, called WebRatio. WebRatio is a composite application development tool that covers not only the front-end design, but also domain modeling, business logic modeling, and process modeling, thus providing an end-to-end approach to model-driven development. In the bibliographic notes we will mention more tools that are either already IFML-ready or can be customized to model application front ends with IFML.

11.1 INTRODUCTION TO WEBRATIO

WebRatio is a development environment supporting IFML. It was created in 2001 for the model-driven development of applications specified with the Web Modeling Language.

The tool comprises several modeling perspectives and includes a code generation framework that automates the production of the software components in all tiers of the application and the connections between the application and external APIs. More precisely, WebRatio focuses on the following main aspects:

- Domain modeling: it supports the design of domain models using the structural features of the UML class diagram.
- Front-end design: it assists the design of IFML diagrams, comprising both built-in IFML constructs and extensions defined by the designer and imported into the tool.

335

- Business logic design: it allows the designer to explode and refine an IFML Action by specifying its internal functioning as a workflow of component invocations, such as data query and update operations, Web API calls, utility functions, and—more generally—any piece of user-defined code imported into the tool.
- Data Mapping: it enables the declaration of JDBC/ODBC-compliant data sources supporting the application, the automatic translation of the persistent classes and associations of the domain model into relational schemas, and the generation of the object-relational mapping (ORM) specifications bridging the classes and associations of the domain model to the data structures of the persistent store. If the database is pre-existing, only the ORM specifications are created.
- Presentation design: it offers functionality for defining or importing presentation templates, typically encoded in HTML5, and for mapping the elements of a View-Containers and ViewComponents to the layout and visual properties of a template.
- Code generation: it automatically translates IFML models and presentation templates into applications built in Java and HTML5, with the front end running on desktop and mobile terminals and the back end running on any Java server, deployed either on premises or directly on public cloud resources.

The workflow of Figure 11.1 summarizes the design process of WebRatio, highlighting the design phases together with their inputs and outputs. The different tasks will be described in more detail in the next sections.

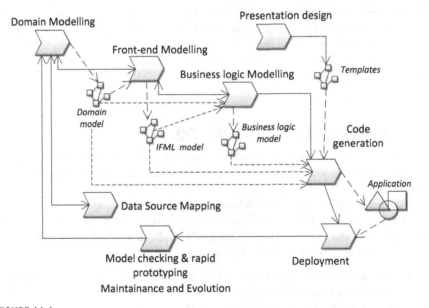

FIGURE 11.1

Development flow with WebRatio.

The software architecture of the applications created by WebRatio exploits the design principles and techniques described in chapter 10 for web and mobile applications. In particular, web applications are built using the MVC pattern. Generic components implement action in the business tier, while HTML5 and CSS presentation rules are used for factoring out the look and feel from the page templates.

Mobile applications are built by translating the IFML model into platform-independent code that is executed directly or through a wrapper in the target device. Presently, WebRatio generates code for the PhoneGap mobile development framework.[1]

In this chapter, we briefly overview the functionalities offered by WebRatio and discuss some advanced features, such as model checking, model-level debugging, cooperative work, automatic documentation, and user-defined IFML extensions. The chapter ends with an annotated bibliograph, overviewing a sample of other tools for the model-drive design of interactive applications.

11.2 DOMAIN MODEL DESIGN

WebRatio provides a graphical user interface embedded as a plugin in the popular Eclipse workbench, which allows designers to compose both the domain model and the IFML diagrams describing the interface of the application.

Figure 11.2 shows a snapshot of the WebRatio user interface, which is organized into the typical four areas of application development tools:

- a project tree (upper left frame), organizing all the elements of the application project;
- a work area (upper right frame), where the specifications are visually edited;

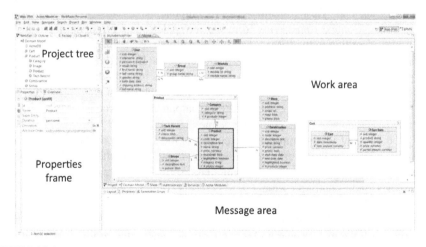

FIGURE 11.2

Overview of the WebRatio interface.

- a property frame (lower left frame), where the properties of individual elements can be set; and
- a message area (lower right frame), where messages and warnings are displayed.

A basic WebRatio application project consists of a single class diagram and of a set of IFML diagrams. In particular, Figure 11.2 shows the WebRatio editor open on the domain model of one of the sample applications shipped with the tool: the "Acme" online shop. The work area visualizes the class diagram. The designer can define classes, attributes, associations, and generalizations. The elements displayed in the diagram are also presented in the project tree, where they are hierarchically organized in folders. The properties of the currently selected element of the diagram are displayed and can be edited in a property frame.

The Acme Domain model comprises both persistent and nonpersistent classes and associations, as specified by the duration property set in the properties panel. The different duration is also highlighted visually in the diagram by the use of a different color.

Classes and associations can be enclosed within Packages to help the organization of large domain models. Furthermore, a default personalization subschema comprising the User and Group classes and the associations representing roles (described in chapter 3) is added by default to the domain model, and the developer can extend it with additional classes and associations.

11.3 IFML FRONT-END DESIGN

The same general organization of the graphical user interface also supports the editing of the IFML diagrams. The design of a diagram is accomplished by picking constructs such as ViewContainers, ViewComponents, Events, InteractionFlows, Actions, and Context dimensions from the tool palette and arranging them in the work area according to the IFML diagram formation rules.

Figure 11.3 shows the IFML work area, open on the IFML diagram that specifies the public site view of the Acme application, which includes multiple ViewContainers, ViewComponents, and Actions. These are also displayed in the project tree, and the properties of the currently selected ViewComponent (the ProductDetails Module in Figure 11.3) appear in the properties frame.

The binding of ViewComponents to classes of the domain model can be specified using the properties frame or a work area menu contextual to the View Component. The designer can select the DataBinding class, set the VisualizationAttributes, and define the ConditionalExpression.

Double clinking the icon of a Module brings up the IFML diagram where the module content is defined, as shown in Figure 11.4. Figure 11.4 also shows that hovering with the mouse over an InteractionFlow causes the information about the associated ParameterBindingGroup to be displayed.

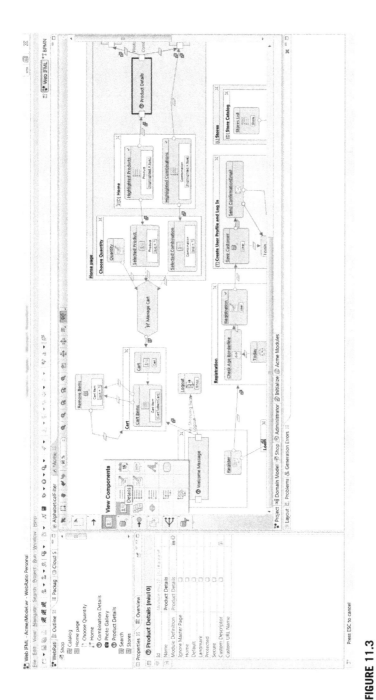

FIGURE 11.3

WebRatio interface for editing IFML diagrams.

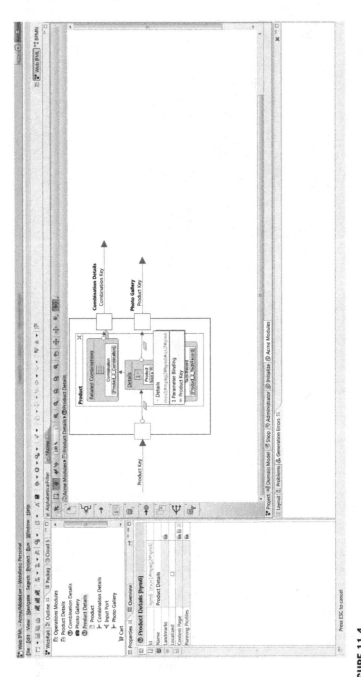

FIGURE 11.4

Interface for defining the content of a Module.

11.4 **DATA MAPPING AND ALIGNMENT**

WebRatio assists the implementation of the data tier for applications that deal with persistent data by associating the front end to the data sources where the content to be published and manipulated resides (Figure 11.5). The data sources supported natively include any system accessible via JDBC/ODBC. Additional data storage platforms—such as noSQL databases, XML repositories, and LDAP directories— can be added by programming and importing within WebRatio the Actions and View-Components for connecting to such data sources.

WebRatio guides the user in declaring the data sources and in mapping the classes and association to tables and columns. The mapping information is stored in ORM mapping files of the underlying ORM system (Java Persistence API and Hibernate ORM formats are supported).

Derived data can be added to the elements of the domain model with the help of a wizard. A code generator translates the OCL expressions of the derived elements into equivalent SQL statements, which can be automatically installed into the appropriate data source in the form of stored procedures or views (Figure 11.6).

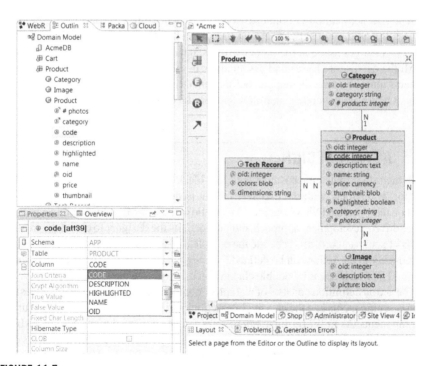

FIGURE 11.5

WebRatio interface for defining the mapping of the domain model onto a persistent data store.

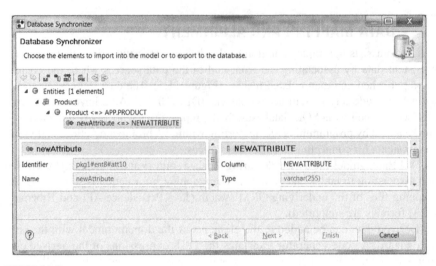

FIGURE 11.6

WebRatio interface for aligning the domain model and the schemas of the persistent stores.

When an application is bound to some persistent stores, WebRatio can be used to check the alignment between the domain model and the physical databases and to reconcile changes made in the model with the database, and vice versa.

All the persistent classes and associations in the domain model and their derived elements must be correctly mapped before generating the code and running the application. Otherwise the code generation may produce incomplete results.

11.5 ACTION DESIGN

IFML treats the application business logic as a black box. The Action, which is modeled only for its interplay with the user interface in terms of parameters exchange and the effect on the visualized ViewContainer. WebRatio embeds IFML design within a broader model-driven development approach and thus permits the designer to define the internal details of actions in order to generate the complete code of the application. The internal functionality of an Action can be defined by using the action definition editor, shown in Figure 11.7, which opens by double clicking on the Action in the IFML diagram.

The action definition consists of a graph of component calls, in which the nodes are business components and the arcs are InteractionFlows denoting the order of execution of components. As in IFML, InteractionFlows can be associated with a ParameterBindingGroup to specify input–output dependencies. Also, different InteractionFlows can exit a component to express different termination conditions, similar the specification of black-box Actions in the IFML diagram. The components that constitute the action definition can be chosen from those predefined in WebRatio or developers can use their own business components, which can be imported into the tool.

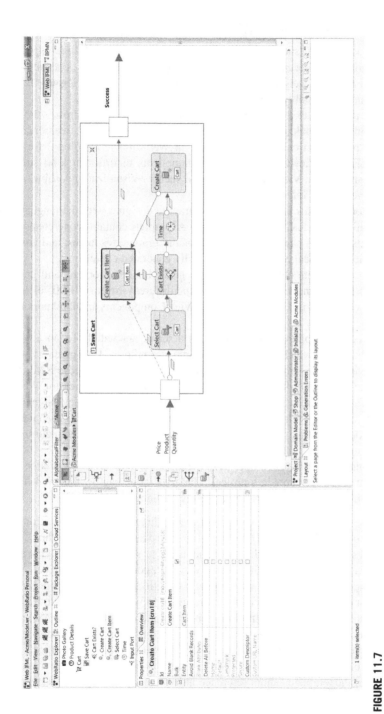

FIGURE 11.7

WebRatio interface for action definition.

11.6 PRESENTATION DESIGN

An essential aspect of a successful user interface is its graphic design, especially when the application is targeted to the general public and thus must be as attractive as possible. IFML purposely ignores the presentation aspects and delegates them to the implementation, possibly supported by tools.

WebRatio incorporates a presentation design functionality that addresses the definition of the interface look and feel with a template-based approach. In essence, the designer can provide an example (a template in WebRatio terminology) for each IFML ViewElement: ViewContainer; ViewComponents of different kind such as Details, List and Forms; ViewComponentParts, such as VisualizationAttributes and Fields; and Events with InteractionFlows.

Presentation templates are created by the graphic designer with the language of choice, typically HTML5, CSS, and JavaScript. A template contains concrete presentation elements, such as page layout constructs and graphic resources, and abstract elements, which are placeholders for dynamically generated content.

Examples of concrete elements are layout grids, banners, footers, and graphic resources. Abstract elements are markers for the different kinds of IFML elements that could be visualized in a template, such as ViewComponents and landmark navigation menus.

In practice, the graphic designer produces a set of annotated files in a source presentation language, which specify an "example of rendition" for a given ViewElement. Such files contain simple directives, expressed as special-purpose XML tags, that denote the insertion of IFML elements produced by the code generator. WebRatio provides functionalities for importing the mock-ups of the graphic designer into the tool and for transforming them into layout templates at different granularities usable for code generation. Figure 11.8 shows the interface of the template import wizard.

The tool also allows the developer to select and associate already available templates to IFML ViewElements in a project. The association can be done at different levels of granularity depending on the generality of the template:

- A template can be specifically designed for an individual ViewContainer or ViewComponent. In this case, the code of the template can reference the individual subelements (e.g., the individual fields or submit events of a Form, the various attributes of a Details or List ViewComponent, or the specific ViewComponents within a ViewContainer). A distinct presentation style can be defined for each of them. This approach is suited to ViewElements with highly sophisticated presentation requirements, because it can apply fine-grain control over the look and feel of each visualized element, but the resulting template is not reusable across projects or different ViewElements of the same project.
- A template can be designed generically for multiple ViewElements. In this case, the code of the template cannot reference individual ViewElements but must express presentation features at a higher level. Usually, the template defines

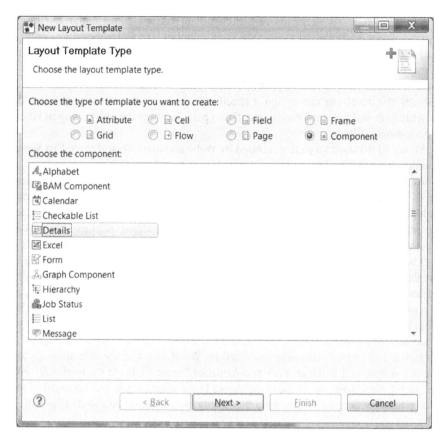

FIGURE 11.8

Layout template import wizard.

the same presentation style for all the ViewElements of the same type (e.g., for all the List ViewComponents, all the Forms, all the fields of a given type), thus providing a uniform look and feel across the interface. This approach is effective for large applications with simple presentation requirements.

- As an intermediate approach, a set of ViewElements can be associated with the same template, as in the previous case, but some rules of the default presentation template can be overridden at the local level of some specific ViewElements. For example, an application could set a default presentation template for List ViewComponents, which could then be overridden for specific ViewComponents. In this way, different presentation styles for the same ViewElement can coexist in the same application or even in the same ViewContainer, yielding a good compromise between uniformity and specificity of presentation. This approach is effective for large applications, with complex presentation requirements.

WebRatio supports all the above-mentioned approaches. In particular, the developer can assign a template at a coarse level of granularity (e.g., for the entire application) and then override such a global default by assigning more specific templates to finer-grain ViewElements at the individual ViewContainer, ViewComponent, ViewComponentPart and InteractionFlow level. Figure 11.9 shows the property panel whereby the developer can assign a specific presentation template to the selected ViewElement and fine tune such presentation parameters as the positioning of labels and the usage of icons.

Figure 11.10 shows a page generated by WebRatio that contains three List ViewComponents published with three different layout templates.

Another aspect of presentation design is the definition of the relative positioning of dynamic content within the interface. An IFML ViewContainer may comprise multiple nested ViewContainers and ViewComponents. The IFML model does not prescribe the actual layout of such elements within the rendered interface. This task is accomplished in WebRatio by means of the dedicated interface shown in Figure 11.11.

The interface consists of a grid- and location-based layout editor. The presentation template associated with the ViewContainer is analyzed, and the abstract locations defined in it are identified. An abstract location is a place where dynamic content can be rendered. The designer can define the positioning system of each location (e.g., by using a grid) and assign ViewElements to the places of the positioning systems (e.g., to the cells of the grid).

Figure 11.12 shows the page generated by WebRatio. The ViewComponents are laid out as specified in the abstract grid model of Figure 11.11. In the rendition, only two ViewComponents out of the three shown in the abstract grid are displayed in the pop-up window, because the user has chosen only one product to be added to the trolley.

11.7 CODE GENERATION

After specifying the domain model and the IFML diagrams, assigning presentation templates to ViewElements and defining their placement in the abstract positioning systems, and mapping the persistent classes and associations of domain model to the data sources, it is possible to launch automatic code generation, which transforms the application models into components for the selected deployment platform. WebRatio supports code generation for mobile platforms and for HTML5-CSS-Javascript web front ends backed by a Java web server architecture.

Before generating the application code, the developer selects the target platform and the deployment host, which can be a cloud resource.

11.7.1 CODE GENERATION FOR WEB AND RICH INTERNET APPLICATION

The web code generator adopts the MVC software architecture presented in chapter 10. The simplest configuration exploits a pure-HTML encoding of the presentation

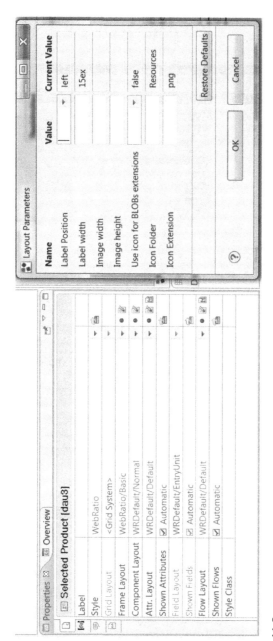

FIGURE 11.9

Assignment of a presentation template (Layout) to the "Selected Product" Details ViewComponent.

FIGURE 11.10

The same ViewComponent displayed with three different layout templates.

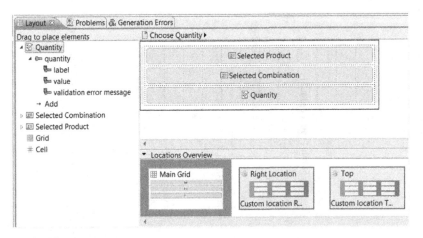

FIGURE 11.11

Interface for relative positioning of ViewElements in ViewContainers.

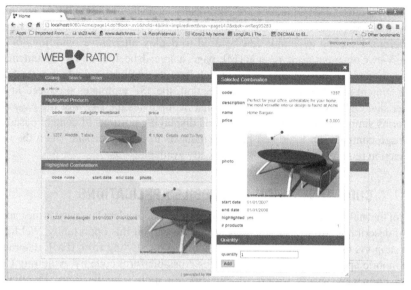

FIGURE 11.12

Page generated by WebRatio, with the layout specified in Figure 11.11.

templates, a Java implementation of the back end, including dynamic page templates for the view, a controller servlet and plain Java objects for the model, and a relational implementation of the data tier. In this configuration, the output of code generation includes:

- A set of JSP templates for the View, including HTML code and JSP custom tags. Each JSP template corresponds to a ViewContainer and is obtained by merging the presentation templates relevant to the ViewContainer itself, the ViewComponents included in it, and their ViewComponentParts, Events, and InteractionFlows. The code generator injects code into the resulting assembled JSP template by replacing the abstract XML elements of the presentation template with concrete Java code for retrieving content from the model objects.
- A set of generic Java components, deployed in the Model, supporting the computation of the content of ViewContainers and ViewComponents and the orchestration of the workflow of IFML action definitions. One generic component is deployed for each type of ViewComponent (e.g., Lists, Details). Such generic components are instantiated with XML descriptors, which specify their concrete properties, such as a query realizing the data binding, the parameters required in input and provided in output, and the visualization attributes. Normally, the developer is not required to edit descriptors. If this need arises, however, for instance to optimize a SQL query, the custom descriptor can be stored in a special directory and will not be overwritten by subsequent invocations of the code generator.
- The configuration file of the Controller.

The produced JSP templates are completely agnostic of the rendition language used, which depends on the presentation template provided by the graphic designer. Therefore, the code generator can be used to deploy alternative renditions of the same ViewContainer, such as an HTML page, a spreadsheet, or a PDF document.

For achieving the responsiveness of rich Internet applications, which refresh the page content selectively upon user interaction, the JSP templates produced at the server side embody an AJAX controller that manipulates the DOM of the page and performs simple actions such as hiding and displaying portions of content based on the page computation logic and pushing requests to the server side when the user interaction requires content that is not already available.

11.7.2 CODE GENERATION FOR MOBILE APPLICATIONS

One of the main advantages of IFML as a platform-independent language is the capacity of describing cross-platform applications. To exploit this opportunity, WebRatio also supports the generation of code for mobile apps, starting from IFML diagrams. The mobile application generator produces cross-platform code by exploiting Cordova/ Phonegap, an open-source framework for mobile applications. Developers write HTML5, CSS3, and JavaScript code. The framework wraps this code within a container (essentially a mobile browser). In this way, "native" apps can be deployed on different mobile platforms (seven platforms are supported as of today). WebRatio generates the HTML5, CSS3, and JavaScript sources from the IFML models and automatically packages them as running mobile apps using the Phonegap services. In contrast to the web and RIA generated applications, the code produced for mobile applications implements all the logics required for page computation in the HTML and JavaScript artifacts deployed in the Phonegap environment. This makes it possible to deploy stand-alone apps that work even when disconnected from the Internet.

11.8 ADVANCED FEATURES

WebRatio includes additional functionalities for model checking, debugging, cooperative work, automatic project documentation, and user-defined IFML extensions.

11.8.1 MODEL CHECKING

One of the benefits of conceptual modeling is the possibility of automatically checking the project for errors at the design level. This feature allows the early verification of the models produced by the designer, saving time in the code generation and in the debugging of the application. WebRatio provides error checking at three levels:

- Domain and IFML Model: this function checks the correctness of the domain model, of the IFML diagrams, and of the action definition workflows; it presents the detected problems, together with their level of severity and hints on how to fix them.

- Domain Model Mapping: this function checks if the persistent classes and associations of the domain model are correctly mapped to the data sources and signals if the databases are misaligned with respect to the domain model due to changes in the UML specification or in the physical data sources; detected problems with the associated hints are highlighted.
- Presentation and publishing: this function checks if all the ViewElements are associated with a presentation template, if all the elements comprised within a ViewContainer have been placed in the locations provided by the presentation templates, and if the deployment server contains all the components needed to run the application; if anything is missing, appropriate warnings are provided, with suggestions on how to solve problems.

Figure 11.13 shows an example of the output of the model checking applied to the IFML diagram. The warnings signal that no ParameterBindingGroup has been found for the Login flow, which may cause the Login Action to remain without the mandatory input parameters of username and password.

11.8.2 MODEL DEBUGGING

Code-level debugging is one of the most popular methods in traditional application development. WebRatio offers a similar functionality for inspecting the runtime behavior of an application, but at the conceptual model level.

The developer can set breakpoints on any IFML model element in order to stop the execution before or after the computation of the element. When a project contains breakpoints, execution can be performed in debug mode, which permits the developer to follow the progress of the computation step-by-step, inspecting the input and output parameter values of ViewComponents as well as the content extracted by ViewComponent's ConditionalExpressions.

Figure 11.14 shows the interface of the model debug perspective of WebRatio. The upper-left frame lists all the pending interaction and internal application events, such as a user event or the beginning and end of the computation of a ViewContainer or ViewComponent. The developer can interact with the interface and step over or into each execution phase and inspect the principal computation variables, shown in the upper right frame. At the same time, the work area and project tree display the status of the execution visually, by highlighting the ViewElements under computation.

11.8.3 COOPERATIVE WORK AND ENTERPRISE SCALE DEVELOPMENT

WebRatio includes project alignment functions, which facilitate the parallel development of an application by a work team. The typical workflow of a WebRatio project consists in developing the data model first and then adding the specifications of the site views necessary to fulfill the application requirements. Site views are natural

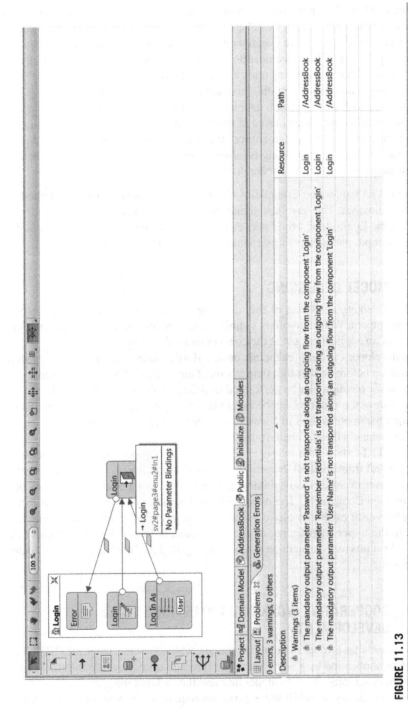

FIGURE 11.13

The model checking function detects problems in the IFML diagram.

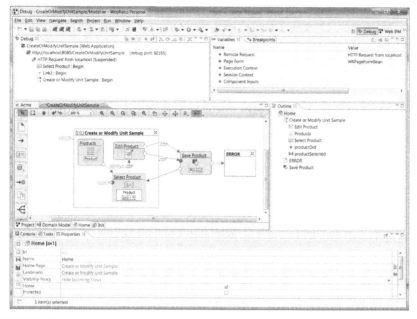

FIGURE 11.14

The model debug perspective in WebRatio.

units of work, which can be independently developed by separate work teams. Therefore, WebRatio includes two functions for facilitating parallel development:

- The import function makes it possible to import the site views of another project into the current project, merging the two projects together. The import function performs a number of consistency checks and transformations that ensure the merged project is the correct union of the two merged subprojects. Consistency checks and transformations are logged into a file and presented as a report to the user, who can accept them or undo the import.
- The export function makes it possible to export from the current project either the data model alone or the data model together with one or more site views. The export function creates a new project, consisting of the exported subschemas. The new project can be evolved in parallel with the original project and then merged back into the original project using the import function.

11.8.4 AUTOMATIC DOCUMENTATION

WebRatio automatically generates project documentation in a format inspired by the popular JavaDoc documentation layout. The document generator is written as a set of customizable rules, which the designer can override and extend to obtain a personalized documentation format. The documentation can be produced in such formats as HTML, PDF, or RTF, and describes every aspect of the project in an easy-to-browse format.

Figure 11.15 shows a sample documentation page, which includes a ViewContainer description. Clicking on each symbol and link opens the documentation page associated with the selected concept. In the example, by clicking on the "StoresList" ViewComponent the user accesses the detailed information of the selected element.

11.8.5 **IFML EXTENSIBILITY**

WebRatio exploits the extension mechanism of IFML and allows developers to create and integrate into the development tool their own custom IFML extensions, such as ViewContainers ,ViewComponents, and code generators.

Custom IFML elements permit the designer to reverse-engineer their interface and business components and make them part of the conceptual modeling and code generation process. Extending IFML requires defining a plug-in implementation-level component and deploying it in WebRatio. The model editor and code generator can then use the new component as any other IFML built-in element.

The definition of a custom component requires addressing both design-time and runtime issues. Adding a custom ViewElement to WebRatio requires the creation of the following artifacts:

- An IFML element definition: this is an XML descriptor file, created with a wizard provided by WebRatio; it contains information that instructs WebRatio to build the proper GUI commands for inserting the new IFML element within the IFML Model, linking it to other elements, and defining the admissible input and output parameters.

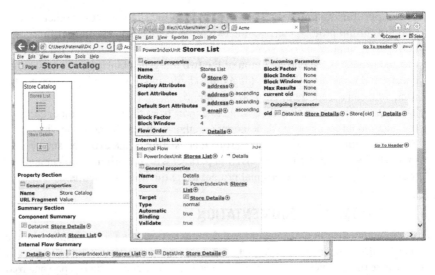

FIGURE 11.15

Example of project documentation generated by WebRatio.

- Validation rules: these are optional rules, encoded following a standard template provided by WebRatio, which enable the tool to validate the usage of the custom IFML element in the IFML diagram and report errors, warnings, and repair hints when some correctness rule is not respected.
- The input, output, and logic templates: if the element is a ViewComponent, which typically requires some processing at runtime, the developer must fill in a standard template to describe the admissible (optional and mandatory) input and output parameters and the optional configuration aspects of the element's implementation; this information is then exploited by the actual implementation code to configure the runtime service that realizes the custom component.
- The presentation template(s): if the element must be rendered in the interface (e.g., a ViewContainer or a ViewComponent), the developer has to provide one or more examples of its rendition in the presentation language of choice.
- The implementation code: an IFML extension is normally encoded as a runtime object, which performs the actual business service for which the extension is designed. The typical case is a ViewComponent, which is implemented as a Java class responsible for input acquisition, content extraction and processing, and output computation.

WebRatio comes with a set of predefined extensions, both general purpose and specific for the development of web applications. Extensions are of two classes. IFML extensions specialize the IFML model elements, according to the built-in mechanism of the language. Action components provide business logic blocks that can be used in the definition of the internal workflow of an IFML Action.

Figure 11.16 shows the interface for managing the construction of a custom IFML extension. The project tree on the left organizes all the artifacts constituting the extension. The work area shows the form for creating the XML descriptor file of the "Hierarchy" ViewComponent extension.

Once a custom extension is completely defined, it appears in the WebRatio tool palette of the IFML diagram editor, as shown in Figure 11.17. It can then be used in the diagram with the standard IFML elements.

11.9 SUMMARY OF THE CHAPTER

This chapter presented an exemplary implementation of IFML built as a model-driven development environment within the Eclipse framework. The described implementation, called WebRatio, is a composite application development tool that covers not only the front-end design, but also domain modeling, business logic modeling, and process modeling, thus providing an end-to-end approach to model-driven development. The chapter also mentions more tools, which are either already IFML-ready, or can be customized to model application front-ends with IFML, through UML profiling or metamodeling.

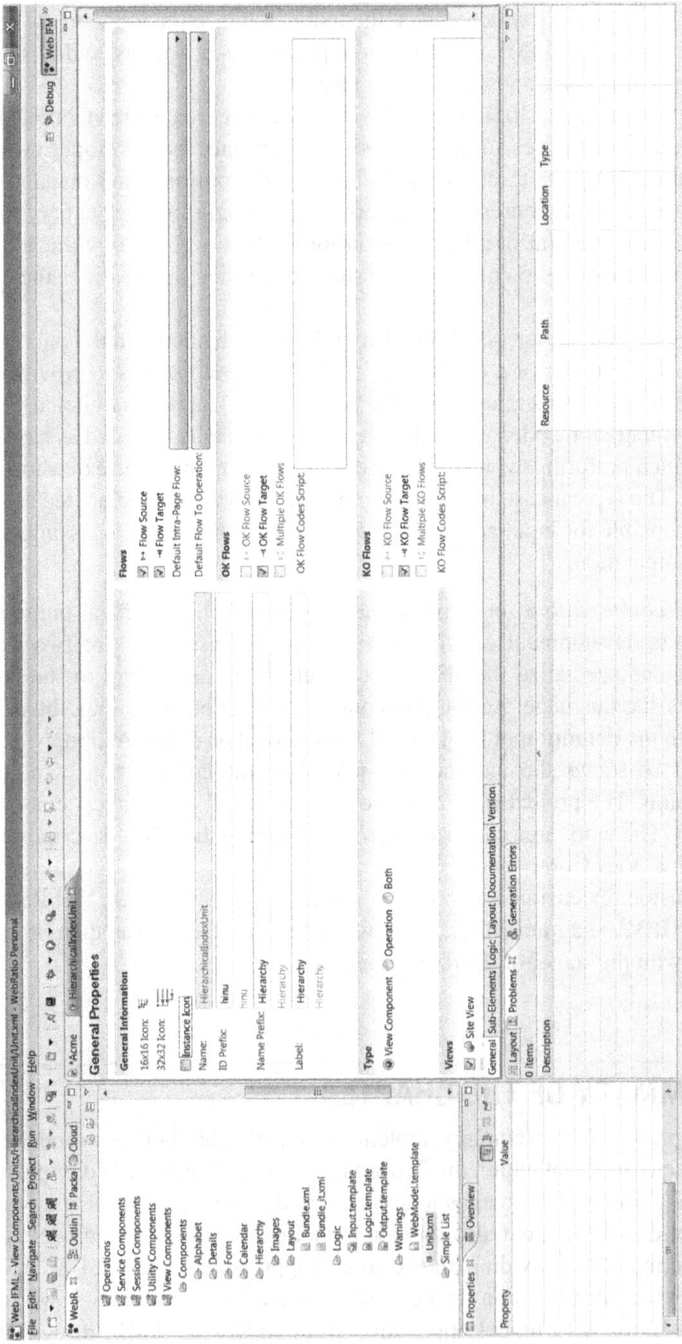

FIGURE 11.16

Form for editing the XML configuration file of a custom IFML extension.

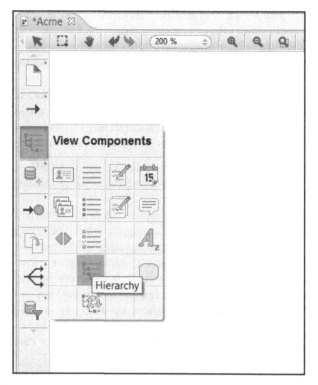

FIGURE 11.17

The custom IFML ViewComponent extension (Hierarchy) of Figure 11.16 in the IFML editor tool palette.

11.10 BIBLIOGRAPHIC NOTES

More information on WebRatio can be found at the web site of the product (http://www.webratio.com/). Usage experience in large scale model-driven development with WebRatio is reported in [FB2014]. An open-source IFML editor for Eclipse is also available (https://ifml.github.io/).

Other tools that support the model-driven development paradigm with a philosophy comparable to that of IFML and WebRatio are listed below.

- Mendix (http://www.mendix.com/) supports the design of multidevice, multichannel applications, based on a domain model, business logic components, and process flows, with a visual modeling approach.
- Outsystems (http://www.outsystems.com/) exploits business process models, domain models, and business logic models to specify application designs that are then mapped to code for mobile and web devices and connected with a variety of backend platforms.

- OrangeScape (http://www.orangescape.com/) focuses on the visual development of business applications offered in a cloud-based, PaaS mode.
- LongJump/AgileApps Live (http://www.softwareag.com/special/longjump/) allows subject matter experts and developers alike to build and deploy process-driven application solutions visually.
- Tersus (http://www.tersus.com/) is an open-source tool for editing visual models and deploying the corresponding web and mobile applications on dedicated server.
- SoftFluent Entities (http://www.softfluent.com/) maps conceptual entities of the domain model to interface components for rapid application development.

UML modeling and code generation tools that support UML extensions can be customized with an IFML profile, exploiting the UML profile representation of IFML described in the standard.

Cross-platform frameworks for mobile application development have become very popular, thanks to the advantage of overcoming the burden of developing multiple versions of applications. Among the most popular ones, we can mention AppCelerator (http://www.appcelerator.com/), and Apache Cordova (http://cordova.apache. org/) and its distribution PhoneGap by Adobe (http://phonegap.com/). While, the former lets developers write native apps in Javascript and then provides a unified Javascript API for all the platforms, the latter operates by wrapping HTML5, CSS3, and JavaScript code into a container (basically consisting in a mobile browser). WebRatio mobile code generation [BMU14] produces code for Cordova / PhoneGap (http://phonegap.com/).

END NOTES

1. http://phonegap.com/.

IFML language design, execution, and integration

12

One of the main advantages of IFML is that it is not a stand-alone initiative insulated from other modeling approaches. On the contrary, IFML is deeply rooted within the Object Management Group model driven architecture (MDA) and, more in generally, within the model driven engineering (MDE) development approach.

IFML is designed to be easily used together with other modeling languages, thus allowing comprehensive system and enterprise modeling.Therefore, to exploit its expressive power for system design, IFML must be put in context within a broader modeling perspective. In this chapter, we describe three aspects that contribute to a deeper understanding of the language:

- The IFML language definition, which the standard specifies formally in terms of metamodel, notation, and interchange format, following the OMG's best practices;
- IFML executability, which expresses the execution semantics of the language and permits implementers to map the conceptual, platform-independent IFML constructs to actual executable behaviors in the chosen user interface platform; and
- IFML integration with other software design languages, through cross-referencing between model elements in different diagrams.

12.1 IFML LANGUAGE SPECIFICATION THROUGH METAMODELING

The IFML language is specified within an official, human-readable OMG specification document, which in turn is accompanied by some technical artifacts:

- The IFML metamodel, specifying the structure and relations between the IFML elements;
- The IFML UML profile, defining a UML-based syntax for expressing IFML models, through an extension of the concepts of the class, state machine, and composite structure diagrams;
- The IFML visual syntax, offering a graphic notation for expressing IFML models in a concise and intuitive way, as shown in the examples throughout this book; and
- The IFML model serialization and exchange format, for tool portability.

Altogether, these artifacts compose the IFML language specification. Each of them is specified according to the OMG standards:

- The metamodel is defined through the MOF metamodeling language (an equivalent ECORE definition is available too).
- The UML profile is defined according to UML 2.4 profiling rules.
- The visual syntax is defined through Diagram Definition (DD) and Diagram Interchange (DI) OMG standards.
- The model serialization and exchange format is defined based on XMI.

A discussion of the complete language specification is outside the scope of this book, but it can be found in the OMG specification document. In the following, we report a few excerpts of the specification.

12.1.1 METAMODEL

The IFML metamodel is defined according to the best practices of language definition, including abstraction, modularization, reuse, and extensibility. The metamodel is divided in three packages: the Core package, the Extension package, and the DataTypes package. The Core package contains the concepts that build up the interaction infrastructure of the language in terms of InteractionFlowElements, InteractionFlows, and Parameters. Core package concepts are extended by concrete concepts in the Extension package to cater to more precise behaviors. The DataTypes package contains the custom data types defined by IFML.

The IFML metamodel reuses the basic data types from the UML metamodel, specializes a number of UML metaclasses as the basis for IFML metaclasses, and assumes that a domain model is represented with a UML class diagram or with an equivalent notation.

Figure 12.1 shows an excerpt of the IFML metamodel that represent some of the elements at the highest level of abstraction. IFMLModel, as its name suggests, represents an IFML model and is the top-level container of all the other model elements. It contains an InteractionFlowModel, a DomainModel, and may optionally contain ViewPoints.

InteractionFlowModel represents the user's view of the application, with references to sets of InteractionFlowModelElements, which collectively define a fully functional portion of the system.

NamedElement is an abstract class that specializes the Element class (the most general class in the model) denoting the elements that have a name. For any Element, Constraints and Comments can be specified. InteractionFlowModelElement is an abstract class that generalizes all the elements of an InteractionFlowModel. As such, it will not be used directly within IFML diagrams. Instead, it is specialized by more precise concepts (e.g., InteractionFlow, InteractionFlowElement). In turn, these subconcepts are abstract, and must be specialized as well. Figure 12.2 shows some concrete subelements of InteractionFlowElement and InteractionFlow, which are the ones that we have actually used in the examples of the preceding chapters.

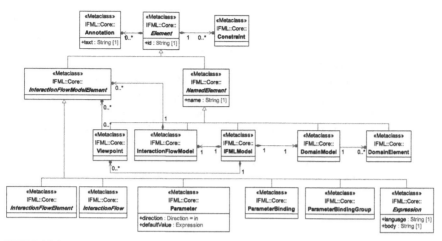

FIGURE 12.1

IFML metamodel excerpt describing the abstract elements of the language.

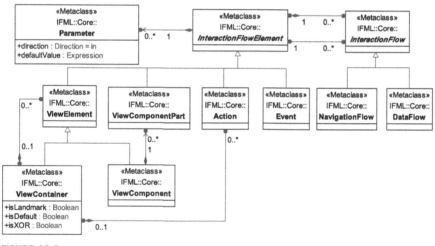

FIGURE 12.2

IFML metamodel excerpt describing some core elements of the language.

All the other concepts of the language and their associations are defined in the metamodel in a similar way.

12.1.2 EXTENSIBILITY

As seen in chapter 7, IFML can be extended by adding new, more refined concepts. To this end, IFML uses the native extensibility mechanisms of UML to allow the definition of stereotypes, tagged values, and constraints on existing concepts, making them more fitting for specific purposes or scenarios. The IFML standard specification document already includes an Extensions package, which exemplifies how the extension mechanism works. In particular, it contains some specializations of the concepts in the Core package. In the same way, users of the language can define new packages containing new constructs to model platform-independent or platform-specific features.

According to the philosophy of the language, not all possible extensions are allowed. Valid extensions should refine or adapt the core concepts to specific cases, specializing their semantics without altering them. The IFML specification explicitly mentions that only the following concepts (and their specializations) can be extended while retaining compliance with the standard: ViewContainer (for defining specific screens or interface containers), ViewComponent (for describing specific widgets or controls), ViewComponentPart (for specifying particular properties of existing or new ViewComponents), Event (for covering platform specific events), Domain-Concept and FeatureConcept (for covering additional content sources), and BehaviorConcept and BehavioralFeatureConcept (for covering integration with additional behavioral models or modeling languages). Extensions of other elements are disallowed by the standard. Any other extended concept will be considered proprietary and outside the IFML notation.

12.1.3 PROFILE, VISUAL NOTATION, AND INTERCHANGE FORMAT

Besides the core packages and their extensions, the remaining parts of specifications describe the UML profile, the visual notation, and the interchange format. The IFML UML profile specifies the IFML elements as stereotypes of UML elements. The diagram notation defines the symbols and graphical rules for the elements that must be represented graphically in the diagrams. The XMI definition defines an XML syntax for the serialization of the models.

12.2 IFML MODEL EXECUTION

This section provides an illustration of the execution semantics of IFML (i.e., an informal description of the kind of computation that an IFML model specifies). Models, like programs, are meant to represent the execution of a computer-based application, so it is important that syntactically correct models, like any program, behave in ways conforming to the intention and intuition of the designer.

An interface is essentially a device that reacts to stimuli (events) by changing its state (transition) and possibly emitting output signals. In an interactive application, the user is the main source of events. A user interacts with the view, which provides a representation of the current status of the system. An event produced by the user triggers the reaction of the system, which possibly executes some Action and causes a transition to a new state, manifested by an update of the view.

The semantics of IFML do not address the internal functioning of the Actions, which can be described separately. Actions are considered black boxes: they are started by a triggering event and terminate by signaling another event (e.g., normal or exceptional termination).

The semantics of a modeling language such as IFML have important applications:

- They allow checking models for the presence of desired properties and the absence of anomalies.
- They drive the construction of model interpreters and code generators, for which it is imperative to know exactly what the model does.

Completely formalizing the semantics of IFML exceeds the scope of this book. This section provides some hints on the subject that are meant to let the designer better understand the meaning of an IFML diagram. For simplicity, we restrict the illustration to synchronous user interfaces (i.e., we exclude the case of asynchronous system events). The bibliographic notes contain several sources that discuss at greater length the semantics of modeling languages, including interaction description languages.

12.2.1 STATE REPRESENTATION

An IFML models describes the state of the user interface and its evolution in response to events. A state of the interface is the set of **visible** ViewContainers and **active** ViewComponents and Events. Intuitively, a ViewContainer is visible if it is in view according to the nesting of ViewContainers in the composition model of the interface. A ViewComponent is active if its content can be determined. An Event is active if it can be triggered.

12.2.2 VIEWCONTAINER STATE

The state of a ViewContainer can be visible or invisible. The set of existing ViewContainers can be represented as an AND-OR tree, that is, a tree where the root is the top ViewContainer and the internal nodes are unlabeled (if the children nodes are displayed together) or labeled with OR (if the children nodes are displayed alternatively). The default subview container of a XOR ViewContainer must also be distinguished (e.g., by marking the corresponding node in the tree). For example, the interface of Figure 6.17 can be represented as the tree of Figure 12.3. Note that, if the

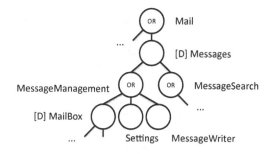

FIGURE 12.3

AND-OR tree corresponding to the interface of Figure 6.17.

interface is page-based, as in a typical web application, it can still be represented as a single tree by adding a dummy XOR ViewContainer at the top, with all the pages as first-level children and the home page as the default sub-ViewContainer of the dummy element.

The tree representation facilitates understanding what is visible when a View-Container is accessed. When a ViewContainer X is accessed, the set of visible View-Containers is given by the union of X and its visible ancestors and descendants, determined according to the following **visibility propagation rules**:

- If Y is the default XOR child of X or Y is a conjunctive child of X, VisibleDescendants(X) = {Y} U VisibleDescendants(Y).
- If X is a conjunctive child of Z, VisibleAncestors(X) = {Z} U VisibleDescendants(Z) U VisibleAncestors(Z).
- If X is a XOR child of Z, VisibleAncestors(X) = {Z} U VisibleAncestors(Z).

For example, considering the tree of Figure 12.3:

- When "Mail" is accessed, VisibleAncestors("Mail") = {} and VisibleDescendants("Mail") = {"Messages", "MessageManagement", "Message Search", "MailBox"}.
- When "Settings" is accessed, VisibleAncestors() = {"MessageManagement", "Messages", "MessageSearch", "Mail"} and VisibleDescendants("Settings") ={} .

12.2.3 STATE OF A VIEWCOMPONENT

The state of a ViewComponent can be active or inactive. A ViewComponent is active when the enclosing ViewContainer is visible and the values of its input parameters are available.

12.2.4 ACTIVATIONEXPRESSIONS

ActivationExpressions add restrictions on top of the set of visible and active ViewElements. If they evaluate to false, an otherwise visible/active element is treated as invisible/inactive. ActivationExpressions can be applied with a finer grain to individual Events, so it may happen that a ViewElement is visible/active but loses its interactivity because the ActivationExpressions associated with one of its Events evaluates to false.

Considering again the model of the running example (repeated for convenience in Figure 12.4). When accessing the e-mail application, the "MessageList" View-Component is active because the enclosing ViewContainer ("MailBox") is visible and the ViewComponent receives the needed parameter from the DataFlow outgoing from the "MailBoxList" ViewComponent (thanks to the PATTERN CN-DEF: default selection, introduced in chapter 5). However, the toolbar with the events for deleting, archiving, reporting, and moving messages remains inactive until at least one message is selected in the "MessageList" ViewComponent, as conveyed by the MessageSet->notEmpty() ActivationExpression.

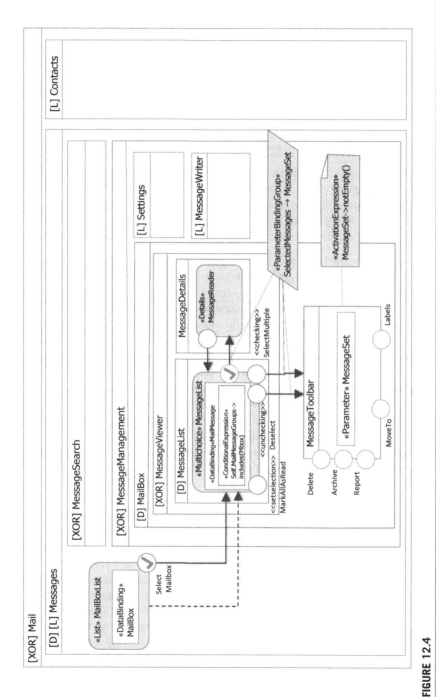

FIGURE 12.4

Model of the e-mail application interface for reading a single message, with activation expression.

12.2.5 EVENT PROCESSING

The execution semantics of IFML dictate how events are treated. Event processing can be regarded as an algorithm that takes as input the state of the interface and an occurred event and computes the next state of the interface. The occurrence of an event has two main effects. It updates the visibility status of ViewContainers, and it updates the active status of ViewComponents within the visible ViewContainers.

12.2.6 VIEWCONTAINER VISIBILITY UPDATE

The initial state of the application can be regarded as an initialization event, which marks as visible the root of the ViewContainer tree. For example, when the application initial event occurs, the root of the tree in Figure 12.3 becomes visible, and so do its descendants according to the visibility propagation rules. During the application usage, two kinds of events cause the update of the ViewContainer visibility:

- **InteractionFlow navigation**: A point-to-point navigation is performed from a source ViewElement to a target ViewElement. When the actual destination of the navigation is a ViewComponent, the target ViewContainer is the one directly enclosing the ViewComponent. When the destination of the NavigationFlow is an Action, the target ViewContainer is the one reached by the InteractionFlow exiting from the termination ActionEvent of the Action. As a result of navigation, the target ViewContainer becomes visible, and the visibility propagation rules are applied to determine the visibility status of the other containers. InteractionFlow navigation can further be distinguished into:
  - **Inter-container navigation flow traversal**: The source ViewContainer is neither among the visible descendants nor among the visible ancestors of the target ViewContainer. This situation appears to the user as a **replacement** of a portion of the view (the source ViewContainer disappears from view and is replaced by the target ViewContainer plus its visible ancestors/descendants). For example, the navigation of a web application falls in this category: all pages are same-level siblings of a (dummy) top XOR ViewContainer, and navigation flow traversal makes the destination page replace the source page.
  - **Intra-container navigation flow traversal**: The source ViewContainer is either among the visible descendants or among the visible ancestors of the target ViewContainer. This situation appears to the user as a **refresh** of the content of a portion of the view: the source ViewContainer remains in view but some other part of the view changes. For example, in Figure 12.4, the selection of a single message from the "MessageList" ViewComponent is an intra-container flow traversal within the "MessageViewer" ViewContainer. The container remains in view, but a part of its content changes because the "MessageDetails" subcontainer replaces the "MessageList" one. Note that the "MessageToolBar" remains in view because it is a visible descendant of "MailBox," which is a visible ancestor of "MessageViewer."

- **Landmark navigation**: A ViewContainer that is reachable due to the Landmark visibility property is accessed. This is equivalent to the navigation of an implicit content-independent InteractionFlow from any of the currently visible View-Containers to the target Landmark ViewContainer.

12.2.7 VIEWCOMPONENT STATUS UPDATE

The status of parameter availability, and thus of the ViewComponents nested within the ViewContainers, is also updated by the occurrence of events, as exemplified in Figure 12.5.

When the "Products" ViewContainer is accessed, the "ProductList" ViewComponent is active. It requires no input, and its content can be computed by evaluating its ConditionalExpression (which defaults to true in this case) over its DataBinding instances (all the instances of entity "Product"). Conversely, as shown in Figure 12.5.a, the "ProductDetails" ViewComponent is inactive. It lacks an input parameter value (the "product" parameter holding the primary key of a Product instance), and thus its content cannot be computed. When the "SelectProduct" event occurs (Figure 12.5.b), it updates the status of the "product" parameter of the "ProductDetails" ViewComponent, which then has all the values of its input parameters defined and becomes active.

The computation of the content of a ViewContainer may be nontrivial. Several ViewComponents may be linked in a network of input–output dependencies expressed through NavigationFlows and DataFlows. Parameter values may be propagated from one ViewComponents to other ViewComponents through several ParameterBindings.

The propagation of computation within a ViewContainer can be schematized by a **best-effort rule**: everything that can be computed is computed. The best-effort rule marks as active all ViewComponents for which the needed input parameters can be determined.

Figure 12.6 shows an example of the best-effort rule. When the "Home" ViewContainer is accessed, the "ProductDetails" ViewComponent becomes active because its container is visible and it requires no input. Next, by the best-effort rule, the "Accessories" ViewComponent also becomes active because its input parameter "product" can be determined from the output of the "ProductDetails" ViewComponent and the (default) DataBinding associated to its incoming DataFlow. Conversely, the "AccessoryDetails" ViewComponent is inactive because its input parameter "selected" cannot be determined from the output of the "Accessories" List ViewComponent prior to the occurrence of the "Select" event.

12.2.8 NAVIGATION HISTORY PRESERVATION

When the user triggers an Event, the content of the destination ViewContainer is refreshed in a way that may depend on the past history of the user interaction. The alternatives for recomputing a ViewContainer (or a part thereof) depends on the

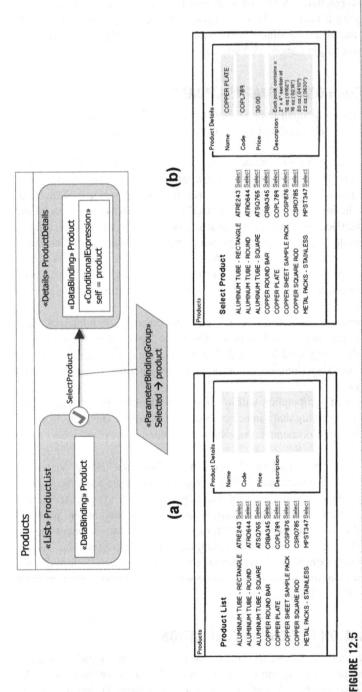

FIGURE 12.5

Example of active and inactive ViewComponents.

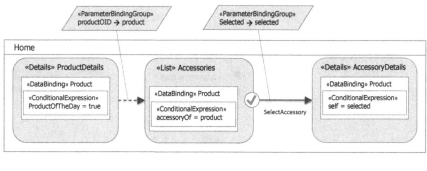

FIGURE 12.6

Best-effort computation of the content of a ViewContainer.

"degree of memory" used for the computation. Two interaction history policies are possible:

- **Without history**: The contents of the ViewComponents are computed as if the ViewContainer was accessed for the first time. The computation without context history may be used to "reset" and forget the choices previously made by the user in a ViewContainer.
- **With history**: The contents of the ViewComponents are computed based on the input history of the ViewComponents existing prior to the last navigation event.

Figure 12.7 shows an example of the effect of the history management policy.

When the "ProductContentManagement" ViewContainer is accessed for the first time, the list of categories is displayed and, by virtue of the default selection pattern, a default product is also shown in the "ProductOfCategory" list. When the user selects a different category, the list of products is updated to reflect the choice. Then the user can delete one product, by selecting it from the "ProductOfCategory" list. After the termination of the "Delete" Action, the "ProductContentManagement" ViewContainer is re-accessed, and the displayed category depends on the history management policy. It is the default category if the policy is "Without history." Otherwise it is the last category selected by the user.

The history preservation policy can be expressed as a general property of the IFML model, which applies to all NavigationFlows. This choice makes the interpretation of the model simpler and the resulting user experience more consistent.

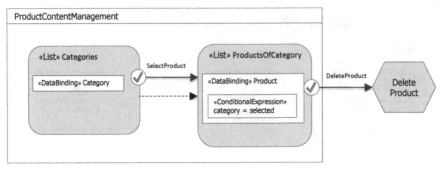

FIGURE 12.7

Example of history-less and history-based ViewComponent computation.

When the need arises to apply different policies, the chosen option can be associated with the NavigationFlows as a stereotype.

12.2.9 PARAMETER VALUES CONFLICTS

Conflicts may arise in the application of the best-effort rule for computing the content of a ViewContainer. A conflict arises when a ViewComponent receives more than one input value for the same Parameter. This could happen due to multiple incoming flows in a ViewComponent or ViewContainer. Such conflicts could be due to multiple navigation events that determine the computation of the same component or to default selection patterns (see chapter 5 and Figure 12.4), which provide values of a parameter at different times (an initial value and then a subsequent value produced by the user's interaction).

A conflict resolution strategy (CRS) specifies which Parameter value is exploited to compute the content of the ViewComponent. Different strategies are possible:

- **Nondeterministic**: One input parameter is chosen nondeterministically at runtime from the set of available inputs.
- **Priority-based**: Priorities are assigned at design-time to the incoming flows (for the ViewComponent or ViewContainer). When runtime conflict occurs, the Parameter value associated with the flow with highest priority is chosen.
- **Specificity-based**: A mix of priority and nondeterministic choice, which exploits priority based on specificity. Specificity of a parameter is assessed according to the following rules:
    - Values which are directly or indirectly derived from the user's current choice, expressed by the last navigation event, are the most specific.
    - Values that depend on the user's previous choices, derived from the history log, are the second most specific.
    - Values taken from system-generated default choices or from DataFlows coming from ViewComponents not affected by the last navigation event are the least specific.

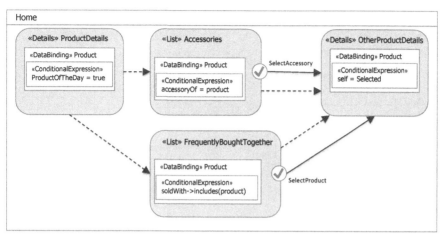

FIGURE 12.8

Example of priority-based conflict resolution policies.

Figure 12.8 shows a case in which the priority-based CSR helps resolve the conflict between multiple default selection patterns affecting the same ViewComponent.

The "Home" ViewContainer shows the "ProductOfTheDay" together with a list of accessories, which could be empty, and the list of products frequently purchased together with the product of the day. To avoid the effect of leaving the interface space dedicated to the "OtherProductDetails" ViewComponent empty at the first access, two default selection patterns are provided: one that selects an accessory and one that selects a related product, in case no accessory list is available. To enforce that the default accessory should be displayed when both the accessory and related products list are available, a priority based policy can be set, giving precedence to the default DataFlow from the "Accessories" ViewComponent.

Figure 12.9 shows a case in which the specificity-based CSR helps resolve the conflict between multiple events that cause the computation of the same ViewComponent in different conditions. The conflict resolution logic requires explaining the order in which ViewComponents are considered for computation.

12.2.10 VIEWCOMPONENT COMPUTATION PROCESS

The interface content computation process is performed every time an Event arises. The process applies the best-effort rule to determine the content of the ViewComponents of the target ViewContainer. Intuitively, the process identifies at each step the set of computable ViewComponents (i.e., the subset of the ViewComponents for which the value of the input Parameters is determined). The computation of a ViewComponent determines the value of its output parameters, which may be mentioned in the DataBinding of other components that thus become computable at the next iteration.

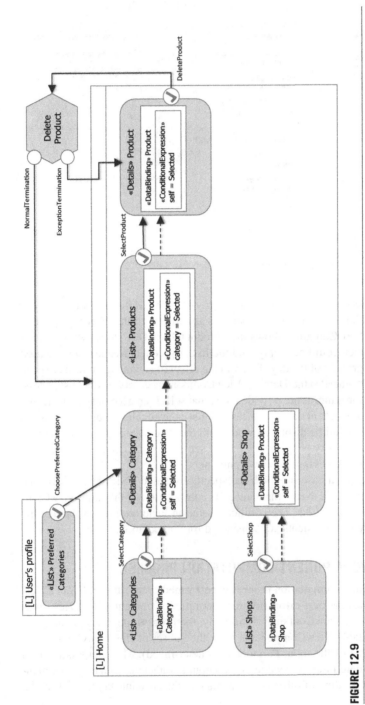

FIGURE 12.9

Example of specificity-based conflict resolution policies.

The following pseudo-code describes the algorithm:

```
INPUT:
- The ViewContainer
- The event that triggers the computation and its InteractionFlow
(if any)
- The parameter values associated with the InteractionFlow (if any)
- The conflict resolution strategy CSR (default =
specificity-based)
- The interaction history policy IHP (default = with history)
- The parameter value history log
OUTPUT:
The sequence of computable ViewComponents
The value of their input parameters
PROCEDURE:
ToCompute = all ViewComponents
WHILE (ToCompute is not empty) DO
  IF a component C exists such that
  (C has no input parameters OR all its parameters have a value AND
  All Components potentially providing input to C have been computed)
  THEN
  Assign to each parameter of C a value according to the CRS and IHP
Compute C and its output parameters using the chosen input values
ToCompute = ToCompute - C
  ELSE HALT
END DO
```

Figure 12.9 shows a ViewContainer on which we illustrate the application of the algorithm for processing several events.

The content of the ViewContainer can be computed in several ways, depending on the actual navigation performed by the user. Each ViewComponent exploits parameters values that are either "current" (i.e., produced by the user's navigation action), "preserved" (i.e., coming from the history of past user's selections), or "default" (i.e.,, determined by a default selection pattern).

12.2.10.1 *ViewContainer access with landmark navigation (or content-independent NavigationFlow)*

The "Home" ViewContainer is accessed via landmark navigation, and thus no initial parameter values are available. Therefore, ViewComponent computation starts from either one of the "Categories" and the "Shops" ViewComponents, which have no input and are computable. Their content is the entire population of the underlying class. Their output is—by effect of the default selection pattern—a heuristically chosen object appearing in the List (e.g., the first object). After the computation of the ViewComponents, both the "Category" and "Shop" ViewComponents have their input parameter settled and thus become computable. When the "Category" View-Component is computed, it provides a category object as output to the "Products" ViewComponent, which becomes computable. After the "Products" ViewComponent has been computed, the default product listed in the "Products" ViewComponent is available as output and can be used as input for the "Product" ViewComponent, which becomes computable. No other ViewComponent remain to be computed, so the algorithm halts.

12.2.10.2 *ViewContainer access after the "ChoosePreferredCategory" event*

The "Category" ViewComponent is the destination of the navigated NavigationFlow and thus the initial assignment of the input parameters includes the object to be shown in the "Category" ViewComponent, which is a "current" value. Computation can start from the ViewComponents that do not require input or from the "Category" View-Component, for which the input parameter is available. Supposing that computation starts from the ViewComponents that do not require input, everything proceeds as in the previous case. The only difference occurs in the computation of the "Category" ViewComponent, which has two possible values for its input parameter: the current object coming from the triggering event and the object chosen by default from the "Categories" ViewComponent. According to the specificity rules, the current value prevails over the default one supplied by the "Categories" ViewComponent. Then the ViewComponents dependent on the "Category" ViewComponent are computed as before. The "Products" ViewComponent will contain the products of the (preferred) category shown in the "Category" ViewComponent, and the "Product" ViewComponent will contain the default product appearing in the "Products" ViewComponent.

12.2.10.3 *ViewContainer access after event "SelectProduct"*

The ViewContainer is computed after the user selects a product in the "Products" ViewComponent. The parameters passed as input to the ViewContainer comprise the input parameter of the "Product" ViewComponent as a current value plus the input parameters of ViewComponent "Category" and "Shop," from the history log as values to be preserved (by default, we assume the "with history" preservation policy). Computation starts from the ViewComponents that require no input ("Categories" and "Shops") and proceeds to their dependent ViewComponents. Due to the specificity rule, history values prevail over defaults taken from List ViewComponents, and thus the "Category," "Products," and "Shop" ViewComponents continue to show the same content they displayed before the navigation. Current values prevail over defaults, and thus the "Product" ViewComponent shows the object selected by the user instead of the default product extracted from the "Products" ViewComponent. In summary, after the "SelectProduct" event, the "Home" ViewContainer shows content that depends on new input (the object shown in the "Product" ViewComponent) and content derived from "old input" (all the remaining ViewComponents). The new input affects the ViewComponents directly or indirectly depending on the user's navigation, whereas the old input is preserved for all the ViewComponents not affected by such navigation, to maximize the "stability" of the ViewContainer.

Note that "old input" does not mean "old content," as the following example demonstrates.

12.2.10.4 ViewContainer access after successful deletion

ViewContainer "Home" is accessed after the successful deletion of a product. The parameters in input to the ViewContainer comprise the input parameters of View-Component "Category" and "Shop" from the history log. Conversely, no input is preserved for the "Product," because such input would correspond to an object no longer existing after the deletion. Computation starts from the ViewComponents that require no input and proceeds to their dependent ViewComponents, whose input parameters are set to the preserved values and not to the default values taken from the List ViewComponents. In particular, the "Products" ViewComponent has the same input as before, because the category object shown in the "Category" View-Component has been restored from the history log, but different content, because the deleted product no longer appears in the List. The default value of the "Products" ViewComponent is then used as the input of the "Product" ViewComponent, replacing the deleted product.

12.2.10.5 ViewContainer access after unsuccessful deletion

The ViewContainer is accessed after the deletion of the currently displayed product has failed. The parameters input to the ViewContainer comprise the output of the Action, which is the OID of the Product object that could not be deleted, plus the input values of ViewComponents "Category" and "Shop" from the history log. The computation starts from the ViewComponents that require no input ("Categories" and "Shops") and proceeds to their dependent ViewComponents. These are instantiated according to the parameters passed as input to the ViewContainer and the specificity rule, which leads to restoring all ViewComponents to their previous content before the triggering of the delete Action.

As a final remark, in the illustration of the ViewContainer computation algorithm, we assumed that the content of ViewComponents is calculated from scratch, even if the ViewContainer is re-accessed with the same input parameters for some View-Components. In a practical implementation, caching mechanisms and more intelligent ViewComponent computation logics can be used to improve the performance of ViewContainer computation by avoiding the recomputation of ViewComponents that have not been affected by the navigation and using the cached results instead of recalculating the content of ViewComponents.

12.3 IFML MODELS INTEGRATION WITH OTHER SYSTEM MODELING PERSPECTIVES

Thanks to its integration in the MDA framework, IFML enables a tight integration with other system modeling perspectives. In particular, three aspects are defined explicitly in the standard: integration with the content model, integration with business logic, and integration with business process models. Further integrations are possible, for example, with platform-specific models, system deployment models, and enterprise architecture models Figure 12.10.

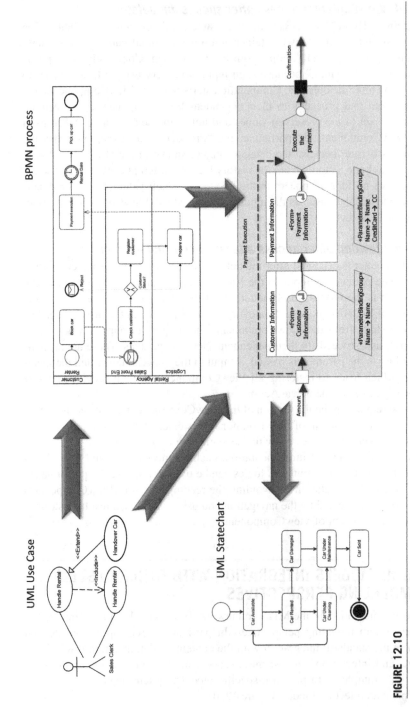

FIGURE 12.10

Examples of integration with requirements and business models.

12.3.1 INTEGRATION WITH BUSINESS MODELS AND REQUIREMENTS

In many cases, system development starts from a requirements model, such as UML use case diagrams, or from a procedural view of the enterprise operations, such as business process models specified in OMG's BPMN. IFML enables the traceability of user interaction models to the requirement specifications that generated them. This can be done by establishing a reference between the requirements model of interest and the IFML model derived from it. Figure 12.12 illustrates the case in which an IFML module specifies the user interaction needed for addressing a use case or a business process task. Furthermore, the execution of an IFML Action or Module may induce some internal state change of the system, whose dynamics is specified in a UML state chart (as also visible in Figure 12.12).

The IFML standard natively provides the possibility of referencing, for instance, a business process task from an IFML module that specifies its user interface. Analogously, references could be defined toward use case scenarios, goal-oriented specification diagrams, state charts, or any other specification model.

12.3.2 INTEGRATION WITH CONTENT MODEL AND BUSINESS LOGIC

The cases of integration of IFML with content models and business logics have been already illustrated extensively in the examples of the preceding chapters. Every time a content binding is specified for a ViewComponent, the integration with the content model is achieved.

As an example, Figure 12.11(a) shows a List ViewComponent that specifies the publication of some contents through a ContentBinding, which establishes a reference between the IFML diagram and the UML class diagram where the "Product" class is defined.

The integration with the business logic is specified when a ViewComponent or Action references a method of a class or a more complex behavior (represented in the language metamodel with a BehavioralFeatureConcept and a BehaviorConcept, respectively). IFML includes dedicated extensions of these concepts for integration with UML. Specifically, BehaviorConcept and BehavioralFeatureConcept are extended respectively by UMLBehaviorConcept and UMLBehavioralFeatureConcept, which allow the designer to directly reference a UML class method or a UML dynamic diagram (sequence, activity, or state chart diagram).

Figure 12.12. shows an example of an IFML model referencing simple behavioral features, such as UML methods from a sequence diagram, and a more complex behavior, such as an UML activity diagram specifying the internal functioning of an IFML Action.

Figure 12.12 contrasts three different concrete syntaxes for integrating an IFML element with an external model: (a) a DataBinding referencing a domain model class,(b) a DynamicBehavior referencing a specific UML method, and (c) a DynamicBehavior referencing an entire UML diagram. The references can be embedded within both ViewComponents and Actions. Typically, the content of a ViewComponent is detailed through a DataBinding, as most of the previous examples have illustrated, but it can also be specified using a DynamicBehavior, which describes the logic to extract or build the content of the ViewComponent.

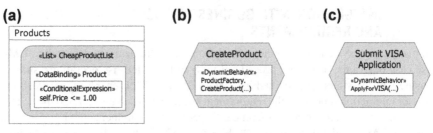

FIGURE 12.11

(a) Integration with content model – UML class, (b) Simple behavioral feature - UML method, and (c) Complex behavior - UML diagram.

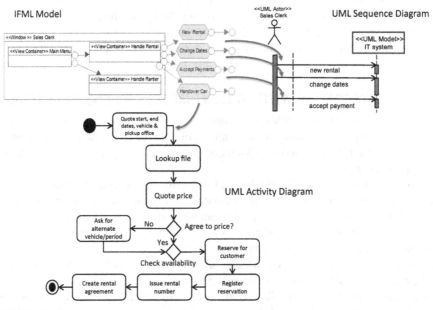

FIGURE 12.12

Integration with simple behavioral feature (class methods) and with complex behavior (UML activity diagram).

12.3.3 INTEGRATION WITH IMPLEMENTATION AND DEPLOYMENT ASPECTS

Finally, one important aspect of IFML is its complementary role with respect to deployment and implementation-oriented (possibly platform-specific) design models. Figure 12.13 shows the typical relation of the IFML model to other alternative system representations. An IFML module is mapped to the elements of an UI mockup, and it shares a common namespace with a sequence diagram describing the interplay between the different architectural layers, described in a UML deployment diagram.

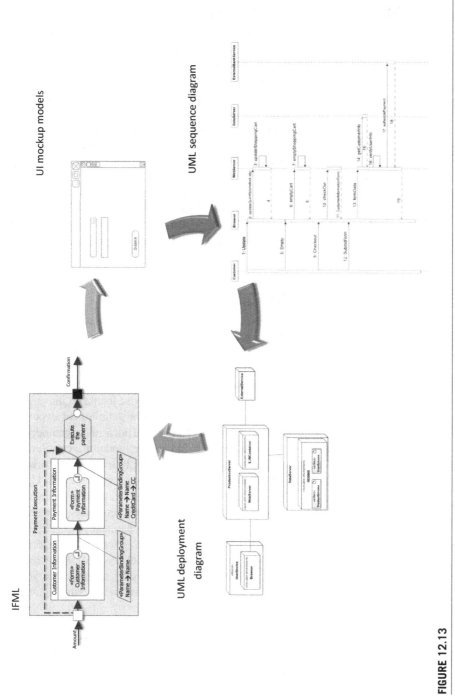

FIGURE 12.13

Integration of the IFML model with implementation-oriented specifications.

12.4 SUMMARY OF THE CHAPTER

This chapter discussed some of the aspects of the IFML language design: the formal definition of the concepts in the IFML metamodel, the notation and model exchange format, the executability, and the integration with models representing other aspects of the system. The definition of the IFML metamodel follows the OMG best practices. It exploits metaclasses and their associations to specify the main aspects of the language.

The IFML execution semantics allow the developer to understand the meaning and behavior of any IFML diagram as that of a machine that takes as input the stimuli produced by the user or by the system and updates the visibility status of the View-Containers and the active status of ViewComponents and Events, thus determining an updated view for the user to continue the interaction.

Designers can integrate IFML with other modeling languages for obtaining a comprehensive view of the system, spanning both the front end and the back end, and for ensuring the traceability between the interaction model and other models built during the requirement collection phase and the architecture design phase.

12.5 BIBLIOGRAPHIC NOTES

Integration of different modeling perspectives for describing completely an information system is one of the most basic practices of model-driven engineering [BCW12]. UML itself supports different diagrams [Fowler03] that complement each other. Some methodologies, such as Model Driven Enterprise Engineering (MDEE), propose a pragmatic approach to integration of OMG and non-OMG modeling specifications, so as to cover all the modeling needs of the enterprise thanks to integrating and relating together multiple and diverse models, through the definition of a vocabulary (SBVR-based) and integrated metamodel. The related idea of megamodeling addresses the complexity that has been observed in real-life model-driven solutions to practical problems. Various experience show how to apply traceability between models, starting from the early phases of requirements elicitation [Brambilla11].

The semantics of interface modeling language is a subject treated in several academic articles [CF01]. Among the early works, [SF89] used Petri Nets to describe static hypertexts, where pages do not access content dynamically. [ZP92] also addresses the navigation semantics of static hypertexts, using Statecharts instead of Petri Nets. [FTM01] introduces HMSB (Hypermedia Model Based on Statecharts) to specify both the structural organization and the browsing semantics of static hypermedia applications, focusing on synchronization of multimedia data (e.g., text, audio, animations, images).

Executable specifications of systems can also be expressed with high-level design approaches like executable UML, initially proposed by Shlaer and Mellor in 1988 [SM88]. The approach is embodied in specifications published by the OMG, specifically the fUML (Foundational UML) [FUML] and the associated action language ALF (Action Language for fUML) [ALF].

Appendix A: IFML notation summary

Appendix A lists the core concepts of IFML and the set of extension concepts specified in the standard, together with their meaning and graphical notation.

Table 1 IFML Core Concepts

Concept	Meaning	IFML Notation	Examples
View Container	An element of the interface that comprises elements displaying content and supporting interaction and/or other ViewContainers	MyViewContainer	Web page, window, screen, pane
XOR View Container	A ViewContainer comprising child ViewContainers that are displayed alternatively	[XOR] MyXorViewContainer	Tabbed panes in Java, frames in HTML
Landmark View Container	A ViewContainer that is reachable from any other element of the user interface, without explicit incoming InteractionFlows	[L] MyLandmark	A login page in an HTML site that is reachable through a link visible on every page.
Default View Container	A ViewContainer presented by default to the user when the enclosing container is accessed.	[D] MyDefaultContainer	The message list pane in a mail application (as opposed to the contact list pane shown on demand)
View Component	An element of the interface that displays content or accepts input	MyViewComponent	HTML list, image gallery, input form

Catching Event	An occurrence that is captured in the model and affects the state of the application	◯ MyEvent
Throwing Event	An event that is launched by some occurrence in the application	⬤ MyEvent
Action	A reference to a piece of business logic triggered from the interface	⬡ MyAction
Navigation Flow	Update of the interface elements in view or triggering of an action caused by the occurrence of an event; data may be associated with the flow through parameter bindings	⟶
Data Flow	Input–output data dependency between ViewComponents, ViewContainers, or Actions	⤍
Parameter	A typed and named value, which can be received (input) or produced (output)	«InputParameter» Parameter1: String «OutputParameter» Parameter2: String
Parameter Binding Group	Set of mappings from output parameters of a source element to input parameters of a target element associated with a NavigationFlow or DataFlow	«ParameterBindingGroup» OutParameter1 → InParameter1 OutParameter2 → InParameter2

User click, form submission, device location change	
Notification after an operation has finished	
Database update, sending of an e-mail, spell-checking of a text	
Navigation from one web page to another, change of tab in a tabbed pane	
Default element of a list (output), displayed automatically in another ViewComponent (input)	
HTTP query string parameters, HTTP post parameters, JavaScript variables and function parameters	

(Continued)

Table 1 IFML Core Concepts—cont'd

Concept	Meaning	IFML Notation	Examples
Activation Expression	Boolean expression associated with a ViewElement, ViewComponentPart, or Event; if true, the element is enabled	«ActivationExpression» MyVar = "MyValue"	Button enabled or information shown only if a condition holds (e.g., if the user has logged in)
Interaction Flow Expression	Expression that determines which InteractionFlow is followed after an event occurrence	«InteractionFlowExpression» If Condition1 then Flow1 Else Flow2	Event triggered after selecting a given value in a ComboBox.
Module and ModuleDefinition	Piece of IFML diagram enclosed in a container (ModuleDefinition), which may be reused by referencing it (through a Module)	«ModuleDefinition» MyModule «Module» MyModule1	Checkout procedure on an e-commerce site

InputPort and InputPortDefinition	Interaction points between a Module and its environment; it collects InteractionFlows and parameters arriving at the module and associates them with ModuleDefinition elements.	*In ModuleDefinition* / *In Module*	The user identity in an order checkout module
Output Port and OutputPortDefinition	Interaction points between a Module and its environment; it collects InteractionFlows and parameters within a module and associates them with the elements outside the module	*In ModuleDefinition* / *In Module*	The transaction confirmation code and message in an order checkout module
ViewComponentPart: DataBinding, Conditional-Expression, ...	A part of a ViewComponent that cannot exist by its own.	«DataBinding» MyDataSource «ConditionalExpression» condition1 «VisualizationAttributes» attribute1, attribute2 «OrderBy» Attribute 3 DESC «Field» Key: String	Fields in a form, DataBinding and ConditionalExpression in a ViewComponent

Table 2 Extension IFML Concepts

Concept Extension Examples	Meaning	IFML Notation	Example at Implementation Level
Select Event	Event denoting the selection of items in a list	(arrow icon)	Selection of a row in a table or of multiple elements in a checklist
Submit Event	Event that submits information in a form	(arrow icon)	A form submission button in HTML
List	ViewComponent used to display multiple DataBinding instances	«List» MyList «DataBinding» MyDataSource	Table with rows of elements of the same kind.
Form with Fields	ViewComponent used to display a form that is composed of fields	«Form» MyForm «SimpleField» MyField1: String «SelectionField» MyField2: String	HTML form with fields
Details	ViewComponent used to display details of a specific DataBinding instance	«Details» MyDetails «DataBinding» MyDataSource	Information about a product on an e-commerce web site, profile of the user

| Window (Modal and Modeless) | A ViewContainer rendered as a window.

Modal: when displayed, it blocks interaction in all other containers.

Modeless: when displayed, it is superimposed over containers that remain active. | «Window» MyWindow

«Modeless» MyModelessWindow

«Modal» MyModalWindow | Desktop window, modal pop-up in HTML, modeless pop-up in HTML |

Appendix B: List of IFML design patterns

Appendix B lists all the design patterns described in the book. The name of a pattern is structured as XY-Z, where:

- X is the category of pattern. For instance, interface organization patterns start with the letter "O," and content and navigation patterns are prefixed with "CN."
- Y is the deployment platform where the pattern originated or is most frequently found. For instance, desktop patterns are labeled with "D," web with "W," mobile with "M." The prefix is omitted for patterns that apply equally well to multiple platforms and for which there is no clearly prevalent platform.
- Z is a mnemonic label identifying the specific pattern.

Name	Title	Description	Section
Interface Organization Patterns			
OD-SWA	Simple work area	Distinguishes a work area where the main tasks of the application are performed along with one or more service areas	**4.8.1.1**
OD-MWA	Multiview work area	Extension of OD-SWA for multiple alternative views of the item in the work area	**4.8.1.2**
OD-CWA	Composite work area	Splits the work area into subregions devoted to different perspectives of the item, presented simultaneously	**4.8.1.3**
OD-MCWA	Multiview composite work area	Combines the decomposition of the work area into alternative perspectives and simultaneous partial views	**4.8.1.4**
OW-MFE	Multiple front ends on the same domain model	Provides different interfaces for different user roles upon the same information	**4.8.2.1**
OW-LWSA	Large web sites organized into areas	Applications that exhibit a hierarchical structure, whereby the pages of the site are clustered into sections dealing with a homo-geneous subject	**4.8.2.2**
OM-MSL	Mobile screen layout	Maps the interface to a top-level grid that contains three regions: the header, the content area, and the footer	**4.8.3.1**

(Continued)

389

Name	Title	Description	Section
Content and Navigation Patterns			
CN-MD and CN-MMD	Master detail and Master multidetail	Presents some items, and a selection permits the user to access the details of one instance at a time	**5.6.1** **8.3.1**
CN-MLMD	Multilevel master detail	Also called a cascaded index; consists of a sequence of lists over distinct classes, such that each list specifies a change of focus from one object, selected from the index to the set of objects related to it via an association role; in the end, a single object is shown	**5.6.2**
CN-DEF	Default selection	Simulates a user choice at the initial access of a list, thus selecting a default instance	**5.6.3**
CN-SOT	Single object toolbar	Content-dependent toolbar that supports commands upon one object	**8.2.1.1**
CN-MOT	Multiple object toolbar	Content-dependent toolbar with commands that can be applied to multiple objects	**8.2.1.2**
CN-DT	Dynamic toolbar	Toolbar with commands that may vary at runtime based on the status of the interaction	**8.2.1.3**
CN-MSC	Multistep commands	Commands that involve multiple interaction steps	**8.2.1.4**
CN-CII	Commands with inline input	Collapses in the toolbar several steps needed to perform an action	**8.2.1.5**
CN-CIM&B	Content-independent navigation bar and menu	Groups commands that do not act upon specific objects but shortcut the navigation or help the user go back quickly	**8.2.1.6**
CN-UP	Up navigation	Refers to some hierarchical structure associated with the interface; it leads the user to the superior element in the view hierarchy	**8.2.2**
CN-BACK	Back navigation	"Back" refers to the chronology of user interaction; it leads back to the last visited ViewElement	**8.2.2**
CN-BREAD	Breadcrumbs	A navigation aid that shows the user location in the application interface	**8.2.3**

Name	Title	Description	Section
CN-PG	Paging	Displays a block of objects at a time and allows the user to scroll rapidly through the collection	8.3.2
CN-PR	Collection preview	Used with CN-PG, provides a preview of the object's location in the sequence and of what comes before and after	8.3.3
CN-ALPHA	Alphabetical filter	Provides an alphabetic filter to partition the collection into chunks	8.3.4
Data Entry Patterns			
DE-FRM	Multifield forms	Form for submitting information through several fields	5.7.1
DE-PLDF	Preloaded field	Variant of DE-FRM where some fields are preloaded with an existing value	5.7.2
DE-PASF	Pre-assigned selection field	Form where the value of a selection field is preselected	5.7.3
DE-DLKP	Data lookup	Data entry task that involves looking up information for filling in the fields	5.7.4
DE-CSF	Cascade selection fields	The data entry task involves entering a set of selections that have some kind of dependency on one another	5.7.5
DE-WIZ	Wizard	Partition of a data entry procedure into logical steps that must be followed in a determined sequence	5.7.6
DE-TDFP	Type-dependent field properties	Provides data entry facilities for form fields of specific data types	8.4.1
DE-RTE	Rich text editing	Provides an enriched text field in the shape of a microapplication that embodies the commands applicable to the text	8.4.2
DE-AUTO	Input auto-completion	Automatically provides suggestions for completing the input based on what the user has already typed in a field	8.4.3
DE-DYN	Dynamic selection fields	Occurs when the application requires the user to input data that have dependencies	8.4.4
DE-INPL	In-place editing	Allows the user to edit content without abandoning the current view to access a data entry form	8.4.5

(Continued)

Name	Title	Description	Section
DE-VAL	User input validation	Checks the correctness of the user input against validation rules and returns appropriate notification message(s)	8.4.6

Content Search Patterns

Name	Title	Description	Section
CS-SRC	Basic search	Keyword search upon a collection of items	5.8.1
CS-MCS	Multicriteria search	Composite search criteria upon a collection of items	5.8.2
CS-FSR	Faceted search	Allows the progressive refinement of search results upon structured multidimensional data, by restricting the objects that match the query based on their property values	5.8.3
CS-RSRC	Restricted search	Restricts the search focus to specific subcollections when searching large collections	8.5.1
CS-SRCS	Search suggestions	Exploits the auto-completion pattern and requires the logging of keywords previously inserted by the users; logged keywords matching the current user input are shown sorted by frequency	8.5.2
GEO-LAS	Location-aware search	Enables search of items that are related and close to the current user position	8.10.1

Content Management Patterns

Name	Title	Description	Section
CM-OCR	Object creation	Enables the creation of a new object in a data storage	6.3.2
CM-OACR	Object and association creation	Creates a new object and sets its associations to other objects	6.3.3
CM-ODL	Object deletion	Deletes one or more objects of a given class	6.3.4
CM-CODL	Cascaded deletion	Removes a specific object and all the objects associated with it via one or more associations	6.3.5
CM-OM	Object modification	Updates one or more objects of a given class	6.3.6
CM-AM	Association management	Used to create, replace, or delete instances of an association, by connecting or disconnecting some objects of the source and target classes	6.3.7

Name	Title	Description	Section
CM-NOTIF	Notification	The interface is updated (typically asynchronously) by the occurrence of a system generated event	6.3.8
CM-CBCM	Class-based content management	Addresses the creation, modification and deletion of an object and its association instances	8.6.1
CM-PBCM	Page-based content management	Supports blogs and page-based content management systems; management of whole pages is allowed	8.6.2.

Identification and Authorization Patterns

Name	Title	Description	Section
IA-LOGIN	Login	Recognizes and checks the validity of a user-provided identity	8.7.1
IA-LOGOUT	Logout	Clears user's authenticated identity preserved in the application navigation context upon explicit user request	8.7.2
IA-CEX	Context expiration notification	The authenticated identity of the user is cleared by the system for security reasons or because of timeout	8.7.3
IA-SPLOG	Login to a specific ViewContainer	Recognizes and checks the validity of a user-provided identity and enables access to a specific part of the user interface	8.7.4
IA-ROLE	User role display and switching	Displays the user role and allows change of role	8.7.5
IA-RBP and IA-NRBP	(Negative) role-based permissions for view elements	Implements (possibly negative) access permissions at the view level that depend on the user's role	8.7.6 8.7.7
IA-OBP	Object-based permissions	Access control is expressed over the content objects and personalization associations in the content model	8.7.8
IA-PRO	User profile display and management	Shows and enables the editing of application-dependent information associated with the identity of an authenticated user	8.7.9
IA-IPSI	In-place sign-in	When the user attempts to trigger an action, the user is warned of the need to sign in and then routed to the login form	8.7.10

(Continued)

Name	Title	Description	Section
Session Management Patterns			
SES-CR	Creating session data from persistent data	Stores information in the navigation session by collecting them from a persistent data source	**8.8.1**
SES-PER	Persisting session data	Creates persistent data from user navigation session data	**8.8.2**
SES-EXC	Session data expiration catching	Handles the asynchronous notification of the expiry of the session to the user interface by causing an automatic refresh of the content	**8.8.3**
Social Functions Patterns			
SOC-AW	Activity wall	Logs the social activity typical of a social network platform	**8.9.1**
SOC-SH	Sharing, liking, and commenting	Enables posting, commenting, liking, and sharing content produced by other community members	**8.9.2**
SOC-FR	Friendship management	Manages a symmetric (friendship) or asymmetric (following) association between users	**8.9.3**

References

[ACM01]   Alur D, Crupi J, Malks D. Core J2EE patterns: best practices and design strategies. Englewood Cliffs, NJ: Prentice Hall; 2001.

[ALF]   Object Management Group. Concrete syntax for a UML action language: Action Language for Foundational UML [Internet]. [updated 2013; cited n.d.] Available from: http://www.omg.org/spec/ALF/.

[Allaire02]   Allaire J. Macromedia Flash MX: a next-generation rich client. San Francisco, CA: Macromedia; 2002.

[Android]   Android Developers [Internet]. [cited 2013 Sep n.d.] Available from: http://developer.android.com/.

[Bales01]   Bales D. Java Programming with Oracle JDBC. Sebastopol, CA: O'Reilly; 2001.

[BBC03]   Bongio A, Brambilla M, Ceri S, Comai S, Fraternali P, Matera M. Designing data-intensive web applications. San Francisco, CA: Morgan Kaufmann; 2003.

[BCN92]   Batini C, Ceri S, Navathe B. Conceptual database design: an entity-relationship approach. Redwood City, CA: Benjamin-Cummings; 1992.

[BCW12]   Brambilla M, Cabot J, Wimmer M. Model-driven software engineering in practice. N.p: Morgan & Claypool Publishers; 2012.

[Bergsten00]   Bergsten H. Java server pages. Sebastopol, CA: O'Reilly; 2000.

[BF14]   Brambilla M, Fraternali P. Large-scale model-driven engineering of web user interaction: the WebML and WebRatio experience. Sci Comput Program 2014;89:71–87.

[BJR98]   Booch G, Jacobson I, Rumbaugh J. The Unified Modeling Language user guide. Reading, MA: Addison-Wesley; 2005.

[BJV04]   J. Bézivin, F. Jouault, P. Valduriez. On the Need for Megamodels. In Best Practices for Model-Driven Software Development Workshop (co-located with OOPSLA 2004 and GPCE 2004) Vancouver, Canada October 25, 2004.

[BLCLNS94]   Berners-Lee T, Cailliau R, Luotonen A, Frystyk Nielsen H, Secret A. The World-Wide Web. Communication of ACM 1994;97:76–82.

[BMU14]   Brambilla M, Mauri A, Umuhoza E. Extending the Interaction Flow Modeling Language (IFML) for model driven development of mobile applications front end. Mobile Web Information Systems Conference: 11th International Conference, MobiWIS, 2014 August 27–29. Barcelona, Spain. Proceedings 8640:176–191. N.p: Springer International Publishing; 2014.

[Boehm88]   Boehm B. A spiral model of software development and enhancement. IEEE Computer 1988;21:61–72.

[Booch94]   Booch G. Object oriented analysis and desing with applications. 2nd ed. Redwood City, CA: Benjamin-Cummings; 1994.

[Borchers01]   Borchers J. A pattern approach to interaction design. New York: John Wiley & Sons; 2001.

[BR82]   Brodie ML, Ridjanovic D. On the design and specification of database transactions. In: Brodie, M.L., Mylopoulos, J., Schmidt, J.W. (eds.) On Conceptual Modelling: Perspectives from Artificial Intelligence, Databases, and Programming Languages, SpringerVerlag, New York 1984: 277–312.

[Brambilla11]   Brambilla M. From requirements to implementation of ad-hoc social web applications: an empirical pattern-based approach. IET Software 2011;6:114–26. http://dx.doi.org/10.1049/iet-sen.2011.0041. IET 2011.

[Brusilovsky01] Brusilovsky P. Adaptive Hypermedia. User modeling and user-adapted interaction 2001;11:87–210.

[CF01]   Comai S, Fraternali P. A semantic model for specifying hypermedia applications using WebML. International Semantic Web Workshop, Infrastructure and Applications for the Semantic Web. Stanford, CA: Stanford University; 2001 July 30–31. Available at: http://webml.org/webml/upload/ent5/1/SemanticWeb01.pdf.

[CFM02]   Ceri S, Fraternali P, Matera M. Conceptual modeling of data-intensive web applications. IEEE Internet Computing 2002;6:20–30.

[CFP99]   Ceri S, Fraternali P, Paraboschi S. Design principles for data-intensive web sites. SIGMOD Record 1999;28:84–9.

[CS13]   Chaffer J, Swedberg K. Learning jQuery. 4th ed. Birmingham, UK: Packt Publishing; 2013.

[CL11]   Charland A, Leroux B. Mobile application development: web vs. native. Communication of the ACM 2011;54:49–53.

[Chen76]   Chen PP. The entity-relationship model: toward a unified view of data. ACM TODS 1976;1:9–36.

[CKLMR97]   Colby LS, Kawaguchi A, Lieuwen DF, Mumick IS, Ross KA. Supporting multiple view maintenance policies. ACM SIGMOD Record 1997;26:405–16.

[Conallen00]   Conallen J. Building web applications with UML (2nd Edition). Reading, MA: Addison Wesley; 2002.

[Conallen99]   Conallen J. Modeling web application architectures with UML. Communications of the ACM 1999;42:63–70.

[CY90]   Coad P, Yourdon E. Object-oriented design. Englewood Cliffs, NJ: Prentice Hall International; 1990.

[Date95]   Date C. An introduction to database systems. 7th ed. Reading, MA: Addison-Wesley; 1999.

[David13]   David M. HTML5: designing rich internet applications. 2nd ed. Burlington, MA: Focal Press; 2012.

[DFAB98]   Dix A, Finlay J, Abowd G, Beale R. Human–computer interaction. 2nd ed. Englewood Cliffs, NJ: Prentice Hall; 1998.

[EN94]   El-Masri R, Navathe SB. Fundamentals of database systems. 3rd ed. Reading, MA: Addison-Wesley; 2000.

[EP00]   Eriksson HE, Penker M. Business modeling with UML. New York: John Wiley & Sons; 2000.

[Erickson14]   Erickson T. The interaction design patterns page [Internet]. [cited 2014 Aug n.d.] Available from: http://www.visi.com/~snowfall/Interaction Patterns.html.

[Fincher14]   Fincher S. The pattern gallery [Internet]. [cited 2014 Aug n.d.] Available from: http://www.cs.kent.ac.uk/people/staff/saf/patterns/gallery.html.

[FFG+03]   Fincher S, Finlay J, Greene S, Jones L, Matchen P, Thomas J, Molina PJ. Perspectives on HCI patterns: concepts and tools. In Ext. Proc. of CHI'2003. New York: ACM Press; 2003. p. 1044–5.

[FKH06]   Falb J, Kaindl H, Horacek H, Bogdan C, Popp R, Arnautovic E. A discourse model for interaction design based on theories of human communication. In: Extended Abstracts on Human Factors in Computing Systems; 2006 Apr 22–27. Montreal. New York: ACM Press; 2006. p. 754–9.

[FLMM04]   Fraternali Piero, Luca Lanzi Pier, Matera Maristella, Maurino Andrea. Exploiting conceptual modeling for web application quality evaluation. In: Proceedings of the 13th international world wide web conference on alternate track papers and posters; 2004 n.d., n.p. New York: ACM Press; 2004. p. 342–3. Available at: https://www.researchgate. net/publication/221022826_Exploiting_conceptual_modeling_for_web_ application_quality_evaluation.

[Fowler03] Fowler M. UML distilled: a brief guide to the Standard Object Modeling Language. 3rd ed. Reading, MA: Addison-Wesley; 2003.

[FP00]   Fraternali P, Paolini P. Model-driven development of web applications: the AutoWeb system. ACM Trans. Inf. Syst 2000;18. 323–2.

[FCBT10]   Fraternali P, Comai S, Bozzon A, Toffetti Carughi G. Engineering rich internet applications with a model-driven approach. TWEB 2010:4. n.p.

[FTM01]   Ferreira De Oliveira MC, Turine MAS, Masiero PC. A statechart-based model for modeling hypermedia applications. ACM TOIS 2001;19:28–52.

[fUML]   OMG. Semantics of a foundational subset for executable UML models [Internet]. [updated 2011; cited n.d.] Available from: http://www.omg.org/spec/FUML/.

[FVB06]   Folmer E, van Welie M, Bosch J. Bridging patterns: an approach to bridge gaps between SE and HCI. Information and Software Technology 2006;48:69–89.

[GBM86]   Greenspan SJ, Borgida A, Mylopoulos J. A requirements modeling language and its logic. IS 1986;11:9–23.

[GHJV95]   Gamma E, Helm R, Johnson R, Vlissedes J. Design patterns: elements of reusable object oriented software. Reading, MA: Addison-Wesley; 1995.

[GLM01]   Génova G, Llorens J, Martínez P. Semantics of the minimum multiplicity in ternary associations in UML. In: Gogolla M, Kobryn C, editors. The Unified Modeling Language: modeling languages, concepts, and tools: Proceedings of the 4th International Conference; 2001 Oct 1–5. Toronto, Canada. Berlin: Springer; 2001. p. 329–41.

[GPS93]   Garzotto F, Paolini P, Schwabe DHDM. a model-based approach to hypertext application design. ACM Transactions on Information Systems 1993;11:1–26.

[GP99]   Gulutzan P, Pelzer T. SQL-99 complete, really. Lawrence, KS: R&D Books; 1999.

[GR93]   Gray J, Reuter A. Transaction processing: concepts and techniques. San Mateo, CA: Morgan Kaufmann; 1993.

[GVBA99]   Grefen PWPJ, Vonk J, Boertjes E, Apers PMG. Semantics and architecture of global transaction support in workflow environments. In: Proceedings of CoopIS '99 1999:348–59. Available at: http://www.informatik.uni-trier. de/~ley/db/conf/coopis/coopis99.html.

[HB11]   Hoober S, Berkman E. Designing mobile interfaces. Sebastopol, CA: O'Reilly Media; 2011.

[HBR94]   Hardman L, Bulterman D, van Rossum G. The Amsterdam hypermedia model: adding time and context to the dexter model. Communications of the ACM 1994;97:50–62.

[iOS]   iOS Dev Center [Internet]. [cited 2013 Sep n.d.] Available from: https://developer.apple.com /devcenter/ios/index.action.

[ISB95]   Isakowitz T, Sthor EA, Balasubranian P. RMM a methodology for structured hypermedia design. Communications of the ACM 1995;38:34–44.

[Jacobson94] Jacobson I. Object-oriented software engineering: a use case driven approach. Reading, MA: Addison-Wesley; 1994.

[JavaSwing]   Package javax.swing [Internet]. [cited 2013 Sep n.d.] Available from: http://docs.oracle.com/javase/7/docs/api/javax/swing/package-summary.html.

[JBR99]   Jacobson I, Booch G, Rumbaugh J. The unified software development process. Reading, MA: Addison-Wesley; 1999.

[Kelly08]   Kelly S, Tolvanen J-P. Domain-specific modeling: enabling full code generation. New York: Wiley-IEEE Computer Society Press; 2008.

[Kiss07]   Kiss C. Composite capability/preference profiles (CC/PP): structure and vocabularies 2.0, W3C working draft [Internet]. [updated 2007 Apr 30; cited 2013 Sep n.d.] Available from: http://www.w3.org/ TR/2007/WD-CCPP-struct-vocab2-20070430.

[Klyne04]   Klyne G, Reynolds F, Woodrow C, Ohto H, Hjelm J, Butler MH, Tran L. Composite capability/preference profiles (CC/PP): structure and vocabularies 1.0, W3C recommendation [Internet]. [updated 2004 Jan n.d.; cited 2013 Sep n.d.] Available from: http://www.w3.org/TR /CCPP-struct-vocab/.

[Kobsa01]   Kobsa A. Generic user modeling systems. User modeling and user-adapted interaction 2011;11:49–63.

[Kopparapu02] Kopparapu C. Load balancing servers, firewalls, and caches. New York: John Wiley & Sons; 2002.

[Kruchten99] Kruchten P. The rational unified process: an introduction. Reading, MA: Addison-Wesley; 1999.

[Laurent01]   St. Laurent S. XML: a primer. 3rd ed. New Jersey: John Wiley & Sons; 2001.

[LVM04]   Limbourg Q, Vanderdonckt J, Michotte B, Bouillon L, Florins MUSIXML. a user interface description language supporting multiple levels of independence. In: Matera M, Comai S, editors. Engineering advanced web applications: proceedings of workshops in connection with the 4th international conference on web engineering (ICWE 2004); 2004 July 28–30. Munich, Germany. Princeton, NJ: Rinton Press; 2004. p. 325–38.

[MR92]   Mannila H, Räihä KJ. The design of relational databases. Reading, MA: Addison-Wesley; 1992.

[MA01]   Menasce DA, Almeida VAF. Scaling for e-business: technologies, models, performance, and capacity planning. Englewood Cliffs, NJ: Prentice Hall; 2001.

[Meier12]   Meier R. Professional Android 4 application development. 3rd ed. New York: Wrox; 2012.

[MBS11]   Meixner G, Breiner K, Seissler M. Model-driven useware engineering. In: Hussmann H, Meixner G, Zuehlke D, editors. Model-driven development of advanced user interfaces studies. Heidelberg: Springer; 2011. p. 1–26.

[MBW80]   Mylopoulos J, Bernstein PA, Wong HKT. A language facility for designing database-intensive applications. Transactions on Database Systems 1980;5:185–207.

[Meyer88]   Meyer B. Object-oriented software construction. 2nd ed. Englewood Cliffs, NJ: Prentice Hall; 2000.

[MPS04]   Mori G, Paternò F, Santoro C. Design and development of multidevice user interfaces through multiple logical descriptions. IEEE Transactions on Software Engineering 2004;30:507–20.

[NB12]   Nielsen J, Bodiu R. Mobile usability. San Francisco, CA: New Riders; 2012.

[Neil12]   Neil T. Mobile design pattern gallery. Sebastopol, CA: O'Reilly; 2012.

[Nielsen00] Nielsen J. Designing web usability: the practice of simplicity. San Francisco, CA: New Riders; 1999.

[Nixon12]   Nixon R. Learning PHP, MySQL, JavaScript, and CSS: a step-by-step guide to creating dynamic websites. 2nd ed. Sebastopol, CA: O'Reilly; 2012.

[NM01]   Naiburg EJ, Maximchuck RA. UML for database design. Reading, MA: Addison-Wesley; 2001.

[PSC12]   Palmieri M, Singh I, Cicchetti A. Comparison of cross-platform mobile development tools. In: 16th International Conference on Intelligence in Next Generation Networks; 2012 Oct 8–11. Berlin. N.p: IEEE; 2012. p. 179–86. Available at: http://ieeexplore.ieee.org/xpl/login.jsp?tp=&arnumber=6376 023&url=http%3A%2F%2Fieeexplore.ieee.org%2Fxpls%2Fabs_all.jsp% 3Farnumber%3D6376023.

[Popescu12] Popescu A. Geolocation API specification, editor's draft (for W3C proposed recommendation) [Internet]. [updated2012 May n.d.; cited 2013 Sep n.d.] Available from: http://dev.w3.org/geo/api/spec-source.html.

[PSS09]   Paternò F, Santoro C, Spano LD. Maria: A universal, declarative, multiple abstraction-level language for service-oriented applications in ubiquitous environments. ACM Transactions on Computer-Human Interaction 2009;16(19):1–19. 30.

[Rabin10]   Rabin J, Trasatti A, Hanrahan R, eds. Device description repository core vocabulary, W3C working group note [Internet]. [updated 2008 Apr 14; cited n.d.] Available from: http://www.w3.org/TR/ddr-core-vocabulary/.

[RB12]   Raj R, Babu Tolety S. A study on approaches to build cross-platform mobile applications and criteria to select appropriate approach. Kochi, Kerala, India: IEEE INDICON Conference; 2012 Dec 7–9. Available at: http://ieeexplore.ieee.org/xpl/mostRecentIssue.jsp?punumber=6410222.

[RBPEL91]   Rumbaugh J, Blaha M, Premerlani W, Eddy F, Lorenson W. Object-oriented modeling and design. Englewood Cliffs, NJ: Prentice Hall; 1991.

[RMB13]   Raneburger D, Meixner G, Brambilla M. Platform-independence in model-based multi-device UI development. In: Proceedings of ICSOFT. 2013. p. 265–72. Available at: http://link.springer.com/chapter/10.1007 %2F978-3-662-44920-2_12.

[RPK11]   Raneburger D, Popp R, Kavaldjian S, Kaindl H, Falb J. Optimized GUI generation for small screens. In: Hussmann H, Meixner G, Zuehlke D, editors. Model-driven development of advanced user interfaces studies; 2011. Heidelberg: Springer; 2011. p. 107–22.

[RS02]   Rabinovich M, Spatscheck O. Web caching and replication. Reading, MA: Addison-Wesley; 2002.

[Sano96]   Sano D. Designing large scale web sites: a visual design methodology. New York: John Wiley & Sons; 1996.

[SF89]   Stotts P, Furuta R. Petri-net-based hypertext: document structure with browsing semantics. TOIS 1989;7:3–29.

[Shackel91]   Shackel B. Usability: context, framework, definition, design, and evaluation. In: Shackel B, Richardson S, editors. Human factors for informatics usability. Cambridge, UK: Cambridge University Press; 1991. p. 21–38.

[Shasha92]   Shasha D. Database tuning: a principled approach. Englewood Cliffs, NJ: Prentice Hall; 1992.

[SM88]   Schlaer S, Mellor S. Object oriented system analysis: modeling the world in data. Englewood Cliffs, NJ: Prentice Hall; 1988.

[SPCJ10]   Shneiderman B, Plaisant C, Cohen M, Jacobs S. Designing the user interface: strategies for effective human-computer interaction. 5th ed. Reading, MA: Addison-Wesley; 2010.

[SR95]   Schwabe D, Rossi G. The object-oriented hypermedia design model. Communication of ACM 1995;38:45–6.

[Starr02]   Starr L. Executable UML: how to build class models. Englewood Cliffs, NJ: Prentice-Hall; 2002.

[SWJ98]   Schneider G, Winters JP, Jacobson I. Applying use cases: a practical guide. Reading, MA: Addison-Wesley; 1998.

[VM10]   Vanderdonckt J, Simarro FM. Generative pattern-based design of user interfaces. In: PEICS '10 Proceedings of the 1st International Workshop on Pattern-Driven Engineering of Interactive Computing Systems; 2010 June 20. Berlin, Germany. New York: ACM; 2010. p. 12–9.

[Voelter13]   Voelter M. DSL engineering: designing, implementing, and using domain-specific languages. N.p.: CreateSpace 2013.

[WK03]   Warmer J, Klepp A. The Object Constraint Language: getting your models ready for MDA. 2nd ed. Reading, MA: Addison-Wesley; 2003.

[Walls11]   Walls C. Spring in action. 3rd ed. Shelter Island, NY: Manning Publications; 2011.

[WW13]   Wheeler W. White J. Spring in practice. Shelter Island, NY: Manning Publications; 2013.

[ZP92]   Zheng Y, Pong M. Using statecharts to model hypertext. ECHT 1992;1992:242–50.

Index

Note: Page numbers followed by "b", "f" and "t" indicate boxes, figures and tables respectively.

Printed in the United States
By Bookmasters